Books by Ann Rule

Bitter Harvest
Dead by Sunset
Everything She Ever Wanted
If You Really Loved Me
The Stranger Beside Me
Possession
Small Sacrifices

The End of the Dream and Other True Cases
    Ann Rule's Crimes Files: Vol. 5
In the Name of Love and Other True Cases
    Ann Rule's Crime Files: Vol. 4
A Fever in the Heart and Other True Cases
    Ann Rule's Crime Files: Vol. 3
You Belong to Me and Other True Cases
    Ann Rule's Crime Files: Vol. 2
A Rose for Her Grave and Other True Cases
    Ann Rule's Crime Files: Vol. 1

ANN RULE

THE END OF THE DREAM

THE GOLDEN BOY WHO NEVER GREW UP

AND OTHER TRUE CASES

Ann Rule's Crime Files: Vol. 5

POCKET BOOKS

New York London Toronto Sydney Tokyo Singapore

The names of some individuals in this book have been changed. Such names are indicated by an asterisk (*) the first time each appears in the narrative.

An *Original* Publication of POCKET BOOKS

POCKET BOOKS, a division of Simon & Schuster Inc.
1230 Avenue of the Americas, New York, NY 10020

Copyright © 1999 by Ann Rule

ISBN: 0-671-79357-8

First Pocket Books printing January 1999

10 9 8 7 6 5 4 3 2 1

POCKET and colophon are registered trademarks of Simon & Schuster Inc.

Front cover illustration by Tom Hallman

Printed in the U.S.A.

For Luke "Ugo" Fiorante
Teacher, Coach, Friend, and Brother

Sometimes the relatives we choose
are as close as those
we are born with.

Acknowledgments

Tragedy and regret are inherent in all true crime stories and, perhaps, in none so much as this one. A number of people set their own welfare aside and helped me try to understand what is really unexplainable. I appreciate their courage and honesty, just as I am grateful to the law-enforcement officers who remembered desperate and dangerous times.

I want to thank Burdena Pasenelli, Special Agent in Charge, Seattle Office, FBI; Norman Stamper, Chief, Seattle Police Department; Sergeant Don Cameron, Homicide Unit, Seattle Police Department; Special Agent Shawn Johnson, FBI; Detective Mike Magan, Seattle Police Department; Detective Sergeant Bob Gebo, Seattle Police Department; Detective Sergeant Ed Striedinger, Seattle Police Department; Sergeant Howard Monta, Seattle Police Department (retired); Jim Stovall, Tom Mason, Ted Forrester, Doug Engelbretson, and Vivian Griffiths.

To all those whose bittersweet memories helped me so much: Robert Kevin Meyers, Roni Morgan, Sarah Rose Morgan, Cindy Geer, Mark Biggins, Marge Violette Mullins, Candee Eddins, Scott Newman.

To *The Seattle Times*, *The Seattle Post-Intelligencer*, and *The Stranger*.

Acknowledgments

To my consciences and guides: Gerry Brittingham Hay, my perennial first reader; Emily Heckman, my new editor, blessed with both an admirable distaste for mixed metaphors and a keen sense of pacing; Joan and Joe Foley, my trusted literary agents for twenty-eight years; Paolo Pepe, the best art director in publishing; Donna Anders, an outstanding suspense novelist, my dear friend, who always lends me an invaluable second pair of eyes and ears at trials and interviews; and my office manager/publicity man, Mike Rule.

To those still involved in erasing all signs of disaster by mud: Larry Ellington, Kimbal Geocke, Martin Woodcock, Don White, Gene Lescher, Kathy and Horace Parker, Dave Bailey, and all the others who have helped me rebuild. While I was writing, they were digging, painting, planting, and re-directing water into wonderful waterfalls. Who could ever have believed it?

And to my favorite people of all: my readers! I appreciate you more than you will ever know, and I read every letter and e-mail that you send and try to respond as quickly as possible. I have a new web site; you can find it on the Internet at www.annrules.com and send me e-mail. For those who have not yet signed up for my sporadic free newsletter (which has updates on what's happening with people from my earlier books *and* news on what's coming next and where I will be lecturing), please send your "snail-mail" (street or P.O. Box) address to: Ann Rule, P.O. Box 98846, Seattle, WA 98198. This newsletter is also available at my web site.

Contents

Contents

Author's Note

In this, the fifth of my True Crime Files, I explore four cases which all ended in the destruction of someone's dream. It might well be argued that *all* criminal acts destroy dreams. But, somehow, the stories I have chosen here left me with more than the average sense of what might have been. I think you will understand as you read them.

The book-length title case is called "The End of the Dream." When I first read about the main characters in a newspaper, I was immediately curious. Even I— who should not be so naive after all these years—kept looking at the handsome and beautiful people whose lives had come to such a sad place and wondered, *why?* I saved the clippings but I didn't really consider doing a book because I was sure I could never convince anyone at the center of the case to talk to me about it.

Still, I have learned that when I am *meant* to do a book, the very people I need to know contact me. That was true of "The End of the Dream," and I found out things—secret things—that amazed me. This case is different from any that I have written about before. It will bring back the carefree days of the seventies as well as expanding on headlines in the nineties. I discovered that it was at the same time tragic and funny, terrifying and romantic, as I heard of wasted talents, crushed dreams, but also of the miracles that evolved and the love that ignited among the ashes of disaster.

"The End of the Dream" will allow you into the lives of Steve, Scott, Kevin, Mark, Mike, Shawn, Ellen, Sabrina, Marge, and dozens of other people who could never have imagined how a long saga would end.

In addition, in this fifth volume you will find three more true cases from my early days as a true crime writer. These three are among the most memorable I have ever covered: "The Peeping Tom," "The Girl Who Fell in Love with Her Killer," and "The Least Likely Suspect."

The wind was a torrent of darkness among the
  gusty trees,
The moon was a ghostly galleon tossed upon
  cloudy seas,
The road was a ribbon of moonlight over the
  purple moor,
And the highwayman came riding—
    Riding—riding . . .

"I'll come to thee by moonlight, though hell
  should bar the way."

—Alfred Noyes,
"The Highwayman"

THE END OF
THE DREAM

The End
of the Dream

Prologue

He knew every square inch of his property, all twenty acres. Every tree. Every building. Especially every secret hiding place. This wild place was, in fact, very close to civilization where houses crowded against each other and malls sprouted mushroomlike from good dirt that should have been left alone. His land, and everything in it and on it, was as close to the perfect home as he had ever imagined. Everything he wanted was here—or could easily be brought here, and he had the ultimate power to protect his trees from the deadly chain saws of civilization.

Eyes closed or stoned or drunk, he could navigate every wooded path as if he had radar in his brain, as if he were a bat sensing any obstacle in its flight. Those who knew him and admired him believed he feared nothing. He had spent his whole life demonstrating that he was not afraid; nothing human could best him.

But the thing in his path clearly was not human. Its red eyes glowed like fiery coals when it reared up in front of him. It was dark as pitch and so suffused with evil that it sucked the breath from his lungs.

He blinked, and it was still there. He blinked again and it was gone.

If he had only seen the black unhuman thing once, he could have found an explanation for it—somehow. With the passage of time, he would have decided that he hadn't really seen it at all. But it had confronted him several times, waiting among the night trees. He was most afraid when the wind forced their branches toward the ground and the sky at the same time, and the rain flung itself toward him like needles. For whatever reason, he knew it was stalking him, and that there might well come a time when it did more than stare at him with crimson eyes.

He was frightened. He could not admit that to his male buddies, but he ran back to his wonderful home, his refuge, and called one of the many women who would be glad to sit all night comforting him. The tender breasts of beautiful women had always made him forget what threatened him. But this night brought no comfort, even though she held him close and listened as he told her about the horror in the path. She offered rational explanations to chase away his vision of death and damnation.

It didn't work. He could not sleep until the sun finally broke free from the mountains that had hidden it all night and the trees surrounding them looked serene and beneficent under the rosy dawn sky.

PART ONE

1

In Seattle, Washington, Thanksgiving is only
rarely celebrated under a brilliant blue sky and
against a landscape rife with autumn colors. More
often than not, the holiday seems to draw memorably
violent storms to the Northwest. Many a turkey has
been coaxed to semidoneness on an outdoor barbeque
because power lines are down. Wednesday, November
27, 1996, was the day before Thanksgiving; the weather was wildly rainy and stormy, with gusts of wind
stripping the trees of their last few leaves. Whatever
smothered sun there had been that day had long since
set, the streets were coils of shiny black, reflecting
yellow streetlights and the red, green, and silver of
Christmas lights.

Late customers hurried into the Lake City Branch
of Seafirst Bank only eighteen minutes before closing.
More than a dozen people stood patiently in the long
lines, most of them so intent on the errands they still
needed to run that they were unaware of what was
going on around them.

The bank's automatic cameras kept clicking away
as they always did, silent, mindless and mechanical.
One camera snapped everyone coming in the door,

7

another caught the bored or impatient faces of people waiting in line for a teller, while another scanned the entire bank. A fourth was aimed away from the tellers' cages toward a central island where customers stood writing out deposit and withdrawal slips. Each frame of the film noted the camera's number, the bank's ID number and name, the date, and the time to the second.

Camera 1-06 recorded the time at 5:42:13 P.M. at the instant a figure appeared at the far right of the frame. From a distance, he seemed only slightly bizarre; he wore both a hooded rain jacket and a baseball cap. A casual observer saw a man past middle age with gray hair; a full, drooping gray moustache; and a prominent chin. His dark glasses seemed odd, considering that the sun had set more than an hour before, and his wide, garish necktie was in dubious taste. He wore cheap tennis shoes, the low black canvas type that predated Nikes and Adidas. A closer look revealed that the body beneath the bulky jacket was too toned to belong to a man in his fifties, and he moved with an almost pantherlike grace. He had to be either an athlete or a dancer.

The camera clicked off seconds and the man approached a line of people. They looked at him with startled eyes and then averted their glances as considerate people do when they realize they are looking at someone with a handicap. Although the man's stride was confident, his face wasn't normal. He appeared to have suffered serious facial burns, and he was wearing either heavy makeup to cover scars or a rubbery mask to prevent additional scarring.

Here, in this neighborhood bank, no one expected

trouble. The robot lenses caught their expressions as the odd-looking man cut between customers waiting in line. One man had an embarrassed half-smile on his face, a woman's eyes shifted momentarily, and a girl covered her mouth with her hand. What they were feeling was just a tingle of alarm. Nothing overtly frightening had been said or done. It was a little rude of the scarred man to slide between people in line, but it wasn't as if he were crowding in. He moved through, toward the back of the bank.

They didn't see the gun. They didn't see the holster strapped under his shoulder nor the knife or the extra gun strapped to his ankle. They certainly didn't see the other strange-looking man. The second man was quite tall, over six feet, and close to two hundred pounds. He wore a khaki parka with a light brown hood. His skin also had a masklike appearance, and he had a bushy moustache, too. The teller closest to him saw that he wore beige gloves and lace-up all-weather boots.

Eyewitnesses are far from reliable, particularly when they are stunned and frightened eyewitnesses. Human perception is skewed by so many things, and people recall height inaccurately more often than not. A man who is frightening may be remembered as being much taller than he really is. "Young" or "old" is relative to the age of the witness. These two strangers would be described as anywhere from "thirty" to "over fifty." Only their eyes were visible beneath their masks and theatrical makeup.

The first man pushed past a bank customer, walked up to a teller, and said, "Step back. Stay away from the counter. This is a robbery."

Of course. Of course it was; why else would there be *two* bizarre-looking men in the bank?

The middle-aged male customer must have looked terrified, because the bank robber leaned toward him and said gently, "Don't panic. Stay calm. This *is* a robbery."

At that point, as if to emphasize his words, he pulled a black handgun about six inches long from his parka. "I'm serious," he said. "If you're nervous, please step out of line and sit down."

The customer and his wife walked gingerly out into the central lobby area and sat down in the easy chairs there. Now, they saw the second man and, when he moved, they caught a glimpse of a gun beneath his jacket that looked like the one the first bank robber held. Although he motioned people to get in line, he didn't use the gun to threaten them.

The first man was efficiently herding everyone from the tellers' lines out into the main part of the bank. He seemed to be in charge; he had an energy field around him that was fraught with danger.

The second, taller, man was very polite, very calm. When he spoke, it was with a southern-sounding drawl. He addressed women respectfully as "Ma'am." The first man, the one in the wild tie, had physically pushed the teller away from the counter. He appeared to be working against a clock.

Neither seemed worried that someone might walk in and interrupt the bank robbery. The bank doors remained unlocked, and new customers actually walked into the bank, unaware that anything was wrong. The tall bank robber had obviously been given the job of controlling the customers and staff. He gestured courteously as he asked people to move into the middle of the bank or into lines in front of the tellers' cubicles. Everyone complied. From the outside, it would look as if business was being carried on as usual.

The smaller man's voice boomed throughout the quiet bank. "Who is the vault teller?"

He seemed to know the inner workings of a bank and the duties of the staff. The big money would surely be in the vault.

A bank employee stepped up and said, "I'm the vault teller. I'll go with you." He led the way through the gate into the tellers' area.

It seemed a very long time before the two men emerged from the vault. Some witnesses thought it was ten minutes; some thought it was half that time. When they came out, the robber who was choreographing the crime carried a shiny blue duffel bag with a rope tied tight at the opening. He tossed it over the gate, and then placed one hand on a low partition and leapt over it effortlessly. Again, his physical agility was incongruous with his gray hair and moustache.

Now, those closest could see that he carried a handheld walkie-talkie radio. He spoke into the radio, saying what sounded like, "Did *you* hear anything?" or "Is *she* here?"

And then they were gone. One customer insisted on following the two bank robbers—despite the pleadings of the others. He ran out into the darkness beyond the streetlights. Inside, they waited with dread, expecting to hear shots. But none came.

No one but the vault teller suspected that they had

all just been part of one of the biggest bank robberies in Northwest history. In less than fifteen minutes, the robbers had managed to carry away more money than most people make in a lifetime.

This was not the first time that these robbers had struck Northwest banks. Far from it. This was at least the *twentieth* bank hit. The shorter man had become the quarry—and the focal point of ultimate frustration—for some of the most skilled investigators in the Seattle Police Department and the Seattle FBI Office. Just when predictable patterns and a distinctive MO began to emerge, he would slip through the invisible net that had been laid out for him. He and any accomplice he brought with him were wraithlike; it was almost as if they ran from the banks and vaporized.

No one knew who they were or what they looked like without their masks. They had to live somewhere; there were probably people who loved them and worried about them. Somewhere, probably within fifty miles of Seattle, they quite likely lived outwardly normal lives.

For the moment, they were known only by the profile they had filled in with their actions and their disguises. The investigators tracking them knew more about who they *weren't* than who they *were*.

Kevin, Steve, and Scott

2

The Gordon* Meyers family were part of a new generation of young marrieds who emerged after the Second World War. The draft and good wages in defense plants tore extended families apart and encouraged people to leave their hometowns and move halfway across the country. Families who had gone generations without a divorce now began to lose their cohesion.

Gordon Meyers was a printer and a lithographer; Joanna was a commercial artist. From the outside, their marriage seemed happy enough. But Gordon became unpleasant when he drank, and he was argumentative and punishing with his wife and children. Only rarely did he praise their successes, while he was quick to comment on their failures. Sometimes Joanna thought that, without him, she and the children might enjoy a simpler and quieter life. The Meyers marriage blew up completely in 1962, and they were divorced. Joanna did the best she could raising their four children, always looking for a better life. Sometimes they found it; more often, they lived a hard-scrabble existence. Their family solidarity made up for what they didn't have in the way of financial stability.

Dana, Steven, Kevin, and Randy Meyers were Joanna's babies. She vowed to do whatever she could to nurture them and allow them to be successful, creative, and happy. Each of them was brilliantly gifted, and that wasn't just a mother's prejudice. It was true. Dana was fifteen at the time of the divorce, Steve thirteen, Kevin ten, and Randy eight.

Kevin Meyers, the third child, second son, recalled his childhood with more humor than pathos, "I thought dog biscuits were cookies—I'm not kidding. They had all the nutrients you needed. And, we ate a lot of mayonnaise sandwiches. Hey, if we didn't have bologna, mayonnaise was good enough."

Although Joanna's children had completely different personalities, they had all inherited their parents' artistic talent. She and Gordon might not have had traits that complemented each other in a way that made for a sound marriage, but they had created remarkable offspring.

Dana, born in Kansas City in 1947, was beautiful, loving and graceful, and a wonderful dancer; compared to other girls taking dance lessons, she was a lily among toadstools. Steven, the oldest son, was born on February 19, 1950. Even as a child, he had a somewhat brooding mien and often looked angry when he wasn't, but he was brilliant. Kevin, who came along in 1953, was cheerfully hyperactive, a natural athlete, and as sensitive as a puppy. Randy, born in 1955, was musically talented and perhaps the most pragmatic of them all. He set his mind on a goal and went for it.

Kevin was a handful. He was born long before

children were recognized as being hyperactive and before anyone knew that reading difficulties were often caused by dyslexia. He could draw or paint anything, but he needed a year to read a book. He *had* to be outside, and he often drove Joanna Meyers to distraction. "Sometimes, she'd put me in my room for some reason, and I would bounce off the walls and yell, 'Lemme out! Lemme out!' I just couldn't stand being caged up."

All the Meyers boys were imaginative and bursting with high spirits. When they watched "Sea Hunt," they hooked vacuum cleaner hoses to their backs and "swam" across the living room rug. They used the couch for a bronco when they watched television westerns. Joanna just sighed and shooed them outside.

Like his siblings, Kevin Meyers was raised in Overland Park, an upscale suburb of Kansas City, Kansas, before his parents divorced. But Kevin almost didn't live to grow up. When he was three, he was hit by a car and barely survived. It was to be only the first of many brushes Kevin would have with death. Perhaps because of this, he was an unusually spiritual child. He recalled "astrally projecting" his mind when he was well under twelve. He thought everyone could do that.

Joanna Meyers had been largely raised by a woman named Martha Ebert—who was not a blood relation, but who was a loving, dear person. As a toddler, Joanna couldn't say "Martha" so she called her foster mother, "Mamoo." Mamoo had always welcomed Joanna's children into her home, too. The little boys liked to watch television with Mamoo. Munching popcorn, they sat on the floor at her feet and watched the screen avidly.

"Mamoo loved 'Dragnet' and 'Perry Mason,'" Kevin remembered. "We liked those shows and she'd let us sit there and watch with her. She loved Lawrence Welk too—but we could never understand why. Every time the bad guy got caught on 'Perry Mason' or 'Dragnet,' Mamoo used to tell us very seriously, 'Remember this, boys: Crime doesn't pay.' We believed her, too."

After their parents' divorce, the Meyers' kids were rudely uprooted from the life they had known in Overland Park. Dana, who seemed years older than she really was, moved into her own apartment in Kansas City. She taught dance while she made plans to go to New York City. Kevin and Randy went to live with their maternal grandmother. She was married to her second husband, a traveling contractor, whose jobs took him all over Kansas. "We lived in this little trailer," Kevin remembered, "And we'd go where the work was. I don't think we went to any school more than six weeks at a time that year."

Perhaps the hardest hit by his parents' split, thirteen-year-old Steven stayed with his mother. He didn't like the man Joanna was dating, even though John Harmon* was quite willing to accept all of Joanna's children. A little over a year later, Joanna and John Harmon were married and they moved to Irving, Texas. Her three boys went with them. Steve hated Texas, and he soon ran away. He was eventually picked up by the police and taken to a juvenile facility. He refused to return to his mother so Gordon

Meyers agreed to let Steve live with him in Kansas City.

Kevin and Randy Meyers were not as overtly rebellious; they simply neglected to go to school most of the time. "We found a treehouse close to the place where we were living," Kevin recalled. "Randy and I spent our time that year fixing it up, and we hardly ever went to school. I flunked seventh grade."

Knowing that he would have to repeat his first year of junior high in the fall, Kevin worried about his father's reaction. Although Gordon Meyers had accepted his oldest son into his home, he had done so reluctantly. He had never supported any of his children emotionally; it was as if he had blinders on when it came to knowing what his children needed. At least Steve was his first son; Gordon looked less favorably upon Kevin and Randy—especially when he heard that they had goofed away a whole school year playing hookey.

"My Mom sent Randy and me to Kansas City that summer—to stay with my dad," Kevin said. "I guess maybe she thought he'd shape us up. We traveled up there with only our laundry bags and our guitars."

Gordon Meyers met his younger sons all right, but he didn't take them home. He was disgusted at their behavior in the school year just past. He told them he was taking them to their sister's place. "You're not coming home with me," he said flatly.

Asked how old Dana was in the summer of 1964, Kevin recalled first that she was well into her twenties. She wasn't—she was only seventeen. He seemed surprised when that was pointed out to him. Dana lived in a tiny little apartment, but she took her eleven- and thirteen-year-old brothers in and cared for them all summer.

"I felt terribly rejected," Kevin recalled, "having my dad turn us away like that."

Steve stayed on with his father, and graduated from Lillis High School in Kansas City in 1968, where he had shown real promise as a sculptor. Across town, Dana was modeling and taking dance classes. Many states away, Kevin was constantly drawing and Randy was taking music lessons. Gordon Meyers' contributions to the family finances were minimal. He had promised to send Joanna $35 a week, but his payments were spotty at best. He was a union man and received a fair salary—which he promptly invested. Raised in the Great Depression, Gordon was more concerned about putting money away for his retirement than he was with supporting his children.

Joanna's dream had always been to find a nice town where her kids would be safe, someplace where she could find a good job and buy a house. The move to the Dallas area had proved disappointing. None of the boys had been happy there. She knew she and John hadn't found the right place yet.

One day, she read an article in a magazine about a model city that had been built near Washington, DC. It was called Reston—Reston, Virginia. This perfect city was the creation of Robert E. Simon, an entrepreneurial millionaire who sold his interest in Carnegie Hall to finance the city of his dreams. It would be within easy commuting distance of Washington, DC. but would still maintain the wholesomeness of small-town America. Rather than being only a bedroom community for Washington, DC, Simon visualized a town where citizens could enjoy recreation, entertainment, shopping, and employment. There would be a low-density buffer on the western edge of Reston, and ten acres of parkland for every thousand people. In Simon's diverse community, all ethnic groups, all races, all classes would be welcome. Located in Fairfax County, the third richest county in America, it would be the first city in the United States to truly welcome middle-class black families.

It sounded like paradise to Joanna Meyers.

Joanna was a small, pretty woman with soft black hair and lovely big eyes; she didn't look very strong, but she was made of tough stuff. She and John had both survived some bad times. John was a brilliant electronic engineer. He had designed and built the first FM radio station in the Kansas City area, but he had lost it through business reverses.

John agreed with Joanna that they should move to Reston. Kevin was thirteen and Randy was eleven when they moved again. The town had a population of ten thousand then, a fledgling project blossoming according to its original plan. It proved to be everything Joanna had hoped it would be. Reston had neat houses, modern townhouses, clean streets, small convenient malls—long before the concept of a shopping mall was generally accepted—parks, bridges, and churches, all located against a background of rolling hills, clear rivers, and trees and fields in a wonderful bucolic setting. Everyone in Reston was treated with respect. Nobody lived "on the wrong side of the tracks."

For the second time, Kevin enrolled in the seventh grade—at Herndon Junior High School. Randy, only a year behind him now, was in the sixth grade at Herndon Grade School. The family rented a townhouse near Lake Anne. John had a new broadcast concept he was eager to explore, and Joanna had found a job as a commercial illustrator for the Arthur Young Company.

Things looked good.

Kevin Meyers was a welcome member of the track team at Herndon Junior High, if a half-hearted student. He was interested in art—and girls—but didn't have the faintest idea how to approach them. Although he wasn't that drawn to the church per se, Kevin soon found his way to the teen meetings sponsored by the Washington Plaza Baptist Church. The meetings were held in the basement of the Reverend Bill Scurlock's home where, rumor had it, it was the best place in town to meet girls. Kevin and Randy showed up one night, spiffed and polished, and voiced their interest in the Baptist Church to Reverend Scurlock.

"A couple of friends said we'd get to meet all the girls in town," Kevin remembered. "That's where I met Scotty. He was the minister's son—two years younger than I was—he ran all over with Randy, but he and I were friends, too. Scott was born the same week that Randy was. They were both a year behind me. Man, we were all wild then. We'd watch some show on television like 'Batman' and we would pretend we were the guys on there. We took chances. We played 'gang tag.' We'd climb up buildings and jump off the roofs, hang from bridges, run around in the dark. Scott was fearless—he'd jump off a two-story

22

building. He could get out of anywhere, and lose all of us."

The boys' lives became the "game," and they sometimes had difficulty separating their daredevil pursuits from reality. All of them, especially Kevin Meyers and William "Scotty" Scurlock, were remarkably physically coordinated and absolutely reckless. They couldn't conceive that they would be hurt—and because of that belief, perhaps, they weren't. They had young bones and young muscles. If their parents had had any idea what chances they were taking, they would have been horrified.

But they all lived in Reston, the perfect, model town, where nothing really bad ever happened. Kevin, Randy, and Scott and the rest of the pubescent boys who went on "death-defying missions" around Reston weren't a real gang. It was decades before street gangs would rear their heads. They were buddies, solid friends who formed loyalties that would last them a lifetime. They were, in a sense, like the boys in the movie *Stand By Me,* awkward socially, a little afraid of girls despite their protestations, and fighting to escape the watchful eyes of their parents. Kevin, however, envied Scott *his* parents.

"It seemed to me that Scott had the perfect family—his mom and dad were nice, and he had cool sisters. I could barely remember when my father lived with us and we were a regular family," Kevin says.

He enjoyed Reverend Scurlock's sermons, even as a junior high school kid. "He had a plan. He had a place where he was leading you, and then he'd get to his point and it all worked. He was charismatic."

Kevin was surprised though when he talked with Scott's dad after a youth meeting. Kevin spoke of his ability to astral project, and the minister was astounded. "I never knew that you believed (in out-of-body experiences) or had any kind of spiritual awareness," he said to Kevin.

"I thought you were a preacher," the skinny kid shot back. "Don't *you* know what I mean?"

"No, no—I've never done what you're talking about."

Kevin walked away, confused. He still believed that everyone felt as he did and that mind travel was a common human experience—especially for ministers. He himself had often "followed" people around with his mind, and he already had a nagging sense of what was the right path and what was the wrong one—not that he didn't sometimes step over the line back then.

3

Scotty Scurlock was a good-looking kid with regular features and a mass of curly almost-black hair. He was the best-looking member of his family, in fact. Sometimes the crap shoot of genetic components falls just right, and a baby so blessed receives the perfect combination of genes that bring with them both physical beauty and high intelligence. Scott was one of those babies. Where his father was a short, stocky man with craggy features, Scott was tall and lithe, and he had the face of a Greek statue, with liquid brown eyes, a classic nose, and full lips. The only outward characteristic Scott shared with his father was his hands; they were as short and stubby-fingered as the Reverend Scurlock's.

Scott was as wild as most "PKs" (Preachers' Kids) are, striving as the other rebellious ministers' children did to prove that he was neither a goody-goody or a sissy. To be perfectly honest, Scotty Scurlock was wilder and more rebellious than most. If Kevin or Randy thought of something dangerous to do, Scotty could be counted on to add an even more outrageous twist. But beneath the surface of the teenage rebel, there was a longing in Scott Scurlock, a sense that he could never hope to have what others had. Sometimes it seemed that his thirst for danger was born out of that longing.

One of Scott's earliest activities that seemed to be only boyish hijinks was, in truth, against the law—if only a misdemeanor. Scott and Kevin Meyers regularly lay in wait to rob early morning delivery trucks. *They* didn't consider it stealing; they thought of it as just one of their games. Hidden from view, the two boys would lie on their bellies on a hill above a road.

"When the pie truck came by," Kevin remembered, "we'd wait until the driver left the truck to make a delivery, and then we'd race down the hill and steal a cherry pie. We'd start on that, but we'd watch for the milkman. When we saw him park down below us, we'd do the same thing—grab a couple of quarts of milk to go with our pie. That was breakfast."

Scotty Scurlock dressed like a ragamuffin; he always would. He wore cheap low-top Converse sneakers; he always would. A few years later, when he and Kevin were old enough to date, Kevin would sometimes comment that Scott's clothes were a little . . . bizarre to wear for social occasions.

"God loves me for my body," Scotty would laugh. "Not for my clothes."

Scott's parents, William and Mary Jane, had lived in Reston almost from its inception. While Bill served as the youth pastor of the Baptist church on Lake Anne's Washington Plaza, Mary Jane taught in the elementary school. Kevin always described Scott's dad as "a Hobbit" because of his blunt, misaligned features. Mary Jane was a plain woman who wore simple clothes, often with knee-high boots. She wore little makeup, and her face was crisscrossed early on with wrinkles because she spent too many hours in the sun. It didn't matter that they lacked classic physical beauty; the elder Scurlocks had made a huge circle of friends and were quickly caught up in the exciting popular culture of the sixties in Reston. They were the leaders that everyone looked up to.

Bill's approach to his ministry was that religion didn't have to be stodgy and bound by musty tradition. His church was alive with new ideas, and he was much sought after as a counselor. Indeed, Reston's founder himself, Robert Simon, considered the Reverend Scurlock a trusted friend. "Bill Scurlock was very important in the early days for me," Simon recalled. "I used to go to him for advice. I can't remember what I'd talk with him about—I didn't have a psychiatrist, so he was the next best thing."

Bill and Mary Jane went to Esalen classes and later embraced those things that signaled New Age religion. They chose mantras and were intrigued by auras. And, since they both counseled others, many people in Reston admired their lifestyle and emulated it.

Bill even studied Rolfing, the vigorous massage that was said to have the ability to free the mind of pent-up memories and emotions through physical pummeling. His Rolfing sessions in the church basement were in great demand.

In Reston, many people in their thirties and forties were questioning old attitudes. The very fact that they had chosen to move to Reston stamped them as people with open minds and vision. The Scurlocks' group of friends were amenable to all manner of communication: intense confrontations, "letting it all hang out," marriage seminars where couples blurted out old resentments and new confessions. While their children were listening to the Beatles, parents searching for something to give their lives meaning were turning to faddish philosophies. Many couples in the Scurlocks' circle were divorced, unable to withstand the truth that emerged at confrontational seminars. Some couples even switched partners. It wasn't just happening in Reston; it was a sign of the times. *Bob and Carol and Ted and Alice* was a smash hit at the movies.

But Bill and Mary Jane's marriage remained intact.

They spent some time at nudist colonies, grew deeply tan, and ate health foods. And they believed in the laissez-faire approach to raising children. Discipline was not a part of their philosophy. Their children were free to choose and to make their own mistakes.

The fact that Scotty Scurlock could discuss *anything* with his father without fearing either punishment or disapproval amazed Kevin Meyers. When Kevin had done something against *his* father's rules, there were no friendly discussions. He had been whipped. "When I lied, I got whipped more. But when Scott asked his father what he should do about something or confessed something he was thinking about doing, his dad just said, 'Do what you think is best, son.' Scott didn't have any rules at all. None. As long as I knew him, he made his own rules. His father taught him to be totally free."

But Bill Scurlock had no rules either. He believed in free will and in the individual's ability to find his own way through life.

Both Kevin and Scott came from families with four children, but while Kevin had three brothers, Scott was the only son. One of his two older "sisters" was really a cousin that Bill and Mary Jane had adopted, and Scott was the third child. He had a younger sister, too. But Scott, of course, would be the one to carry on the family name. He was his father's immortality, and the Reverend Scurlock clearly doted on Scott and secretly smiled at his antics. Even when Scott, at age fifteen, "borrowed" a van and took several friends on a joy ride to the ocean, nobody in his family was very upset. That was just Scotty.

Scott had certainly inherited his father's charisma. He was smart and clever, and he was movie-star handsome, better looking with every year he grew older. Physically, he was still the marvelous change-ling child dropped into a plain family. More than that, he had a glow about him, a wild, rakish charm that well-nigh hypnotized anyone who came close. He was kind and considerate and infinitely amusing and attractive. Everyone wanted to be his friend.

"I certainly liked Scott well enough then," Kevin Meyers said. "But I think I liked the feeling of his house more; it was almost like being a part of a real family. I envied him."

Joanna Meyers wasn't really in the Scurlocks' social circle, although she knew them. They were parents of a similar age, raising children in the same era, but the Scurlocks were stars while Joanna and John lived a quieter life. Joanna was a serene woman who seldom found reason to disparage anyone else. She simply viewed the Scurlocks as alien creatures whose lifestyle was completely dissimilar to her own. She had to laugh once, however, at Mary Jane Scurlock's attempt at watercolors. Mary Jane's admirers thought her paintings were exciting, while Joanna, a watercolorist herself, quickly realized that Mary Jane's efforts were amateurish at best.

Perhaps it was only that *anything* the Scurlock family did seemed bigger than life. They were the perfect family to live in Reston—special, brilliant, talented, and much beloved by their friends. The town was new and open to limitless opportunities and avant garde ideas, and so were Bill and Mary Jane.

Although Scotty Scurlock played basketball at Herndon High School, it was his friend Kevin Meyers who became the real athletic star. He had been "discovered" in seventh grade at Herndon Junior High. Ever the hyperactive kid, Kevin was clambering in the girders high above the gymnasium when Ed Zuraw, the track coach at Herndon High School, happened to look up. Zuraw didn't shout at him to come down; instead he marveled at the kid's agility and thought he saw the makings of a pole vaulter.

Athletics and Ed Zuraw saved Kevin Meyers from a life without purpose or ambition. Ed kept an eye on the kid over the next few years, and recruited him for the Herndon High track squad. Zuraw completely turned Kevin's life around, giving him a belief in himself he had never had before. Kevin became a champion vaulter.

When he was a freshman, lean and tautly muscled, he placed fourth in the Virginia State meet by jumping fourteen feet, six inches. After that, he won every meet for the rest of his high school career. He became second in the nation as a senior when he sailed over a fifteen-foot-three-inch bar. He was offered track scholarships at a number of colleges.

Ed Zuraw instilled a strong sense of discipline and positive thinking into his athletes and none of them believed in these philosophies more than Kevin Meyers. Kevin would compete in some very difficult circumstances. Even though he cut his leg severely once during a meet, he insisted on vaulting again—and he won.

Quite naturally, Kevin's best friends in high school

were other pole vaulters. One was Bobby Gray. Another was Dan Becket. The trio formed their own little "fraternity" during high school. Still, over the years, the age difference between Kevin and Randy shrunk. Kevin's friends become Randy's friends and vice versa. Maybe it had something to do with the spirit of Reston, Robert Simon's dream that all kinds of people could live together in harmony and friendship.

Even though there might be periods where they didn't see each other and lived thousands of miles apart, so many of those boys from the early days in Reston would remain linked throughout their lives.

Oh, but they would go into adulthood kicking and screaming; some of the gang tag group simply didn't want to grow up. It wasn't that they wanted to be Peter Pan. They modeled themselves, instead, after Captain Hook. With the wisdom of retrospection, their hedonistic, foolhardy adventures—which continued long after they should have outgrown them—quite possibly set them up for tragedy. Nobody can take as many risks as they did and emerge unscathed. The piper must be paid.

Both fate and circumstance would dictate who they would become. One of the boys of Reston would develop a deep social conscience and a belief in God that pulled him continually away from the games that never stopped. Another would go in an entirely opposite direction. Even so, not one of them would escape chaos and disaster. It is the way fate singled them out and wrote the scripts of their lives that is baffling.

4

Steve Meyers suffered the most damage from living with a father who seemed unable to give much of himself to his boys. His father laughed at Steve's dreams of being an artist and told him he had better face reality if he expected to earn a living. He showed little, if any, admiration for Steve's talent. Gordon Meyers' words hurt Steve far more than the whippings he administered. Despite Joanna's pep talks and her belief in Steve, his father constantly undermined his self-confidence.

After his mother and brothers moved to Virginia, Steve followed them to Reston and enrolled in college at Northern Virginia College in Fairfax. He stayed close to the family until 1970, studying political science and literature at Northern Virginia College. Most of the young people who lived near Washington, DC, were interested in politics because they had matured in the shadow of the Pentagon. There were people living in Reston whose names were household words in American political circles; living so close to the national center of government, local kids formed opinions early on about politics.

1970 was a year filled with disenchantment with old values. Richard Nixon was in the White House, students were demonstrating against the war in Vietnam, and National Guardsmen shot into a crowd of students at Kent State, killing four of them. Young men either went to college, to Canada, or to war; many of them decried big business as much as they did big government.

Steve stayed in college and tried to conform, to study subjects that would lead to the kind of job his union-man father would approve of. But it didn't last. He longed to work with his hands and create objects of beauty.

In the summer of 1970, Steve traveled to England to attend Emerson College in Sussex where he studied his true love: art. He was an incredibly talented young man—and already possessed the gifted hands of an artist twice his age. He was a sculptor. He studied sculpting and art in England for two years, where he also worked with developmentally disabled children.

In 1972, while his brother, Kevin, was graduating from high school back in the States, Steve Meyers met a German architect, Ingleberg Schule, and moved to Vinterbach, Germany, where he would serve an apprenticeship in furniture design and cabinet making. He studied with Schule for three years. Steve carved and smoothed tables that had no legs, but were rather intricate puzzle pieces of ash and maple that nested together to make a base for smooth tabletops. His chests and armoires were softly chiseled and shaped so that it seemed his fingers had left their imprint in the hollows. No one but Steven Meyers could have built these pieces. His technique was so distinctive that he hardly needed to sign them.

Steve was very thin in those years. He had black

beetling brows that gave him the look of a darkly brooding artist. Kevin looked a lot like Steve, though it was as if they were opposite sides of a coin. Steve's side was shadowy while Kevin's was bathed in sunshine.

After learning everything he could in Germany, Steve Meyers moved to Norway to a village in the Telemark Mountains. There, he restored antique furniture so deftly that even a trained appraiser could scarcely detect the places where the old pieces had been renewed. He loved the precious woods and sanded and smoothed them with care. Eventually, Steve moved to Oslo and, at last, had his own studio where he designed furniture. He also returned to sculpting.

Critics were enthusiastic about Steve's work. It would have been difficult for them to picture him as one of Joanna Meyers' four rowdy kids—the kids who ate dog biscuits for cookies when times were lean and who had moved from one place to another while their determined mother searched for a secure home. Steve Meyers had blossomed into an artist who seemed capable of creating *anything,* whether he coaxed his pieces from wood or from marble—from glass or from steel. All the bad times seemed to be in the past.

In Norway, Steve met a woman who made him abandon his austere, rather lonely life. Her name was Maureen Lockett.* They lived together and, with Maureen, Steve moved to Carrara, Italy, in 1978. In 1980, Maureen and Steve had a baby daughter— Cara.* Steve was almost shocked by the love he felt for the tiny, perfect child with a cherub face. And she worshiped her father. Cara looked like a Botticelli painting, and, early on, she showed talent for dance just as her Aunt Dana had.

Steve never planned to return to America—not for good. He was in his element in Europe, where the masters had studied and painted and sculpted. He would visit his mother, certainly, but he never planned to go home to America to stay. He had everything he needed in Italy.

In the middle years of the seventies, all of Joanna's children had taken steps toward the forefront of the art world. It seems hardly possible that two parents could have produced *four* children with so much talent, but Joanna and Gordon had. Beyond the fact that the children shared a tremendously creative sense, they also looked like one another. A woman who met Kevin and Dana many years later recalled that she was shocked to see how much they resembled each other. "She was a beautiful girl, and he was a handsome young man—but their faces—their *faces*—were like twins . . ."

Dana *was* beautiful. She went to New York to study dance and joined the chorus line of the Rockettes, the famous Radio City Music Hall dancers. Ironically, though Dana was the first of the Meyers to become a professional in the arts, she was the one who cared the least about her career. All she really wanted to do was marry and have children. Dana longed to care for children, her own and others'.

* * *

Kevin Meyers graduated from Herndon High School in 1972. Ed Zuraw helped him decide which scholarship to accept, and he settled on Tempe Junior College in Arizona, where he continued to excel and break records. One day, however, in the last meet before the Arizona State finals, Kevin misjudged his speed and the height of the bar when he sailed over at almost fifteen and a half feet. It would have been another record, but he kept on going and crashed into the bar's standards beyond the pit. He ruptured both his ankles. The tendons were almost snapped and his ankles hemorrhaged. It would be six weeks before he could stand, much less pole vault, so he wouldn't be able to compete in the state finals.

But he was young; he healed as good as new, and his extraordinary talent as a pole vaulter returned. He spent some time in the summer of 1974 with his father, painting houses to earn some money. When he told his father that his greatest wish was to go to school in Hawaii, Gordon Meyers surprised him. He not only didn't laugh, he said he thought he could do something to make that happen.

"My dad went inside the house, made a few phone calls, and within a day, he told me it was taken care of. I had a scholarship to the University of Hawaii!"

The offer exceeded all of Kevin's dreams. He accepted at once. The kid who had bounced off walls back in Kansas would now live in paradise. He would receive room, board, books, and tuition.

Back in Reston, Kevin ran into Scott Scurlock at a party. Scott was with an absolutely beautiful girl named Corrinne. That didn't surprise Kevin—Scott usually had a fabulous-looking woman on his arm.

Although they hadn't seen each other for years, they talked and caught up and Kevin mentioned that he was on his way to Hawaii. Scott said he had been in Israel, living in a kibbutz, and that he'd always wanted to go to Hawaii.

Kevin wondered what a Baptist guy would be doing in a kibbutz, but Scott had always been up for some new adventure.

"How much is the plane fare to Hawaii?" Scott asked.

"I only know the one-way fare," Kevin said, "and that's two hundred and fifty dollars."

"I might come over someday," Scott said.

Kevin didn't think much of his comments. They were making small talk at a party.

Although the University of Hawaii supporters were far more enthusiastic about football and baseball than they were about track and the money allocated for track facilities was minimal by comparison, Kevin Meyers figured he'd died and gone to heaven when he got off the plane in Honolulu in the autumn of 1974. He loved Hawaii, the coaching staff, and the chance to turn out for the sport that consumed him.

He cashed his first scholarship check at a bank near the Puck's Alley shopping mall in Honolulu, and he was tucking the money into his wallet as he walked out of the bank into a fine misty rain. Just at that moment, a bus arrived from the airport and pulled up in front of the bank.

Kevin looked up and saw a familiar figure alight from the bus. The man wore frayed shorts, an old T-shirt, and he was barefoot. He had a faded Boy Scout knapsack on his back.

It was Scott Scurlock.

Scott had always had a way of turning up in the oddest places, as if he had dropped out of the sky. Kevin would learn never to be surprised to find Scott tapping on his door or rapping at his window. Now, Scott stepped down, as casually as if they weren't thousands of miles from Reston.

"How you doing, Bubba?" Scott said.

While they had been good acquaintances before—mostly for the purpose of gang tag when they were in junior high school—they were about to became best friends. They were fated to be the best of buddies, true friends, and mischievous partners. Scott dubbed Kevin "Thunderbolt" because he was aggressive and fearless—especially about approaching women. He had long since lost his shyness. Scott called himself "Lightfoot" because he had a certain athletic grace and stealthy ability to seem almost invisible.

For as long as he could remember, Kevin had wished for a friend who would be as close as a brother. Somehow, his own brothers had never filled the empty space he carried inside. And, from the moment Scott Scurlock stepped off that bus in Hawaii, acting as if it were the most reasonable thing in the world for him to be there, he and Kevin Meyers formed a bond so strong that it would stand the test of time and good and bad fortune. Nothing short of death or a cataclysmic metamorphosis in one or the other could ever break it.

5

Scott Scurlock quickly landed on his feet in Hawaii. His main employment was with a company called Hawaii Plant Life and Privacy Fences. He worked for a man named Warren Putske, who quickly realized how competent Scott was and made him a supervisor. Putske shared a huge house with several others, and he turned the basement over to Scott.

Warren Putske was an entrepreneur and sometime politician who was ten years older than Scott. Besides owning Hawaii Plant Life, Putske ran for public office as "The Uncandidate," who promised "If elected, I promise to do nothing!" He always got his share of votes from people who appreciated his honesty.

Scott didn't have enough money for a car at first, so he bought a bicycle to get around. "The fact that he picked up women for dates riding a bicycle didn't bother them at all," Kevin said. "He found another beautiful girlfriend right away. He used to tell me that riding double on a bike only 'warmed his women up good' by the time they got to the movies."

Scott applied for modeling assignments and was hired often. He was certainly handsome enough to make it as a model—or even as an actor. He was a man having a love affair with movies—he saw almost every film that came out—and he would have jumped at the chance to act, although he didn't pursue it.

Aside from his gardening job, most of Scott's employment came about because of his looks and his innate charm. For a while, he also worked at the Honolulu Airport as a "lei greeter." His assignment was to kiss female passengers as they walked through the arrival gates, and put leis around their neck. For Scott, it was like stealing money; he adored women, all women—or so it seemed.

Kevin Meyers concentrated on track. He vaulted sixteen feet that first year at the University of Hawaii. The son of the Reverend Bob Richards—the legendary track star—visited the University of Hawaii and taught Kevin how to vault over seventeen feet. He was reaching heights that would have been unheard of even ten years earlier.

And then, suddenly, after only a year, it was all over. Maybe it had been too perfect to last. The university cut the track program out of its budget so that they could build the Hula Bowl. They had no reason to pay a pole vaulter's tuition and expenses any longer—even if he was one of the five best in America.

Kevin Meyers was not only terribly disappointed, he was stuck. He didn't want to go back to the mainland, and, if he had, he had no money for airfare. A kid named Leon, one of the other pole vaulters, told Kevin he was renting an A-frame out in the jungle. There wasn't any water there or even any windows, but it had four walls, a roof and mosquito netting over the holes where windows were supposed to be. Leon offered a room to Kevin while he tried to figure out a way to survive. It was almost impossible for anyone to starve in Hawaii, although the variety of food available to someone on a tight budget was limited. Kevin was subsisting mostly on bananas.

"I moved in, and then I came home one day and found the place was overrun with goats! Big goats, baby goats." Kevin laughed. "They were standing on each other's backs trying to eat the last of my stalk of bananas."

Kevin went over to see Scott, and Scott got him a job landscaping for Hawaii Plant Life. Scott's basement bedroom had bunk beds and Kevin moved into one of them. This would be just the first of the many times that Kevin and Scott shared living space. The arrangements certainly weren't lavish, but, for Kevin, it sure beat fighting goats for his dinner.

Although Scott Scurlock had the bearing of a man who feared nothing, there *were* things that frightened him. Dark things. The first time he told Kevin that he sometimes felt that a kahuna was stalking him, his friend thought Scott was kidding. But he wasn't. Scott had heard of the Night Walkers who roamed the islands when the moon was hidden and there was no light at all. He had heard that one had to get out of their way or he would die—only to be swept up in their path and become one of them, doomed to walk forever in the dark.

Scott always kept some sort of weapon nearby—a club or a knife. One night, he took a shower, after setting his club just outside the curtain where it was handy. As he turned on the water, the basement went dark. Terrified, he raced to the light switch and flipped it back on. No sooner was he back in the shower than the basement went dark again. When Kevin came home, he found Scott waiting outside, his club held close. The "dark things" had frightened him, but he could never actually describe them.

Kevin didn't laugh at Scott. Whatever haunted him was real—at least to him.

Warren Putske had a lot of trust in Scott and gave him quite a bit of responsibility in carrying out big jobs for Hawaii Plant Life. Although Kevin was a good worker, he was, by his own evaluation, more of a "wild man" and Putske viewed him with a wary eye—particularly after he rode a few times in the company truck when Kevin was at the wheel. Kevin drove a truck the way he pole vaulted—throttle wide open. When he got out alive, Putske vowed never to ride with Kevin again.

Despite his unique personality, people had always liked Kevin Meyers—but for different reasons than why they liked Scott Scurlock. Scott mesmerized people where Kevin was as friendly and sincere as a puppy dog.

Bill Pfiel, who had been one of his track coaches at the University of Hawaii, was also a tomato farmer. He had leased five acres of prime agricultural land and two houses on the north end of the island of Oahu.

He knew that Kevin's living arrangements were tenuous, and he offered the smaller house on his acreage to him for $270 a month. Even better, he said he would give Kevin the first four months free if he painted the house and landscaped the hard-packed earth that surrounded it.

Kevin grabbed the place, and he asked Scott if he wanted to go partners on the project. The house sat on the opposite end of the ranch from Pfiel's place. It had a magnificent view of Waimea Bay and the salt breezes stirred the coconut palms so that they almost sang. The place would be nearly free if they both chipped in. No rent for four months, and then only $135 apiece. Pfiel loaned them a dump truck to move their belongings over to the farm. They gathered up bits and pieces of furniture, books, and personal belongings and moved onto the barren-looking spot.

Things began to look up almost immediately.

The men who thought of themselves as Thunderbolt and Lightfoot were about to embark on a lifestyle that any young man in his early twenties might aspire to. They were both handsome and smart and healthy and without a care in the world. Both of them were in peak condition. They were tanned, their hair and beards were thick and luxuriant. And they were still utterly fearless daredevils. They had no bonds—no wives or children, no parents within five thousand miles.

It was 1975, an era of adventure and free love for many young Americans, but for none as much as Kevin and Scott. They were on an endless vacation.

"We had four rules we lived by," Kevin said: "See Beauty; Have a Blast; Do Good; and Be Free!"

The tomato farm grew whatever was in season: tomatoes, of course, and squash and green beans. Shark's Cove and Waimea Bay were only a couple of minutes away. Bill Pfiel's agreement with Kevin and Scott also included work in the fields for them—at minimum wage—whenever they wanted to make a little extra money.

They dubbed their end of the ranch "The Shire Plantation" after the Hobbit fantasy in *The Lord of the Rings*. Their life was as close to perfect as that of the fictional Hobbits whose homes were cottages surrounded by flowers and who lived in peace and harmony. Hobbits never fought or argued; they farmed, ate six meals a day, and simply enjoyed life.

"We had everything we might ever want," Kevin recalled. "We had 'The Shire,' we didn't have to work more than a couple of days a week unless we wanted to. Almost everything we needed to eat grew on the property, and somebody had a potluck meal every night someplace. We could swim and body surf and jump off cliffs into whirlpools."

Landscaping "The Shire" wasn't difficult. Hawaii Plant Life had a contract to take care of all the flowers and bushes at the Kahala Hilton. The hotel specified that all their plants would be torn out periodically, and replaced with fresh vegetation. Neither Scott nor Kevin could bear to see anything living thrown away, so they carted the rejected plants home to The Shire Plantation.

"Anything would grow there," Kevin recalled. "If you spit a melon seed off the porch, you'd have a melon vine flourishing the next time you thought to look. We threw a seed out from an acorn squash and it wasn't long before we had two hundred squashes. We took so many squashes to the potluck suppers that we weren't very popular for a while. If we planted something at ground level, in nine months we could reach our hand off the porch and pick the fruit. We had every kind of plant you could imagine growing on our property. Hibiscus and Birds of Paradise and orchids and tropical flowers. We planted coconuts and had a row of coconut palms." (Twenty years later, when Kevin returned to Hawaii, he found that The Shire Plantation was no longer visible because the trees they had planted had grown so high around it.)

Scott and Kevin began to take great pride in the lush gardens they were creating. Sometimes, Kevin thought that the place must be blessed. He noticed one day when he was approaching The Shire by a winding road high above it that the peculiar conformation of timbers on the roof made a perfect giant cross.

It seemed fitting.

The casual attitude of the tomato farm allowed workers to pick produce naked. Scott, of course, had grown up in a family that embraced nudity and Kevin had no problem at all with it. The young women who lived in the big house and picked tomatoes or whatever else was in season had slender and perfect bodies too, and they didn't balk at working without clothes. Shut off from roads and the stares of tourists by thick foliage, the pickers moved gracefully through the fields with little more on than the bandannas they tied around their heads. Their nakedness wasn't so much sexual as it was free.

"We called them the Earth Girls," Kevin said. "They were vegetarians, they didn't shave their legs or under their arms, and their potlucks were always organic. They liked to come over to our porch, though, because we had the best sunset view. They taught us how to make perfect pizza dough with their bread starter. We made pizza out of everything—even 'cauliflower pizza.'"

In truth, Kevin and Scott were living more of a hedonistic existence than the serene life of the Hobbits they chose to emulate. They were far more prideful and obsessed with their bodies. They attached rings to the telephone poles in back of the house and spent hours doing gymnastics, building their biceps until they had the definition of competitive body builders.

"We were show-offs," Kevin remembered. "When the Earth Girls called us for dinner, we did handstands out of our chairs." The pictures they took of their finely honed bodies remain: Scott Scurlock, naked, lifting himself with only his hands gripping the arms of a spindly looking wooden chair, his legs straight out in front of him, and an insouciant, faint smile on his face to prove to the camera that it took so little effort.

Thunderbolt and Lightfoot craved a certain amount of excitement, and they sought out adventures that were not that different from their early days in Reston when they raided the pie trucks and the milkmen. It didn't matter that they had been thirteen then, and now they were twenty-one. They were grown men, bigger and far stronger than in the early days, but they were still full of mischief.

One afternoon, they were driving the landscaping truck when they spotted a sign that read "Catholic Banana Farm." They looked at each other and grinned, mouthing *"Catholic Banana Farm?"* They had to investigate. The next moonlit night, they drove through the massive and unguarded gate, and found acres and acres of ripe bananas. Cutting them would not do permanent damage; the plants left behind would regenerate.

The temptation was too great. They worked all night, hacking off banana stalks as tall as they were, and loading them into the truck. "We had enough bananas for everyone we knew," Kevin Meyers remembered. "Maybe too many. We'd show up for the nightly potlucks each holding a stalk of them, and people began to groan when they saw us. It was worse than the acorn squashes."

It seemed that the more adventures they had, the more Kevin accepted Scott as his "brother." "I loved him. He *was* the brother I'd been looking for. He always had time for me, and he never minded my being around. He always called me 'Bubba.'"

Although neither Kevin nor Scott recognized it, they were living out a magical time in their lives, one that could never be replaced once it was gone. One day melted into the next. They went to movies, and almost always preferred the films that were full of myth, swashbuckle, and romance. They played chess and sang and strummed duets on their guitars. The two of them liked to impress guests by playing "Blackbird" as a duet. Two decades later, Scott could still pick up his guitar and play "Blackbird" flawlessly. It was a haunting song, the words those of a man longing for his freedom.

It was odd that Scott so identified with the lyrics; he had, perhaps, more freedom than almost any man alive. Kevin felt some faint sense of urgency; he knew where he was headed—his life would be devoted to his painting. It might be five years—or even ten— before he could realize his ambitions, but he had no doubt in the world that he would be an artist. For the moment, he fixed up a studio in the basement of The Shire House.

Scott was less focused. He knew his dad expected him to get his four-year degree and find a well-respected career, but he felt no particular time pressure about going to college. He was a prodigious reader and very intelligent. He had always been good at science, and he thought that one day he would become a doctor.

Scott made a pretty good living with Hawaii Plant Life, although he would have preferred to have made it as a model. He had a display on the wall at the Shire Plantation with photographs of himself taken at modeling jobs. He still greeted women at the airport from time to time. His friend Marge Violette asked him once if he minded kissing the older women, and he shook his head and grinned.

"Scott had no sense of age with women," she recalled. "He liked kissing young women and he liked kissing old women. The only difference was that he wouldn't ask the older ones for their telephone number or which hotel they were staying at."

Marge Violette was a New Jersey girl, originally, but she had been born with a wanderlust. She worked at various desk jobs for TWA for a while in New York City. Then she was assigned to Hawaii, and was stationed—happily—in Honolulu from 1969 to

1975. When the company downsized and she lost her job as a reservationist, she decided to spend a year in South Dakota. She had always enjoyed a complete change in lifestyle, and South Dakota was nothing like Hawaii. Still, she had a great time there.

But Marge missed Hawaii and she came back to visit her friend Bill Pfiel in the spring of 1976. She was in her middle twenties, slender and pretty. She wore her thick black hair parted in the middle and caught up with two rubber bands. Hers was the ubiquitous look of the seventies, that long straight hair, a T-shirt without a bra, and either shorts or a long skirt.

The extra rooms at The Shire Plantation were open to anyone who happened to be passing through. They never knew who might move in next. Bill Pfiel told Marge he thought she would like the young men from Virginia who lived there. Since she would be living with them, she hoped that she would.

Marge met Scott first; Kevin was away on a two-week trip. Scott's hair was naturally black, but it was sunburned almost blond in places, and came down to his shoulders. His face had been softer and more boyish back in Reston—now, it was a man's face, chiseled and handsome. He had a short beard, and he wore a blue bandanna tied around his forehead. He stood just under six feet and he was browned by the sun, with a washboard stomach and well-defined biceps. Marge noted that his voice was a deep, masculine rumble and that his grammar was perfect.

On the first night she met Scott, Marge recalled that they walked down to the beach. They sat there and talked for four hours, "Until long after the sun set," she remembered. "The sky was black and we could see the stars. It was so pitch black that we could hardly see to find our way back."

She recalled being utterly mesmerized that first night. Scott was so interested in everything she had to say, and she found everything he had to say fascinating. He told her that he divided his time between The Shire and a house in Honolulu that he shared with four other men. He spoke of his modeling career and about his family back in Virginia. It was hard for Marge not to feel romantic about a stranger who poured out his heart to her in the velvet darkness of a Hawaiian night. She found Scott exciting and attractive.

"I quickly became infatuated with him," Marge admitted. "Anyone would have. We spent almost two weeks getting to know one another, but people kept telling me that I hadn't met anyone until I'd met Kevin."

Marge Violette was bewitched by Scott, but she wasn't in love with him; she soon realized that he would be emotionally dangerous. He was clearly not a one-woman man. Scott never promised fidelity and she never expected it. He would go off to his town house in Honolulu often. She had no illusions that he wasn't dating other women. She simply enjoyed watching him, listening to him, hearing him play "Blackbird" on his guitar. She studied his face in the firelight the way someone might watch a completely handsome actor in a movie. He was like quicksilver, impossible to trap or to hold.

But the others who hung out at The Shire Plantation were right about Kevin. "When Kevin showed up," Marge recalled, "he stood in the doorway and he filled the room. He was even more intense, if possible, than Scott was."

The two men were so alike. Even their voices were so similar that, if she closed her eyes, she found it impossible to know which of them was talking. Yet, at the same time, Scott and Kevin were completely different. Scott was *too* handsome, *too* perfect. Any woman who truly fell in love with him was asking for a broken heart. It wasn't that he was shallow. He wasn't—but he was ephemeral. She knew that one morning he would be gone. If not gone entirely, gone from her. Kevin was solid, a man who was deeply committed to his art. He seemed to be more of a jokester and hedonist than Scott was, but, underneath, he clearly knew where he was going. He was always looking for a job where he could use his talent, and his heart was in his little basement studio.

"It was Kevin I really fell in love with," Marge remembered. "I would have married Kevin in a minute if he'd asked me, but he didn't; he wasn't ever cruel, but he kept reminding me that he and I didn't have that kind of a relationship. There were other women he wanted—not me."

Kevin's brown hair was bleached flaxen from salt water and the sun, and it blew in the sea wind. He was a little taller than Scott, and probably twenty pounds heavier. Marge watched them together, and marveled at what close friends they were. They laughed about the same things, remembered the same things, and told hilarious stories about what bad little boys they had been back in Virginia.

"There was no leader and no follower between Kevin and Scott. They were both so full of energy. They were intrepid and unassuming," Marge said. "That could describe them both—'intrepid and unassuming.'"

The two men always signalled to each other with hawk cries, and beyond their Lightfoot and Thunderbolt nicknames, Scott called Kevin "Bubba." Kevin called Scott a half dozen names, "Willy," "Willie-Boss," "Tarzan," and "Wilbur." Scott liked "Willie-Boss" the best. He liked to be in charge.

Kevin and Scott were dedicated, tireless hikers, and they explored Hawaii's most isolated spots, stumbling across secret places. They hiked from Lahaina to the Halekala Crater to the Seven Sacred Pools. They walked along pig paths, through jungles, and along the sea. They could be tormenting—almost sadistic—about it, especially when they offered to lead friends on hikes. For them, the steep climbs and the tortuous crawls through overgrown pig paths full of thorns and sharp branches were easy. Their charges begged for mercy before the hikes were over and lived to rue the day they signed up, returning covered with scrapes, cuts, scratches, and bruises.

The buddies swam and snorkeled and bodysurfed. They found a cliff at Koko Head where the ocean churned violently seventy-five feet below. Only the very reckless would leap from there, but Scott and Kevin cannonballed into the white surf below over and over again.

From then on, they demanded an "initiation jump" from any visitor who came to stay at The Shire

Plantation. On the way from the airport, they stopped beside the roaring ocean and refused to budge until their hapless visitors jumped. Only Scott's parents were allowed to decline. And Marge.

"We got almost everyone else to agree to jump," Kevin smiled, remembering. "But they didn't realize that was only part of it; once they were airborne, they had to figure out how to get out of the surf below and then find a way to make it back up the hill."

"They could never make me jump," Marge remembered. "I told them that I was there to take pictures, and I couldn't get the camera wet."

More menacing even than the precipitous drop were the sea caves in Shark's Cove below. Kevin and Scott found an underwater tunnel that they called "The Dragon's Mouth."

"You could barely see light at the end of the tunnel, and, if you held your breath and swam through," Marge said, "you were on the ocean side of the cove when you came to the surface."

When molten lava had hit the water long before, it had curled The Dragon's Mouth into myriad stone fingers. Some of the tunnels even went far back into the cliff itself. Holding their breath, the two men trusted that they would pop up out in the ocean before they ran out of oxygen. Marge went with them once and almost drowned before she could find an outlet to the path she had chosen to take.

Marge remembered one of the things Scott had told her on the first night she met him. When they spoke of the things they wanted to accomplish, he had told her the one goal he truly wanted to realize was to save a life. And he did. "It was a doctor . . . from the mainland who was on vacation," she said. "The man had gone out too far and couldn't get back . . . I never met the person, but Scott did see the doctor again. He took Scott out to dinner and Scott took him cliff jumping."

The three of them got along great in a platonic way that spring of 1976. Marge kept house and added a woman's touch to The Shire. While they planted flowers outside, she brought them into the house. Often Kevin and Scott had work to do in Honolulu for Hawaii Plant Life and they came home only on weekends. They were glad to find that Marge had taken care of everything in their absence. If Kevin knew that she had romantic feelings for him, he avoided any discussion about it. Things were perfect the way they were.

On one of their hikes, Scott and Kevin came across a field of marijuana and they realized it would be a much bigger score than the "Catholic Banana Farm." In their island social circle, good marijuana was highly desired. The group frowned on cigarettes, but not on pot smoking. They selected their marijuana the way a generation older might have picked a fine wine. (Scott himself preferred female, sencea pot.)

They lived in a place and during an era where their youth happily isolated them, and they were benignly alienated from anyone over forty. So, when they found the field of illegal marijuana, they made plans to liberate it.

This time, they returned to the field with a beat-up

old car to bring home a load of "produce." They cut the mature marijuana plants and piled them onto the roof of the car, and when they could get no more in the front and back seats, they filled the trunk to bursting. They had less than a mile to drive to get back to The Shire. Literally buried in pot, they peered over the fragrant leaves and steered precariously down the road.

"I went into Scott's room late that night," Marge said. "And there were Kevin and Scott in a room filled with marijuana plants they had cut down. They were pulling the leaves off the stems and asked me to help them. There was this very intense energy in that room."

Watching them, Marge shook her head slowly, strangely revulsed by the smell of their sweat in the warm room. In the previous weeks, she had put a lot of house plants in Scott's room, and they had all been thriving. Now, she saw that they were suddenly limp and wilted.

"Look what you're doing to them," she scolded Kevin and Scott. "Look around and see them. They're practically crying out—they're scared that they'll be the next to be pulled out of the soil and have their leaves torn off. I can't even stay in this room."

Scott looked at her as if she'd gone crazy, but Kevin understood what Marge was saying and bent his head. She could tell he felt bad.

"The next day, the pot was gone," she said. "With some extra care the houseplants all survived—the orchids and all."

Kevin never knew where Scott had gone to sell the

leaves they'd spent all night stripping. But, somehow, Scott had known just what to do. The next day, he handed Kevin $2,000. Kevin was dumbfounded. It had been a long time since he had had anywhere near that much money. They laughed uproariously. They hadn't taken all the "hippie's crop," but they had taken enough to make a bundle of money. To them, it wasn't stealing; it was more like a chess game.

Marge and Kevin and Scott were a happy trio. They showed off and she took pictures. She forgave them for the marijuana incident. In June 1976, some friends of Kevin's docked their boat in the harbor. One of the men, Rich, had gone to high school with Kevin. Kevin asked Marge if she wanted to go out with them to a Mexican restaurant. The sailors hadn't had real food or drinks or fun for a long time. Marge agreed to join them.

Rich was quite taken with Marge that night, and later when he came out to stay on the tomato farm. The attraction was to be the end of the good times that Kevin, Scott, and Marge had shared. The crew of the sailboat explained that they alternated choosing new crew members, and it happened to be Rich's turn to pick someone to sail with them for the next three weeks.

Kevin said he wouldn't mind going, but Rich shook his head. "Nope. This time we want a woman. We're sick of looking at our own ugly, bearded faces. I pick . . . *Marge.*"

Marge smiled and nodded. It would be another adventure. South Dakota, then Honolulu, and now, the open sea. Anyway, this leg of the trip was to be a short one. She only planned to sail with them to Fiji, and she had enough money to buy a plane ticket back to Hawaii.

"Once in Fiji, I decided to stay with the boat and sail to New Zealand," she recalled. "The boat was staying there six months. My money for a ticket from Fiji to the U.S. would buy me a ticket back from New Zealand too . . . the owner had no problem with my staying on the boat as an unpaid crew member."

As it turned out, Marge stayed with the boat for fourteen months. They sailed on to Tahiti and then back to Hawaii, arriving in Honolulu in October 1977. Two decades later, she remembered the day well. There was a heat wave in Honolulu and they went to the movies to escape the heat. "We saw *Star Wars.*"

When Marge Violette had sailed out of Honolulu, she didn't realize that she wouldn't be coming back for more than a year. She had simply stepped out of Kevin and Scott's perfect world onto a sailboat. But in the interim, an invisible curtain had dropped between them: She would see Scott Scurlock only once more in the seventies, and that was when she stopped over in Honolulu briefly after her long cruise.

"Scott took me and another girl to a Halloween party," Marge recalled. "I wore leotards with wings attached to my arms and went as a butterfly. Scott may have worn a plaid shirt and gone as a lumberjack—but on this I'm not sure. . . . There were a lot of University of Hawaii students there. . . . It was one of the nicest parties I have ever attended."

Marge's brother was getting married back in New

Jersey, and she left for the mainland the first week of November 1977. In the years ahead, Marge kept in touch with Kevin and saw him once in a while. On one occasion, she took a train across Canada to see him in Edmonton, and she visited him in Virginia and met his mother. Years later, when Marge got engaged, she called Joanna Meyers to tell her. Joanna blurted, "Oh, I'm sorry—it's just that I always hoped you and Kevin would get married."

It was different with Scott. Marge would not cross paths again with Scott for seventeen years. When they did meet again, their worlds would be completely changed.

6

Joanna Meyers' children had not only left home, it looked as though they were going to settle in far-flung corners of the world and she might never see them all together again. Dana was in New York, Steve in Italy, Kevin in Hawaii, and now Randy, too, had headed off to Europe. He would make Italy his base for a very successful career writing musical scores for movies. Their homecomings would be infrequent but wonderful. Joanna was always so glad to see any of her children. She was proud and grateful. Somehow they had come through the fire of her stormy marriage and had grown past the ego-damaging neglect of their father.

Dana was married now—to the stage director of the New York City Ballet Company, Peter Gardner. And although Steve wasn't married, he had settled down with a woman. But neither Randy nor Kevin had shown any signs of permanent romantic commitments.

Of all the children, Kevin seemed the most unsettled, the searcher who knew that he wanted to paint and that no other career would suit him, but he hadn't found a spot where he could set up a real studio. He was younger than Dana and Steve and not as disciplined as Randy. And, by all accounts, he was having a wonderful time in Hawaii. He wasn't thirty yet. There was time.

Just when it seemed that all the Meyers were going to be fine, small things started to go wrong. There was the slightest creaking in what had seemed to be a solid structure. It was like finding a fissure in a wall left behind by an undetectable earthquake. The damage seemed minuscule, but deep inside, there was a fault that would one day make itself known.

Kevin Meyers trusted Scott Scurlock completely. Although he liked almost everyone he met, there were only a handful of people he trusted completely. Scott was one. They were best friends, brothers, co-conspirators, adventurers together. Kevin would recall those days and say, "I honored Scott's path—I honored him."

They still had little money, but they didn't need

much. Their landscaping jobs paid them enough to rent The Shire and buy what they needed. They weren't joined at the hip; Scott spent time in Honolulu, and Kevin took short trips to Edmonton, Alberta, and sailed with his friend Rich. But The Shire was their home base; it was the most stable, dependable, welcoming home either had ever found.

But then their perfect way of life hit a roadblock. Kevin's job with Hawaii Plant Life was phased out, the tomato farm was in a fallow period, and he didn't have the money for his share of the rent. He didn't miss the jobs, though. He had made up his mind to believe in his skill as an artist. But Scott didn't have enough to pay for both of them, and he said, "Bubba, we're in trouble. We haven't got the rent."

"Don't worry," Kevin said. "I'll get the money."

At that moment, the phone rang. Scott answered and handed it to Kevin, saying, "It's for you, Bubba."

It was Michael Lau, who owned a wonderful tourist attraction called Paradise Park. Kevin had put his bid in to do some murals at the park, even though he'd never painted a mural in his life. But Lau didn't know that and he hired Kevin on the spot to paint a seventeen-by-fifty-five-foot mural at Paradise Park. He would pay him $3,000.

This amount of money was unheard of in their world, but Kevin accepted the commission without betraying the excitement he felt. It would mean leaving The Shire for a long time, but it was necessary if they hoped to continue renting their home.

"I wasn't going to waste any money renting another place," he recalled. "I bought a tent from somebody for $150 and found a place out in the jungle next to a stream. It was gorgeous, and I ended up living there for six months."

Kevin painted thirteen murals at Paradise Park. It was fortunate that he was an athlete; the murals rose so high above the ground that he had to be both an acrobat and a painter. The wall he created in the Bird Theater looked so real that you had to touch it to tell it was a painting. A crystalline waterfall cascaded over lifelike rocks and banana leaves and crimson halacoya shaded the "water."

One night, there was a violent tropical storm and Kevin woke up in his tent to the sound of trees crashing down all around. When he ventured out at dawn, he saw that a huge coconut palm had fallen inches from his tent. Rather than being frightened, he felt blessed. He was alive, he had finished his assignments at Paradise Park, and he had more money than he had ever made in his life. Most important, he had proved to himself that he could, indeed, make a living with his art.

Kevin Meyers had come to believe in signs and omens. Some unseen hand had saved him from being crushed by a falling tree in the jungle. He was free now to go back to The Shire.

Kevin's homecoming was not what he expected. On the surface, everything looked the same; the gardens they had planted were, if possible, even more lush than they had been. But, as he walked through the property, Kevin felt the hairs prickle at the back of his neck. He looked closer and saw that someone had cleverly planted marijuana in sheltered pockets of space between The Shire's gardens. The pointed leaves hid themselves among the coleus and the hibiscus plants, but they were there, as luxuriant and thriving as everything else they had planted.

Kevin turned to Scott with a question in his eyes. "Who planted it?"

Scott grinned. "I did. See how it blends in? I hid it so well that no one will ever see it."

It was one thing to rip off somebody else's illicit field of pot; it was another to *plant* the illegal drug in front of their home. Scott couldn't understand why Kevin was upset. And Kevin couldn't explain that growing marijuana on the land that Bill Pfiel had leased was a betrayal that could bring them all down. This wasn't like stealing cherry pies, or bananas, or even somebody else's marijuana. This was fouling their own nest.

Kevin didn't want to be at The Shire. His friend Rich was sailing to California and needed him to crew. Kevin accepted. He hoped that when he came back, things would have returned to normal.

But a Pandora's Box had been opened, and there was no way in the world to close it. Scott wasn't at all deterred by Kevin's shock and disappointment. He simply went ahead with his bumper crop of marijuana, reaping it when it was ready, rolling the leaves and preparing to sell it. It was his second foray into the world of drug dealing, only *this* time Scott was selling his own product.

Perhaps because he had no real experience in the cultivation of marijuana, Scott Scurlock was clumsy. Bill Pfiel found out about the forbidden crop. It would be difficult not to notice that the gardens of

The Shire Plantation were full of growing things one day, and virtually decimated the next. When Pfiel and the owner of the tomato farm verified what was going on, they evicted Scott. By the time Kevin returned, Pfiel knew that he had had no part in growing the illegal plants, and Kevin was still in favor—to a degree. But since Kevin had brought Scott to The Shire, he was now somehow tainted too.

"They told me that I could move back in—but everything had changed," Kevin Meyers said. "They wanted triple the rent and, for that, I could only rent the basement where I'd had my old art studio. Somebody else was moving in upstairs. It wouldn't be The Shire any longer. That part of our lives was over."

Scott left Hawaii to return to Virginia to sell the marijuana he'd grown. Kevin moved in with some friends, staying in Hawaii only long enough to finish one final mural commission.

"It was all ending," Kevin recalled. "I had about $3,200 left, and I headed for Canada to live with Ron Jackson—one of the guys from the University of Hawaii track team. I didn't know when I'd see Scott again—if ever."

Kevin Meyers spent the next few years traveling between Edmonton, Alberta, where he ran youth hostels during the summer, and Virginia, where he spent winters. He didn't see Scott Scurlock, although he heard that he'd gotten a job with the county back in Reston as a building inspector. That would be the kind of prestige job that Scott's dad would approve of.

Kevin wanted to live full-time in Virginia, if he could find some broken-down place that he could remodel into a studio. It had to be broken down because he knew he would never be able to afford anything in Fairfax County that was even faintly livable. For the moment, though, he had to make do with, somewhat ironically, an old pie truck. He fixed that up, lived in it, and sold it for $1,500. Then he bought a van from his old coach, Ed Zuraw. He saved his summer money, and fitted out his van as a studio. It doubled as his home.

Kevin Meyers and his brother Steve shared similar talent and ambition, but Steve was way ahead of Kevin in terms of selling his work. Even with the good traits they shared, they also seemed to share a kind of family curse; when things looked bright, something always came along to cast a pall.

Much to the amazement of the villagers in Carrara, Steve had renovated an old building in the Italian hamlet where he lived. He had rescued what seemed to be an unsalvageable structure and made it into a home and studio. He loved his studio, his family, and his career. It was 1982 when Steve's steady climb to critical acclaim and fortune as a sculptor in Italy hit several broken steps. A propane explosion in a kiln destroyed his home, all of his works in progress and most of his personal possessions, along with irreplaceable works of art. It was a tremendous blow for Steve. He had wrenched something out of nothing, made it into a studio and home full of sunlight, only to have it disappear in one terrible moment.

Steve didn't have the money or the heart to rebuild. While Maureen and their daughter waited in Italy,

Steve returned to America to try to find a way to sell art pieces on commission. He was welcomed into galleries—in Washington, DC; New York; Houston; just as he had been welcomed in Oslo, Milano, Stuttgart, and Paris.

It would be slow, he knew—but he would make it all the way back—and beyond.

Steve Meyers returned to Italy, and boxed up everything he had left. He shipped his belongings to Kevin to store, and, in the spring of 1983, Steve brought Maureen and Cara to Virginia. They lived one month with Joanna, while Steve looked for an old house he could afford. He was in his early thirties, strong and healthy, and he believed he could make a new life for his family.

Steve found an old farmhouse that needed massive clean-up and carpentry work in Great Falls, Virginia—close to where Kevin hoped to find a place. He transformed it into both a home and a studio.

But his hope of recouping his losses and keeping his "family" together soon faded. Suddenly, nothing was right. His relationship with Maureen was rocky and growing more so every day. They had lost everything that had made their lives romantic and fulfilling. It was as if the explosion had blown up more than their physical possessions; it had blasted them apart too. Living day after day in the midst of disarray and building supplies, it was almost impossible to remember their sunny studio in Italy.

Their relationship shriveled like a grape left too long to ripen in the sun. Maureen told Steve she no longer wanted to live with him. He stared at her uncomprehendingly as he realized all that would mean. He thought he could not bear to live without Cara. But, dully, he knew he would have to. Alone, he couldn't take care of her. The most he could hope for would be visits. Nothing would ever be the same again.

Steve finished the farmhouse so that it was pleasant and quite livable and left Maureen and Cara there while he returned to Italy to salvage a few last pieces from his ruined studio in Carrara. In May of 1984, Steve had an exhibition of his work by the BMS Studio d'Arte at the Spoleto Festival. Dana and Peter Gardner had divorced, but Peter was still a friend and patron, and he wrote the cover notes of the brochure that described Steve's work:

> In confronting the works of Steven Meyers for the first time, one is struck by the apparent diversity of styles. Yet . . . there is a subtle denominator which makes viewing the sculptures a coherent experience. . . . The use of light, as if the illumination of matter by spirit heighten(s) our awareness of shadow. . . .
>
> At The National Academy of Design in New York, the recent exhibition of Meyers' "The Tomb of Lazarus" threw this aspect of his work into dramatic relief. The white marble was once again worked to translucency. . . .
>
> These themes of love, death, spirit and matter are always in Meyers' sculpture to varying degrees. . . .

Inspired by great poets and writers, Steve Meyers often referred to classic literature to explain his work.

One piece was inspired by H. Miller's poem, "Fragment,":

> We are never whole again, but living in fragments
> And all our parts separated by thinnest membrane.

Steve and Maureen were separated by more than that. If either of them had hoped that absence might make them realize that they really did love each other, they were disappointed. It really *was* over between them.

Lonely, Steve had met another woman while he was traveling in Italy—a woman who had been living in Brazil. Her name was Diana Gerhart.* There was definitely an attraction between them, and Steve hoped they would meet again. At least their meeting showed him that it was possible for him to find love again. In the meantime, he missed his daughter terribly.

Steve Meyers didn't know Scott Scurlock. He had never gone to high school in Reston, and he'd never really lived there at all. When he first moved to Virginia, he had gone to college, and then he had headed to Europe. He may have heard Scott's name— as a friend that Kevin had lived with in Hawaii—but he would have known nothing about him.

Steve planned to gather up whatever he had left in Italy, return to the United States, and find a way to revive his career. His fondest hope was to win custody of Cara, although he didn't think that would ever be possible.

When it first burst from the forest floor in the fall of 1971, Evergreen State College in the Washington State capital of Olympia, was criticized by the state's more staid and established colleges. Detractors called it a "kiddy college," and claimed Evergreen was only for hippies and dropouts who weren't really serious about getting an education. Evergreen *did* attract artists and musicians and freethinkers, but it would one day take a respected place in the hierarchy of higher education in the Pacific Northwest.

Having been raised in a home where avant garde thinking prevailed, it wasn't surprising that Scott Scurlock was attracted to Evergreen. Nobody in his family was a conformist, and he himself certainly was not. Scott had had his two years living the life of a carefree bachelor in Hawaii, with more adventures than most men ever know. He had soon grown bored with his Fairfax County building inspector job.

Bill Scurlock thought it was time that Scott settled down to studying, and he approved of his enrolling at Evergreen in 1978. If Scott ever hoped to find a serious job, he was going to need a four-year degree. Scott assured his father that he would get his bachelor's degree. He had lost enthusiasm about getting his

MD. He had scholarships and loans when he entered Evergreen to study biochemistry.

The Evergreen College campus in the late seventies scarcely resembled any other in America. It was still the forest primeval it had been only a short time before. Fir and cedar trees crowded next to paths between buildings, and huge stumps remained from early logging days. When Scott Scurlock started there in the early 1980s, it was as verdant a forest as a "tree hugger" could wish for.

Scott first lived in student housing, and then he found a little gray house to rent on Overhulse Road NW outside of Olympia. He was attracted to the house because it sat on nineteen heavily treed acres, close to Evergreen but with a comforting sense of complete isolation from civilization.

Although Scott Scurlock had survived the cliff jumping, and other daring stunts in Hawaii, he came close to death in Olympia. "Scott was driving his Volkswagen bug and he almost died in it," a friend remembered. "A truck ran a red light and creamed him. He scooted right underneath the rig and it almost took his head off. The bug was smashed—I mean *smashed;* he should have died. That was his moment. I think his angels saved him."

After a brief hospitalization, Scott Scurlock was as good as new. But the accident did not slow him down or sober him. He wasn't a typical college kid; he was nearly twenty-five and he was used to traveling and living a high life. College scholarships weren't going to pay for that.

Scott had always had a knack for making friends. He kept those he had—even though his antics sometimes caused temporary estrangements—and he made new friends constantly. He was the center of any number of social circles. There was an energy—a vibrancy—that surrounded him.

As he moved through his twenties, Scott Scurlock only grew more handsome. With his thick and wavy dark hair and perfectly balanced chiseled features, he was catnip to women. And he loved women—in great numbers. It may not have been in him to maintain a monogamous relationship, or it may have only been that he had not found the one woman who was right for him.

But Scott always had male friends too. As much as he loved women, he probably was more comfortable in the company of his male buddies.

While Scott studied chemistry at Evergreen, he was also learning how to augment his income by reducing an intricate chemical formula into a much-sought-after product: crystal meth.

"Crystal meth" is a delicately distilled form of methamphetamine, a popular and expensive street drug. It is, essentially, "speed." The drug accelerates users' metabolism, generates a feeling of well-being and power, and negates—at least for a time—the need for sleep.

Scott wouldn't be producing the stuff solely for personal use or just for his friends. If he was going to distill purified speed and take the risks that came with the process, he would have to set up an efficient distribution system. Scott had met someone on the campus, a tall man with waist-length hair, who taught him everything he needed to know about extracting the methamphetamine from the prescribed chemicals. Together, they worked on what Scott would always call his "experiments," pretending to be zealous students carrying out class projects.

The money that would inevitably result from Scott's hidden lab would pay for the thing he loved most: travel. Scott had always had itchy feet. Even while he was attending college at Evergreen, he took off as often as he could, determined to travel the world over.

Kevin Meyers crisscrossed America and Canada often in his van. He had named it "Azland" for the magic lion full of energy and strength in the *Chronicles of Narnia*.

He left Banff and headed for Washington State. He hadn't seen Scott Scurlock for more than three years, but he knew he lived in Olympia and he had his address. Kevin arrived late one night and parked beside a Volkswagen outside the small gray house. He fell asleep in the van, waking the next morning to the sound of someone outside. Sliding the side window open, Kevin peered out and saw Scott. He was sitting on the bumper of the Volkswagen putting on a pair of Converse tennis shoes.

Time had seemingly stood still. Scott was wearing the same cheap shoes he'd worn back in the days of gang tag when they were in junior high—the same shoes he'd worn in The Shire days. Scott was unaware that Kevin was watching him—he didn't even know he was there, and he apparently hadn't noticed the Virginia tags on Azland.

Kevin poked his head out and shouted, "You can't

see the wizard today!" a line from a long-standing joke between them.

Scott looked up and grinned. "Bubba!"

"The past was forgotten," Kevin recalled. "All the bad stuff about the marijuana and losing The Shire. It had been years, but we were friends again. He was the same Scott I'd always known."

Or so Kevin hoped.

Scott took Kevin to the Evergreen campus and showed him around. He ended the tour by taking Kevin to his private lab. He laughed as he pointed to the sign on the door: it was the international symbol that indicates the presence of radioactivity. He told his old friend that he kept it there to be sure he had privacy.

In retrospect, Kevin realized that Scott was testing him when he took him into the lab. "He was watching me to see if I saw anything unusual about the place. I didn't have any idea what you were supposed to have in a chemistry lab. It looked normal enough to me."

During Kevin's visit, he would sit on a stool in the tiny lab and work on watercolors while Scott did whatever it was he needed to do on his "experiments."

He didn't know that they were in a bootleg laboratory—and that the radioactive sign was to keep anyone from checking it out, including the college janitors. Inside, Scott Scurlock was manufacturing a vital ingredient of crystal meth, using the facilities and the chemicals that belonged to Evergreen State College.

"Scott made drugs right there under their noses,"

Kevin recalled. "Even all these years later, they're probably going to freak when they find out. I found out later that he had his own set of keys to most of the rooms in the chemistry building. He got everything he needed. The school taught him chemistry, and he used it."

If Scott needed something that was behind one of the few doors he didn't have a key for, he used skills he'd learned back on the days of gang tag in Reston. He would crawl through the ceiling and along the rafters, taking apart heating ducts if he had to, and dropping down into nearby labs to take what he needed. Nobody ever suspected him; nobody even missed what he took.

It was ironic. Scott Scurlock was a student who had the intelligence and, perhaps more importantly, the intellectual curiosity and innovative ability to work on mankind's problems—this was a man who read scientific journals avidly. But he chose to make drugs instead of helping humanity. Even though he often talked about the need to find cures for AIDS and cancer, Scott was too busy filling the orders of drug dealers he had contacted in and around Olympia to do more than talk.

Kevin inadvertently came close to blowing Scott's cover. He forgot his paint kit one day and went to Scott's lab. The door was locked and he asked one of the janitors to let him in so he could retrieve it. The janitor didn't notice anything unusual either. "Boy, was Scott mad at me when I told him I'd had the janitor let me in. And I *still* didn't know why."

Scott was making money simply from selling a vital component of crystal meth, and that, he told friends he trusted, was the most important thing to him. That was where he got the drive to study as hard as he did. "These are the *keys* that are going to make me money," he bragged. "All these students are here, trying to get some stupid *degree*. Who wants a degree? What are you going to do with it? Go get a job for $45,000 or $50,000 a year with a chemical company, and you'll be sitting there putting test tubes in line and growing things in petri dishes. Bullshit. That's boring."

Even more than his revulsion at the thought of being strapped for money, was Scotty Scurlock's horror at being bored. He had rarely been bored in his life. Everything had come easy for him—good looks, health, excitement, pleasure, beautiful women, and sex.

Scott never did get his college degree although he went to classes regularly or sporadically at Evergreen for six years.

8

Steve Meyers left Italy for what he believed would be the last time in 1984. His travels took him to Paris, and there he found Diana Gerhart. He had not forgotten her. This time there was no question about their feelings for one another. Steve took Diana back to Italy in 1985, and they began to live together. They loved the warm lazy days, the evenings where they sat in a street cafe, sipping red wine and eating pasta while they talked as earnestly as if they had just met each other.

Steve was in love again, but it only made his already complicated life more complicated. He wanted to be in America so that he could spend as much time as he could with Cara, who was five years old now. But Diana was a Brazilian citizen and needed the proper papers to emigrate to America. She couldn't even visit until Steve arranged for that, so reluctantly, he left Diana behind in Europe and came home to obtain the paperwork that would let her travel to the United States with him.

In the autumn of 1985, Diana Gerhart joined Steve in Virginia. They had some hard times ahead of them, although Steve was making some progress in selling his work. That year, he had a one-man exhibit of his sculpture and furniture at Unica Design in Bethesda, Maryland, and he showed his work at the Studio Garden Show in Great Falls.

Steve returned to antique-furniture restoration, but always with the hope that one day he would be doing his own sculpture and building his uniquely designed furniture exclusively. He had to go where the work was and so he traveled frequently.

But Steve always kept in touch with Cara. He wanted her to know she had a devoted father. This caused tension with both Maureen and Diana; his ex-lover and his fiancée pulled at him, making it difficult for him to arrange visits with Cara.

Steve had an exhibition in May 1986, in the posh Georgetown section of Washington, DC. It was titled

"Into the Twilight," and featured his incredible sculptures made of marble and steel. And in the fall, Diana Gerhart and Steve Meyers were married. Interestingly, the Reverend William Scurlock, Sr., Scott's father, presided over the ceremony. Steve hoped that the fact he and Diana were married would show he was maintaining a stable home. His dearest wish was to have Cara come live with them.

By the time Steve came home to Virginia, Kevin had finally found the ramshackle house he was looking for in Great Falls, Virginia. He and Steve were alike in that way; they could see possibilities where no one else could, and they were creative workhorses, willing to put sweat-equity into something that would one day be beautiful.

Kevin's dwelling had been built long before the Civil War, with various owners slapping layer after layer of peculiar facades over what had once been a classic log cabin. There was no running water, and a large family of snakes lived in the ceiling. But it didn't matter; it was his.

In a way, Kevin had come full circle. Steve was back in his life, and so was Scott. Bill and Mary Jane Scurlock were still living in Reston during the eighties, and Scott came home for Thanksgiving. He'd been there just in time to help Kevin move into his Great Falls home. Scott slept on the floor there, and, for a day or so, it was almost as if they were back in Hawaii, "brothers" and best friends. But they were a decade older, and they had gone in different directions.

They promised to stay in touch, and they did.

* * *

Back at Evergreen, Scott was gearing up to go into full crystal meth production. He couldn't actually make the stuff in the university lab; the chemicals produced a noxious smell like cat urine. Some meth labs were set up in trailers out in the woods, some particularly stupid "chemists" set up temporary labs in motels—but the smell almost always gave them away.

Scott paid people he met to find deserted houses far from town where he could actually put the chemicals together and start them cooking. Once he found a likely spot, he set up elaborate venting systems to carry the pungent odors produced high into the trees until it was blown away by the next brisk wind.

The crystal meth project brought in more money than Scott had hoped, and he liked the element of danger. What he was doing was a criminal offense, and Scott enjoyed watching true-life police dramas on television, feeling it would help him keep one step ahead of the police. (Later, "COPS" would be one of his favorite programs.)

One thing, however, that Scott never worried about was that he would be betrayed by his dealers. The small army of men and women who took the speed from him and fanned out to Seattle and Tacoma to the north, and the Olympic peninsula to the west seemed, to him, to be only extended members of his loyal crew. While some might consider friendship among drug dealers and manufacturers to be a paradox, Scott didn't. Just as he felt no guilt about the product he was selling, he took pride in his team.

As his crystal meth network expanded, Scott often traveled all the way back to Reston, Virginia, to deliver his product to a dealer there. His Virginia connection was an old school friend who had lived an apparently straight life, but who had very expensive tastes. His friend, known only as "Hawk" to everyone but Scott, was ready to take all the product Scott wanted to sell to him. Scott flew into Dulles Airport, handed over the crystal meth, and got right back on a plane to Washington State without ever leaving the airport. He could wake up in Olympia, fly the round-trip across America, and return to sleep in his own bed.

Sometimes, though, Scott stayed longer in Reston, visiting his parents and sisters, catching up with old friends. He visited Kevin and saw that he had per-formed miracles with the dilapidated house he had bought in Great Falls for $45,000. The original log cabin beams were exposed now, and he had remor-tared so that there were no chinks to let in the winter wind. And the snake nests under the roof were all gone.

Kevin's Great Falls home, which he called "Spring-Vale Studios" had the most serendipitous ambiance for painting that he had ever found. His work was going better than he could have dreamed. His paint-ings of the sea and sky were selling almost as fast as he could finish them.

The Washington Gallery of Fine Art sold one of Kevin's canvases, which depicted a mighty, crashing white wave rolling over a beach of black sand, for $2,000. By 1984, Capricorn Galleries in Bethesda had featured Kevin's paintings in two shows. Both of them were immediate sell-outs, and the gallery urged him to return with more paintings.

Kevin saw Scott fairly often since he usually came by Kevin's studio when he was visiting Reston. During one of Scott's visits, Kevin's older brother Steve happened to be home too, and the two were finally introduced. Kevin bragged about what a skilled sculptor and carpenter Steve was and Scott invited Steve to come work on the property in Olympia that he hoped to buy soon.

Steve's income was sparse at that period in his life, and he seemed interested when Scott suggested he come out to Washington State for a few months. The compensation he offered was attractive, and the project sounded good. It didn't concern Scott that he didn't even own the acreage on Overhulse Road; the owners were several states away.

Scott shared the rented gray house on Overhulse Road in Olympia with his friend Mickey Morris.

"I'd been looking around for a place to build in the woods," Mickey recalled. "Scott had the same dream, so we put our heads together and came up with this idea to build a platform in the trees."

They had seemingly endless space on the acreage, and Scott thought it would be fun, and profitable, to build a treehouse in a cluster of evergreens. He had walked out in the woods and noted a circle of cedars, a natural location for the treehouse he envisioned.

"It started out as a really small idea," Mickey said. "We built this massive platform, and while we were doing it, we just kept getting more and more donations of wood. People would say, 'Well, we're tearing down this house, and you can have the wood.' We ended up with this huge stockpile of wood.

"We built with all hand tools. Essentially, we were squatters. It started off very innocent and low-key . . . we just never planned on building this major structure."

Scott and an assortment of old and new friends carried on the building project. Some of the materials for the first treehouse were paid for with meth money, but Scott confided to a friend that he had also stolen lumber from deserted old houses, tearing the places apart to take what he wanted. If anyone cared, they never heard about it.

That first treehouse proved to be a highly successful project, so much so that Scott and Mickey moved into it as a full-time residence. They sublet the little gray house to a young woman named Julie Weathers.*

Julie Weathers was also an Evergreen student, but she was very different from many of Scott's friends. She was one of the "Greeners," the members of the student body who embraced health food and the preservation of all things natural. Vegetarian, of course, Julie wore clothes made only of cotton, linen, and wool. She smelled of clean soap and fresh air.

Moreover, she was the perfect embodiment of the kind of woman Scott Scurlock had sought all his life. She came from Montana, and she was a tall, slender girl with flaxen hair that fell straight and gleaming to the middle of her back. Her body was absolutely perfect. Julie wore Levis and cowboy boots and Guatemalan shirts. She had a Bo Derek or Linda Evans face, clear-eyed, open—and beautiful.

It was probably inevitable that Scott would fall in

love with Julie Weathers. He let her keep her horse on the property, and he loved to watch her ride bareback. She was all grace and fluid movement; this was a woman that even he could be faithful to.

It might seem that a man could not make his fortune manufacturing a pungent-smelling, forbidden drug, and, at the same time, be consumed with a love for nature and personal fitness. But Scott was always a man who believed that he *could* have it all; he didn't see that many of his activities were at cross-purposes, that if one succeeded—the other must fail. His personality, always bifurcated into diverging loyalties, developed deeper fissures. He saw himself as a true friend, a protector of the weak, a loyal son, and as much an advocate of natural resources as any "Greener" at his college. A large part of Scott Scurlock really wanted to be *good*.

At the same time, Scott's pursuit of worldly wealth continued undiminished. He was catering to the weaknesses of his fellow human beings and dealing with some of the sleaziest members of society. Anyone but Scott would have had great difficulty reconciling the two sides of his nature—but he was apparently quite able to partition off sections of his mind. When he was with Julie Weathers, he was the complete naturalist; when he delivered his product to his dealers, he was a cunning businessman.

It may have been just too crowded in that first pilot treehouse project. Whatever the cause, Scott and Mickey had a disagreement and Mickey moved out. Even though he and Scott parted company, Mickey's picture would hang on one of the tree walls for the next ten years. Nobody ever bothered to take it down. It was as familiar as the Winchester rifle Scott always kept by the door.

Mickey continued to be a reminder that Scott had not—as he liked to claim—built the first treehouse all by himself. "It would have been better for his big image," Mickey said, "to have built it by himself. I think whenever he would see me, it would remind him that he didn't do it himself, and he really hated that."

Sometime after Mickey left, Scott decided that the treehouse needed major upgrading. He and his helpers took ladders and broke into lumberyards at night, taking the boards and beams they needed.

"You're kidding," a friend laughed when Scott told him about the midnight lumber thefts. "Doesn't that take a lot of energy to get those heavy boards back to your place? Wouldn't it have been easier just to buy the stuff?"

Perhaps. But, for Scott Scurlock, there was the excitement of stealing what he needed. Anyone could buy a 2-by-12-by-16-foot board, but few had the guts to steal them—nor the sheer physical strength required to run through the woods in the dark with a board that size on their shoulders. Scott and his henchman would go without a night's sleep to steal $200 worth of lumber.

"He wanted to do anything that took balls to do," his friend said. "That was what he was about."

Scott's treehouse was so unique that word about it reached *The Seattle Times. The Times'* Sunday paper had a section that featured unusual homes in the area—everything from millionaires' penthouses to refurbished 1920s bungalows to houseboats and log cabins. The treehouse in Olympia was, however, a first.

Scott agreed to let photographers and a reporter visit his home high among the branches, but he asked not to be identified. That wasn't an unusual request; many of the featured homeowners preferred to remain anonymous. They didn't want their homes to become stops on somebody's Sunday drive. Scott, particularly, wanted to keep his world private.

Even so, Scott couldn't resist posing for *The Times'* photographer. A shot taken from high above showed him sitting in an Afghan-draped easy chair. The photograph was of a good-sized room with a table, range, refrigerator, and wood stove. Two huge multi-paned windows revealed the tops of tall trees just outside. Scott was almost thirty at the time, but he looked nineteen. He didn't bother to tell *The Seattle Times* that he wasn't really the owner of the property on Overhulse because, in his mind, the place was already his.

Despite the favorable publicity his treetop home had received, Scott's treehouse still needed a great deal of refurbishing and remodeling. He recognized the fact that he wasn't a skilled carpenter, even as he claimed to have been the sole builder of his treehouse.

Although Scott first offered a carpentry job to Steve Meyers, it was Kevin who agreed to accept a temporary job during the summer of 1984. But what Scott wanted from him had little to do with building or carpentry.

The offer came in the middle of a conversation back in Virginia earlier that spring. Scott approached the subject in an oblique way, saying, "If I present you with this situation, would you participate?"

Kevin stared at him confused. *What* situation? And then, before giving any more details, Scott said, "I have to think about it. I'll let you know."

When Scott *did* tell Kevin what he had in mind, it sounded innocent enough. He said he had rented some property south of Olympia, near the Mima Mounds. (The Mima Mounds are literally thousands of "blisters" of grass-covered earth that dot the landscape for miles. No one knows where they came from or whether they were caused by some accident of nature or by human beings.) Scott told Kevin he needed someone to watch the place for the summer. All Kevin would be required to do was sit by the swimming pool and paint pictures.

Kevin Meyers was a bluntly honest man, and he made no effort to whitewash what Scott eventually proposed to him. He wasn't naive enough to think Scott would give him a free summer just so that he could paint; he knew Scott planned to use him in some way. But that was OK; they would both get something out of it.

Kevin wondered why Scott had had to "think about it." Was he to be a front for something illegal and had Scott actually felt guilty about bringing him into what was going on? Or was it that Scott had to decide if he trusted him or not?

"The thing about Scott was that, whenever he was involved with something that might rebound on him, he didn't touch it himself. He was always the 'middleman' between the middlemen between the middle-men," Kevin mused. "But his friends loved him enough that they didn't want to know what he was up to and they really didn't care."

Kevin had pressing problems himself that made it easier for him not to look too closely at what Scott was up to; he needed financial help that summer. Despite his success, Kevin wasn't making enough with his art to do the work on SpringVale that he wanted to. "I just couldn't get ahead because I couldn't afford the building materials. Whatever money came in just evaporated."

There were other reasons that made Scott's offer enticing. Kevin loved the Northwest in the summer, and he wanted to vault in a Masters' track meet in Eugene, Oregon, in August. So it *did* sound like the answer to both Kevin's monetary problems and like an adventurous summer to boot. Most compelling of all, Kevin loved Scott. He remembered the halcyon days in Hawaii a decade earlier. "He and I laughed more together than any friend I ever had."

Shoving down any suspicion, Kevin headed west from Great Falls, Virginia.

He saw that the treehouse was in the embryonic stage of yet another transformation. He could appreciate the challenge posed in rebuilding the treehouse and the sheer fun in doing it. Even so, Kevin noted wryly that Scott still used his "cosmic carpentry," rather than any sound principles of building. It drove Kevin Meyers nuts to see Scott's strongman approach to carpentry. If Scott wanted a tree limb gone, he was as likely to attack it with a machete as with a saw. Some of the structure was flimsy and unsafe, but Scott only laughed when Kevin pointed that out. He shrugged—Scott had always taken shortcuts and that hadn't changed.

But other things had. On this visit, Kevin was troubled as he sensed that Scott was heading down "a dark path." Scott made no effort now to hide the fact that he was heavily involved in some kind of drug business, but he spoke of it euphemistically. He always referred to what he was doing as just another "experiment."

Lots of Scott's experiments had failed. Kevin remembered when he had tried to grow marijuana—using Gro-lites—in a space he'd hollowed out beneath the old barn. That had been a joke. Even though Scott hid the excavation with bales of hay, everyone along Overhulse seemed to know what he was up to. And then his cannabis plants were flooded out by underground water. He'd finally admitted that he couldn't grow nearly enough pot on his own acreage to make any profit.

Although Kevin never walked back into the Mima Mounds behind the house where he painted, he soon suspected what went on there. He figured that Scott must have a huge crop of marijuana someplace back among the mounds and the wooded property. But what Kevin didn't actually see for himself, he wouldn't have to acknowledge. He spent his days painting canvases in the harsh light that reflected off the pool of the rental house.

What he was doing gave him an uneasy feeling nevertheless. So many times that summer, Kevin berated himself for accepting Scott's offer. Scott made the mortgage payments on Kevin's house in Virginia, but he never paid him so much as a dollar that summer that he could put in his pocket. He was completely dependent, and he hated the feeling. Nothing Kevin painted was memorable or up to his usual standards. He knew why; he was corrupting the thing that meant most to him.

Kevin would have been utterly lonesome if Scott hadn't insisted he have some kind of a guard dog with him. "He gave me a couple of hundred dollars and told me to go buy a dog," Kevin said. "I bought this huge, long-haired Belgian Shepherd who had been a working guard dog, but he had been locked up in a cage at some kennel. His name was Max, but I changed it to B-I-G-D-O-G. That dog was supposed to be dangerous, but he was so glad I rescued him from the cage that he almost caused me to have an accident on the way home because he was sitting in my lap, licking my face."

Kevin made a point of not asking Scott specific questions. When they were back at the place on Overhulse Road, sitting around a campfire, waking up to the pureness of dawn over Mt. Rainier, it was easy for Kevin to convince himself that Scott hadn't changed as much as he feared. Scott still loved nature and their long hikes; he still railed against the wickedness of clear-cutting timberland. They rented movies and cheered for the heroes. They forced themselves to be complimentary when Julie Weathers served vegetarian meals—strange conglomerations of mushrooms and herbs coaxed into soufflés that invariably fell flat.

They winked at each other and laughed—just the way they always had, forcing their expressions into innocent stares when she accused them of making fun of her.

Scott and Julie drove Kevin down to Eugene for the Masters' track meet, and cheered when he leapt over sixteen feet and narrowly missed taking a first-place medal. Onlookers were amazed that he still had such power at the age of thirty-one. It was a good trip, and the three of them laughed a lot.

Even though Kevin Meyers grew disillusioned with his best friend, he had forgiven Scott many times. There was a bond between them that was far closer than that between blood brothers. Kevin loved Scott and hoped that one day he would change. Scott was just too special not to metamorphose into the kind of man he was fully capable of being.

Scott continued to entice his old friend to join him in unplanned escapades. They went to Mexico together in early 1985 and discovered Xalapa on Mexico's eastern coast, just north of Veracruz. A decade fell away as they hiked through strange terrain, calling to each other with familiar crow caws, which signaled there was no danger ahead. They leapt off thirty-foot rocks into four feet of water, full of an almost-forgotten derring-do. They explored the ancient Zempoala Ruins.

"Scott had angels around him, still," Kevin remembered. "He was still so lucky. Somebody had to be watching over him."

One day, they were racing through a thick forest where the tree roots were as thick as a man's thigh. Scott was leading the way. "He was about to leap over a cluster of roots," Kevin said, "when a hawk suddenly flew down right at him. He stopped in his tracks. I caught up with him and we looked past the roots to the spot where he was about to leap. There was a huge rattle snake coiled there."

Even Scott was pale and quiet for a few minutes. If he hadn't been stopped, he would have landed on the snake.

A few months later, Scott asked Kevin if he wanted to go to Nicaragua with him. "Come on," Scott urged. "We'll be tourists. It will be cheap. We can do it on dollars. . . ."

The trip to Nicaragua changed Kevin Meyers' life; he had never seen such abject poverty and he felt guilty and helpless. The life of the poor in Nicaragua seemed so much worse because the rich had so much. For years after this trip, Kevin Meyers would become agitated at the memory of the injustice he saw during those days in March 1985.

But the trip was Scott's adventure, so it was fraught with danger and excitement. And Scott had been right when he said they could live like kings on very little money.

"It was supposed to be a tourist scene there, but nobody else could afford to be there," Kevin said.

They stayed in an ocean-front hotel for a week, paying $5 a night for a room. Frugality was everywhere: toilet paper rolls were cut into fourths and the soap was carefully pared down into small pieces.

They swam in the clear ocean waters of Nicaragua, wearing fins that had cost them $80 a pair. "A factory worker at Uni-Royal down there was making $200 a *year*, for working ten hours a day," Kevin recalled.

"But with a pair of fins like we had, he could have made a better living spear-fishing."

They were bodysurfing one day, and Scott didn't like the way his fins worked, so he borrowed a butcher knife and began cutting them down. A little boy nearby watched with horror. He thought the crazy American was destroying something worth pure gold. Scott tossed him the fins and they watched the boy run home whooping with joy.

The waves were so far out that Kevin and Scott were disappointed with the bodysurfing anyway, and, as the sun set, the wind churned the sand until it pricked their eyes. They walked back a hundred yards to where they had left their rented car and found it was locked tight. Neither of them had the keys.

"The closest town was ninety miles away," Kevin said. "We weren't going to find a locksmith. I was blaming Scott for losing the keys, and he was saying I had them. Finally, Scott just said, 'Let's go find the keys.'"

"Look at it out there," Kevin said. "The beach is twenty-five miles long and you can't even see the tracks we just made. The keys are gone."

Scott grinned at him and walked confidently to a spot on the beach as if he could somehow hear the keys calling to him. "He reached down—right by his feet—and he came up with the keys. He had some instinct, something more than anyone else. He was the luckiest guy I ever met."

Long before the hawk that warned Scott of the snake and the keys in the sand, Kevin had become used to Scott's incredible, uncanny luck. When he gambled, he never lost and he never won small. The first time he became aware of Scott's startling luck was during a company poker party at Hawaii Plant Life.

"I wasn't there," Kevin recalled. "I was still in college, and I didn't have enough to buy even a beer, much less gamble. And I hadn't started working for the company yet. But Scott went with the three bosses. He had his $250 paycheck and his lucky leather hat, his lucky shirt, his lucky pants. He *cleaned out* the bosses—winning *thirteen* straight hands! They thought he couldn't win hand after hand—but he did. They all went broke and quit. All he'd had going in was a bicycle, and he comes driving up to see me in a TR3. He'd paid $2,400 of his winnings for it, and he still had money left over."

Scott claimed to have magical chants. And when he played pool or cards, he'd mutter things like "Ooomsha . . . Ooomsha" and "Alligalla, Walligalla" and he managed to convince his opponents he'd hexed them.

"I saw him once in Vegas after he'd put down ten bucks," Kevin laughed. "And he won $20 . . . $40 . . . $80, $160, $320, $640. And on and on. I was real proud because I'd won $180. He said, 'That's pretty good, Bro.' I was so proud of my little $183 from the blackjack table. I was Don Knotts, saying 'Look, Andy!' And here comes Andy, sticking out his chest and pulling $500 chips out of his jacket pockets. I've never seen anybody win like that. I guess he had $15,000 on him and all from one $10 chip. That kind of money would have changed *my* life."

Scott often went to Las Vegas to bet "the parlay" on the sixteen football games slated to be played the following weekend. "It was like 100-to-1 odds," Kevin said. "You put a hundred down, you get ten grand. He won that thing five or six times."

The lost key episode in Nicaragua could have been a disaster, but, with Scott's luck, it wasn't. And their evening only got better; they ate at a local restaurant where a steak and lobster dinner cost a dollar, an ice cold Mexican beer ten cents. They left dollar tips for their ten-cent beers, and the waiter was ecstatic.

There was no doubt that Scott Scurlock was blessed with uncommon luck. He seemed then, and always, to be invulnerable to the forces that could bring an ordinary man down. And they both needed Scott's luck later that night. They went out to jog in the moonlight, their bellies full of beer, steak, and lobster. They hadn't run very far into the black, moonless night when they heard the boom of a high-powered gun. It was just one shot, and they didn't think much about it; it could have been a family quarrel or some local feud.

The second shot kicked up the sand near their feet, and a voice called "Halta!" Kevin and Scott were wearing shorts and their feet were bare. Kevin tentatively called out, "Turista, turista!"

They couldn't see the man who called out, but then a flashlight followed by long shadows came closer to them. "I counted thirteen shadows," Kevin remembered. "The oldest of them was about twenty-five and the youngest twelve, and they all carried machine guns. Russian-made AK-47s. They were really proud, and really poor. We didn't know it then but the CIA had come in invading from the ocean just north of there and blown up a water treatment plant that they thought was an oil refinery. These people came down with cholera. So many of them got sick . . . and here we were, strangers, running in the night."

Scott signaled Kevin that they had to make friends. They didn't have a passport and they were clearly Americans.

Scott said, "Reagan" with disgust in his voice, and drew his finger across his throat. Kevin spit as he too said, "Reagan."

The men with machine guns watched them warily. Finally, one of them said something in Spanish, and the others put their guns down.

"We found out quickly that nobody jogs in Nicaragua," Kevin said. "You either walk or you run."

After every new adventure with Scott, Kevin headed back to Virginia, grateful to be home in his log cabin studio. There, he felt renewed as he worked.

9

Scott, who had never ended a relationship with a woman unless he chose to, lost Julie Weathers. He had had scores of women, but Julie Weathers' beauty was recognized not only on the Evergreen campus but all around the city of Olympia. Together, they made an exquisite couple—Scott with his classic features, muscular body, and dark curly hair; Julie, tall and slender and as fair as Scott was dark.

Julie knew about the marijuana plots, but that wasn't what drove her away from Scott. She left him for another woman.

Scott was dumbfounded. And bereft. When he first suspected Julie had taken a female lover, Scott simply could not believe it. But then he was a man on fire who had to have proof, so when Julie left one evening to visit Ursula Ving,* Scott followed her. After she went into Ursula's house, he climbed a tree outside the bedroom window and watched in horrified fascination as Julie made love with a woman.

He had seen them there—*together*—and he could no longer deny what seemed impossible. His beautiful "Greener," his woman who had smelled like clover and sunshine and the wind in the cedars, was a lesbian.

Scott's male ego may have suffered a profound blow because he had once tried to "convert" another beautiful lesbian student at Evergreen. A female classmate and no fan of Scott's recalled that situation to *The Stranger,* a Seattle publication:

"My most outstanding impression of Scott Scurlock is that he was an asshole. I was in class with him at Evergreen—a full-time program. We met five hours a day, three or four days a week, for a term.

"Scurlock was extremely handsome in a slick kind of way. He was rugged and outdoorsy, with a big head of curly black hair and tight jeans. And he was a jerk, a real jerk. Scurlock and a buddy of his in this program were in love with this woman in the class. She was incredibly beautiful and turns out she was a lesbian. They would sit around talking about her, how they were going to convert her. They sat around ogling this woman in class. It was like it really bugged him that a woman he wanted could care less about him. He (was) the cave man: 'Me want her.'"

But even Scott had not been able to seduce the beautiful lesbian.

Scott wasn't used to losing women, and his close friends remember how changed he was after Julie Weathers left him. There was a bitterness about him now, a hard edge they had never seen before. The fact that Julie chose a *woman* over him did terrible damage to his sense of self-worth and his masculinity.

After Julie left, Scott didn't seem to care about anything but money. Money afforded him the income that he needed to live his life exactly as he wanted. He sometimes explained that it was the actual *spending* of money that gave him satisfaction. He spent most of it on his journeys, he gave some of it away, and he bought whatever he wanted—technical gadgets, guns, tools, books, furniture. Once he spent $3,000 on a lie detector. It was just something he was curious about. But he rarely bought clothes. Sometimes he would buy L.L. Bean clothes, but he wore them until they were old and scruffy. He still wore the same cheap Converse All-Star sneakers. The thing was that Scott Scurlock was so *beautiful* that no one noticed what he wore.

Scott still laughed and he still behaved outrageously at times, but there was a side of himself that he kept hidden now. Kevin could be talking to him and see some door close behind his eyes. Suddenly, he wasn't Willy Boss at all: now eighty percent of him was the same old Scott; twenty percent of him was a complete stranger.

Disappointed and wanting not to believe what he already knew in his heart, Kevin had proof in the summer of 1986 that Scott was involved in a lot more than growing marijuana. One day he accepted Scott's invitation to go for a ride. Scott drove far out into the isolated counties beyond Olympia. They were on a modern freeway, but the fir forests crowded up on both sides, and there were logging roads that snaked through stands of trees so thick that they shut out most of the sun.

Kevin was gripped with a bleak kind of curiosity. He sensed that this trip was not one of their boyish adventures. Now he suspected that Scott was manufacturing crystal meth on a massive scale.

Scott turned his 1972 red-and-white Ford pickup— a truck indistinguishable from any logger's—again and again until they were speeding along some logging road so far off the beaten path that Kevin would never be able to find it again. Scott slowed and pointed to a beat-up sixties' model Ford van. A man got out and walked toward them. He was a good twenty-five years older than they were, bald-headed, wiry, almost emaciated, with sweat beaded on his flushed face. He didn't look particularly menacing, though. He was grinning.

"This is Captain Pat," Scott introduced the stranger. "He works with me."

Kevin nodded. The guy had the twitchy look of a longtime drug addict. Captain Pat gave Scott a package wrapped in a garbage bag and sealed with duct tape. Scott took it and tucked it down between the truck's seats as he drove off. When they were some miles away, Scott pulled over and peeled off part of the wrappings.

"It was $250,000!" Kevin recalled. "That man gave Scott a quarter of a million dollars. Scott told me he had a whole network of people working for him. He gave them the crystal meth, and they went out and sold it. Out of Olympia. Up to Seattle. Over to the coast. Even Virginia."

Kevin was amazed. Why wouldn't a druggie with $250,000 in his hands simply have taken off for parts unknown? But this guy had been so proud to give it to Scott. He sighed; wasn't that the way *everybody* felt about Scott—wanting to please him and to be part of his inner circle?

Kevin had always wondered if Scott was bragging when he had hinted about the scope of his drug business. Now, seeing the money, he saw with sickening clarity that Scott had not exaggerated.

He *was* making a fortune. And Kevin knew "Hawk"—Scott's contact back in Reston, Virginia, too; he had always figured the guy was a legitimate businessman who was making such a good salary that he could pay for the new house he had custom-built. Now he realized that Hawk had to be part of what was going on in Washington State. Who else might be involved?

Scott could be so seductive. Kevin knew that Scott would die for him; they had come close many times before. He also knew that somehow Scott had the ability to corrupt, to ferret out other men's weaknesses and entice them with money. Something in Scott needed to make others beholden to him.

Kevin winced. Now *he* was beholden. He'd accepted Scott's offer to pay his mortgage that summer. He had accepted Scott's generosity for their trips to Nicaragua and Xalapa. He wondered what he would owe Scott.

They stopped near a beach on the Pacific Ocean and skipped rocks and ate lunch. Kevin could hardly digest his food knowing that Scott had a quarter of a million dollars hidden in the ratty upholstery of the truck.

While Kevin had begun tentatively to move toward a more spiritual life, Scott's journey was just the opposite. It was a reality that ate at Kevin when he allowed himself to think about it; he longed for a return to the world they had once known. But once Scott told him about his crystal meth operations, he seemed obsessed with telling his old friend everything about it.

It was soon apparent that most of Scott's close coterie of friends knew about his crystal meth business. He was proud of the money that was rolling in. Another friend recalled that one day, Scott climbed the stairs to the treehouse and plunked down a shoebox that had been decorated with buttons, glitter, sequins, and bows. "Scott set it down on the table," the man recalled. "He lifted the lid and there was more money in there than I'd ever seen in my life."

Scott had another "partner" in the business, apparently—a man a half dozen years older than he. Where Captain Pat looked the part of delivery man, the "partner" dressed in three-piece suits with expensive ties. He was a silent contributor, matching Scott dollar for dollar when they purchased the raw materials. Apparently this man had ways of obtaining the basic ingredients and the necessary apparatus from drug-supply companies—without arousing suspicion. He wasn't anyone Kevin knew, or wanted to know.

Scott was into another world, a dangerous world. "Scott always had to be the best at everything," Kevin explained. "Whatever it was—sports or money or whatever. But success had to come fast for him. One time, he invested a little money in the stock market, but he had no patience, and he lost money. I think it bothered Scott that one of the guys we went to school with in Reston was a millionaire in computers while the rest of us—even Scott—were way behind."

Scott always kept meticulous—if phony—records. Notations of his "purchases" and "expenses" were all filed in neatly labeled folders in a cabinet in the gray house. He told Kevin that he always paid his taxes, too. That is, he paid taxes on what he *declared* as his income, the income of a carpenter. As far as the IRS knew, Scott's annual income was about $24,000. He was careful never to buy a new car, preferring nondescript used models. He never wanted to be in debt to anyone, so he paid his bills punctually each month.

The property on Overhulse Road was about to be transformed into a Northwest version of The Shire Plantation in Hawaii. Only this time, Scott planned to own it. There was the gray house, the barn, the outbuildings, and the treehouse, and Scott intended to spare no expense in his plans to remodel it all. But the most important remodeling would be to the treehouse. The first treehouse had been only a shack compared to the one Scott envisioned. He intended to use some of the $250,000 to put a down payment on the place when the time was ripe.

Scott planned to eventually rip out seventy-five percent of the original treehouse that had been built in the seven cedars. Those cedars remained, but the new and perfected treehouse would be built in and around forty-seven trees. There would be a working bathroom, a tub, and planked walkways that extended far back into the forest. There would be decks and ladders and look-out spots. Kevin suggested that Scott call his carpentry business "Seven Cedars," and he did.

Despite everything, it was easy—most of the time—to pretend that Scott hadn't changed. He drank a little more, maybe. Life around Seven Cedars was essentially about having a good time. Kevin teased Scott about the place, calling it "Peter Pan Land." The boys who played there were growing older. Scott was well over thirty now, but he was little changed from the twenty-year-old who had hopped off the bus in Hawaii. His heroes, real and fictional, surrounded him. N. C. Wyeth's painting of Robin Hood hung over his king-sized bed in the treehouse. "He liked to think he was like Robin Hood," Kevin said. "But he really used his money to impress people. He spent most of it on himself, and the money he gave away was what he gave to waitresses."

Waitresses loved Scotty Scurlock. He *was* a big and flamboyant tipper, although he had a system. Scott would tip pretty waitresses $100 the first time they served him, even if the check was less than $15.

"After that, you don't have to tip them any more than normal," he would say, smiling. "They still remember you as 'that big tipper.'"

Scott liked Gardner's Restaurant, Ben Moore's, Louisa's, and the Bud Bay Restaurant in Olympia. They were spots where he didn't have to dress up—even though he preferred to drink Dom Perignon and Cristal champagne—and where he was always greeted warmly. He was, after all, "the big tipper."

Other than that, Scott's generosity didn't come without a price tag. The plane tickets, the free rent, and the vacations he gave to his friends came with implied debt. Whether it meant that his friends had to work on the treehouse, the barn, the gray house, or in the marijuana fields; whether they were expected to participate in his newest experiments or provide company for him when loneliness caught up with him, those who shared in his wealth and his hospitality somehow knew that, someday, they would owe him.

10

During one of Kevin's visits to Olympia, he
helped Scott develop a rope system using horizontal
ropes and pulleys that would let them swing like
Tarzan between trees 70 feet above the ground. It
began in the treehouse itself and ended 185 feet out
into the woods. Scott commented that he needed it
for a "getaway in case of a shoot-out."

"Shoot-out?" Kevin asked, puzzled.

"In case the cops come," Scott explained. Kevin
realized Scott was serious.

"Who gets to test it?" Kevin asked, pointing to the
rope escape.

"You do," Scott laughed.

And Kevin did test the intricate system high in the
air, although, uncharacteristically for him, he was
terrified. "I dropped thirty-five to forty feet straight
down before that rope got taut. It was like jumping off
the top of a building."

Kevin swung to one tree forty feet away and he had
to inch his way back hand over hand, finally scissoring
his legs over the line for a more secure purchase. Like
most of Scott's brainstorms, the rope system was far
from perfected; if Kevin had lost his grip, he would

have fallen six stories. But he was still in good shape, and he made it back to the safety of the top deck of the treehouse.

After Kevin tried the ropes, and proved they were basically safe, Scott swung out, too. Kevin filmed him on a camcorder. The videotape is reminiscent of Lightfoot and Thunderbolt, together again. Their images appear on the amateur video slightly out of focus and tilted. Their shouts of "Hey Bubba!" sound like kids calling to one another.

They still hiked, and both of them remained in peak condition. No matter how he might indulge in drugs or alcohol, Scotty Scurlock was obsessed with maintaining his body like a perfectly tuned machine. He kept a note on his refrigerator door, "Spirit ain't spit without a little exercise!"

They climbed snow-packed Mount Rainier wearing only shorts and tennis shoes. Although it was unheard of, they took no provisions with them, not even water. Scott had always maintained that there would be water when they needed it. And, so far, he had been right.

Once he had hiked the Grand Canyon from the north rim to the south rim, with the best marijuana he could find his only provision. Much to the park rangers' amazement, Scott completed that dangerous solo hike. He found water along the way, drinking deep from small waterfalls. He never got sick, and he never took a misstep. He trusted that some divine providence looked after him, and apparently it did.

It was like the time he and Kevin had climbed up a sheer cliff near Havasu Falls near the Grand Canyon.

Copper miners long-since dead had left a kind of ladder attached to the steep walls that led to the mine, its rungs five feet apart.

Kevin and Scott both made it up to the top of the miners' ladders just fine, but Kevin felt himself weakening in the heat as they came back down. There was only one way down, and he realized that if he couldn't swing off the last rung, he would fall forty-five feet down to rocks and cactus—and quite probably his death.

"My muscles were exhausted, I was out of gas and I was trembling," Kevin remembered. "But old Scott was still doing fine. He swung out and he could have been free—but he could see I was in trouble. He showed me what I had to do. He put the rope in front of me and showed me how to swivel out with a straight arm and drop. I still couldn't see how, but he got me down step by step. He saved my life."

Although Scott had won their latest contest, for once he didn't crow about it. He had seen how close Kevin had come to death.

Their hikes and their climbs together were an integral part of their camaraderie. Kevin just laughed when he saw how Scott shocked other climbers on Washington's Mount Rainier. "Once, when we climbed Mount Rainier—of course without taking any supplies—Scott offered some other climbers twenty dollars for a sandwich. And more money for water. They looked at us as though we were crazy in our shorts and sneakers, but they sold Scott the sandwich."

* * *

After Julie left him, there were many women in Scott Scurlock's life. Oddly, for a man as handsome as he was, he didn't necessarily pursue beautiful—or even pretty—women. Indeed, most of the women who now managed to bind him to them for more than a night or two were basically plain, although they wore a lot of makeup and had "big hair."

His friends quickly spotted the women Scott would home in on. Whenever a woman would walk into a bar with heavy makeup and hair piled high, they laughed and chanted, "Mousse alert. Mousse alert. Scottie's going for it."

But as Scott had told Marge Violette years before, he simply enjoyed women. Over the years, he bedded scores of them. Some said he was a perfect lover, and others maintained he was only average. And some women found him curiously asexual, not even interested in necking.

Scott had one fetish; he kept photographic souvenirs of the women he dated. Some women posed naked willingly in seductive poses; others appeared unaware that they were being photographed. By using mirrors, Scott was able to put himself in the scene too. He saved a series of photographs of a clearly identifiable woman performing oral sex upon him, and other shots that showed fairly tame episodes of missionary-position intercourse. Scott collected more than a hundred photographs of himself with a variety of lovers. Some of them were artistic, most were simply pornographic.

Neither Scott nor his women ever expected the pictorial records of sex in the treetops to become public knowledge, although he often showed them to his friends and even to his father. It was almost as if Scott needed to prove to Bill Scurlock that he was a successful womanizer. The elder Scurlock was far from shocked; rather, he complimented Scott on his prowess. Undoubtedly, the girls who had been delighted to be led up the ladder to Scott's bed, who had unknowingly—or cheerfully—posed for his camera, would have been mortified if they had known that their private pictures had become trophies.

A lot of people would eventually see Scott's collection. One woman, whose job it was to catalogue them as evidence, remembered her shock as she recognized an old friend. "I was packing them up when I went, 'Wait a minute! That's Cissy Mendoza'*—my childhood friend from Olympia. Only she was taller and she was naked. . . . She was in the shower, bending over, posing for Scott's camera."

Sometimes, Scott allowed hippies to live in the gray house free—with the understanding they would take care of his property while he was gone. But they almost always left the place worse off than it was when they moved in. He didn't have it in him to evict the "Granola Eaters," as much as he despised what they represented. Scott hated to have anyone dislike him. He usually waited until one of Kevin's visits and asked him to throw the squatters out. Kevin was glad to do it.

"Scott really couldn't stand hippies," Kevin remembered. "He hated seeing those guys standing by the freeway with signs that said, 'Will work for food.'" He'd say, "Why don't they carry a sign saying, 'Too lazy to work—give me money.'"

Nevertheless, the people who camped on Scott's twenty acres couldn't be described any other way. Kevin called them "Scott's hangers. They'd linger around Scott for all the energy he poured out."

The only squatter Scott liked was a squirrel he dubbed "Roscoe." Roscoe was probably a female, and had a definite proprietary interest in the treehouse. He—or *she*—always found a way in while Scott was gone and helped herself to any food left behind. Scott enjoyed the audaciousness of the tiny squirrel and laughed when he came back to the chaos Roscoe left behind. Crackers, beans, and potatoes all over the expensive Turkish rugs, cupboard doors open and dishes broken. Scott didn't care.

Roscoe was the closest thing Scott had to a real pet; he had no patience or sense of responsibility to another living thing. Having a real pet would interfere with his ability to walk away from his life in Olympia whenever he chose. Sometimes stray cats wandered in and turned half-feral out in the woods, and when Kevin was around, he brought his dog. But Scott had no steady woman, no child, no pet, no bonds of any kind.

Kevin believed Scott's obsession with freedom would never change. That was why he was utterly amazed to hear in late 1987 that Scott was planning to get married. Scott told him his fiancée's name was Pam* and Kevin assumed that it was the Pam Scott had dated in Olympia after Julie left. She was a warm, pretty young student who had lived in the gray house for a while. *That* Pam was someone Kevin approved of; he believed that she really loved Scott. But Kevin soon learned the bride-to-be was a *different* Pam. Scott referred to one Pam as "The Queen of Spades" and to the other as "The Queen of Hearts."

And it was the Queen of Spades that Scott was going to marry. He told Kevin he had met her while he was on a trip to Mexico. She was a wealthy Catholic girl from California who was vacationing with her parents. Scott had taken photographs of Pam in various stages of undress, and when he returned from Mexico, he was eager to show her beauty off to his friends.

"Look at this wonderful woman I found," he told Kevin, as he handed over a stack of photos.

What does a friend do in that situation? Kevin knew he was being asked to compliment Scott on the new woman, so he looked through the pictures slowly and deliberately, searching frantically for something positive to say. She had a great figure and dark hair done in a huge bouffant style, but her features were sharp. "She had a real long, pointy chin."

Kevin murmured vague congratulatory phrases. He wasn't much concerned. It wouldn't last. Since Julie, Scott never lasted very long with any woman—not even the good Pam—and this one would go away soon enough, too.

But this Pam didn't go away. Scott seemed determined to marry her.

Scott had concluded that it might be best for him to choose a woman who either didn't ask questions at all or who didn't care what the answers were. The Queen of Spades didn't mind that he had plans for a huge network of crystal meth dealerships. All that mattered to her was that he had money.

"He knew he should have married the one with the good heart," Kevin said regretfully. "She might have saved him. But he chose to go with the Pam who was corrupt, and it just got worse. She changed him for the worse. She really changed him."

Kevin was painting at SpringVale in Great Falls in 1987, and he heard that Scott was in town and he stopped by the elder Scurlock's condominium on Lake Anne to see him. He bounded up the steps to see the front door was wide open, and he could hear sounds from inside. He was in the doorway before he realized that Scott and Pam were naked and engaged in a sex act in the room just beyond.

Too late to turn back. Kevin bent his head and knocked loudly on the door, calling, "Hey, Scott—" Pam leapt up like a frightened deer and fled into another room, completely mortified. Scott wasn't embarrassed at all. He turned, grinned, and shouted, "Hey, Bubba! Come on in. Just hang on for five minutes. We're getting married in five minutes. You're just in time to be the best man."

Anyone could have come to the door, but Scott didn't seem to care. In fact, he had *expected* his father to show up. Bill Scurlock was going to preside over the wedding ceremony, which, indeed, he did. It wasn't a particularly auspicious occasion. Scott wore raggedy shorts; Pam wore a bathing suit. Kevin wore a look of bemusement. They stood on the dock at Lake Anne where Scott and Kevin had swum so many times as boys.

Reverend Scurlock said the words and the ceremony was over in minutes. Pam and Scott's honeymoon was more impressive. They took a trip around the world, and he bought her a $12,000 necklace in South America.

But their honeymoon lasted longer than their marriage.

Why Scott married the Queen of Spades is a puzzle that no one who knew him well could understand. Maybe he felt that he should experience everything once—even marriage. He and Pam certainly had an intense and uninhibited physical attraction for one another. She was smart and fit into the mold of the plain woman with a good figure that Scott seemed drawn to. And she never nagged him about his "experiments" or his secret business meetings. But it is unlikely that he loved her or that she loved him.

Pam was anxious for Scott to purchase the Overhulse property. The owners lived two states away, and they didn't plan to return to Washington. They were, seemingly, unaware that property values had soared in the Northwest in the late eighties. Their twenty acres were worth more than $200,000 now. But Pam Scurlock typed up an offer of $90,000, with $25,000 down, and mailed it to them. The owners accepted, and Seven Cedars belonged to Scott and Pam. Scott figured a mortgage was the best indication of a solid, responsible citizen. He never missed a payment.

For all of his suspect activities and his often wobbly moral sense, there was something in Scott Scurlock that seemed to long for the kind of love he saw in the movies he watched so avidly. After Julie Weathers, after the woman Kevin called the good Pam, true love was a concept that he could no longer grasp intellectually or achieve in his own life. Perhaps he hadn't even felt it with Julie. Had she sensed that and sought a deeper commitment with another woman? Possibly. Did Scott expect he might find it with the dark Pam?

If he did, he was disappointed. The marriage ended in acrimony and haggling over money. In the end, Scott told his friends that he had to buy his way out of being married to Pam. The Queen of Spades knew too much about him.

According to Scott, he finally met Pam in Las Vegas. He had reserved a room for her at Caesar's Palace, where he always stayed when he was in town, but there was nothing romantic about this meeting. He walked into the room with a sum of $20,000 in cash to settle their accounts. They had a tacit agreement. If she kept her mouth shut, the money was hers. If she chose to betray him, Scott allowed her to think that her life wasn't worth five cents.

Would Scott Scurlock have hurt Pam Scurlock— really? No one will ever know. She went away quietly, and her absence seemed to cause barely a ripple in his life.

Although the Queen of Spades was out of Scott's world within a few years of their meeting, she *had* done some subtle permanent damage. Or, perhaps more accurately, they had each done damage to one another. Scott had never been blessed with much of a conscience, and he had been taught to be a free thinker who made his own rules. Pam's acceptance of his lifestyle helped erode his character further. Even though he no longer thought about *her,* being with Pam had made him more of a hedonist.

He seemed unable to escape his descent into what seemed to be outright sociopathy. But it didn't have to be that way. So many people loved Scott Scurlock. "He was one of those people that you just wanted to make happy," an old friend recalled. "He didn't get angry. The minute you met him, you wanted to be friends with him. You didn't want to be a lamb to follow after him, but you just did anyway. I only saw him get really angry once. And that was at his wife."

11

Bill Scurlock was ready to retire as the eighties came to a close, although he had no intention of giving up his religious work entirely. He and Mary Jane announced to their congregation and neighbors in Reston that they were moving to Sedona, Arizona, one of the bastions of New Age philosophy. The general belief was that if there was intelligence in outer space, or psychic communication or conversations to be held with those who had gone on before, Sedona would be the most advantageous location. There they hoped to have a closer connection to the God that they referred to as "The Great White Light."

Kevin Meyers attended the going-away party

thrown for the Scurlocks. He had long since learned that the Scurlocks were the complete opposite of fundamentalists. The Scurlocks talked of a religion that allowed the widest of personal choices; they approached it much as they had approached child rearing. There were no rules *except* to say there must be no rules.

Sometimes Kevin found the New Age fads were laughable, and he teased Mary Jane or Bill. So did Scott, although they did it so subtlely that Scott's parents often didn't recognize the bite in their jokes. "If they'd known about all our Rambo ways," Kevin laughed, "they probably would have thrown both Scott and me out."

At the Scurlocks' going-away party, Kevin walked up to Mary Jane and three other women as they discussed the current thinking on mantras in Sedona. "I heard them talking about color—they were saying that 'This year, the color in Sedona for auras is orange and yellow . . .' for bringing the god into your soul. They were saying it would be important for the shakras of the earth to wear a lot of yellow and orange.

"I thought what a crock of shit. I walked up and said, 'Hey, I just got back from a spiritual session in Arizona, and it's all shifted. The color's green now. Wear nothing but green.'"

The women turned to him, fascinated. "Oh, really?"

He had them. "Yeah," Kevin continued. "Green. The color of Franklins."

"What?"

"Benjamin Franklins. One hundreds? You got a pocket full of those green babies, you always feel good!"

The women laughed.

The Scurlocks bought a home in Sedona with a clear view of the cliffs where the Red Rocks Church stands. It would become more and more stately through the years as they made improvements. Most of the residences close by were in the half-million dollar range, and their neighborhood was marked by an artificial waterfall of brilliantly colored water that flowed endlessly from the barren desert.

Scott often visited his parents and helped his dad remodel the house. He was generous; he told friends he'd given them a significant sum of money and helped them redo the basement so that students attending their seminars could stay there. The house, lovely to begin with, became more and more valuable.

It seemed to those who observed the Scurlocks that there was a close bond between Bill and Mary Jane and their only son—particularly between Bill and Scott. Scott clearly wanted his father to be proud of him. Kevin always felt that Scott needed to share the clever plans he made and carried out, although he could not say whether Bill Scurlock knew about his secret life.

The Scurlocks drove the stretch between Sedona, Arizona, and Olympia, Washington, regularly. Usually Scott seemed pleased to see his parents drive up. He was close to them and to his sisters. He always made sure the gray house was cleared out of whatever temporary residents were living there so that Bill and

Mary Jane could use it. One summer, he promised his mother she could buy a vacuum cleaner for the gray house. The Electrolux salesman brought all his equipment and did his dirt-dumping demonstration. Mary Jane had to wake Scott up to get the money for the vacuum cleaner, which cost a thousand dollars. "Get two," he said impatiently, peeling bills off a thick roll. "One for you to take home and one to leave here."

Bill and Mary Jane Scurlock visited often, proud of their only son. His father always enjoyed seeing the improvements on the treehouse, and, later, on the gray house. As a grown man, Scott clung to many of his father's teachings. He had always forbade outright negative emotions. Scott had never been allowed to say, "I hate." He had been taught that he could only say, "I dislike." He never "hated" anyone. He caught himself many times saying "hate," and with the rote lessons he had learned as a child, corrected it to "dislike."

Sometimes, Bill Scurlock came alone for a visit. He returned Scott's favor when it came to remodeling. Bill did a lot of work on the barn at Seven Cedars. He was a good carpenter himself, and the exterior turned out beautifully with a distinctive V design of two-by-fours that Bill had used to face the building.

On one of Bill Scurlock's solo visits in 1988, there was a near tragedy in the treehouse. Kevin was also visiting that summer, and he and Scott were working on a walkway high up in the trees that Scott called "the stairway to heaven." He had planned to install a Jacuzzi just beyond the top step of the walkway.

Scott's enthusiasm for building was hardly blunted by ordinary safety precautions. He and Kevin had worked until dark one night on the "heaven" stairway, and the base for the newest steps was close to seventy feet off the ground. They threw two-by-twelve boards out until they could be attached to one of the cedars that made up the central core of the treehouse. The two extra feet beyond the holding trees were very strong, strong enough to make each base. They had nailed in all but the top step securely. "Scott said, 'We're just going to put one more step in,'" Kevin recalled. "And I said, 'Man, it's dark'—but you can't tell him. So he put the top step in, but he toe-nailed it. That's sticking it in just enough to hold it, until you're ready to secure it. It would be really dangerous for anyone to put weight on it."

And there were no guard rails at all; Scott just didn't think they were necessary.

While the younger men slept in the next morning, Bill Scurlock was up early and set out to see how the carpentry had progressed the night before. He walked up the stairway to heaven, unaware that the top step was only tacked in. When he put his weight on it, it gave way and he plunged straight down.

Bill Scurlock was able to throw his arms out and grab tree branches, but he still dangled six stories up in the treetops. He cried out to his son, and Scott woke instantly and clambered out as close as he could get to his father. Bill Scurlock was in his sixties and in terrible pain.

"Dad," Scott said, trying to sound calm. "I want you to inch toward me. You can do it."

It was a terrible moment. If Bill Scurlock fell, he would surely die. Following his son's directions, he managed to move himself backward through the boughs and finally turn around so that Scott could grab him. He was bruised for weeks.

It was a near-miracle that Bill Scurlock was alive. Had he fallen, the impact of hitting the needle-carpeted forest floor below would have been like hitting concrete from six stories up.

Scott was badly shaken. He had warned his father very explicitly not to go out on construction in progress. He was gray-faced as he confided to Kevin, "If my father had died, I would have burned down this treehouse until it was only ashes."

12

In the spring of 1989, Steve Meyers moved to Chicago to set up a studio there. He knew that Diana wouldn't be coming with him. Their marriage was over; it had lasted less than three years. Diana had already filed for divorce in Virginia.

Steve bought an old warehouse on Milwaukee Avenue in Chicago and stayed with a friend until after Christmas. He leased out a section of the warehouse while he renovated the rest. Steve didn't see the mess and the dusty beams. Instead, he saw high ceilings, huge windows, and brick walls that would one day make a fine background to display his new sculptures. He saw the cozy space that might be a perfect room for Cara.

He purchased a huge piece of pure white marble, thirteen and a half feet tall and six feet wide at its base. To everyone's amazement, he got it off the truck and into his new studio by himself, using winches and rollers. He could see a magnificent work inside that marble, waiting to be released.

In 1989, Kevin Meyers shuttled between the people who mattered most to him. His mother, his brother and sister, and Scott Scurlock. Kevin visited Steve in Chicago and traveled farther west. When he got out to Olympia, he was shocked at the change in his old friend. Scott, who never let *anything* bother him, was anxious and upset.

Captain Pat, Scott told Kevin, was dead— murdered. Scott said that Pat had kept an old trailer deep in the woods of the Olympic Peninsula. He described it as a bizarre site, junky and isolated. Pat had decorated the site with naked baby dolls, nailing them to trees. It was a practice he had never explained, and one that Scott hadn't asked him about. Now Pat was dead.

"Somebody shot him in the head," Scott confided, "when he was sleeping. Nobody knows who."

Kevin could see that Scott was genuinely frightened. It was as if he had never really grasped how dangerous drug dealing was. If Pat had been shot because of his connection to the crystal meth operation, Scott figured that he himself might be in danger. Except for his fears about ghosts, Kevin had never known Scott to be afraid of anything. Certainly not anything concrete.

But Scott had other concerns. He said Pat's murder had cost him an awful lot of money. He had been preparing for a new "experiment," and he had entrusted the expensive ingredients to Captain Pat.

"I bought $100,000 worth of chemicals I needed for the next experiment," Scott said. "I gave them to Pat, and he buried them around his place in plastic containers. He didn't tell me where because I didn't want to know—not then. Now, I've got all that cash invested in those chemicals, and I can't find any of them."

Kevin just stared at Scott, wanting to believe this was only an overactive imagination at work. $100,000 worth of chemicals buried in the ground? That hardly seemed possible. But Scott was frantic.

Scott assured Kevin he was out of the crystal meth manufacturing business for good. It was too dangerous and unpredictable. Kevin knew he meant it. Now that Captain Pat was dead, Scott had caught—perhaps for the first time—a glimpse of his own mortality.

Scott still had his "stashes," however, of both money and drugs. He had once explained to Kevin how he stockpiled his product. He put the meth into white plastic buckets, sealed them with duct tape, and buried them around the property on Overhulse Road. He said he was like an Indian covering up a trail; he brushed the dirt with boughs so that the ground over the white buckets was left with no trace that anything had been buried there. Somewhere, Scott had perfect diagrams that would lead him to the buried drugs. He figured he had a supply that would last for at least a couple of years—maybe more. Whenever he needed money, all he had to do was dig up a bucket of meth.

He would be very, very careful now, however, about where he sold it. He didn't want to end up with a bullet in his head like Captain Pat. The drug stashes gave him some time, but Scott would have to find another way to make the kind of money he needed to continue his high-living lifestyle. Kevin feared that it probably wasn't going to be a job in some corporation's chemical laboratory.

He tried not to think about it as he turned his van east toward Denver, where he planned to visit his sister, Dana, before he went home to Virginia. They were all headed for a new decade. The boys who raced around Reston in the sixties leaping off buildings were going to be forty before too long. How could that be? Despite his frequent misgivings about what Scott was up to, Kevin had thought somehow that Peter Pan Land in Olympia, Washington, would go on forever.

But Kevin had always believed that his sister Dana was the wisest and best human being he knew. During their visit in Denver, he confided some of the things that had gone on with Scott over the years they'd been best friends.

Dana listened for a long time and saw that Scott had often humbled her proud little brother. "Kevin," she said softly, "Scott's not your friend. Don't you realize that friends don't treat friends like that?"

He didn't want to believe her, but, inside, he knew she was right.

* * *

Kevin was one of only two of Scott's longtime friends who resisted his tremendous influence. The other was Bobby Gray, who, long ago, had pole-vaulted with Kevin at Herndon High. Kevin had introduced him to Scott. "I told him, 'Scott, you've got all these *huge* plans, you need a professional builder—and Bobby's the best.'" Bobby had joined Kevin almost every year for the trip to Washington. Each of them had been enthusiastic workers during the treehouse-building summers, but they had both stubbornly maintained their own lives back on the East Coast.

It turned out that Bobby and his wife, Penny,* already had a link to Scott. Penny's parents had been very good friends of Bill and Mary Jane Scurlock's when they all lived in Reston. When Penny was a teenager, her family had been invited to a nudist gathering where the Scurlock's attended. She told Bobby later that she had been shocked by the sight of the Reverend Scurlock in the altogether.

It became a favorite inside joke for Bobby and Kevin. Kevin laughed when he heard about Penny's experience, and asked Bobby what a nudist getaway was like. Bobby scratched his head, and finally said deadpan, "Well, she said it makes you appreciate clothes!"

Although Kevin considered Scott the best friend he'd ever had, and he expected to head west to visit the treehouse regularly, he had held back on giving up too much of himself. So had Bobby.

But, in that summer of 1989, Scott asked Kevin for one last favor. On the surface, the favor seemed innocuous enough, and Scott's request came when

Kevin stopped in Denver on his way back to Virginia. He was visiting Dana and her second husband and their two sons. Dana was teaching ballet and was saving for her dream of running a day-care center that she would call "Rose Garden." She seemed so happy.

During that visit, Kevin called Scott to see how things were going in Washington. Scott asked him to come back to Olympia and buy a Chevy four-by-four truck for him. Scott said he would give Kevin the cash to go buy a truck he had already picked out. That was all. He didn't have to register it in his name or anything. Since he wasn't in any tearing hurry to get back home to Virginia, Kevin agreed to fly back to Washington.

On the plane from Denver, he met the woman who would change his life. She was a lovely woman who had soft blue eyes and thick blond hair. Her name was Ellen Hasland,* and she told him she had been visiting her family in Colorado and was on her way home to Seattle. She was a single mother raising three daughters.

Ellen had a sweet calmness about her, the exact opposite of Kevin's nervous energy. She listened to him talk about his ambitions in the art world, and about his family. He listened less—he was a man whose energy made it difficult for him to listen—but he heard enough to tell him that he had finally found the woman he had been looking for. He was thirty-six, still single, while Ellen was a little younger. But she seemed older and so much wiser.

There was the unspoken agreement that they wouldn't say good-bye when their plane landed. They made arrangements to see each other again; it didn't matter that they lived on opposite coasts.

Over the next two years they saw each other as often as they could. Kevin came out to Washington; Ellen visited in Virginia. Scott had also met his girlfriend of the moment while flying. She was a flight attendant named Cindo. Cindo told *The Stranger* some years later about their affair: "He said he lived in Olympia, and we exchanged numbers, saying we'd try to bump into each other again. After that, when I had Seattle overnights, I'd call him and we'd usually get together. Sometimes we'd rendezvous in Vegas. We'd stay at Caesar's and Scotty would have everything arranged. He was first class all the way. He told me that he did some construction, some general contracting. He was *so* talented. He was also a writer and photographer— he traveled all over the world to take pictures. I didn't really know if he had family money or what. It wasn't something that was really of interest to me. We stayed at the nicest places, we ate at the finest restaurants, and there always seemed to be plenty of money."

Cindo was the perfect girlfriend for Scott, and she would always remain impressed with him. "Scott was real intelligent, and he used to read a lot, and he wrote poetry. He was really interested in environmental concerns. He was always interested in conservation and taking care of the land. He would *never* litter. He seemed to give back to the planet by growing things. I really admired his deep convictions to do that."

Cindo was, of course, describing *exactly* the image of himself that Scott strived to project. He wasn't a writer and he wasn't even a very good amateur photographer—but he enjoyed creating the illusion that he was.

13

Back in Chicago, Steve Meyers began to work again. Chicago wasn't Carrara, but the feel in the warehouse energized him. He visualized it as a magnificent place. And he remained optimistic. He still had his talent and he still hoped to have Cara with him. He thought he could provide a better home for her than her mother.

Steve contacted Scott Scurlock and said he was ready to come to Olympia, Washington, to do carpentry work for him. In the summer of 1990, Steve arrived in Washington State, bringing Cara with him. Scott welcomed them both.

There were several buildings now on Scott's twenty acres: the gray house, a Prowler trailer that Scott's folks had left for him to fix up and sell, a thirty-two-foot storage shed, and the barn that had possibilities but needed more work. Steve stayed for three weeks working on the barn. The Meyers brothers—perhaps because they had had virtually homeless years as children, saw a wonderful dwelling in almost every solid old structure they encountered. Were it not for their soaring artistic gifts, they would have made a good living as contractors.

After only three short weeks, Steve and Scott became good friends, and Steve moved into the rarefied inner circle of Scott's world.

Kevin recognized this and felt a dull sense of dread. There was, of course, nothing he could do about his fears for Steve. Steve was his own man, and bullheaded at that when he wanted to be.

Steve Meyers retained an attorney and filed for custody of Cara. He refinanced his Chicago building so that he could build a bedroom for her, a charming feminine oasis in the midst of the warehouse. They needed a proper bathroom too, so Steve designed one with a Jacuzzi and Grecian urns. When Scott heard about Steve's massive building project, he volunteered to come to Chicago and help. Scott said he would do whatever he could to help Steve obtain custody of his little girl.

Steve was tremendously grateful to Scott and accepted his help. A skeptic might suggest that Scott *knew* how much that would mean to Steve, and that it would create a symbolic debt.

In the late summer of 1991, after some acrimonious legal wrangling, Steve was granted temporary custody of Cara and he brought her to Chicago. Steve had paid for Cara's ballet lessons—seeing in her the grace that he had once seen in his sister Dana. He vowed that she would continue to have the best lessons available. Although he could scarcely afford it, he enrolled her in a private school. But she wasn't happy there and he transferred her to a neighborhood school program for gifted children.

Steve had lost two studios—one in Italy and one in

Virginia—and he had lost the two women he loved. But now he had his daughter with him. He asked for nothing more.

He was not to have that. When Maureen and Steve went to court the judge saw an attractive young mother living in suburbia—opposed to an artist father living in a warehouse located in an industrial section of Chicago. On the surface, which would provide the more stable home for a ten-year-old girl? The judge granted custody of Cara to her mother.

Steve Meyers was inconsolable. He knew that Cara would grow away from him. He had done everything he could to protect her and to keep her with him. And now she was gone from his life.

In his legal fight to gain custody of Cara, Steve had spent everything he had; even the huge pillar of white marble had to be sold. When he had paid his lawyer and court costs, he had nothing left. He had no choice but to file for bankruptcy in the last months of 1991. That meant his warehouse/studio/home would be lost, too.

Once more, Steve Meyers had no place to work, no place to live. And now, it seemed that he had no one to love, although he would love Cara to his dying breath.

In the spring of 1992, Steve Meyers received a phone call that seemed to bring with it the answer to his immediate problems. It was Scott Scurlock. Scott knew that things weren't going well in Chicago, and he had an offer. He suggested that Steve move to Olympia. Scott had work for him to do; the gray house needed to be completely upgraded. The treehouse project needed work, too. Scott said that there would be a place for Steve to live, rent free, on Scott's own acreage.

"How am I going to get my stuff all the way out to Washington?" Steve asked.

"I'll get a rental truck and come get you. Bubba will help."

It seemed like Steve's best—and only—option.

Scott drove a van to Chicago and helped Steve move a load out of the warehouse. They drove back to Olympia, and then Steve returned to Chicago for the rest of his belongings. Kevin had agreed to drive back to Olympia with him. Steve was so broke that Kevin used his own Sears card to pay for the Ryder truck.

At the end of August 1992, Steve Meyers looked around the warehouse for the last time. And then he got behind the wheel of the van full of his belongings and headed for Olympia, more than two thousand miles away. Kevin and Steve took turns driving, and the one who wasn't behind the wheel slept in an eighteen-inch-wide strip at the back of the truck on a folded mat.

When they got to Seven Cedars, Steve tore the Achilles tendon in his heel as he was unloading the truck, and had to be taken to the Black Lake Medical Clinic. It was an excruciatingly painful injury, and he would have to be on crutches for at least a month.

Kevin returned to his acreage in Great Falls, Virginia, somewhat gratefully, although he felt a strong sense of unease about Steve living on Scott's land. He knew how persuasive Scott could be and that Steve's being down on his luck made him vulnerable. He hoped that Scott still remembered how frightened he was when Captain Pat was killed—a murder that had never been solved. If Steve just helped Scott redo the gray house and shore up the barn, this could be a good time for him to regain his bearings.

Scott lived in the treehouse; there was no question of Steve making it up the ladder with his injury, and so he lived in the gray house. When he was more mobile, he would start putting marble counters into the kitchen and the bathroom. Later, he would finish the barn.

Something deep inside Steve Meyers had died when his daughter was taken away from him. He had been a man of humor, a man with a ready smile and an expansive imagination. Now, he was bitter and defeated.

He had tried to make it by playing by the rules of society. He had failed. Now he was as open to suggestion as a man could be.

PART TWO

Mark

Here the hand and here the Heart,
    Some melancholy bloom
  Must start,
This flowered dream both
  Sweet and tart.
Since you must stay
  And I must part . . .

                     Adieu,
                       M

          —Mark Biggins

14

Scott had several close friends in and around Olympia. Probably Mark Biggins was the closest. Mark had been in and out of Scott's life for seventeen years. And like Steve Meyers, Mark had endured some rough times. But he and Scott were as opposite as men could be; Scott was lightning and impulse—Mark was sentiment and dogged loyalty. One was a warrior, the other a philosopher.

Mark was an old friend from Scott's years at Evergreen College. He was a big, gentle man, a guitarist and poet, a wanderer whose prodigious physical strength belied his tender heart.

Mark Biggins and Scott Scurlock had met in 1981 when they were introduced by one of Scott's housemates. Though Scott had gone to college mostly to please his father, Mark had wanted to become a teacher and, ultimately, a writer. He had majored in English literature.

Whether Mark knew *everything* about Scott Scurlock in those early days is unknown. Perhaps Scott kept him in the dark—as he had Kevin Meyers. Although Scott had become very open about his drug making in the late eighties, he had been quite secretive when he was in college.

Later—much later, Mark *did* know.

Mark Biggins was born in Mankato, Minnesota, one of seven children, and the oldest son of a devout Irish Catholic family. He grew up in St. Cloud with his four sisters and two brothers. His father worked for the government and his mother taught in Catholic school. The Biggins family was exceptionally close, and they preserved the memories of the growing up years of Mark and his siblings in countless albums of photographs: children playing in the Minnesota snowdrifts, swimming, celebrating birthdays, observing First Communion, opening Christmas presents. They were as American and middle class as any family who ever lived. There is a poignancy in those early pictures of Mark, who was a cherubic toddler smiling up at the camera.

The Biggins children were impressed with the need to develop a strong work ethic. They had to; that was the only way they were going to get through college and survive in the world. Intelligent as they all were, it was up to them to pay for the advanced education that a teacher's and government clerk's salaries couldn't cover.

Mark was a popular, cheerful boy with a keen sense of humor. He was a gentle kid. He brought home injured animals and tried to nurse them back to health, and he sobbed when he lost them. He grew up quickly and stood a head taller than his father.

Mark Biggins went to Tech High School in St. Cloud, Minnesota. He was an altar boy in his church—The Church of Corpus Christi—and he won several achievement awards from the St. Cloud Chapter of Kiwanis, International. In high school, he played football, baseball, basketball, and wrestled. Talented musically, he had roles in a number of school plays and one of the leads in Tech High's production of *Guys and Dolls*. When Mark and his brothers turned sixteen, their father took them hunting. His brothers enjoyed the sport, but Mark could never bring himself to shoot a living creature.

When he graduated from Tech with honors in 1972, Mark had no real sense of what he wanted to do in life. He enrolled in Duluth Area Vocational Technical Institute where he studied broadcasting. The next year, he switched to St. Cloud University where he took pre-med courses.

Quite probably, Mark wasn't that interested in becoming a doctor or a radio announcer; he longed for something more. Even then, he had a strong social conscience, and he wrote poems and essays about the less fortunate in society. His heart bled for the poor, for children without love, for policemen who were in danger. He seemed far more aware of the pain that is inherent in many lives than most nineteen-year-olds.

In 1974, Mark's closest friend's father perished when he fell under a train. Mark's friend was so grief stricken that he committed suicide, and this was quickly followed by a sister's suicide. Mark himself was so distressed that he could no longer function in school, and so he dropped out of college. He moved in with his dead friend's mother, serving as a buffer against the morbidly curious outside world. He cooked her meals and sat with her during the long evenings. He wrote "Thank You" notes to those who had attended the funerals and who had brought casseroles and flowers.

Mark Biggins himself was too traumatized to go back to college. In 1974, when he was twenty, he began hitchhiking across the country. Accompanied by friends, he headed west, seeking the serenity that he assumed existed along the Pacific Coast. He and his companions weren't that different from a lot of young people in their twenties then; together, they made up a ragtag army sweeping west across America looking for some elusive dream that might come true in California or Oregon or Washington.

Like his peers, Biggins had been only a child during the sixties with its student riots, hippie culture, and rampant rebellion. But in the seventies they were all precisely the right age to feel disenchantment with society. Now, Richard Nixon had been impeached, Patty Hearst kidnapped *and* turned renegade herself, and the war still raged in Vietnam. It was an age of broken dreams and promises for the young, and many sought geographical solutions—or the temporary euphoria of drugs—to ease their troubles. For Mark, who had seen too much death too soon, finding peace was paramount. He smoked marijuana and drank, unaware that he had little tolerance for either.

Unlike many of his fellow travelers, Mark Biggins never felt alienated from his parents. He always kept in touch with his family back in Minnesota.

He was a dreamer, but he was also a worker. That was fortunate because nothing, beyond his native intelligence and musical talent, would ever come easy for Mark Biggins. He stood well over six feet and weighed more than two hundred pounds now. He resembled the poet he aspired to be with his mop of curly hair and soft brown eyes, but his muscular build looked more like that of the basketball star he had been. When Mark and his fellow hitchhikers reached Estes Park, Colorado, on the eastern edge of Rocky Mountain National Park, Mark put down tenuous roots. He moved in with a group of people who had come west from Chicago, and he found plenty of work painting houses.

Still, after ten months, Mark Biggins headed home to St. Cloud. He hadn't found what he was looking for in Colorado. He ran a gas station for eight months in Minnesota, but his wanderlust whispered in his ear and he soon started thumbing rides west again. In 1975, he made it all the way to California. He traveled up and down the coast for four months, writing poems and playing his guitar, but even California failed to fulfill him. He made trips to New Orleans and Brownsville, Texas, always touching base with his home in Minnesota.

Finally, Mark Biggins found the place he had envisioned. He was enchanted with Washington State from the moment he arrived. In 1976, he moved to Forks—a logging town in Clallam County, Washington. The logging industry was booming in the mid-seventies, and Mark found work as a choke setter for cedar mills in Forks and La Push. He also split cedar shakes. It was dangerous work, but he was young and very strong.

Clallam County is a triangle of land, located in the far northwest corner of the Olympic Peninsula. It is surrounded by the sea—the Pacific Ocean to the west and the Strait of Juan de Fuca to the north. The area is misted with fog and rain; its heroes are lumberjacks and fishermen.

Mark Biggins worked hard and made a good living in Forks. He rented a cabin and settled into the life of a woodsman and logger. A year later, Mark met a striking town girl named Annie,* who was eighteen and nearly as tall as he. They fell in love and began a complicated and chaotic relationship. Mark and Annie would be connected through the next fourteen years, perhaps for the rest of their lives. However, theirs would not be an idyllic love story. Their goals were different, but, unhappily, one of the things they *did* share was a weakness for alcohol. At first, neither of them recognized the danger signs of addiction.

Once Mark Biggins had a home of his own up in the woods country, he was generous in sharing it. One of his friends from St. Cloud, Glenn Jansen, moved to Forks, looking for work. But the Marine Corps veteran had picked the wrong time to arrive in town; in July of 1978, most jobs in the forest were shut down because of the threat of fires in the woods due to a record-breaking hot, dry summer. Glenn was camping out and near the end of his cash reserves when Mark offered help.

"I was living in a tent as fall approached," Jansen remembered. "Mark helped me find odd jobs at some of the cedar shake mills. He also gave me food for a few weeks when my money ran out."

Mark Biggins found a cabin in La Push that Jansen could afford. "He was a godsend to me that summer and I am forever in his debt for his helping hand," Jansen wrote one day, remembering their friendship. The two young men became fast friends.

Helping out those who were temporarily down on their luck wasn't unusual for Mark. He was a man who seemed to feel an obligation to look after anyone who had hit a rough patch. When Pete Shelkin's girlfriend broke up with him just as their travels brought them to Forks, the Virginia native found himself alone in the isolated logging town thousands of miles from home. Mark befriended Pete, found him a job, and even shared his own home until Pete was able to afford his own apartment.

Logging was not the ultimate career choice for Mark Biggins. Even though he made excellent money in the mills during the late seventies, he had never planned to abandon his education. Once he had found his equilibrium, he knew what he wanted to do with his life. In 1980, he obtained student loans that allowed him to attend Evergreen State College.

It was a point of pride with him to keep current on his loans, so he lived in Olympia, but traveled the 130 miles to Forks and logged during his summer and Christmas vacations. Mark would be one of the few college students in America whose student loans were completely paid off by the time he graduated.

The friendship between Mark Biggins and Scott Scurlock began then at Evergreen and remained intact through the years, even though Scott was a devout "tree hugger" who deplored the clear-cut logging that was, for a time, Mark's source of income. They played their guitars together, and they discussed literature; Scott had a remarkable library—which was full of tales of adventure and derring-do. Pictures of the two friends in the early days show Mark towering over Scott as they stand in front of a tangle of trees on Scott's Overhulse Road property.

15

Olympia, Washington, is a small town—despite being the state capital. A young woman named Ren Talbot* became acquainted with both Mark Biggins and Scott Scurlock in the mid-1980s when she was in her early twenties. But she had no idea that they knew each other. Eventually she dated Scott, but it was Mark whom she came to admire.

Ren was working down on the piers in Olympia rebuilding wooden boats when she met Mark in 1983. She had grown up racing sailboats, and the job of refurbishing old Chris Crafts was a natural for her. She had dropped out of college to go skiing in Colorado, and then headed home to Olympia. She was a tall, almost skinny woman with beautiful eyes and classic cheekbones—but she didn't see herself that way. "I was this deadhead hippie, with a little pixie haircut," she laughed, recalling those years. "Mentally I was about sixteen."

Mark Biggins was working in the warehouse right next door—making tiny well-crafted cedar boxes for Eddie Bauer's sportswear company.

He noticed Ren when she rode her bike past his warehouse. He found out her name and called out to her one day as she rode by. "Come to find out," she remembered, "he and the guy I was seeing then—a musician—used to jam together. And then I met his girlfriend, Annie. I thought she was wonderful."

Ren and Annie became fast friends and they often sunbathed, talked, or went swimming together. "Mark was always logging," Ren said. "I just remember that they were *always* struggling financially. We *all* were."

Ren noted that Annie drank a lot, but it was a time when almost everyone in their crowd did. They played pool and pinball and danced. Before she met Mark and Annie and their friends, Ren had been part of what she considered a "real cool" group of "trust-funders" from the East Coast, all in their twenties. "I thought they were just the cat's meow—getting $5,000 a month from their moms and daddies to live on.

"When they weren't around, I hung out with Mark and Annie. I'm ashamed to say it, but when the 'trustfunders' were around, I'd act like I didn't know Mark and Annie because Mark was exactly what I was running from. He was so much the working-class, honest John walking into the Fourth Ave with his suspenders on and his Lee 88s and his 'If you ain't a

logger, you ain't shit' cap. And his 'Hey, darlin—
how's it goin'?' and 'I think you've had too much to
drink, and I'm gonna drive you home.' He was always
taking care of people. He was too much like my dad,
my uncles, and my grandad."

Ren was annoyed and embarrassed by Mark's big
brother-like protectiveness. She wanted to be one of
the psychedelic, tie-dyed, hippie trustfunders danc-
ing around like flower children. She was struggling so
hard to get away from the good, honest, working class
and here was Mark Biggins hanging around, looking
after her.

She saw how much in love he was with Annie, and
she with him—but they were always arguing about
something. Or Annie was. She would threaten to leave
him often. And then Annie got pregnant. She and
Mark were both Catholic and Annie was anxious to be
married, but Mark dragged his heels. But fatherhood
changed him and Mark was thrilled when Lori* was
born in 1983. Just as Steve Meyers was utterly devoted to Cara, Mark idolized Lori. Whatever his own
dreams might have been before her birth, Lori now
came first. Mark and Annie were married in a modest
ceremony in the Unity Church in Olympia in 1984.

Their fussing and arguing continued as it had
before they were married. Even so, anyone who knew
them could see that they were in love. Everyone
thought of "MarkandAnnie" as a couple who would
be together forever, despite all their financial troubles
and their spats.

In 1985, Mark was working at Hardell's plywood
plant in Olympia. He got the job through a man

named Mitch Evers,* who was dating Scott's sister, Debbie. Debbie was now attending Evergreen College.

But the Bigginses' financial situation was more desperate than anyone knew. Even though Mark worked hard at any job he could get, there were inevitable layoffs. Mark kept a journal that noted both good and bad times in his life. For some reason, he saved the crumpled, lined notebook page he had written on a particularly bleak day. Half seriously, half comically, he jotted down his troubles.

Bad Luck, nothing but bad god-damn luck! Get away! Get the fuck out of my life! Now! Got no job and no leads on any jobs. Had to borrow 170 bucks from one girl, 50 bucks from a guy and 50 bucks from another guy. The battery in my car went tits up, the tires are bad and I don't have a spare. I need an oil change. This chick approached me in the library one day last quarter, said she didn't have her library card and wanted to know if I'd check a book out for her with mine. I did. Yesterday, I got a bill in the mail for that book. Applied for food stamps at the beginning of this month, got approved. Today is the 13th and they're still not here. Some screw up in the mail. Been calling their office everyday for the last week and they're so messed up. There's never anyone available to talk to you when you call, so they take your phone number and say they'll call you back and never do! And that's after you've been put on hold for 5 minutes. Our phone bill is due, there was a screw up there too; they tacked last month's bill onto this month's bill. The electric bill is due as well. We're almost out of food. My mother-in-law and my sister-in-law will

141

be here tomorrow and are going to think I'm a
poor provider and with good reason. I got stung
on the bottom of my left foot and it swolled up so
big I couldn't wear shoes without limping. I'm
out of cigarettes. My car gets about 8 miles to the
gallon. My daughter has huge fever blisters on
her legs from sweat and urine being trapped in
her plastic pants. My wife's softball team won
only one game all season. I went to every game
but that one. They had a game tonight and now
she's out drinking with the girls and the way
things are going will probably get a DWI. Go
away bad luck—get away, get out of my life!
                                        Now!!
                        6/13/84 Olympia, Wa.

By the time he ended that piteous recitation, Mark
Biggins' sense of humor had obviously kicked in. But
it was clear that he had no talent for making money—
or, perhaps, for handling the money he did make.

By 1985, Ren Talbot was working as a nanny for a
very wealthy family. "Annie came over one day and
told me, 'I'm going back to Forks with my daughter.
Mark and I are splitting up.'"

Ren was shocked. She had never imagined that such
a thing would really happen. When she ran into Mark,
she saw he was utterly bereft. He was sitting in an
Olympia bar drinking shot after shot and crying.

He was determined, though, not to give up on his
marriage. Mark commuted several days a week, almost a three-hundred-mile roundtrip, so that he could
be with Annie and Lori in Forks. They were his world.
Less than a year later, Mark moved back to Forks to

work at the Sunshine Shake Company. There were no teaching vacancies in Clallam County, and nobody in Forks could see the value of a degree in English literature.

Although he was doing his best to keep his marriage together, it was a losing battle. Annie had too much to drink one night and announced that she was taking Lori and moving to California to live the beach life with her sister in Oxnard. Sober the next day, she was still resolute about leaving. Mark couldn't make her stay. He stayed behind to work, but he was crushed, and once again full of despair. He was still a devout Catholic who didn't believe in divorce. Four months later, he was so lonesome for Lori that he packed up and moved to Oxnard.

Annie, who had been enjoying her single life in the city near the Port Hueneme Missile Test Center, agreed to give their marriage another try. She must have known, however, that Mark had followed her to California to be with his daughter, not with her. They found a studio apartment where the rent was $600 a month, far more than they had paid in Forks. Mark found a job buying and selling squid. It was a smelly, onerous occupation and he longed for the clean smell of sap and sawdust.

It was inevitable that their reconciliation would fail—and it did. When Mark and Annie Biggins' marriage completely disintegrated in late 1987, he called Scott Scurlock. Mark had been drinking and sounded almost suicidal as he told Scott his life was over; he had lost his wife and daughter. Once more, it was Scott who stepped in to help a buddy glue together the shattered pieces of his life. (After a year, Scott's marriage to Pam was wavering too, but *he* was more relieved than grieving.)

Like Steve Meyers, Mark wanted to gain custody of his daughter and make a home for her, but he had no assets. He was elated when Scott offered him a job in Olympia. He told Mark he could come back to Washington and he would give him a place to live. Scott said he would pay him $1,000 a month to live on the property, work on construction, and watch the gray house whenever Scott was away. It was an offer quite similar to the one Scott made to Steve Meyers four years later, and Mark grabbed it.

Why Mark Biggins didn't find a job where he could use his college degree is an obvious question. He was back in Olympia where his degree meant something, but he didn't look for a white-collar job. He was, perhaps, too dispirited to try. Seven Cedars was a safe hiding place, the cozy rooms high up in the treetops a perfect spot for introspection and healing.

And there was marijuana and crystal meth to be had without any hassle. Mark had a weakness for addictive substances, anything to take the sharp edge off his anxiety and depression.

Of all the choices he made in his life, the decision to work full-time for Scott Scurlock may have been the most disastrous in Mark Biggins' life; without knowing it, he had given up the reins of his own destiny.

Scott traveled a great deal during 1987 to 1990. He had circled the globe with Pam before their marriage ended. Later, he went to Florida, to Nepal, and, with

Kevin, to Mexico and Nicaragua. Mark Biggins became Scott's partner in Seven Cedars Construction, working to build the remodeled treehouse and watching over the twenty acres while Scott was away. But Mark became more than just Scott's business partner; somehow, someway, he had lost the ability to think for himself, and Scott's values and Scott's needs superseded his own.

On some level, Mark realized this. He was drinking a lot, although drinking didn't make him serene or happy—it made him morose and suicidal. He drank to celebrate, to have fun, to escape. He drank for the sake of drinking. Sometimes, he charted his physiological response to alcohol—back pain that he took to be evidence of kidney and liver damage, nausea and headaches. Sometimes, with the maudlin tears of a man deep in his cups, Mark wrote letters to Lori— letters he never sent—begging her not to drink when she grew up.

One dark night in the winter of 1987–88, he sat high up in the swaying treehouse and downed drink after drink. He believed that he was on a binge that would end only with his death, and he felt incapable of stopping it. He wrote to Lori, a mournful dirge of a letter:

> My darling daughter . . . I fear I may never see you again. I fear I may die tonight. I want you to know one thing. I love you more than life itself. I love you more than I can say. I love you more than anything on earth. . . .
> If I survive this night I will stop drinking and come and live with you. Sober for the rest of my

life. If I do not survive this night, I pray to God that you will understand what I am trying to say to you here. I hope that you can forgive me for not finding the strength to stop before it was too late. You have got to believe me when I say it was not for love of you—it was for lack of love for myself. It was a disease I could not overcome. . . .

Mark prayed aloud to live, and he did, but he never really overcame his addiction to alcohol; he only tamed it slightly. He never mailed the letter to Lori Biggins, but he saved it to give to her when she was grown.

In mid-1988, Mark moved into the gray house. He had a place now for Lori, and Annie let her move to Washington to live with him. Having her with him assuaged much of the guilt he carried. She attended grade school in Olympia. In 1989, Mark met Traci Marsh.* Traci was an upbeat but nervous woman who wore no makeup and had her dark hair cut in a short shag cut. She had a wry sense of humor and she got along well with Scott and Mark's other friends. They were a mismatched couple, though; Traci was even more interested in having enough money to live comfortably than Annie had been. But Mark didn't care; he loved her anyway.

Traci moved in with Mark and became a stepmother to Lori. They lived for awhile in the Apple Park Apartments in Olympia. Oddly, although Mark's marriage to Annie was over for all intents and purposes in 1987, he never divorced her. Annie got along well with Traci, and the three of them "co-parented"

Lori without problems, although the child lived most of the time with Mark and Traci. Traci waited tables, and Mark picked up handyman jobs. Lori was a beautiful, calm little girl who seemed perfectly adjusted to having three "parents."

16

Ren Talbot met Scott Scurlock about two years after she met Mark and Annie Biggins. Although she wanted so much to be part of the hippie crowd, Ren was fairly naive at twenty-two. In 1985, one of her best friends lived with a man named Ewell Fletcher.* Ewell held semi-open houses at his place in Olympia. Ren had no idea that he was a drug dealer—not until a long time later. It was through Ewell that she met Scott, although she didn't realize at the time that Scott was Ewell's source for crystal meth; she had thought he was simply one of Ewell's huge circle of acquaintances. She remembered Ewell saying, "I have to turn you guys on to Scott—this guy who lives in a treehouse."

"So he took us out to meet Scott," Ren recalled. "I wasn't that impressed at first—but then Scott started coming around to my place. And he started talking to me a lot. Believe me, I was *not* much then. I had tank tops, levis, hiking boots. I was a real tomboy, hiking all the time. I couldn't understand why he pursued me. Now, I think I know—it was because I was working as a nanny for the richest people in Olympia. He liked being around people like that. . . . They lived in this mansion, and I lived in a little cabin next door."

Like most women, Ren found Scott attractive and captivating, and she was pleased by his interest in her. She visited the treehouse property a few times, completely unaware that Scott and Mark Biggins were acquainted.

"I was amazed to see Mark working near the barn one day," Ren said. "He was from one part of my life and Scott from another. I said, 'Hey, Biggins,' and he said, 'Hey, Talbot,' but he ducked behind the barn. I don't know what it was—why he acted that way. I think maybe he didn't want me to be part of that world out there—Scott's world."

Ren Talbot and Scott "hung out" together a few times—you couldn't even call them dates—and she developed a crush on him, probably because he didn't make *any* romantic moves. She finally invited him out to dinner. Their one big date—to a Moroccan restaurant in Seattle where diners sat on the floor and ate with their fingers—turned out to be a bore. "He just sat there like a bump on a log," she recalled. "And he wouldn't participate in any in-depth conversation at all. He would be attentive to what I had to say for a minute or two, and then his eyes would veer sideways and he'd be scoping out the other females in the room. And I ended up paying the check."

Afterward, Ren begged Scott to take her to a

nightclub called The Rainbow. Her friends' band, "Heliotrope and the Riders of the Purple Sage" was performing there.

"When we walked in, the place was filled with everybody from Olympia. He didn't like that. He turned around and walked straight out. He never liked to be in a place for very long where he knew people and they knew him," Ren said. "I wanted to stay so I told him I'd find my own way home.

"A couple of days later, Ewell Fletcher called me to say his girlfriend—my friend, Hattie*—hadn't shown up at his place in three days and he was frantically worried about her. I found out she'd been with Scott in his treehouse. She told me they didn't even have sex, but that she'd had a wonderful time. She said Scott cooked for her, and that he gave her champagne and caviar. Real champagne and real caviar. I never went out with him again."

Scott had always been a man who wanted what he couldn't have. When he realized that Ren *really* didn't want to date him again, he seemed to show up wherever she was. He would sit at the bar at the Bud Bay Cafe or Louisa's and stare at her. Sometimes he sent drinks over to her table. She would lift her glass in appreciation but she never invited him to join her.

"But Scott had this weird energy," Ren recalled. "This may sound strange—but I could always sense when Scott had walked into a restaurant, even when my back was turned to the door. His presence was electric, and you could just tell he was in the room."

Although Scott dated scores of women in Olympia,

it was essential to him that he be unforgettable to *every* woman he fancied. Ren was sitting on the tailgate of a pickup truck once and he came up to her and forced her to kiss him. She sensed it was just a conquest kiss, and, angry, she kicked him in the groin and sent him reeling back from the truck.

After that, Scott left her alone, although she would run into him from time to time. "One day," she recalled with a faint smile, "he came out to the place where I was the nanny. The wife of the couple I worked for was very attractive, and Scott came walking up their long driveway carrying a dozen roses. I asked him what he was doing, and he said they were for my boss, 'for Mother's Day.' Only it wasn't Mother's Day. It was *July*. I knew he just wanted to impress her. And annoy me."

Ren wondered sometimes what Mark Biggins and Scott Scurlock could possibly have in common— although Scott said they'd both gone to Evergreen. She wasn't really connected to either one of them any longer, and she rarely thought about them.

Mark considered Scott one of his best friends. Despite his shadowy enterprises and his self-indulgences, Scott seemed to be the truest of friends. When Scott was flush with money, he always shared what he had; when he was broke, he still made an effort to help. He had a kind of Tom Sawyer appeal; he made even hard work seem enjoyable. When Tom didn't want to whitewash a fence, he made his peers think that he was doing them a favor by handing them the brush. Scott was like that. He could never have built the first treehouse or upgraded it without the help of his friends—but none of them ever felt that they had been taken advantage of. Scott gave them crystal meth—just the right amount—and it wasn't unusual for his crew to work around the clock. His next door neighbor once asked him where *he* could hire such an enthusiastic crew of builders, and then looked puzzled when Scott laughed out loud.

When the builders finished a project, they usually started a bonfire, cracked open beers, and roasted hot dogs and marshmallows. They seemed as wholesome a bunch of carpenters as any to be found. But more often than not, they also smoked some of the good marijuana Scott always had. They were all close to forty, but they were frozen in time, boys with tinges of gray in their hair, boys who clung to the better times in the past or who yearned for better days to come.

Since the day he met Ellen Hasland, Kevin Meyers had an even more compelling reason than Scott to come to Washington. He had put his SpringVale studio up for sale, and had, in fact, sold it for the almost unbelievable sum of $240,000! The buyers gave him $30,000 down and paid him $1,800 a month, with a balloon payment of $210,000 promised one year after the sale. He had never had so much money in his life. Indeed, for the first time, it was *Kevin* who had money—and Scott who did not.

The crystal meth that Scott had buried in white plastic buckets was almost gone, and Kevin began to see that Scott didn't know how to live without money. Along with Ellen and her daughters, Kevin often visited Seven Cedars, and, as far as they could tell, Scott was still living high on the hog. He still bought every gadget he wanted, took trips, and was the local waitresses' darling.

It was 1990 and, clearly, a *lot* had changed in Scott Scurlock's life. He was edgy, and whatever calm exterior he managed to maintain was studied. Sometimes, his face in repose was a study of melancholy— all the classic planes and shadows a mask of despair. But then he would seize control of himself and be the Scott everyone was used to.

At the end of another halcyon summer in the Pacific Northwest, Kevin went home to Great Falls to collect his balloon payment, only to find that his buyers had failed to obtain financing. He took the place back, relieved—in a way—to have it. He decided to stay in Virginia, and urged Ellen to consider moving east. On one coast or the other, they needed to be together. Kevin knew his savings wouldn't last forever—now that the sale on his place had fallen through. He still wasn't able to remodel his studio at SpringVale in the way he visualized, his taxes were getting higher because his place sat smack dab in the middle of where DC bigwigs were building and buying all around him. Even as much as he loved it, he didn't know how long he'd be able to hold on to SpringVale.

Scott noted Kevin's concerns about his financial situation. Just as he had with Steve and Mark, he came up with what seemed to be a magnanimous offer. "If you sell your place in Great Falls," he told Kevin, "you can move out here. You can remodel the barn and turn it into an art studio. I'll sell it to you for $50,000."

It seemed like a great idea. Kevin could get enough cash out of his Virginia studio to pay Scott and have enough left over to support himself until he began to sell his paintings in the Northwest. His brother and his best friend were in Olympia, and the woman he loved was in Seattle, only sixty miles away.

Kevin had a mission too. He had talked to Scott before about using his acreage to build low-cost homes for people in need. Nicaragua had changed Kevin Meyers. He had seen abject poverty and he had vowed to do what he could—if not in Nicaragua, then in America. It could be a money-making project for Scott too. He knew Scott needed money badly. All his meth stashes were gone. All the buried money. Everything was gone.

Whatever doubts Kevin Meyers had were overwhelmed by his excitement about starting over in Washington State. Ellen wanted him to come west. So did Steve and Scott. He put SpringVale up for sale. Within a few months, he sold it—this time for good—and packed up everything he owned. When he finally arrived in Washington, it was the high summer of 1990. This time, he felt he would be there forever.

"Except for Ellen, it was a terrible mistake," Kevin remembered, wincing. "I rolled into Olympia and drove up to Seven Cedars and no one was there. I found Scott, Mark, and Steve at The Keg restaurant, but it wasn't like I expected it to be. It was awkward. I told Scott I had the $50,000 to buy the barn, and he acted as if he'd forgotten all about our agreement. He wouldn't look me in the eye. He finally muttered something about 'Those options are on the back burner now.' I felt like the odd man out. Their minds were on something else—something that obviously had nothing to do with me."

Still, once Kevin settled in, things seemed better. Scott wouldn't accept his money, but he let Kevin set about remodeling the inside of the barn to use as a studio.

It was a huge barn. The front was wood, but one summer Bobby Gray had reinforced the back with heavy underground bunkers formed of concrete. Kevin built a twenty-four-foot workbench, a sixteen-foot art table, and installed track lighting and a sink. Steve helped by installing a wide door that opened smoothly on rollers. Kevin couldn't help being proud of what he had accomplished. Every bit of workmanship was like a piece of fine furniture. He knew he didn't have his brother's craftsmanship, but he countersank every screw and lovingly sanded the wood.

Scott seemed too busy to check out his work, but Kevin expected him to be pleased when he saw the final result. Even if he didn't own the barn yet, Kevin knew he would be happy painting there.

Kevin commuted from Ellen's apartment most days. Often, he stayed over at Scott's place, sleeping in his van. Sometimes Ellen and her girls—who were nine, ten, and twelve in 1990—came down for week-ends. The kids loved the treehouse; they would climb up the steps and then slide down the forty-foot pole over and over. And they loved the woods, and they adored Scott.

Scott liked Ellen, and she liked him. But she was a highly intuitive woman and she saw sadness in him, even some desperation. He told her he wanted flowers everywhere and gave her the money to bring back armloads of them. She filled every container she could find with fresh flowers and placed them around the treehouse and on the deck. She kept the hanging fuchsia baskets watered and free of deadheads. When the Scurlocks visited, they were very taken with Ellen, and teased Scott, saying, "Why can't *you* find a woman like that?"

Scott only grinned and spread his palms wide in a gesture of defeat. And they all laughed.

On the surface, everything seemed fine. But Kevin knew Scott better than he had ever known anyone. And something was wrong. He tried again and again to get Scott to talk about his idea for utilizing some of the Overhulse acreage to build clean but cheap housing. Scott only stared at him with disinterest.

Kevin tried to persuade Scott to sell him a few acres on the far side of the property so he could at least build a place for himself, but Scott refused. Kevin even reminded him of the slogan they used to share, "To increase the joy, we must share it."

"You share it, Bubba," Scott said. "I've got things to think about."

One day, Kevin was walking toward the treehouse

when a bullet whizzed past his ear. He dropped to the ground, flattening himself. He looked up and saw Scott high up in the trees with a 30-30 rifle cradled in his arms, an inscrutable look on his face. As incomprehensible as it was, he realized that Scott had shot at him.

"What'd you do that for?" Kevin called, bewildered.

"You didn't give the crow caw."

"You *knew* it was me."

Scott shrugged and disappeared inside the treehouse. Kevin turned around and went back to work on the barn, shaken. It was the awful thought that his best friend, the man who had faced death with him more than once, had actually fired a gun in his direction. And for no reason at all.

Nothing was working. The land was wonderful and the barn had great potential as a studio. Why, then, did his heart feel like a stone in his chest? He didn't know Scott any more. He still "honored" him as his friend, but he was puzzled by the coldness and the cruelty he sometimes glimpsed in the man who had once had the biggest heart in the world.

Kevin buried the memory of seeing Scott cradling the Winchester rifle, and continued to work around the place. He installed a septic system for the treehouse bathroom that was right out of *Swiss Family Robinson* and Scott was pleased. Kevin worked mostly on the barn, though, taking great satisfaction in the way it was shaping up. He knew Scott would love it when he had it finished. He learned otherwise one day when Scott brought his sister Karen into the barn. Kevin was eagerly pointing out the improvements he had made, when Scott dismissed him with a half-wave of his arm, and walked away.

Bill and Mary Jane Scurlock visited that summer, but even their visit didn't lighten Scott's mood. Scott didn't even bring Bill by to look at the barn. After the Scurlocks headed back to Arizona, things continued to be strained at Seven Cedars. "Something ended the day I called him out to show him that I'd finished the barn," Kevin said. "I could tell right away he didn't care about it. He was desperate because he didn't have any money. Even in that state, he wouldn't say he 'hated' my studio. But I'd left a bunch of beans soaking in a half-gallon milk jug on the barn floor so we could make tortillas later, and he yelled at me that they were rotten—"

Suddenly, Scott kicked the jug. For an instant, the scene seemed Daliesque, gelid, the air full of water and beans. And then they fell like so many fat bugs all over the remodeled barn, Kevin's art table, easels, sink—everywhere. Kevin and Scott stared at each other, one in a rage; the other humiliated and shocked. Finally, Scott turned on his heel and walked out. Kevin realized at that moment that Scott had never intended to let him have the barn to paint in. Almost two decades of committed friendship were now history. Kevin had to accept that they weren't friends now—not in the way they had been. Scott had always been Willie-Boss; now he wanted to be more than that. Everyone on the place—everyone *except* Kevin—tiptoed around Scott, waiting for orders, waiting for approval, waiting to find out when they could breathe or sleep or take a crap. But Kevin remained his own man.

Mark Biggins was the caretaker of Scott's empire, and for a long time, he had done a good job. He built fences and cleared away brush. He watched over Seven Cedars while Scott traveled. He collected his $1,000 a month and had free room and board. But, when Traci moved in, things didn't work as well. They needed more space. So now Mark lived off the place, as did Kevin. Kevin quit work on the barn and quietly moved his painting supplies back to Ellen's place. They still came down to visit; Kevin couldn't bring himself to walk away completely. The good memories were still too strong.

17

It was 1991 and Scott Scurlock was no longer a big spender. Now more than ever, he lost himself in adventure movies, identifying with both the good guys or bad guys, whoever handled their lives the most deftly. Scott watched certain movies many times. In 1991, he was mesmerized by *Point Break* with Patrick Swayze and Keanu Reeves. The lead characters were so like himself, Kevin, Steve, Mark— and the others who called Seven Cedars home.

Swayze played Bodie, a surfer-cum-bankrobber; Reeves a kind of renegade FBI agent who was caught halfway between the world of the splendid surfers and the uptight senior agents who lectured him. *Point Break* was antiestablishment—it was all about taking chances and the renegade camaraderie of a group of men. Bodie's gang of bank robbers called themselves the "ex-Presidents" and wore latex masks of Ronald Reagan, Richard Nixon, Jimmy Carter, and Lyndon Johnson. They didn't seem so villainous, really, the way they leapt on counters and waved the guns they never used. It was an inside joke; the damned politicians in Washington, DC, had robbed the working stiffs, and now they were robbing the banks, *the* symbolic center of greedy big business.

At some point, and no one can now say when, William Scott Scurlock, thirty-nine years old and at the end of his financial tether, visualized himself standing in place of Patrick Swayze. In his mind, he stepped into the movie and became its hero.

He began to study adventure movies in earnest, as if he believed that screenwriters really knew how to outwit cops and FBI agents. *FX* was another major influence on him. It taught him how to use makeup to disguise himself so completely that even his mother wouldn't recognize him. He rented that movie so many times that he almost wore it out.

"Look," he told friends, "*look* how they can change. Watch it again. . . ."

"It's a *movie,* Willie-Boss," someone said. "It's not real."

Why wasn't it, Scott asked. Why couldn't movies be

real? He had been a film nut as long as they had known him. He was caught somewhere between myth and the most brutal depictions of reality.

Scott Scurlock, born in 1955, had always taken great pride in the fact that he was a direct descendant of Doc Scurlock, who rode with Billy the Kid in another place, another time. Half joking (or seeming to half joke), Scott had once suggested to Mark Biggins that they should pull a bank robbery.

Biggins figured he was kidding, and laughed. Now it seemed not to be a joke at all. Scott kept studying movies about bank robbers, and he became obsessed with books about famous bank robbers. He learned everything that he could about what had worked and what had not. Still, he was more influenced by movies and folklore, fables and fiction, than by the gritty reality of *real* bank robberies. Instead, he became entranced with the infamy and the folk-hero stature of these men, letting his mind skip past the ghastly black-and-white photographs of their morgue photos, their heads propped on wooden blocks and bodies full of bullet holes, while proud lawmen posed next to them.

Scott had groomed both Steve Meyers and Mark Biggins to the point that they would do what he asked. In a sense, they no longer had wills of their own—although *they* might have argued that they had. By being first their friend and then their benefactor, Scott had reeled them in. What followed next seemed natural and right. He was headed for another adventure, a different kind of experiment, and he would share the game with his friends, just as he always had.

In the spring of 1992, Scott began to talk seriously about emulating his Great Uncle Doc. He approached Mark one night when the two of them were drinking. Mark Biggins realized that this time Scott was not talking about "What ifs?" He was talking about when and where. "Let's rob a bank," Scott said enthusiastically. It was a conversation that Mark could never have imagined being part of. He tried to kid Scott out of it, but it didn't work. Scott said he had scouted out a bank in Seattle and had already worked out a plan.

There is no question that Mark Biggins should have walked away. But he didn't. He was broke; Traci had been after him to make more money so they wouldn't have to live like paupers. Lori needed things. He agreed to go with Scott to look at the bank.

Sometime in the middle of June, the two men drove to the Madison Park area of Seattle. It was a good distance from downtown—and from any of the Seattle Police Department precincts. It was, however, also a good distance from the entrance to a freeway and a quick getaway. Scott had thought about a number of variables, but he hadn't considered their escape very carefully.

By the middle of June 1992, everything seemed to be in place for Scott Scurlock's plan. It was actually a rather stupid plan, full of pitfalls, a script that might have worked in a movie but had little basis in reality.

Scott enlisted Traci, too, who was far more eager to be involved than Mark, who got queasy at the very thought of it. Scott outlined his plan to them; Traci would be the driver and Mark would be in charge of crowd control. Scott and Mark would go into the bank wearing disguises and carrying guns. They would wear gloves so they wouldn't leave fingerprints. They would scoop the cash packets out of the tellers' trays and be out of the bank before anyone knew what had hit them.

Their first target was the Seafirst Bank at 4112 Madison Avenue. Traci drove Scott's blue van and dropped Mark and Scott off a block away from the bank shortly before noon on Thursday, June 25. Scott wore makeup and a fake nose; Mark wore a Ronald Reagan mask. Their weakest link was their getaway vehicle. Scott didn't want to use his own van because it could be traced back to him. He told Mark to watch for a customer who drove up in a car that looked dependable but not flashy—and to remember that driver. Once in the bank, and during the robbery, Mark was to take the person's car keys. Then they would leave in the designated car, ditch it, and meet up with Traci at a prearranged spot.

"Nobody will ever know what we arrived in," Scott explained.

Mark watched a customer drive up to the bank in a blue 1991 Cadillac, and memorized what the man looked like: *White male . . . medium height . . . graying red hair. . . .*

"Let's go," Scott breathed, and, suddenly, they were in the bank. Scott leapt up on the teller counter, just like Bodie had in *Point Break,* shouting "This is a hold-up. Don't anybody move!" Then he jumped nimbly behind the line of tellers. Mark watched as Scott scooped cash out of the tellers' drawers.

Mark thought he must be in a dream. He felt the gun in his hand and waved it around, aware of the fear that was almost palpable among the customers and the employees. He told the customers to lie down on the floor. He just wanted to be out of there. Like a sleepwalker, he walked to the tellers' area, and was ready to grab money as Scott had instructed. But then he looked at his hands and saw that he had forgotten to put on gloves. They were still in his pocket.

Scott finished gathering money and ran back to Mark, "You have the keys?"

"No . . . no, I forgot."

"Let's get them," Scott barked and Mark walked to the man who'd driven the blue Cadillac. "May I have your keys, sir? Don't worry. I won't hurt your car."

The man was lying facedown on the floor, and he had to dig in his pants pocket awkwardly to find his key ring. He handed over his car keys, and Scott and Mark ran from the bank. As they neared the door, Scott turned around and said, "As long as nobody sets off the alarm, we won't have to come back and shoot anybody," and then he grinned and shouted, "Thank you! Have a nice day."

They got into the Cadillac, and Mark tried to start it, but he was so scared that he only ground the motor. It felt like hours before it finally started. When it did, he drove to the parking lot where Traci was supposed to meet them.

Only she wasn't there.

Mark was terrified. He had known all along that it wasn't going to work. They abandoned the stolen Cadillac and raced down an alley. A huge dog, chained in an adjacent yard, lunged at the fence and Mark felt its breath. He practically ran up Scott's back. He heard Scott laughing. He was *enjoying* this.

They had talked of a backup meeting spot, and they leapt over a fence onto the golf course of the extremely posh, gated Broadmoor community. Golfers saw them coming—two men in masks carrying a bag of money—and they stopped, open-mouthed, in midswing. Incredibly, nobody tried to stop them.

At a little stone restroom, Scott stopped to wash off his makeup. Traci was where she was supposed to be this time. The two men leapt into Scott's van and Traci headed toward the northernmost floating bridge connecting Seattle to Mercer Island, then eased onto 405 South until it merged with I-5. They were on their way to Olympia and the treehouse. No one was hurt, and they had a bag of money— $19,971 to be precise.

Scott and Traci shouted with excitement all the way home, while Mark sobbed, "I'm *never* going to do this again. Never."

Scott looked at him in the rearview mirror, his eyes full of disgust. "Traci," he said. "You are going to be my Number One Man to rob banks with. We can't deal with you, Biggins. You lost it in there. You were shaking. You are one lousy bank robber."

It was clear that Scott and Traci were riding an adrenaline rush, triumphant that they had actually done it. As soon as they got back to Seven Cedars, Mark went into the house and packed his and Traci's belongings in suitcases and duffel bags. He carried them out to their ancient station wagon. When everything was packed, he went to get Traci. Thank God, Lori was with her mother in California.

"We're going, Traci," he said. "We're moving. We're never going to do anything like that again."

"You don't even have your share of the money," Scott said, incredulously.

"I don't want it. Come on, Traci."

"I'm staying with Scott," she said. "I'm his Number One Man."

It took every persuasive tactic that Mark Biggins had to get his girlfriend away from Seven Cedars. She had the same glitter of excitement in her eyes that Scott did as they counted out and divided the money. Once she grudgingly got in the car, he headed toward Oregon, where they stayed one night in a motel. The next day, they drove to Idaho and east into Hamilton, Montana, near the Bitterroot National Forest. During the entire trip, Mark kept his ear tuned for sirens, expecting to see flashing blue lights behind him.

It seemed impossible, but apparently they had gotten away clean. Mark and Traci stayed for a few weeks at the Lost Horse Resort, and it was an edgy, tight-lipped time between them. In August, they rented a tiny house in Darby, Montana. Mark got a job building log cabins. They made friends with people in town, and on the surface they seemed to be an ordinary young couple struggling to make ends meet.

But Mark needed to find out what was happening back in Washington. He had to know if anyone was looking for him. He made phone calls, but he couldn't find Scott. He finally got in touch with some friends who said that, as far as they knew, Scott hadn't been arrested for anything. Why would he be? He'd been off on some trip, but he was doing just fine. In the meantime, he had someone else handling all the stuff that Mark used to do: Steve Meyers.

After a while, Mark began to think that they truly had missed disaster with the elusive luck that so often had abandoned him. Nobody came looking for him. No police knocked on the door of their little place in Darby. He dared to take a deep breath.

Mark had good reason to breathe easy. If he and Scott never pulled another bank robbery, the chances were excellent that they wouldn't be caught. All the FBI had were four electrostatic lifts of latent fingerprints (single fingers) from the bank counter, two photographs of shoe prints, and five dust prints of shoes. No two witnesses seemed to agree on what they looked like—beyond the consensus that they were both male and probably white. Age estimates varied from twenties to mid-fifties, and some thought that Scott was thin while others said he had a potbelly. Most of them remembered that Mark had worn a Ronald Reagan mask, and one woman saw curly hair on the back of his head.

Anyone who has studied witnesses' memories of events knows that under severe stress, such recall is often flawed: six people witnessing the exact same scene will often give as many descriptions. And that is what happened on June 25, 1992.

However, the FBI lab's criminalists compared some of the shoe prints they had lifted at the bank with known treads and deduced that they came from a "Converse All-Star brand, or another brand having a very similar outsole design."

Scott had worn All-Stars since he was a kid. He had hiked the Grand Canyon and climbed Mount Rainier in Converse All-Stars. Now, he had worn them in another "sport," and left behind physical evidence that he was completely unaware of. Not Nikes. Not Reebok. Scott would one day regret that he had such undying brand loyalty.

PART THREE

Mike and Shawn

18

One of the ironies of true life "cops and robbers" is that, given other circumstances, the hunted and the hunters might well have been friends. Often they have backgrounds that are not as dissimilar as we might expect. And yet, somewhere along the line some added ingredient, some catalyst, or even some genetic predisposition makes some favor the law while others flaunt it.

The detective who dedicates a good portion of his waking hours to tracking a high-profile offender carries—always—an image in his mind of whom he is looking for. He may be wrong, of course, but, amazingly, he is often right. The "successful" criminal focuses on protecting his identity, while the investigator tries to think like the man he hunts. In the end, it almost seems as if their hearts have synchronized to beat at the same rate and they draw breaths at the same time; one leads and the other steps in his tracks. Ultimately, they end up in the same place at the same time. They have become fraternal—if aberrant—"twins."

Almost every law officer who becomes obsessed with—and possessed by—the desire to capture a particularly adroit criminal dreams of the moment when they will meet face to face. Surprisingly, most elusive felons hunger, albeit subconsciously, for such a meeting.

The bank robber who would come to be known only as "Hollywood" had not one but two spectacularly adept investigators on his trail. Of all the Northwest lawmen who would mobilize to track and trap him, Shawn Johnson and Mike Magan wanted him the most. Although they were as different in temperament and technique as any two men could be, they would unite in what became a surpassingly baffling investigation.

Mike Magan is tall and muscular; Shawn Johnson is tall and lanky. Mike was a football star; Shawn a basketball star. Mike Magan's lineage is pure police, while Shawn Johnson is the first law-enforcement officer in his family.

And Mike was a Seattle police officer while Shawn was an FBI agent. To the layman, that probably doesn't mean much. To a working cop or agent, the old antagonisms between city cops and "the Feds" haven't quite dissipated. During the long reign of FBI Director J. Edgar Hoover, "the Bureau" was viewed as elitist by most police departments. City and county police detectives grumbled about sending their information to the FBI because they claimed it disappeared into a great black hole, and there was no reciprocation. They were sometimes justified. With the abdication of Hoover, the Bureau and local cops began to work together with far more give and take.

Hollywood was a trophy kind of criminal, clever enough and elusive enough to become the kind of big fish that any cop would love to land first. Most of the working cops in the Northwest would come to know about Hollywood and his gang, and they all pondered how they might catch him if he showed up in their jurisdiction. But perhaps most of all, Mike Magan and Shawn Johnson wanted him. Each of them wanted to be the one to put the handcuffs on Hollywood, the first to read him his rights.

Still, neither of them had a fix on what he looked like, who he was, where he lived, or where he would strike next.

1987 was a crucial year for both of them; Mike Magan was graduating from the Washington State Criminal Justice Training Center and about to become a rookie office on the Seattle Police Department. Shawn Johnson was attending the FBI Academy in Quantico, Virginia, and never had reason to give Seattle, Washington, a thought.

That same year, less than an hour's drive from Quantico, Scott Scurlock was marrying "The Queen of Spades," in Reston, Virginia, while three thousand miles away from Quantico, Mark and Annie Biggins' marriage was breaking up. Steve and Kevin Meyers were both living in Virginia, too—and Steve was enjoying a new marriage.

But as far back as 1987, a certain synchronicity of circumstances was beginning to line up and intersect. It was happening as quietly as a gentle breeze sliding through bare winter branches. It would be almost a decade before the tragic quintet of players would actually meet. All of them were so intent upon the lives they were living then, they had no time to look ahead; none of them could have foreseen what was to come.

We know now where Scott Scurlock, Mark Biggins, and the Meyers brothers were from the fifties to the late eighties. Where were Mike Magan and Shawn Johnson?

Actually, Mike and Shawn were nowhere at all in the fifties; they weren't even born until the next decade. Shawn Johnson was born in Red Wing, Minnesota, in February 1961 and grew up a few miles east of there in a hamlet called Cannon Falls. In Quantico, he would be geographically close to Scott Scurlock. As a child, he grew up a short distance from Mark Biggins. Shawn was seven years younger than Mark, but both were sons of working-class Minnesota families and both were good students and athletes.

While Mark Biggins had six siblings, Shawn had only one; his sister was seventeen years older than he and about to graduate from high school when he was born. Shawn grew up as virtually an only child. He was a tall skinny kid, a little bit shy. Like Mark Biggins, he would always be soft-spoken.

Shawn Johnson graduated from Cannon Falls High School in 1979, and started college at Winona State University that fall. Winona State is located near the shores of the great Mississippi River a few miles south of the falls that drop the St. Croix River into the Mississippi. He graduated in 1983 with a Bachelor of Science degree in criminal justice. His sister was an attorney, and he planned to be one, too.

But in the summer of 1983, Shawn did an internship with the St. Paul Police Department. He found he loved police work. Still, he went on to law school at the William Mitchell College of Law in St. Paul. Halfway through law school, Shawn married his college sweetheart, Marie.

During his years in St. Paul, Shawn Johnson had done a variety of internships—with a corporate law firm, a prosecuting attorney's office, and two years with an insurance defense firm. As his graduation approached in 1987, he had every intention of going into the practice of law in one specialty or another. But he always remembered his internship with the St. Paul Police Department, and he realized that he was more intrigued by the challenges of police work than with practicing law.

The FBI came to the law school campus every year, recruiting agents. The Bureau sounded interesting to Shawn; if he were to become a special agent, he would have an opportunity to combine his longtime interest in investigative work with his training in the law. And so in his last year of law school, Shawn Johnson applied to the FBI.

He had just graduated from law school and was preparing for the Minnesota bar exam when he learned he had been accepted into the FBI's twelve-week training program in Quantico. He asked for—and was granted—an extension so that he could take the bar exam. He passed on his first try.

A new lawyer, Shawn Johnson was soon a rookie FBI agent, reporting to FBI headquarters in Quantico in August of 1987. It was the hottest, muggiest time of the year to run the obstacle courses in Virginia, but

Shawn wasn't sorry he was there; what he was learning was riveting.

Eight weeks into the training, Shawn got his assignment: Seattle, Washington. "I had to look on the map," he admitted. "I knew it was someplace out west, and I thought it was on the Pacific Ocean. I found out it wasn't."

So the Johnsons headed west. They arrived in November, the beginning of Seattle's six-month rainy season.

Shawn Johnson's first assignment in Seattle was with the Green River Killer Task Force, an intense serial murder investigation that ended in bitter disappointment after bitter disappointment. Shawn arrived when detectives and FBI agents were winding the failed investigation down. More than four dozen young women had disappeared in the Seattle area between July 1982 and April 1984; most of their skeletonized remains had been found in lonely gravesites located in ever-widening circles around the Seattle-Tacoma airport. The victims (all but four) had been identified, but never avenged.

The Green River Task Force had once had several dozen investigators working in a high-pressure boiler room of leads, tips, and follow-ups. After four years, when no viable suspect had been found, the task force began closing down.

Shawn Johnson worked for three months with another FBI special agent and Seattle Police and King County detectives who were still assigned to the task force. "We were basically pulling out," he recalled, "but it was still interesting for me—coming right out of Quantico—to work on a case like that."

The search for the Green River Killer was a gripping learning experience for the scores of detectives who took part in it, even though at this writing, all the murder cases are still open, and the manpower assigned to follow leads consists of only one and a half detectives. Everyone who worked on the task force came away with a deep understanding of serial murder and the devious mind of a brilliant sociopath. They just never found *the* brilliant sociopath who committed the Green River killings.

Shawn Johnson was assigned next to the FBI's violent crime unit. There was no lack of such crimes in Seattle; Shawn worked bank robberies, extortions, kidnapping, and parole violations for a year. "We were always busy," he recalled.

Marie Johnson seldom knew exactly what her husband's daily work life was like—not unless she overheard "war stories" at social events where he and other agents got together. It was just as well she didn't know. He made a point of not bringing his work home; some of the cases he investigated were very dangerous.

From 1989 to 1994, Shawn worked counterintelligence and counterterrorism. This was during the Goodwill Games and the Gulf War. "There was always something going on," he says—a deliberately vague understatement. He will not say—he *cannot* say—*what* was going on. Those five years taught him a lot about the more sinister and dangerous attributes of terrorists.

By this time, the Johnsons had two toddlers at home. Shawn spent his off-duty time with his family and pursued his avocation as a scholar of the Civil War. Immersing himself in the lore of a war that ended more than a century ago was a way to step out of the war against crime he lived everyday. At work, his life was far different than it might have been had he opted to become an attorney in Minnesota. At first, both he and Marie had been homesick for Wisconsin and Minnesota, but gradually they grew accustomed to Seattle's sometimes endless rainy season, bought a home in West Seattle, and settled in.

In January of 1994, Shawn Johnson was reassigned to the violent crimes unit. Among the many cases that were thorns in the sides of agents and local detectives who worked robberies, there was a bank robber who had come to be known as Hollywood. He was so good at disguise and escape that he sometimes seemed to be more a ghost than a man. By the beginning of 1994, he and his accomplices had hit seven banks and stolen more than $400,000.

When Shawn Johnson looked over the charts that represented Hollywood's crimes, it was obvious that he was perfecting his "craft." In 1994, the bank robber in the mask wasn't yet in the most-wanted class; he was only one among too many bank robbers in Seattle. But he seemed to be coming up through the pack, making himself more infamous with each bank he hit.

19

Michael Patrick Magan was born on September 21, 1962. The Magans had come to America from County Langfar, the village of Killahsee. Mike came from so many generations of Irish cops that the strong blue line was almost genetically bred into him. His great grandfather—the *first* Frank Magan was "Lieutenant of Roundsman" for the New York Police Department. His grandfather, Frank R. Magan, was a New York City Police officer and later a New York City fireman. His father, Frank III—born in Brooklyn, raised in Queens—joined the New York City Police Department in 1958. He was on the Tactical Patrol Squad, the first in America. All the patrolmen on the special squad had to be over six feet; at over six-feet-six, Frank III qualified easily.

Where Scott Scurlock's great-great uncle Doc had ridden with Billy the Kid, all of Magan's male ancestors rode with the law.

Just as preachers' kids often rebel, so do cops' kids. It can be rough on a kid when his old man represents all that is moral and legal. But that didn't happen to Mike Magan. All he and his big brother Jake ever wanted to be were police officers, and they couldn't wait until they were old enough to join the force.

Susan and Frank Magan III, Mike's parents, were the least likely couple to meet. She was a naive, extremely devout Irish Catholic girl from Butte, Montana, who attended Catholic school in Butte and left home to attend strict St. Mary's College in Leavenworth, Kansas. Big Frank Magan, of course, grew up in Queens. The petite blond and the towering Frank met in Seattle in the mid-fifties at a party one of Susan's friends gave. All they had in common was a devout Catholic faith and a certain independence of spirit.

Frank convinced Susan to marry him and move to New York City, and she loved it, but in 1962 when Jake was almost two and Mike was about to be born, they moved back to Seattle, "because it was a better place to raise kids." It was, and they had three—Jake, Mike, and Molly. Like the Scurlocks, the Magans had no set rules for their youngsters. But their lifestyles were vastly different; while the Scurlocks were immersed in New Age religion and the laissez-faire attitudes that went with it, the Magans' kids all went to parochial schools where the nuns and the Irish Christian Brothers could be tough. Both families taught by example, letting their youngsters make their own decisions.

Susan Magan recalled that she and Frank never had trouble with Jake, Mike, or Molly—nothing beyond some "egg-throwing incidents" with the boys. Her older brothers were much stricter with Molly than their parents were. She felt lucky if she could ever have a date without her big brothers watching over her.

Mike Magan barely survived childhood. Susan took him shopping at the A&P when he was four, and she was terrified when he suddenly started gagging and choking in agony. One of the store employees had been changing the price tags on merchandise, using acetone (nail polish remover) to remove the old labels. Foolishly, he had used a pop bottle to hold the acetone. When he set it down for a moment, he put it right next to bottles of *real* pop. Little Mike saw it there, open, and took a big gulp of "pop."

He was rushed to Children's Orthopedic Hospital by ambulance. Doctors told Frank and Susan Magan that he might die, and if he didn't, there was a strong possibility that his lungs had been irreparably damaged. "He inhaled some of it," the doctors warned. "You have to understand that his lungs were burned."

Mike was released after five days in the hospital, hardly the worse for wear. *He* didn't realize how desperate his condition had been. And his lungs developed just fine.

Susan always worked, but she was home before school and after school because she was a drama and speech teacher at a private preparatory school for girls. Later, she also opened her own catering business.

In 1980, when Mike was a senior in high school, Frank R. Magan II moved in with his son's family in their home in a suburb in the north end of Seattle. He was an irascible character who usually thought his grandsons the finest boys on earth. He believed Susan was an angel. Stories of Grandpa Frank's eccentricities still send his family into gales of laughter. He had a prized 1964 Mercury Marquis that he revered so much (despite its rapidly disintegrating condition) that they called it "Baby Jesus" behind his back. Mike drove it once and was afraid it would explode from sheer gas fumes alone.

Once when Grandpa Frank's sister, Agnes, a most devout and sheltered nun, was coming for a visit, he took Mike and Jake aside and cautioned them, "Now, boys—my sister Agnes is coming and she doesn't like cuss words—"

Mike winked at Jake and said, "Well, what's the ##@@$$$ big $$###&& deal about that?"

"Boys . . . Boys, she's a Rosary Hill Dominican nun!" Their grandfather implored.

"Well," Jake said, jumping into the joke, "I'll try not to say **&&%%%—but I don't know if I can @*+++%% help myself . . . I might forget."

After they'd blurted out every swear word they could think of, they began to laugh and he realized it was a joke. No matter how they tormented their grandfather, they loved him fiercely. And, of course, they were on their best behavior when Sister Agnes came to visit, never saying so much as "darn" in front of her.

Mike made good use of his time as he waited to become a Seattle Police Officer. He graduated from O'Dea High School, and went to college at the University of Washington, where he played offensive guard on the Washington Huskies' Rose Bowl–winning football team in 1982.

He had a number of jobs to pay his way through school, one of them driving a Coor's beer truck.

Like everyone else who became involved in this case of intertwined lives, 1987 was a watershed year for Mike Magan, too. While Shawn Johnson was preparing to graduate from law school and join the FBI, Mike became a Seattle police recruit. He was a member of the 307th class of Washington State's Basic Law Enforcement Training, and he graduated on February 25, 1987, from the Criminal Justice Training Center. His grandfather Frank was there to proudly pin on Mike's badge.

When Frank II was eighty-eight, he became terribly ill. He had faced death innumerable times as a cop and a fireman. Back in New York, he and his partner, Barney Kelly, once fell several stories down an elevator shaft in a burning building. Now, in the hospital, he asked his son how bad off he was, and Frank III said, "This is worse than that time in the elevator shaft with Barney."

It was. Mike Magan said his good-byes to his grandfather. The old man smiled at the end, gazed around his hospital room and gave individual advice to everyone gathered there. Then he murmured, "It's payday," and died.

Mike Magan's serial number was 5094, and there was never a rookie policeman more excited about hitting the streets as a full-fledged officer. The Seattle Police Department made no mistake when they hired Mike Magan. He was twenty-four years old, still in the peak of condition necessary to play college football, and possessed of that instinctual "gut feeling" and computerlike memory that every superior cop has. All he needed was experience, and he was about to get plenty of it.

The first time Mike's name hit the Seattle papers was at Christmas, 1987. He and his partner, David Lishner, were called to a downtown hotel at 10 P.M. on Christmas Eve, where a distraught and depressed thirty-one-year-old man was poised to jump from a fourth-floor window. He wouldn't let them in the room, but when Mike and Dave heard glass shattering inside, they broke down the door. From that point on, they moved with agonizing slowness and kept their voices soft and nonthreatening.

The man had cut himself on his face and arms and was bleeding heavily as he perched precariously outside the window in the icy rain. Mike Magan crept as close as he could, talking quietly, "There are better things to live for—" he said. It took him several minutes to convince the would-be suicide to come back toward the window. When he did, the two officers grabbed him and pulled him to safety.

Assigned to the North Precinct, Mike Magan worked everything from purse snatchings and home burglaries to accidents and rapes. In April 1989, he spotted a driver who was known to be a black tar heroin dealer. A "wants and warrants" check showed an active warrant for the man, and a search of the car turned up $22,885 hidden in the car. Mike's elation at finding the drug money—which was held for evidence—was matched by his frustration when no drugs were found. The driver laughed as he said, "You lost. I'm going to California to *buy* drugs, but you didn't find drugs in my car or the rest of the cash." Mike had to let the dealer go, but minus almost $23,000.

In 1990, Magan was assigned to work at the Goodwill Games in Seattle. He was also moved to a Community Police Team and to bicycle patrol. The Seattle Police Department was discovering that the immediate and visible presence of officers on bikes had a powerful impact on prostitution and drug trafficking that had infiltrated family neighborhoods in the north end.

Mike and his new partner, Chris Gough, teamed up with local residents to rake and sweep up drug paraphernalia and other detritus left by dealers and prostitutes. The sight of officers working alongside residents impressed citizens who had almost given up. Backed by police interest, neighbors turned out to take back their streets.

In 1991, Mike Magan was nominated for the annual Jefferson Awards, which are given out by *The Seattle Post-Intelligencer*. These awards go to six Washingtonians who have "most enriched the lives of their neighbors and helped communities through voluntary public service."

Mike's nomination read:

> Innovative Seattle police officer who conceived the project to close North Seattle's Nesbit Street in Licton Springs from 6 P.M. to 6 A.M., an area of high crime, drugs and prostitution, to all but

residents. It works. Magan is available to everyone, 24 hours a day, or off duty, to counsel
teens, parents, or anyone else.

Mike was still only twenty-eight, although his hair
had turned completely gray. This was a genetic trait—
not a result of his four years on the force. His gray hair
was deceptive, however; he and Chris Gough were
chasing down suspect cars on their bicycles. Between
February 25 and March 31, 1992, they made four
arrests for suspicion of narcotics, one for fraud, one
for theft, five warrant arrests, two for drinking in
public, two for criminal trespass, one for concealed
weapon, one DWI, one for obstructing, one reckless
endangerment, two for shoplifting, one violation of
court order, two for investigation of child neglect, and
six for "stay out of areas of prostitution" in the
Aurora Avenue corridor alone. And this exhaustive
list didn't include the other neighborhoods where the
two officers in bicycle shorts and helmets had become
a familiar sight.

They were so good at what they did that they were
nominated twice by their supervisor—Sergeant Howard Monta—for the Officer(s) of the Month Award.

If the community along the Aurora Avenue corridor
had had their way, Mike Magan and Chris Gough
would have been patrolling on their mountain bikes
(and in a patrol car when Seattle's rains were too
drenching) until they retired from the force. The bikes
made them approachable and available. Chris and
Mike even became something of a tourist attraction,
posing patiently for the cameras of visitors to Seattle.

Their legs were like steel and their lung capacity was phenomenal. No one would ever have imagined that Mike was once a little boy whose doctors feared for his lungs.

Mike Magan wouldn't have been honest if he said he was totally satisfied staying on bike patrol. Although patrol officers—in cars, on foot, and on bicycles—are almost always the first on the scene of a crime, even a homicide, they ultimately have to hand it over to the detectives to investigate. Some are quite content to do that. Others feel a sense of frustration because they cannot follow a case through to arrest and trial. Magan was one who hoped one day to be in a detective unit—preferably Homicide and Robbery.

By the early 1990s, there were an inordinate number of bank robbers working the Seattle area—so many that Seattle had jumped to the fourth spot in the country in terms of the number of bank robberies, an incredible fact given that there are many cities with much larger populations.

Special Agent Shawn Johnson knew why. "Where Marie and I came from—Minnesota and Wisconsin—there are taverns on every corner. Most big cities have a 7-Eleven or a gas station on the corners—but Seattle has a bank branch on almost every corner."

20

In early summer 1992, Scott Scurlock had pulled off a single successful bank robbery, and it had only whetted his appetite for more. He realized early on that he would have to do it better. He had replayed the bank robbery over and over in his mind, looking for flaws. Trusting that he and Mark could steal a getaway car hadn't been clever. What if the guy had fought giving them the keys? What if the blue Cadillac hadn't started at all?

And Mark sure hadn't turned out to be the ideal accomplice; he'd been terrified while they were in the bank, and so full of angst when it was over.

Scott's first bank robbery had showed him that there were more variables than he had visualized. He could see that robbing banks was going to be a lot like playing chess. He would simply have to anticipate any eventuality. Most of all, he had to be sure that he was anonymous, that no one in a bank would ever know what he really looked like.

Since his initial bank heist had worked so well, Scott had the audacity to return to the *very same bank* two months later. On August 20, 1992, late on a Friday afternoon, he walked into the Madison Park branch of the Seafirst Bank alone. One of the tellers who had handed money to him in June recognized him almost at once as the same man who had robbed her before. But no one else made the connection.

Once again, the bank witnesses all estimated his age differently; one thought he was forty-five, another guessed he was in his fifties. Everyone agreed he had graying blond hair and a blond-gray mustache. Some thought it was his real hair; others suspected it was a wig. He wore a dark green baseball cap and a gray sports jacket.

The "aging" robber had ordered everyone to lie on the floor, and warned them not to follow him. He had apparently been doing his homework because this time he ordered the teller, "Don't put any dye packs in."

(Any bank robber who survives for long knows that tellers keep stacks of money with a hidden pack of bright orangey-red dye stuck between a packet of bills in the drawer where they have their cash. The dye packs activate when they are carried beyond a certain point in the bank, and they explode—covering the robber and his loot with dye that will not wash off for more than a week.)

The bank surveillance camera didn't activate in time, and none of the tellers managed to slip in any marked bills or any dye packs. So far, so good—but he didn't get as much money as he had the first time: only $8,124.50.

The FBI was charting the gray-haired bank robber's movements, and they didn't have to wait as long for him to hit again. On September 3—only two weeks later—a man burst into the U.S. Bank in West Seattle at 12:30 P.M. He moved with a certain fluid grace toward the teller counter, pointing his black handgun at the bank employees and customers. "This is a robbery. Keep calm. Everybody keep quiet. Don't move. I want all the tellers to put the money on the counters."

This time, the dozen witnesses described a younger man—in his thirties. He had worn jeans, a light-colored T-shirt, and a pale blue sport jacket. And, incongruously, high-top red sneakers. Some had seen only the blond wig, while one observant teller saw the curly dark brown hair beneath it and even the razor burn on his neck from a recent shave. But everyone remembered the surgical gloves he wore, and the baseball cap that said "DARE" on it. That was an ironic touch; those hats were handed out by police to promote their "Dare to keep off drugs" program for kids.

Nobody could really see the robber's face; some recalled only thick makeup, while others thought he wore a translucent mask *over* makeup. He wore opaque sunglasses that obscured his eyes. Once the money was on the counter, he moved quickly, sweeping stacks of bills into a black vinyl bag. He seemed to know his stuff. When he saw that a teller had given him only one stack of bills, he ordered her to produce the money from a second drawer. She did.

Still, one of the tellers had surreptitiously activated the bank's camera and silent alarm and another had pushed a stack of marked bills toward the lone robber.

He was in and out of the bank rapidly. As he walked toward the double doors, he called back, "Everyone lie down on the floor. Nobody look out the windows, or I'll come back and shoot."

Believing him, no one moved. A teller managed to peek under her arm and saw the bank robber turn left outside the doors. But then he was gone. And he had taken $9,613 of the bank's money with him, some of it in "bait" bills.

It was, of course, Scott. He had now made a mistake, a small one, yes, but he carried away the marked packet of bills.

The fourth bank robbery by a slender, remarkably fit man happened only eight days later. On September 11, he was back in the northeastern part of the city— at the University Savings Bank in the Laurelhurst neighborhood. Again, it was at the end of the week— Friday—and around noon: 12:10 to be exact.

His MO and his outfit were virtually the same as the last time. This time, his image was caught on the bank's cameras in excellent detail; the funky gray-blond wig and mustache didn't match the lithe, muscular body and he definitely moved like an athletic younger man. His voice was described as harsh and deep, but that could have been influenced by what he was saying.

"It's a robbery. Get the money out. Put the money on the counter!" When one teller hesitated, he turned to him and said, "You too. I don't want any dye packs. I want your backup money, too."

The man with the black gun asked again for "back-up money."

"That's all I have," the Customer Service Teller said, as he emptied his second drawer, deftly slipping bait bills into the stack of money. The man in the strange, translucent mask said, "Look at it this way. If I was going to cash a five-thousand-dollar check, where would you get the cash?" He leapt effortlessly onto the counter so that he could watch the tellers closely.

The male bank officer had no choice but to take out a reserve box of cash and put it on a back counter. The robber grabbed the box and vaulted back over the counter.

He was ready to leave, but first he forced everyone to move to the center of the bank and lie facedown on the floor. "You guys lay down on the floor," he said. "And don't look up for twenty seconds or I'll come back and shoot someone."

The bank robber was gone within those twenty seconds. He had sounded deadly serious about shooting and everyone obeyed his time limit. They didn't know if he had someone outside the bank, watching. He had seemed supremely confident, *and* well informed, a professional. He knew about the dye packs, and about the reserve money. If he knew about bait bills, marked so that he could be linked to them if he tried to spend them, he didn't mention it. But his take was dropping; this time, he only got $5,739.

On October 5, he hit in West Seattle again. It wasn't the end of the week; it was a Monday at 10:15 A.M. when he strode into the Great Western Bank. He wore the blond wig and mustache, the "DARE" baseball cap, the sunglasses, but he had substituted a white shirt and wild tie for the T-shirt, and he wore a windbreaker jacket. The see-through mask was gone, replaced by skillfully applied theatrical makeup that included a large hooked nose. Instead of surgical gloves, he wore black gloves.

He had never yet left fingerprints and he apparently didn't intend to. He was clearly operating on the premise, "If it ain't broke, don't fix it," as he used the same general language to demand money and to warn witnesses not to follow him. This time, he asked for the "vault teller," something he had never done before. When a female teller stepped nervously forward, he demanded that she take him into the vault, where he evidently knew the large amounts of cash were kept. Once there, he instructed her to give him hundreds, fifties, and twenties only. As he ran from the bank, he carried a blue nylon duffel bag. It contained $27,423.

The bank's surveillance cameras caught it all, and FBI special agents continued to form a profile of this unknown man. They did it by carefully questioning every bank employee, every customer in the five robberies. No detail was too small since they couldn't know which minuscule part of his pattern might help them catch him.

In October of 1992, Scott Scurlock had become a star of sorts in the Seattle area—though, of course, no one knew his name. The "Rat on a Rat" program featured him on one of their bulletins and offered a thousand-dollar reward for any information on a: "Male, white, 30s, 5'11", 165 lbs., sandy brown hair, makeup on face, black semiautomatic pistol."

The picture used was the blurred frame of a bank's

camera, and despite his makeup and false hair, he looked for all the world as if he'd come straight from central casting.

He would have liked that.

Scott's sixth bank robbery in 1992 was so remarkably successful that it must have even stunned him.

It was Thursday, a week before Thanksgiving, when the man who had become all too familiar to the Seattle Police Robbery Unit and the FBI walked into the Seafirst Bank in Hawthorne Hills at 11:40 A.M.

He announced, "This is a robbery. This is no joke, folks." Then he asked the tellers to step away from their drawers and the customers to move to the center of the bank. He instructed the drive-in teller to move back from her window, and made sure that her microphone was turned off.

"Who is the vault teller?"

No one answered.

He racked back the slide on his pistol, chambering a round. *"Now,"* he said, menacingly, "who is the vault teller?"

A young female teller, whose name was Patti, stepped forward, "I am," she said quietly. She was frightened. Her manager handed her the keys to the vault, and, despite her fear, Patti showed some spirit when she turned toward the man in the grotesque makeup and said, "I would like someone to go back there with me."

"Fine," he said, and the woman manager of the bank moved to the teller's side. The trio walked toward the vault, the women trembling.

Once back in the lonely stillness of the vault, the teller had trouble with the combination to the safe.

Her hands were shaking so much that her fingers kept slipping past the code stops.

"Calm down," the robber said with a trace of humor in his deep voice. "I'm not going to hurt you."

"I'm sorry," Patti whispered. "I'm just scared to death."

Again, the robber told her she was safe, that he wouldn't hurt her. But his voice was a little impatient now; the clock was ticking, and he had no way of knowing what they were doing out in the rest of the bank. He needed to be gone.

Patti finally got the safe open and stepped back.

There was so much money inside that the bag the bank robber carried wasn't big enough to hold it all. He ordered Patti and her manager to find him another bag. There wasn't one large enough in the vault area, so Patti went out into the bank and brought back a canvas bank bag.

"Do you have dye packs in here?" the robber asked abruptly.

"We don't use them here," the manager lied. But she could see there were no dye packs in what he was grabbing. His hand hovered for a moment over a stack of bait money—as if he knew what it was—and then he left it where it was.

Laden down with the two full bags of money, the man in the DARE cap and checked black and white pants seemed about to leave. Then he turned back. Everyone froze. But he only said, "Don't trip any alarms for thirty seconds—or I'll come back in. Now everybody get down on the floor." And then he was gone.

But the vault teller realized that this masked strang-

er was now a rich man. He had just walked away with
$252,000.

It was a week or so later—almost Thanksgiving in
1992—when Mark Biggins and Traci Marsh saw
Scott Scurlock again. He showed up at their door in
Darby, Montana, grinning broadly. While Mark and
Traci were barely getting by, Scott looked to be
thriving. He told them that all of his worries were in
the past; he had money again. He was not the Scott
they had known during the last months before the
Madison Avenue bank robbery. He was the old Scott
again. Confident and magnanimous. He looked
around their grungy small house, peeled off a stack of
bills, and handed them $5,000. Mark didn't want to
take it—but Traci reached for it eagerly.

During Scott's four-day visit at Thanksgiving 1992,
they found out why he seemed on top of the world. He
confided that he had robbed five more banks since
they had fled Washington.

And he allowed them to believe he had done it all
by himself, without a partner (like Mark) or a driver
(like Traci). He told them that everything just kept
getting better. In fact, during his last robbery, he had
carried away $250,000—a quarter of a million dol-
lars!

Mark could only stare at Scott with a mixture of
wonderment and shock. He had been so revulsed by
the bank robbery they had committed together that he
could not imagine anyone would want to experience
that level of anxiety, terror, panic, and guilt again. But
Scott seemed happy and supremely confident.

They had a good evening together, picking away on their guitars while they sang their old songs, and growing more mellow with each drink. Scott regaled Mark with anecdotes about his success as a bank robber. Mark stared at him and felt the little hairs on the back of his neck stand up.

Where were they all going? He had to admit that the money Scott had given him felt good in his pocket. He and Traci were living in a small mountain cabin that had fleas in the summer and cracks in the walls where the wind whistled through in the winter. Traci complained continually about their living conditions. It was a familiar feeling for Mark, being poor and a lousy provider. Christmas was coming, and he had nothing to give Lori. He didn't even have a way to get to California to see her.

Mark was constantly worried about Lori. Sometimes, when he talked to Annie on the phone, Mark worried that she was drinking again. He had to find a way to be with Lori and look after her.

And now, here was Scott grinning at Mark, inviting him in. It was all there, ripe plums for the taking. The stupid cops didn't know what the hell was going on. Scott was even able to philosophize about why robbing banks wasn't much of a moral problem—it wasn't like they'd be stealing from the bank's customers; they would get their money back from the insurance company. So what was so bad about spreading the wealth around a little? Scott was such a good talker that he made Mark dizzy.

If Mark didn't let his conscience niggle at him, it would be easy for him to view Scott as Willie-Boss.

Good, solid, dependable Willie-Boss—the same guy who had taken him in and given him a place to live and food to eat. They had been friends for more than a decade; they'd been through a lot together. If Scott had been able to rob five banks all by himself and never been caught, it couldn't be all that dangerous.

Scott opened the door wide and Mark stepped through. This time, there was no way, ever, of going back. In time, everything that mattered to Mark would be lost to him, but it would happen so insidiously that Mark wouldn't even realize it was gone until it was too late.

Scott Scurlock was playing in the big time and he loved it. He had stolen $302,899.50 from banks in five months. He no longer had to worry about money. He felt invincible, and he managed to persuade most of the men who had been his friends for decades that they were invincible too.

21

In late 1992, the "Take Charge Robber" in the clear mask, makeup and DARE cap was only one of a number of bank robbers that the FBI and Seattle Police Department were tracking. The nickname Hollywood had yet to be coined.

And, by the New Year, he seemed to have disappeared. After a half-dozen bank jobs, and a take of more than $300,000 between late June and mid-November of 1992, he could well afford to move on or retire. He could be dead, for that matter.

There *had* been a bank robbery in Olympia, Washington, in December of 1992 that bore some similarities to the ones the man in the mask had carried off. But this one was just different enough to confuse authorities.

On Friday, December 18, a tall man wearing a wig and sunglasses had walked onto the Seafirst Bank on Black Lake Boulevard outside Olympia. He had a pistol, and he ordered customers to sit on the floor while tellers filled up the two plastic bags he had brought with him. He didn't leap on the counters, and he didn't seem to have the dramatic flair that the Seattle bank robber had. Besides that, his physical description wasn't the same. The Olympia robber was taller and huskier, and the little tufts of his own hair that showed beneath the cheap wig were curlier and lighter.

When Scott Scurlock found out about the Olympia robbery, he was angry. He had not given permission to any of his accomplices to act alone, and Scott liked to be in control. He had sent plane tickets to Mark and Traci so that they could fly to Washington in December. He knew that things in Montana weren't working out for them and he had flown them in, ostensibly so Mark could put insulation in the gray house. But Scott had also wanted their help with another bank robbery. However, their arrival had coincided with a visit to Seattle by President Bill Clinton, which was not a propitious time for a bank robbery; the city was crawling with security. Scott had called off their plans, and he gave Mark and Traci a car to drive back to Montana.

Once there, Mark was frustrated and in despair. He had been disappointed when Scott canceled the December robbery. Scott didn't need the money, but Mark did. He was right back where he had started, instead of being with his daughter for Christmas. Most of the $5,000 that Scott gave him at Thanksgiving was already gone for back bills.

Mark's desire to show up at Christmas as a generous Santa overrode his memory of that first, horrible, goof-up bank robbery with Scott back in June. He and Traci drove back to Olympia, while Mark worried about his desperate financial situation all the way. They arrived at Overhulse Road on December 15, 1992. Scott wasn't in the gray house or in the treehouse. Steve Meyers, who had been staying in the gray house, was gone too. They waited for three days, but Scott didn't show up. It was typical of Scott—he never told anybody where he was going.

And so, improbable as it seemed, it was Mark Biggins who had robbed the Seafirst Bank on Black Lake Boulevard in Olympia, and, in doing so, he broke most of Scott's rules. For one thing, this was the bank that Mark had *patronized* when he lived in Olympia. Yes, he and Scott had talked casually about robbing it, but Scott had decided that pulling a job so close to home was foolhardy.

But, with Traci encouraging him, Mark took one of Scott's pistols and set out to rob the Olympia bank.

He was clumsy and nervous, but he got away with it. Mark walked out of the bank with $47,000. He felt almost as nauseated and guilty as he had the first time—but not quite as much. Now loaded with money and presents, Mark and Traci drove to Oxnard and spent Christmas with Lori and Annie. Lori was nine years old now. She was tall like both her parents, but she resembled Mark the most.

After New Year's Day, Mark and Traci returned to Montana—but only for a few months. At Christmas, Mark's fears about Annie's drinking had been confirmed. His little girl was taking care of her mother, when it should have been the other way around. He couldn't bear for Lori to live like that.

In the spring of 1993, Mark and Traci left Montana and moved to Ojai, California. Mark was determined to get a legitimate job and to use the money from the Olympia bank robbery sparingly. It was to be a stake—not a way of life. He had helped Scott bury money around the Overhulse Road property, and now he buried most of the bank money in Ojai. If he concentrated on the thought that he had done it to make Lori's life better, it eased his conscience. He was in massive denial.

Mark got a job in a company that manufactured equipment for producing leather clothes for motorcycle riders. Traci took a paraplegic man into their home and cared for him. They immediately moved Lori in with them, and Mark saw to it that she could be a little girl again. He cooked her breakfast every morning, walked her to the bus and picked her up afterward. It was just like old times.

Mark taught Lori to play the flute and the trombone. With her father helping her with her homework, it wasn't long before Lori was getting straight *A*'s.

Mark also taught Lori how to play basketball. Like her dad, she was a superior athlete who played the game so well that, by the time she was in the eighth grade, she would already be courted by college recruiters. Lori Biggins adored her dad as much as he did her; she was blossoming now.

Whenever Annie needed a place to stay, she was welcome in Mark and Traci's home; Mark was careful never to disparage Annie to their daughter.

Of course, there was a sharp dichotomy now in Mark Biggins' ethics, a schism that he was able to blur by drinking or using speed. He did this when his daughter was asleep or away. No one has ever argued that he wasn't a caring, attentive father. He would have died for Lori without question, and he tried to give her everything she needed. That he partially provided for her with money he had obtained by robbing two banks was a memory he tried to bury.

When Scott found out about Mark's solo bank robbery, he was furious. If Mark had been caught, the gun would have been traced back to Scott. The whole damn operation would have been over. But after one angry phone call blasting Mark for being an idiot, Scott slipped out of Mark's life.

Mark hoped that he would never hear from Scott again—that everything that smacked of that old life could just be forgotten. He still had a lot of affection for Scott, but he knew that he probably wouldn't be able to say no to him if he showed up with some exciting proposition. Nobody could say no to Scott.

That was the thing about him: he could make almost anything seem reasonable and possible and do-able.

Scott Scurlock had never had to approach strangers to help him carry out his plans, whether it was stealing bananas, building a six-story treehouse or robbing a bank. He had his friends. While Mark Biggins had run off to Montana after the very first bank robbery in June 1992, Steve Meyers had been grateful to accept Scott's invitation to move to Olympia. Arriving in August, Steve had, of course, been hobbled by his torn Achilles tendon until well into September.

But Scott had been understanding, and he gave Steve the gray house to live in, rent free. When Steve could move about a little, he and Scott had worked on the house. Steve didn't know where Scott was getting the money for the top-of-the-line building supplies, or for the frequent trips he took—and he didn't ask.

In late September, when Steve was finally off crutches, Scott asked him to travel to Las Vegas and Reno to place bets on sporting events for him. Steve knew this was a way to launder money so that it couldn't be traced. Again, Steve didn't ask questions.

Each weekend then, during the final months of 1992, Scott gave Steve a packet of cash—up to $20,000 at a time—which Scott had harvested from plastic containers he had buried around the property on Overhulse Road. Steve then went to Las Vegas or Reno and placed bets on both teams in a game; he wasn't betting to win—he was betting to launder the money and by wagering on *both* teams, he could limit his losses to five percent, the bookie's take. Most of his bets were for $1,100 or $2,200. He always registered under his own name; in Reno, he stayed at the Hilton or Harrah's. In Las Vegas, he checked into Caesar's Palace, Scott's favorite hotel.

At the end of each weekend, Steve Meyers flew back to Washington State, and turned entirely different bills over to Scott. None of this "clean" money had ever been in a bank vault in Seattle.

Steve tried to concentrate on the workday weeks at Scott's place, and not the trips to Nevada. The beat-up gray house had benefited tremendously from his labors. The interior of the house had metamorphosed from that of an old farmhouse to a modern residence with all the lavish trappings of any new home in Seattle's fancier neighborhoods. Some of the floors were polished hardwood with a high gloss Swedish finish. Thick beige and moss green carpeting covered others. Whole sections of walls had been replaced with rich wood paneling.

Steve had had to walk away from his warehouse-studio in Chicago, but now he worked on Scott's place as carefully as if it were his own. Steve's precise and artistic tile counters transformed the kitchen and bathroom. All the cupboards and drawers in the kitchen were new, and there were enough brand new appliances to please any gourmet cook.

The bathroom was a work of art with a sunken Jacuzzi tub and a shiny ebony toilet and bidet—all with gold fixtures. Steve designed the wall surrounding the Jacuzzi with dull earthtone tiles above and gleaming azure tiles beneath and on the floor. He had even cut a perfect diamond through the wall and installed a mirror that reflected the beauty of his work.

Scott's walls were hung with numerous maps. A man who loved faraway places would naturally choose to surround himself with maps. He also collected Bev Doolittle prints, all of them typical of her work where nothing was what it appeared on the surface. An Indian princess gazing serenely wasn't just that; wild things and eagles' wings were there in her hair and in the trees behind her. A wolf with yellow eyes wasn't really a wolf. If you blinked, you would see an Indian brave painted within the eyes.

With the help of his friends who came for summer work parties—and the friends who came to stay longer—Scott's house, treehouse and myriad outbuildings were fitted with "hidey holes," places deep behind closets, in walls, and behind stairways. He had more guns hidden there than anyone realized, and satchels, suitcases, boxes, and containers with blank labels. No one thought anything of it.

There hadn't been a bank robbery since November 19. In early December, Scott had flown up an electrician friend from California to rewire the house. He had also brought Bobby Gray and his wife up from Florida to do some more concrete work. Bobby was someone whom Scott cultivated, always making sure that he maintained a connection to him.

For that holiday season of 1992, when Mark Biggins had headed for California, almost everyone from the old gang on Overhulse Road scattered for family reunions. Scott himself drove to Sedona to be with his parents and sisters. Steve went to Denver to visit

Dana. Dana, only forty-four, had been diagnosed with non-Hodgkins lymphoma, but she appeared to be in remission. Her family was hopeful.

"Dana was the best of all of us," Kevin recalled. "She was the one who deserved to live."

Kevin had gone back east in October to pack up his life in Virginia. He spent a month in Reston, putting in a new bathroom for his mother. Then he pulled a trailer with the last of his possessions as he headed west, encountering a number of blinding snowstorms. He had stopped in Denver to see Dana over Thanksgiving, and she assured him that she didn't expect him to come back again for Christmas.

No one realized how ill Dana really was. Within a short time, the damnable cancer cells would invade almost every organ in her body and they would lose her.

Steve Meyers drove back to Olympia after Christmas through Reno, stopping to bet on the Super Bowl. Scott was home when he got back and they began working on the house again. For the first month of 1993, the two men worked companionably as the rain drummed on the shake roof.

Kevin, who had been Scott's closest friend for years, was rarely at the treehouse anymore. He lived in Seattle with Ellen and her girls. He had remodeled the girls' bedroom with bunk beds and built-in desks so that they had room to move around easily even though Ellen's apartment was small. Scott had donated the lumber; Kevin tried to remember the generous things Scott still did. But there was a wariness between them now, a distance that had developed since the incident with the bean pot in the barn.

Even with his brother, Steve, Kevin felt alienated. The men who came and went on Overhulse Road had quietly but firmly shut him outside. He wasn't sure why, but sometimes he was gripped with a shadowy premonition that frightened him. He worried for Steve, who was spending Christmas without the hope of seeing his daughter, and Kevin wasn't sure where Mark Biggins had gone. He hoped wanly that when summer came, they would all gather around the campfires again.

22

Marge Violette—now Marge Mullins—who had met Scott and Kevin eighteen years before in Hawaii, had kept in touch with Kevin, visiting back and forth, but she hadn't seen Scott since the magic time they had all shared at The Shire. Her world was now far removed from theirs; she was no longer the carefree hippie girl she once was. In February of 1993 Marge was living in Los Angeles, and was in the midst of a divorce. She had three young sons—seven, eight, and nine—and she didn't want to raise them in Southern California, especially not as a single mother.

Marge had thought about relocating to Washington State, and she contacted Kevin and asked about coming up for a visit. She knew vaguely that Scott was living somewhere in Washington since Kevin had talked about Scott's treehouse there. Now, Kevin said that Scott was traveling in Mexico, but that he wouldn't mind if she and her boys stayed in the treehouse. Marge was a little leery about that, but she knew her sons would love to at least see it. She told Kevin that she would stay at a motel, and he said he'd be glad to drive her around to look at the area.

"But Scott's not the same as he was, Marge," Kevin warned her. "You wouldn't want to spend too much time around him. He's on some kind of a negative trip. He's gone farther along a dark path."

"What do you mean—'a dark path?'"

Kevin wouldn't explain what he meant, and she didn't press him.

Marge and her sons flew up to Washington. They got a motel room in Olympia. She was not about to climb up into a six-story treehouse with three little boys until she checked it out.

She called the number Kevin had given her for Scott, and got an answering machine. A woman's chirpy voice said, "Hi there! This is Bob and Linda, and we're not home right now." Marge didn't know any Bob and Linda. When she told Kevin he'd given her the wrong number, he laughed. "That's how Scott screens his calls. That's his number all right, but he doesn't answer the phone much. Just leave your number; he's back from Mexico and he said he'd call you."

One of the ways Scott controlled his friends was by

being virtually unreachable by phone. He would either unplug his phones so that they rang futilely, or he let the machine answer. Often, the only phone that worked on the place was the one in the barn. Oddly, the only time Scott plugged in his phone line in the treehouse was when he was entertaining a woman. Then, he seemed to be somehow pleased by the interruption and he carried on long conversations while the woman of the moment waited for him.

When Scott got Marge's message, he did call her back, and she and her boys came out to the treehouse to visit. When she saw Scott, she felt the years drop away. It was as if she'd only said good-bye to him the day before. Scott didn't look that much different; he still smiled the same way. She was acutely conscious that she was a forty-five-year-old woman, with some streaks of gray in her hair, and some extra pounds around her hips. Scott didn't seem to notice. He was as sweet to her as he'd always been.

"We clicked right away," she recalled. He was the same Scott who had sat with her on the beach in Hawaii as they talked about what they wanted in the future. Only she had grown up and he hadn't. He grinned at her boys and they crowded around him, fascinated.

That first night, she and Scott planned to take the three boys out to a restaurant. As they drove past one of his neighbor's places on Overhulse Road, Scott saw a "For Sale" sign and said, "I'll come back when it's dark and take it down."

"You can't do that, Scott," she said, laughing.

"Sure I can," he said, grinning. "And I will."

Marge let it pass. She didn't know how much Scott

hated to see "For Sale" signs along his road or that he was engaged in a war with his neighbors. He believed the signs were early warnings that housing developments would follow. He was always afraid that someone would come and cut down the forests that made the real world seem miles away from Seven Cedars.

Thurston County authorities had already come sniffing around his treehouse, threatening to tear it down. Scott had stopped that by going to attorney Shawn Newman. It turned out well enough; Newman exchanged some letters with the county and they had backed off—at least for the moment. Newman was a man devoted to preserving the habitats of wild animals and to conservation, so he and Scott had something in common. Newman's receptionist accepted a few dates with Scott.

But Scott continued to knock the signs off their posts as soon as they were nailed up. He had one neighbor, Greg Smith—who was a minister on the Evergreen campus, and lived a quarter mile away—who had real estate signs on his fences.

The two had a running battle. Every time Smith nailed a sign up, Scott would tear it down. On one curious evening, Scott went to Smith's place and demanded that he stop putting "For Sale" signs on the road. "He was the scariest guy I ever met," Smith recalled. "He was cursing and screaming and threatening me just because of the signs."

Smith called the Thurston County Sheriff who went to Scott's place and told him he couldn't pull the signs down. Except for getting a ticket once for doing "wheelies" in a parking lot, it was the closest Scott came to having trouble with the law.

Now, Marge thought Scott was half-kidding. She recalled how he had shot out street lights in Hawaii because they ruined the night, and how he routinely broke the speed limit. He had always had such a sense of entitlement.

They took Marge's boys to see *Aladdin*. Then they went out to dinner. The video game in the lobby of the restaurant wasn't working, so Scott said he would take the boys to Tilt, a video arcade at the mall.

Marge's sons were so excited. She watched, bemused, when Scott handed each of them a $20 bill to play the games. They were speechless; they'd never had so much money. Once the kids were settled, Scott led Marge to a nearby bar where they could have drinks and keep an eye on the boys.

"I had a Margarita without salt," she recalled. "I can't remember what Scott had. He told me about a woman he was dating in Olympia who had a son, and then about another one he was having an affair with in Switzerland, a woman he hoped to see soon. I offered him one of the 'buddy tickets' I got from TWA— where he could fly to Europe for under $50."

Kevin had told Marge that he thought Scott might be involved in something illegal, although he didn't know what it was, so she warned Scott now that if she got him a buddy ticket, he mustn't try to use it for anything suspicious because he would be sure to get caught. "With that kind of a ticket, you and your baggage would almost certainly be separated," she cautioned.

Scott looked at her innocently, and smiled. He still had beautiful clear blue eyes, fringed by long lashes. He could make anyone believe anything, she thought.

They talked softly, playing catch-up for all the years. They both loved to travel. Marge said she'd been snorkeling in Fiji, and Scott said he'd been to the Seychelles Islands and to Europe and Mexico many times.

"He told me that when he first went to Evergreen, he took a lot of science classes—he wanted to study medicine. He wanted to find a cure for cancer," Marge recalled. He told her that one of his close relatives had had cancer and he wanted to cure it. "But then he said he learned a lot about making drugs, and how easy it was. That was when he dropped out of pre-med. It seemed to me that not all the drugs he made were legal."

"I stopped 'smoking' a long time ago, Scott," she told him. "I don't smoke *anything* now. I quit using drugs of any kind years ago. I rarely drink. You wouldn't know me. When I got pregnant with my first son in 1982, I wouldn't even take over-the-counter medicine."

He smiled and shrugged. It occurred to Marge that they barely knew each other anymore.

He lifted his glass and gave her a long beautiful toast about old friends whose paths had drifted apart, but who still had much in common. She laughed, remembering: "It ended with, 'And may all your orgasms be long ones,'" she said, "but the way he said it, it wasn't even sleazy or suggestive."

They had another drink, and Scott confided in Marge that he was involved in "some international bank scams."

"Do you mean something with computers?" she asked, not sure that he wasn't teasing her.

"Something like that." He didn't say any more.

Marge Violette never dreamed that he might be involved in *robbing* banks. She assumed Scott was doing some kind of computer scam—maybe going into some escrow account with billions of dollars for a few days, earning interest, and switching back to his own account. He didn't say anything that alluded to that kind of fraud, though. A long time later, she said, "I never thought that Scott was *going in the front door of banks to get the money!*"

She still saw the Scott who had stolen bananas and marijuana plants. He had always been mischievous and he loved to break rules, but he was never truly crooked. He was treating her and her sons so wonderfully. He was a nice man.

Marge's boys came running back; they had spent their $20 bills. Over Marge's protests, Scott handed out three more. The kids stared at him in awe—but they took the money and ran back to the video games.

Scott liked the kids, and he invited Marge to bring them out to his place on Overhulse Road.

While they visited, he was the perfect host. He asked only that the boys take their shoes off before they went into the gray house; he said he and Steve had sanded the floors and they hadn't had a chance to varnish them yet. Marge found the house charming and cozy. Steve was putting the finishing touches to marble counters in the kitchen, and the bathroom was practically a showplace. She was impressed.

One thing bothered her, though. During her visit, Steve and Scott talked so much about gambling. They both seemed to be obsessed with it.

Scott led them to the treehouse. Marge's sons

looked up into the treetops, as if they couldn't believe their good fortune. This was a playground that any little boy would wish for. They climbed up, awe-struck, and then Scott showed them how to slide down the pole to the ground. He went first, balancing them on his shoulders, so that his body would keep them from falling.

It was as if he hadn't aged at all. He was Peter Pan, frozen in time, still full of adventure and derring-do. He was the fourth "boy" playing in the treehouse, as he urged Marge to let them all slide down the pole. "They can do it," he soothed Marge. "Let them try." And, indeed, they could.

Scott told Marge that while he enjoyed having her boys around, he never planned to be a father. "This is no world to bring a child into," he said bleakly.

Her sons used a camcorder to capture the treehouse to show their friends and Marge talked more with Scott. He seemed very concerned about her, and she had to admit it felt good to have a man show such compassion. She was going through a rough divorce, and Scott said that he wanted to give her enough money so that she could hire a good divorce attorney.

Smiling, she shook her head. That wasn't necessary. "I've read my divorce papers very carefully and I know I can use our joint bank account to pay for my lawyer," she told him. "I've already found a good one."

And then Scott surprised her with another generous offer. "You can live in the gray house," he said. "You can all move up here."

"Steve's there," she demurred. "I wouldn't want to put him out."

"I need a nice respectable family living there. The price is right," Scott urged. "We'll work it this way. You can give me a check for $1,000 every month, and *then* I'll give you back $900 in cash."

Why on earth would Scott want to rent a newly refurbished house for $100 a month? He wasn't coming on to her—it wasn't that. Nor was he offering her charity.

(Later, Marge realized that Scott needed to have some nice honest income to show. His income from rent would go into his bank and show $12,000 a year. And her TWA salary would be easily traceable and explainable.)

As warm as he was, Marge saw that there was something secretive about Scott. On the one hand, he was so open and loving. On the other, he simply shut down. When she started to stroll around his property by herself, he caught up with her and warned her not to go into any of the outbuildings—not even the shed that housed the washer and dryer.

"Why not?" she asked, puzzled.

"Well, some have power—and others don't."

That didn't make much sense, but she didn't press him. And she didn't so much as look into the barn or any of the various buildings. Marge did see his income tax forms lying out on his desk. "I snuck a peek," she admitted. "At first, I thought he had listed his income at $200,000, but then I saw it was only $20,000. It said his occupation was 'odd jobs' and it was part-time," she said. "But he *lived* as if he made $200,000."

Marge Violette Mullins didn't take Scott up on his offer to move into the gray house, as tempting as it was. There was something chilling about it. "I didn't really know what he was doing, what he was involved in," she explained. "But I knew in my heart that sooner or later, he would have my boys working for him, and something in me *knew* that would be disastrous."

Scott didn't seem upset or resentful when Marge turned down his offer. When she and her sons left after a week's visit, she wondered if she would ever see Scott again. She returned to her world, saw her divorce through, and, in the autumn, moved to the Midwest.

Steve Meyers stayed on at the gray house, and, in February 1993, Scott left again for Europe. He didn't need Marge's buddy ticket. He had enough money to go around the world several times—if he chose. On this trip, he was away for three months.

Back in Olympia, there *was* a woman in Scott's life, just as he had told Marge. Her name was Maren* and she was a cool and lovely blond, the mother of a small son. She was one of the many women over the course of his life who genuinely cared about Scott—and one of many who had no idea at all about who he really was. As much fun as he was, as tender as he could be in private moments, he kept her at an emotional arm's length. There were moments when he would just shut down, his face closed and somehow melancholy.

But, of course, Scott was not faithful to Maren. Nor to any woman. He had another girlfriend in Switzerland whom he had met on a previous European jaunt. His friends called her "Swiss Cheese." She was a rather plain, bright woman who was much more than a lover to Scott; she was a banker. Through her, Scott had access to Swiss bank accounts. She would even become one of the many female travelers who visited at his treehouse in the woods.

Scott met women all over the world; some of them were only fleeting romances, and others stayed in his life. Some were, quite simply, prostitutes. Although he had never lacked for willing women who were thrilled to have sex with him, he maintained a network of contacts with prostitutes around the world. Once, he had tried to convince Kevin that any man needed the experience of paying for sex from time to time, but Kevin couldn't understand his reasoning.

Scott came home to Olympia in late spring, just as Steve Meyers left for Europe. Steve visited his brother, Randy, and then traveled through Greece and to Prague. He didn't go to Italy; he had nothing there any longer. It would have been too difficult emotionally to see where his first real studio had been, where his daughter was born. The studio and his daughter were both lost to him.

Despite the murky life that had captured him, Scott still welcomed his old friends. They gave his life a sense of normalcy, even though those who knew him best noted that he never really met their eyes. Everything was the same and yet nothing was the same; being with Scott in Olympia could be an edgy thing. They all laughed and drank more than they had before. At the Bud Bay Cafe, they sat on the deck during endless sunlit afternoons and long into lavender/peach-tinged evenings as the sun went down.

Scott was often with Maren, and he posed with her

as she wore a white-lace dress and a big white straw hat that only a beautiful woman could carry off. He wore the same clothes that the "take over" bank robber had worn: a pale T-shirt under a sports coat and his ubiquitous Converse sneakers.

Now, Scott was more careful than ever to avoid the appearance of wealth, knowing full well that a new car and new clothes might alert someone watching. He drove his old white van. He could have easily paid off the mortgage on the property on Overhulse Road, but he deliberately made his payments month after month as any normal working stiff would. His exterior remodeling was done at a measured pace—so that no attention would be drawn to the place. (He didn't know that some of the patrons at Bud Bay had concluded he must be a drug dealer to tip the way he did. They were right—but long after the fact.)

Even as the gray house improved, parts of the treehouse began to fall away. Once he'd built it, Scott rarely took care of anything, leaving wood and rope and *things* to rot in the wind and rain of Washington State while he bodysurfed on some golden beach halfway around the world, or, if he was in residence, he stayed inside and watched videos as the winter storms pounded the treehouse.

Paradoxically, Scott treasured certain items of no particular monetary worth: the Norman Rockwell address book that he carried with him for years; a painting of Kevin's that he had rescued from the trash barrel once; blurred photographs.

And some things didn't matter. The guitar that had been Scott's in Hawaii had followed him all over America and it was the "official treehouse guitar," but only because Kevin had boxed it up a long time ago and sent it from Hawaii to the Scurlocks in Reston. One night, Mark Biggins had been a little drunk and stepped on it, snapping the neck. Kevin got it fixed, thinking it had to mean a lot to Scott after all the years he'd played "Blackbird" on it. It didn't; Scott never even remembered who had broken it and who had fixed it.

Mark *could* play that guitar. He could sing the lyrics to a thousand songs, and he had a beautiful voice. Whenever he felt down, Kevin had tried to remind him that he had his voice and his remarkable memory for lyrics. "You could walk in anywhere and people would be glad to hear you sing," Kevin told him. "You're the *piano* man. You're the *guitar* man."

Mark was sweeping the barn once when Kevin told him that. He had been surprised and pleased. "You mean that? You really think I could?"

"Absolutely. No question about it," Kevin said. "I honor you for that. You've got all of Dylan in your head—you've got all those lyrics. That's something very few people have."

But Scott had always discouraged that kind of conversation. "Kevin, cut it out," he'd said, annoyed. "Mark hasn't got any life purpose other than to work for me. That's the way it's going to be. Don't fill his head full of that shit."

That tableau stayed forever in Kevin's memory. In an instant, Mark had changed. He'd looked down at the ground and started sweeping. Kevin had been shocked—and furious. Probably for the first time in his life, he had wanted to hit Scott for the way he treated Mark. That wasn't necessary.

Now, in the summer of 1993, Mark was long gone, and Kevin wasn't sure where he was. Scott had a group of about a dozen people whom he spent time with. Kevin and Mark weren't even in the inner circle any longer, although Steve was. Kevin wasn't resentful of that—he was glad Steve had found some *place* to be.

Steve and Scott did some mountain climbing that summer. Steve's Achilles tendon had healed completely, and they were both in remarkably good shape for two men who drank as much as they did. Staying in prime shape was an obsession with Scott. He would not allow himself to go to sleep drunk; he ran it off—jogging until his head cleared.

A woman Steve had met in Prague in the spring came to visit. He took her to Las Vegas and then to the Grand Canyon. They were gone for a month, but Scott stayed home; summer was the best time in the treehouse. There was no rain to leak through, the whole place smelled of cedar, and the decks were abloom with planters and cut flowers that Ellen had brought down.

Steve and Scott finished the inside of the gray house, and Scott asked Kevin to paint the outside. It was a putdown for Kevin—like asking a surgeon to carve a turkey—and he didn't really want to; that wasn't his kind of painting. But Scott kept asking him and eventually, he agreed to do it, and he did a great job—using a paint sprayer. Still, when Scott came to inspect the job, he pointed out flecks of paint on a bush near the front door.

Kevin's grin faded as Scott began to berate him—in front of Ellen, belittling him for being a lousy painter. It was like the time he'd humbled Mark for the way he swept the barn floor. Kevin might have taken Scott's abuse if it had been just the two of them. But he would not allow Scott to do that to him in front of Ellen. Of all the women who came to Scott's place, Ellen was the one Scott respected the most. Kevin wondered if Scott had had him paint the house just so he could have this moment.

Kevin shouted at Scott angrily, and Scott backed down, surprised. But then Scott turned around and he was smiling. It was all over. Still, it was another crack in their broken friendship.

One day in the fall of 1993, Kevin was batting tennis balls with Steve and Scott at the Evergreen campus. It was a beautiful day and they were together, but they weren't *truly* together. An invisible fence had gone up. Their dreams were eroding. Steve wasn't working at his sculpture, and Kevin's studio was gone too—although he was still painting at Ellen's place. Kevin felt like an interloper between his own brother and the man who had been his best friend.

Out loud, Kevin said, "I wish we could have the old magic days again when we were all free and creative."

For him, it was far more than an idle wish; it was more a prayer. Neither Steve or Scott commented. They continued to hit the tennis ball back and forth. And then the ball disappeared somewhere in the space between them. Each of them thought one of the others was playing a joke. But the ball was simply gone.

Kevin walked up to the net, looking for it, and so did Scott and Steve. It wasn't on the ground or on the sidelines.

After ten minutes of searching, Kevin glanced at his racquet. The ball was *there,* wedged tightly in an impossible spot, the triangle where his racket handle met the strings. He had neither felt nor seen the ball catch itself there.

"In that moment," he remembered, "I knew something beyond whatever power I might have was in effect. Something was rolling too fast down the hill and nothing I could do would stop it. We were *never* going to get the magic back again."

23

Down through the years, turf wars, jealousies, and proprietary interests have been part of the politics of law-enforcement agencies. It is a tense arena where men and women risk their lives as a part of their jobs, and their difficult cases become part of them. They see things that no one should ever have to see, and they are witnesses to pain and tragedy and pointless sacrifice, to perversions and unimaginable, unconscionable greed. Because they care so much, they sometimes become obsessed.

Thirty years or more ago, a dog-in-the-manger attitude about sharing evidence and information was more common than anyone admitted. Some of the most infamous cases in criminal history—including the Manson murders, the Hillside Strangler, the Atlanta child murders, and the Son of Sam case—were hampered by the hesitancy of one police agency to share information with another. In the 1990s, no department has the luxury of being territorial any longer. Being a cop today is much more difficult than it once was. With the advent of gangs and pervasive drug use, no law enforcement agency can afford to be an island.

In 1993, the pressure was on in the Seattle area. There were enough major crimes—particularly robberies and bank robberies—for the FBI to suggest forming a task force. The Seattle Police Department agreed. This task force would allow many police agencies instant access to each other's personnel and special knowledge. It would be comprised of the very best officers for the job from a number of departments—both local and federal: six FBI special agents, four Seattle Police detectives, and two from the King County Sheriff's Office. The smaller police departments in the county would participate, along with HUD (Housing and Urban Development), the Secret Service, the ATF (Alcohol, Tobacco, and Firearms), and the DEA (Drug Enforcement Administration). This new task force would be housed in the FBI's "annex" on the 28th floor of 1000 Second Avenue in downtown Seattle.

Foremost among the task-force goals would be to remove Seattle from its spot near the top of the list for bank robberies in the United States. In addition, the task force would work to solve other other serious crimes; unsolved cases—including homicides—

would be among them. It would be called the Puget Sound Violent Crimes Task Force.

Still, the main focus of the task force would be to wage war on the army of bank robbers who were thumbing their noses at cops in and around Seattle.

There were a lot of investigators who wanted to be on the task force—among them Mike Magan. For six years, except during the most inclement weather, he had spent his patrol time on a bicycle. Although he had never caught a bank robber and didn't know much about that criminal specialty, it was something that had been at the back of his mind for years. Getting an assignment to the task force wasn't going to be quick or easy. Mike was enthusiastic but realistic: he doubted that he had a much of a chance. He wasn't even a detective yet, although he had completed his compulsory time on patrol, and he had been on the detective eligibility list for three years.

Helping to clean up a neighborhood ridden with drugs and prostitution would have been satisfying to any good cop, and Mike had had some some exciting moments. He had chased a bully, who beat and robbed vulnerable shoppers and transients, for eight blocks, although he was on a bicycle and the robber was in a Chevy Nova. He got the license number that led to an arrest. He was becoming so adept, in fact, in identifying robbery suspects that he often worked with the Seattle Police Department's Robbery Unit.

During February 1993, when Scott Scurlock was traveling in Europe and renewing his romance with the Swiss banker in a snowy resort, Mike Magan was working bike patrol in the rain in the north end of Seattle. A number of women had been attacked and sexually molested as they rode their bikes on the popular Burke-Gilman trail near the University of Washington.

The precinct commander assigned the day-watch bicycle officers to stakeout the trail. The next day, Mike was riding the trail when he spotted a man who had removed half of his clothes. When he tried to question the man, he fled. Mike caught him. The suspect admitted to the Burke-Gilman assaults and to an extensive criminal history of indecent exposure, burglary, resisting and obstructing officers.

Mike Magan's file in the Chief's office was thick with commendation letters from the public and from other police agencies, and he was grateful for that. He loved his job, but he was thirty-one years old and he had the roaring energy and drive that young cops have. The adrenaline of a police chase is a strong motivator, and he found that he thrived in that edgy milieu. Mike didn't take unnecessary risks, but he was never more alive than when he was responding to an emergency.

His wife, Lisa, knew that. She knew that he wouldn't be happy if she worried or put a guilt trip on him. They had met in November 1990, at Nordstrom's, where Lisa was in charge of the cosmetics department. Mike approached her as directly as he would have any suspect, and she found herself accepting a date. He had a forceful personality, but she was as independent as he. They made a great pair.

Sometimes, Lisa grew impatient when Mike called off their plans because he had to meet an informant or somebody in trouble, but she always forgave him. If she worried about him—and she did—she never let him know it. Being a cop was who Mike was. That was part of why she loved him.

Shawn Johnson would be assigned to the Puget Sound Violent Crimes Task Force almost from the beginning. His style was very different from Mike Magan's—he was more low key and reflective. If Mike got the assignment he longed for, that would be a plus; investigators stalking a common enemy work together more effectively when their personalities are *not* similar. They bring more to an investigation. Although FBI Special Agent Shawn Johnson and Seattle Police Officer Mike Magan might someday find themselves tracking the same suspect, they would come at him from a different angle.

But, first, Mike Magan had to find a way to get on the task force.

It was nearing November 1994. Like every cop on the Seattle Police Department, Mike Magan and Chris Gough began to hear radio reports of bank robberies. "We'd *pedal* up on our bikes," Mike laughed, "and arrive ten minutes after the fact, not exactly in a position to do much good. I said to Chris, 'You know I've *never* caught a bank robber.' Chris had about ten years on me on the force, and he said, 'I've caught two or three,' and he went into this long spiel telling me how great it was chasing them down."

"Let's work on this," Mike said. "Let's get some surveillance photographs from the FBI agents."

Mike Magan knew that the FBI was looking for take-charge bank robbers who all had nicknames. There was someone called Abe Lincoln and Partners and someone dubbed Hollywood who worked with at least one other guy. Mike made a few notes on the most likely suspects. Sooner or later, it seemed as if all the bad guys in the western half of the United States would show up along the Aurora corridor and he and Chris had a huge network of friends and informants. They decided to see what they could do to catch themselves a bank robber or two.

After the Key Bank in Northgate was robbed, Mike and Chris talked to two special agents. Mike gave them his card and asked if he could have some FBI bulletins describing the suspects.

At about the same time, their supervisor, Sergeant Monta, asked Mike and Chris if they'd like to work plainclothes for a while and investigate a bank robbery in the tiny north end suburb of Mukilteo. It was November, the winter rains had begun, and working plainclothes in an unmarked squad car was preferable to riding their bikes through mud puddles and pelting rain. They assured Monta that they would be delighted to look for the Mukilteo bank robbers.

"Sure, we will," Mike said. "But who are we looking for?"

Howard Monta gave them the name of a suspect: Nick Donteri,* who was believed to be living in Ballard. They obtained a picture of Donteri and went to the residence where he was supposed to be, but it turned out he had only been using the address. Nobody knew where he was. Chris and Mike had no luck at all locating Donteri. They told the resident

FBI agent in charge of the bank robbery investigation that they had run out of leads.

Even so, Mike Magan's eerie knack for snaring bank robbers had begun. He and Chris Gough drove to the Starbuck's on Aurora Avenue to get a cup of coffee. They strolled in, and Mike locked eyes with a man standing several feet away.

"I knew him, but I didn't know from where," he recalled. "We just kept staring at each other over the sugar and cream."

Mike whispered to Chris to go to the car and check the "Wants" bulletin. Chris did and gave him a thumbs down gesture. The familiar-looking man was getting into his truck when Mike and Chris strolled over and identified themselves as police officers and asked him what his name was.

"Nick . . ." he said, a bit nervously.

Immediately, Mike Magan *knew*. This was Nick Donteri.

"Donteri!" Magan yelled, drawing his gun.

It had been two years since Donteri had posed for the booking photo they were working from, and he had shaved his moustache and cut his hair in the interim. But his eyes gave him away. He surrendered without a fight.

"I'd caught my first bank robber," Mike Magan remembered. "I thought, 'Hey, this is going to be easy. It's pretty sweet, making arrests like this, if they all go down this way.'"

They would *not* all go down like that; Magan didn't know it then, but chasing bank robbers was about to become his job, his hobby, and his obsession.

24

Being a bank robber had been Scott Scurlock's job, hobby, and obsession for more than two years by the time Mike Magan arrested the Mukilteo bank robber. Scott's first bank robbery had been a thrill, a pure adrenaline rush that made jumping off cliffs and meeting up with boy-soldiers in Nicaragua seem as innocuous and unchallenging as the mornings he and Kevin used to steal pies in Reston. In a sense, it was as if Scott had spent his whole life searching for the kind of thrill he experienced when he walked into the bank on Madison Street in Seattle.

There had been next to no chance that he wouldn't do it again. Just as Shawn Johnson and Mike Magan loved what they were doing and never considered other careers after they became working lawmen, Scott Scurlock had discovered if not a career, a challenge that seemed to satisfy his need for excitement and danger.

He had carried off six successful bank robberies in 1992 and escaped all of them with enough money to last him for a long time.

However slapdash Scott might have been about some areas of his life, he viewed robbing banks as an intricate venture from the very first. He learned from every robbery, and he grew more accomplished each time.

Who helped Scott after his first robbery with Mark and Traci? It couldn't have been Steve—because Steve hadn't moved from Chicago until August, and then he had a torn tendon that kept him on crutches. It couldn't have been Kevin, or, rather, it *wouldn't* have been Kevin; Kevin had let Scott know what he thought about illegal activities and his disapproval had bounced him right out of Scott's inner circle. The accomplice might have been one of Scott's women, but, if it was, no one ever saw her.

Mark Biggins had been in Montana until he came back in December and pulled his own clumsy—and very lucky—bank robbery. After that, he stayed in California. Indeed, Mark didn't see Scott for most of 1992, and would not for all of 1993 and 1994.

It had been a year since Scott's last robbery on November 19, 1992. He had no more money for Steve to "launder" in Nevada. In a year's time, Scott had managed to spend more than $300,000.

It was time to begin again.

Scott was totally unaware, of course, that this time he would be pitting his skill, brains, experience, and strong athletic body against a whole task force of men—and women—who were just as smart as he was. Maybe smarter. It would never again be as easy as it was the first year.

Once again, Scott Scurlock needed an accomplice. His first choice was Bobby Gray. Bobby was still living in Florida, working hard to keep his concrete business growing. Scott figured that he was temptable. Bobby had known trouble in the past; he'd seen the inside of a prison after a drug conviction. And he owed Scott. Bobby's dream of having his own concrete operation had come true because Scott had loaned him $25,000 to buy his first concrete pumper. It was a used rig, but it worked fine.

Now the time had come, as it did with almost all of Scott's "loans," and he called it in. Bobby fit the profile that Scott envisioned as an ideal accomplice: savvy, agile, and smart. Scott called Bobby and offered him more money than Bobby had ever had—all for a few hours work. After listening long enough to Scott's persuasive argument that this would be a fail-proof operation, Bobby was convinced. Scott immediately sent him a round-trip ticket to Seattle.

But, as Bobby would recall later, he was on his way to the airport when he passed a Toys R Us store. He caught a glimpse of a rack of new bicycles outside. Like the friends Scott had recruited in the past, Bobby Gray had a daughter whom he adored. His little girl wanted a bike, but he hadn't yet seen his way clear to buy her one. Now, he thought, *If things go wrong, I may never see my daughter again. But I can at least leave her something that will make her happy to remember me by.* He wrenched the steering wheel and turned left into the Toys R Us parking lot. He bought the bike and headed for home to give it to his daughter.

But when Bobby got home and looked at his family, he had a searing glimpse of reality. His daughter didn't need "more money than you've ever seen"; she needed *him*. He picked up the phone and called Scott. "I'm not coming."

Scott was stunned, and then furious. "You get out here on the next plane," he said menacingly, "or else . . ." and he slammed the phone down.

Bobby stayed up all night, worrying about what forces Scott was about to call down on him. Nothing happened. The next day, he called Scott, and said, "Or else, *what?* I'm still here, and I'm not coming to Washington."

Scott had cooled down. He apologized and said he hadn't meant the threat *literally*.

Bobby was never sure.

Bobby Gray stayed in Florida and worked long, punishing days in one of the hardest areas of the construction business. By 1996, Bobby would own four concrete pumping trucks and he was well on his way to becoming wealthy. Even so, the tragedies that seemed to stalk everyone close to Scott Scurlock also followed Bobby.

Amazingly, Scott turned next to Kevin, who had stubbornly resisted him. When Kevin asked him what he had in mind, Scott said he couldn't tell him any details of what was involved or what the project was. He asked Kevin to trust him.

"He only said," Kevin recalled, "'I guarantee you that you will make more money than you have ever had in your *entire* life. All it will take is one afternoon. *One afternoon.* I am talking about a quarter of a million dollars, Bubba.'"

It wasn't even a decision for Kevin Meyers. He stared back at Scott and felt only sadness. He didn't want to know what Scott's project was. Whatever it was, it couldn't be good. Anything that would make him $250,000 in one afternoon could most certainly also put him in prison. When Kevin shook his head slowly, Scott didn't seem angry. Scott knew him well enough to know Kevin could not be persuaded when he had made his mind up.

It wasn't long after that strangely inscrutable meeting that Kevin Meyers' fears about what Scott was involved in were confirmed. He was in Florida, looking for a piece of property he could afford, when he stopped by to see Bobby Gray.

"Bobby told me that Scott was robbing banks," Kevin said. "He told me Scott tried to get him into it, and how he had changed his mind at the last minute. Maybe I knew it all along and tried to deny it. I don't know what I thought before that. But, once Bobby told me, it all fell into place. I couldn't turn Scott in. How could you turn the guy who had been your best friend all those years in to the police?"

Kevin knew that danger was like a drug to Scott; it always had been. How many times had Scott repeated the creed he lived by? "If I die, I die, Bubba—but it's better to go out as a flame than to live as a flicker."

Kevin's concern for his brother Steve grew. Kevin had said "No," and Bobby had said "No." Steve was still living in Scott's house, and Kevin felt sick with this knowledge. He tried not to think about it—but someplace inside, he *knew*.

He was, of course, correct. Steve Meyers became Scott's accomplice in his escalating assault on Northwest banks. At first, it was just to be one bank. Scott asked Steve to go with him to do surveillance on the very same bank where Scott had netted a quarter of a million dollars the year before: the Hawthorne Hills branch of Seafirst. Of course, he had no guarantee that there would be that much in the bank a year later.

Nevertheless, Scott and Steve made several trips from Olympia to Seattle to observe activity in and around the bank on North Fifty-fifth Street. He liked the location; it was out of the way without a lot of traffic—but it was close to a number of businesses in the neighborhood. All those commercial accounts probably meant that the bank kept substantial cash in the vault most of the time.

Scott insisted that they go in separate cars, so that no one would be able to link them. They would be only average looking men walking by the Hawthorne Hills Bank.

Ironically, detectives and FBI agents were going over surveillance pictures with a magnifying glass at the same time Scott and Steve were doing their own surveillance. As unaware as he was of the men who hunted him, Scott may have felt a little nervous; he hadn't robbed a bank for a year. This one had been easy the first time, but he must have suspected that they would have beefed up their security in the interim.

Once again, it was Thanksgiving time. Scott was waiting for it to rain. He preferred to work on dark rainy afternoons in the autumn because there would be fewer people venturing out to do their banking. It would also be harder to identify him in his vehicle, and he felt that people in general—even police—were groggier on a rainy day, lulled by the thrumming sound of drops hitting the roof of their squad cars and the whish-whish of the windshield wipers.

Scott didn't want to use his white van this time. Nine months earlier, he had given Steve cash to buy a used yellow Renault. Steve had worn gloves during that transaction, as Scott instructed, but he hadn't asked questions then. Now, he knew why. This was the car Scott would drive in the bank robbery.

Scott wanted to put his makeup on in Olympia and then drive to Seattle disguised as an older man with a moustache. Through a rain-streaked car window, he would look completely normal. Afterward, he would make use of the two plastic bags he carried—one with mineral spirits to take off the fake nose, chin, and cheeks, and one with soap and water. Although it took him almost two hours to put *on* his makeup, he could get it off in minutes. If anyone stopped him, he would look completely different from the "bank robber."

Scott outlined the plan to Steve. They would drive the sixty miles to Seattle in two different vehicles. Steve was to park near the bank with a police scanner and one of two portable Motorola radios Scott had bought. If a silent alarm should go out and the police responded, he would hear it on the police frequency and alert Scott, who would be carrying the other radio.

"When I'm through," Scott explained, "I'll say 'I'm out' on the portable. I'll meet you near the freeway and we go home."

It rained hard on Wednesday, November 24—Thanksgiving Eve, 1993. They headed for Seattle, arriving about 11:30 in the morning.

With Steve monitoring police calls, Scott walked

briskly into the Seafirst Bank, Hawthorne Hills branch, for the second November in a row. The bank manager spotted him and his first thought was that he must have been badly burned and had tried to cover his scars with makeup. *Poor guy.* And then he noticed the black gun in the man's right hand.

Scott no longer bothered with the tellers' money. He knew exactly where the real money was now. He announced, "This is a robbery. Who's the vault teller?"

"He's on vacation," the manager said, and the bank robber seemed to accept this. "I have the keys, but it's only my second day here," he lied, "and I don't have the codes."

"Then open up the teller drawers."

The Seafirst manager thought rapidly, trying to thwart the robber. "I'm sorry," he said, "I don't have the keys to that area either."

But, as luck would have it, two bank employees, unaware that a robbery was in progress, walked out of the vault where they had been counting money. They carried stacks of bills in their arms. The man with the grotesque makeup on his face couldn't smile, but there was a grin in his voice as he spotted them and said, "What do we have here?"

Scott Scurlock's phenomenal luck had held. It was almost like the card games in Hawaii and the football parlays in Las Vegas. Once more, he had stumbled onto the mother lode.

He ordered the bank manager and the two tellers back into the vault. He pulled a lime green bag out of his tan parka. He stuffed it full of money. Every few moments, he darted a look out into the bank itself to check on what was happening there.

"Who has access to the money in the ATM?"

The bank manager shook his head. "No one does."

Apparently satisfied, Scott prepared to leave. But first he motioned to a bank courier who had just walked in, unaware, and he put the courier into the vault with the other employees. Then he told the customers in the lobby to stay where they were for a full minute.

"If I hear an alarm," he warned, convincingly, "I'll come back and someone will get hurt."

Once again, nobody disobeyed his orders. By the time the bank employees emerged from the vault and called corporate security, Scott had vanished.

Scott parked next to Steve at a prearranged location ten blocks from the bank. He quickly removed his makeup and then he tailed Steve's car as he zoomed onto the freeway entrance there. It was a piece of cake. They stayed on I-5 until they took the off-ramp just south of Olympia that was only minutes from the treehouse property.

Scott and Steve drove both their cars into the barn, closed the doors behind them and counted out the money there. Scott may have been a little disappointed; he hadn't gotten as much as he had the year before. But it sure wasn't bad: $98,571.

He handed Steve his share: $5,000. Scott explained that this was a fair split. *He* was the one who took all the chances. He planned everything, and it was he who had gone into the bank. He was the one who risked getting shot or arrested or recognized.

They were exhausted—more from the tension of the day than any physical effort—and they saved the clean-up for the next day, when they pitched out or burned the clothes and other items that they felt were too recognizable to use again.

Back in the bank, the FBI reviewed the tape from the bank's cameras, the frames showing a now-familiar—if bizarre—face with a grotesque mask and false chin and nose, topped by a blondish red wig. There was something about the robber's stance, something that marked him as an athlete even in the grainy bank footage. But try as they might, they could not see beneath the mask and the makeup.

Taking $15,000 to launder, Steve Meyers left for Las Vegas a few days after the robbery. Back on Overhulse Road, Scott filled his plastic buckets, and reburied them on his land. Now there was enough cash for many, many rainy days.

Steve moved to San Francisco before Christmas to live with the new woman in his life. She was a flight attendant whom he'd met on one of his many flights between Seattle and Nevada. Her name was Sari* and she was originally from Croatia. The plain fact was that Steve didn't want to live in Washington State any longer. Like Mark Biggins, he sought a geographical solution in an attempt to avoid Scott's plans. Except for Kevin Meyers and Bobby Gray, no one seemed able to flat out tell Scott "No" and make it stick. Neither Steve nor Mark were truly weak men—but circumstances and fate had made them both susceptible to Scott's persuasive arguments.

Kevin and Scott prepare to leap off Koko Head; they feared nothing but boredom. In top shape, they constantly challenged each other. *(Courtesy Marge Violette Mullins)*

Water-Spirit, Kevin Meyers' work two decades after The Shire days. *(Courtesy Robert Kevin Meyers)*

THE END OF THE DREAM

Scott Scurlock, at age 21, on the front porch of The Shire, naked in paradise and about to do a handstand. Scott could do nine, Kevin only seven.

Although his name was in the papers constantly, this feature on the treehouse was the only clipping Scott saved. *(The Seattle Times, 1986)*

Mark Biggins in California, 1994. He had hoped never to be called back to Washington State.

Scott's treehouse in Olympia, Washington.

Scott tacked N. C. Wyeth's illustration of Robin Hood above his bed in the treehouse.

THE END OF THE DREAM

The treehouse interior.

One of Steve Meyers' pieces. He could sculpt everything from wood to marble, classic to avant garde.

When Steve Meyers saw this wanted poster—with a $50,000 reward—he feared it was only a matter of time before they would be caught.

THE END OF THE DREAM

"The Hollywood Bank Robber" is caught on a bank security camera.

Mark Biggins and his daughter Lori.

Mark Biggins, left, and Scott on the treehouse acreage in 1988.
(Mark Biggins collection)

Steve Meyers with his beloved daughter Cara.

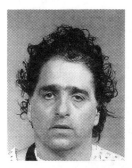

Steve Meyers, the sculptor whose arms were critically wounded by gunshots, faces a bleak future as he poses for the police camera in Washington's King County Jail infirmary.

Mark Biggins, eyes filled with tears, photographed in the King County Jail infirmary days after the near-fatal shoot-out with police.

Scott Scurlock, September 1995, atop a mountain—one of his favorite places to be.

THE END OF THE DREAM

Seattle Police detective Mike Magan with the loot.

The hidden makeup room in the barn at Seven Cedars.

The escape van, riddled with bullet holes. This window was broken from the inside as the robbers returned police fire.

FBI Special Agent Shawn Johnson with some of the last bank loot.

THE END OF THE DREAM

The camper in Mrs. Walker's backyard, where Hollywood fought his final battle. Police made a shocking discovery when they got inside.

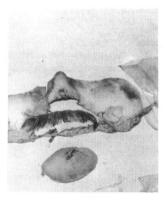

Police found the prosthetics and makeup used by the robbers in the back of their getaway van.

Scott Scurlock makes headlines once again.

(The Seattle Times, November 30, 1996)

Detective Lt. Jim Stovall of the Salem Police Department. Stovall's knowledge of body language eliminated a prime suspect in the murder of Kay Owens. *(Ann Rule)*

Detective Vern Meighen of the Salem Police Department who, with his partner Detective Tom Mason, listened to an incredible murder confession seven years after the fact. *(Ann Rule)*

THE PEEPING TOM

Kay Owens, 26, lived in the tiny duplex, center. Her VW wagon is parked at the left of the picture. The voyeur who watched her gained entry into her home through the window just to the right of the VW. *(Police photo)*

The killer slit this screen and entered Kay Owens' duplex. *(Police photo)*

THE GIRL WHO FELL IN LOVE WITH HER KILLER

Snohomish County detective Jerry Cook, who went to Easy Oakley's home to arrest him and found him sound asleep. *(Ann Rule)*

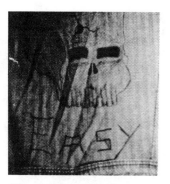

"Easy" Oakley liked to draw skulls on jail coveralls, including "bullet holes" to show where he had shot his victim. *(Police photo)*

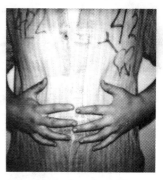

Easy poses for the jail camera after he deliberately cut his arm to fake a suicide attempt. *(Police photo)*

Snohomish County detectives Doug Engelbretson, left, and Vivian Griffiths investigated a brutal attack with an unbelievable ending. *(Ann Rule)*

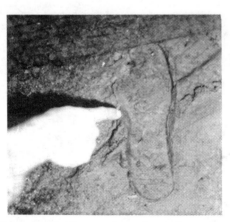

A Snohomish County detective points to a small footprint and a tire mark at the spot where Barbie Linley was raped and then shot three times in the head. *(Police photo)*

AN UNLIKELY SUSPECT

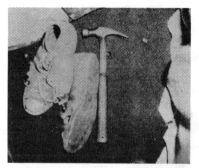

When the body of his stepmother was found in John English's bedroom, there was a bloodstained hammer next to it, along with John's battered sneakers. *(Police photo)*

Next to the Englishes' bed in the master bedroom detectives found all manner of bondage paraphernalia. *(Police photo)*

This mobile of anatomically correct nude dolls in bondage positions was found hanging in the bedroom of 14-year-old John English. *(Police photo)*

AN UNLIKELY SUSPECT

King County detective Ted Forrester worked the bizarre crime scene in the murder of Vera English. *(Ann Rule)*

King County detectives lifted John's mattress and found a collection of pornographic pictures. *(Police photo)*

Steve Meyers had no plan to participate in another bank robbery, but he didn't plan *not* to, either. He had deluded himself into believing that the man on the other end of the Motorola short-wave radio wasn't *really* a professional bank robber. Scott wasn't going to do it forever, and Steve tried to tell himself that he had been there only to look out for a friend.

Once in California, Steve began to sell some of his art again, and looked around for a studio. If he could only get established there. But the fact was, everything moved too slowly, Steve was soon out of money; the $5,000 Scott had given him hadn't lasted very long, so when Scott called and asked Steve to meet him in Reno to talk about the next robbery, Steve went. He gambled with the money Scott gave him. Steve was becoming addicted to gambling, exhilarated by the ambiance of the smoky casinos in Las Vegas, Reno, and Lake Tahoe.

Scott? Scott's whole life was a gamble against long odds.

Early in January 1994, Steve capitulated and drove back to Olympia. A few weeks later, he took part in his second bank robbery. On January 21, 1994, he and Scott headed for a U.S. Bank—the Wedgwood branch—which was in the same neighborhood as the bank they'd robbed only two months earlier. It was a Friday. It was raining. It was 11:25 A.M. Everything was going according to plan.

A day earlier, Scott had left a car parked in Seattle with a key under the bumper, ready for him to drive to the Wedgwood district. He had sent Steve out to buy it from someone who had placed a small ad in a local paper, and it was as plain as peanut butter. But it now had a brand new battery and good tires.

Scott drove it to a parking lot a block north of the bank. Steve parked *his* car a block south, and listened to his police scanner as Scott entered the bank. In a very short time, he heard Scott on the Motorola, "I'm out. . . . Let's *go!*"

Steve pulled out and headed for their meeting location, but the little hairs on the back of his neck stood up when he heard the police scanner crackle out the address of the bank Scott had just robbed. He realized how close they had shaved their time. In only a few minutes, Scott would have been trapped coming out of the bank. But everything seemed to be OK; he saw Scott's car accelerate up ahead and disappear around a corner.

But then Steve lost radio contact with Scott. All the way back to Olympia, he wondered if Scott would be there when he turned into the Overhulse Road property.

Scott wasn't there. Steve's heart pounded. If the police had Scott, it would only be a matter of time before they knew about *him.*

It wasn't long, however, before Scott's van came up the driveway. Steve could see that he was not happy. Nothing had worked right. Scott said he hadn't been able to get into the vault because the teller with the combination wasn't there. And then, some wise guy teller had tripped the alarm and had had the balls to tell Scott so.

Scott rarely got upset—but Steve saw that he was, now. They counted the money he did get in the barn.

There was only $15,803 and Scott gave Steve $5,000 of that. They might as well not have bothered.

The chances are that Scott might not have scheduled another bank robbery so soon if the take had been better. As it was, Scott was anxious to go to Seattle and chose another, more profitable, location. But there was another reason; Scott didn't want to let a near-failure stay on his record. It was more than just the money.

How could the investigators who were trying to stop the bank robber know *which* bank he was going to hit next? When the FBI agents reread all the witness interviews and reports, they could see that he had established a pattern which was becoming easy to chart. He liked the northeast part of Seattle—with only two forays into West Seattle. But there were so many banks in the north end of Seattle. Where would he go next? The best strategy seemed to be to wait for the physical evidence he would leave behind the next time, or the next. Fingerprints. A car license plate number. A clear photo that someone might recognize.

One thing seemed likely. The robber vanished so quickly after each incident that he probably lived in the north end of Seattle and was able to return to the safety of his home almost immediately. If this were true, somebody in the neighborhood was sure to notice certain repetitive activity and connect it to the bank robberies.

On February 17, 1994, Scott Scurlock pulled off a foolhardy bank robbery. He returned for the third time to the Hawthorne Hills branch of the Seafirst

Bank. He had always found gratifying stacks of money there. But he was also a familiar face—or rather, a familiar *mask*—in the beleaguered bank.

Once again, it was a Thursday. It was snowing, weather rare enough in Seattle that locals who don't have to drive in it usually stay home. He changed his MO only by going in earlier. The bank was barely open for business at 9:45 A.M. when Patti—the same vault teller whom he had terrified in November—looked up to see a nightmare returning. She recognized him, almost with disbelief, saw again the way he moved like an athlete or a graceful animal. How could he chance coming back for a third time to the same bank?

He strode toward the teller's counter, protected now by a bandit barrier. His eyes swept the bank and he saw that one teller was on the phone. He turned to Patti and told her to make the other woman hang up. Then he looked at the drive-in window teller and barked, "Get her out of the window!"

He wanted the vault teller, but Patti told him that the new vault teller was the woman who'd been on the phone. He herded them both toward the vault. Patti could smell his acrid sweat, and she knew, for all his calm demeanor, that he was nervous. He cleaned out one vault, and then instructed them to open "the lower vault."

Funny how familiarity diminishes fear. Patti wasn't as frightened this time, and she looked at the man's strange face, curious about what he looked like beneath the puttylike makeup. He looked up suddenly and caught her. He said, "Don't look at me. Keep your eyes on the ground."

"You really like it here, don't you?" she asked.

"Yeah," he said in a deep voice, "but I don't think I'm coming back here anymore."

Patti hoped devoutly that he meant it.

He did mean it. But he had planned very, very carefully so that this final dip into their vault was flawless and rewarding. Scott and Steve had driven Scott's blue van to Seattle the night before and parked it near the bank. On the day of robbery, Scott had driven up a "drop car," an untraceable older white station wagon. But—when he ran from the bank—Scott headed for his own van, leaving the station wagon for someone to tow away. It was as clean of prints, hairs, fibers, bits of paper, as any vehicle could be. He had seen to that.

Scott could well afford to lose his small investment in the station wagon. Back in the barn, he and Steve Meyers counted the money, elated at the size of the take. It was enough that they didn't have to think about another bank robbery for a long time. When he walked out of the Hawthorne Hills branch of the Seafirst Bank for the third time, Scott had carried away $114,000. He had now stolen almost $475,000 from one neighborhood bank alone.

Seafirst security mobilized to stop the daring day-time robber who had hit them yet again, despite the deterrents they had installed. They had him on camera, but that was the only place they had him. They didn't believe he would come back to this particular branch—but that didn't mean he wouldn't hit one of their myriad branches in the Seattle area.

Who *was* he? Who was the man who seemed fixated on one small neighborhood bank? None of the bank employees knew him, or they *believed* they didn't know him. None could really describe him. By the time Scott had rolled down the interstate, he had wiped all the makeup off his face and he looked like any guy driving south on I-5.

Scott planned never to use the same drop car more than twice, and he decided that it wouldn't be Steve who bought the next anonymous car. They looked too much alike. They were both dark, about the same size and age, and both of them had very heavy eyebrows that almost grew together at the bridge of their noses. He would have to get someone else to buy a good solid—but forgettable—used car for Steve to drive in the next job.

After the robbery, Steve drove back to San Francisco. He returned to sculpting, but with the dull sense that a hand would tap on his shoulder at any minute. There was no question any longer if there would *be* a next job. There would always be another bank robbery waiting in the wings.

25

Disillusioned with his oldest friend and sick at heart, Kevin left the Seattle area. He said good-bye to Ellen, promising to come back. He needed time to think about where his life was going, and there was a

woman in Oklahoma—half mystic/half spiritual
teacher—who welcomed him as a student. Kevin
chose his own solitary road, not sure where he was
headed. When he returned from Oklahoma, however,
he was amazed to see his paintings take on a new
grandeur, a luminous quality. On his last camping
trip with Scott, they had slept under the stars on one
of the San Juan islands and awakened to a majesti-
cally shrouded sunrise. Kevin's photographic memory allowed him to recreate that scene in a huge
painting he called "San Juans at Dawn." In "Water-
Spirit," he painted the ocean, as blue as the sky,
endlessly rolling toward the shore. All of his work was
suffused by golden light.

In Oklahoma, it had been easier for Kevin to shut
his mind to whatever mischief Scott and his brother
were up to. He knew Ellen still saw them occasionally.
She had a heart gentler than any he had known other
than his sister Dana's, and she'd reported to him that
Scott and Steve seemed somehow sad and lost. Kevin
wasn't worried that they could draw Ellen in; she was
too good, protected by some spiritual light that kept
the worst traits of human nature from touching her.

Although the FBI, police agencies and bank security teams kept their eyes on the lookout for the bank
robber whom they had now dubbed "Hollywood"
because of his elaborate makeup, he seemed to have
gone to ground during the spring of 1994. Looking
back over the nine bank robberies he had carried off
so far, they compared notes on all the surveillance
photos and his MO. His approach never varied; he
said the same things, carried what appeared to be the

same gun, and vanished each time he stepped through the bank doors.

They noted that he had disappeared for a whole year—November 1992 to November 1993. Would it be another year until he struck again? Or was he just watching and waiting?

It wasn't another year; it was only five months. On July 13, 1994, the Hollywood Bank Robber carried out his tenth robbery at the First Interstate Bank on Seattle's Queen Anne Hill. The neighborhood was new for him, located very close to the downtown section of the city and on the west side overlooking Elliott Bay.

It was on a Wednesday, at 10:45 in the morning, and the bank's manager was having coffee in the break room when she heard a commotion in the lobby. She walked quickly into the main banking area and approached a man from the back. He was shouting something.

"I'll have to ask you to leave—" she began.

And then he turned around and she found herself thinking, *"Not again."* Her bank had already been robbed twice in six weeks and it had only been three days since the last hit. She didn't recognize this robber, though. Without appearing to study him, she memorized his clothing and his face: he wore a brown jacket, a baseball cap, and what was clearly a wig and fake moustache. He had a salmon-colored mask that obfuscated his features, and his improbably large nose and chin seemed to be fashioned from rubber.

She saw that he had something in his gloved right hand, something black, rectangular, and about five inches long—but it wasn't a gun. As the branch manager stood there, surprised, he waved the thing at her and spat out, "You know what this does to you, lady?"

He moved his finger and the mechanism made a snapping or whirring sound. For a moment, she thought it might be a toy; she could see green flashes coming out of the top of it. It wasn't a gun and nothing struck her, but whatever it was, the object in his hand looked dangerous. She nodded as he asked her to take him to the vault.

He had already robbed the tellers, showing them a handgun—and ordering them not to put in dye packs. "And don't activate any alarm. I'll know," he'd warned. "I'll hear the clicking."

But he had *not* heard the click as one of the tellers tripped a silent alarm. The robber ordered everyone on the floor while he took a teller and the manager into the vault.

Once there, the manager was dismayed to see that a longtime bank customer, a woman over eighty years old, was calmly going through her safe deposit box, unaware of any danger. There were four of them now in the small area, three women—one elderly—and a nervous bank robber. When she realized what was happening, the old woman had the great presence of mind to say nothing; she only paused with her hand resting on her papers and watched quietly. The robber pulled out a blue-green bag and directed the bank employees to load it with money from the vault. They filled it with $111,796.

When they emerged from the vault, the robber

looked around the bank and realized instantly that someone was missing. A woman customer had managed to slip out the door and flee. Her call for help would be superfluous, however. Seattle Police patrol units were already racing toward the Queen Anne bank in response to the silent alarm.

But not soon enough. The man in the mask was gone.

The frustrating thing was that the witness statements were sickeningly familiar and sparse in detail. There was no question it had been Hollywood. They had him on camera—*again*. He had once again managed to avoid the dye-pack bills, but he'd taken the bait bills. If he tried to spend them, they might just lead the task force to him.

Scott Scurlock had reason to feel secure and smug. Ten robberies and no slip-ups. What he didn't realize was that, with every bank robbery, his chance of being caught grew. The sheer odds of chance said that something, sometime, would go wrong. Even Willie-Boss wasn't impervious to that.

And something had gone wrong on Queen Anne Hill. Someone had seen him as he left the bank. A woman living a block from the bank was pulling weeds in her front yard on that Wednesday morning in July. Parking is at a premium on Queen Anne Hill, and strange vehicles stand out. She noticed a dark blue van—a Ford Aerostar—parked across the street and thought idly that she hadn't seen it before.

Some ten to fifteen minutes later, she saw a man walking rapidly toward the van. He was carrying "a greenish mesh bag." As she watched, the man hopped into the unlocked driver's door and sped off down the street.

No, she told disappointed FBI agents—she had not been able to get a license number. No, there was something about his face that kept her from really seeing him.

A newly hired bank teller at the Interstate Bank told the investigators that he had not been on duty at the time of the robbery—but he had seen something unusual the evening *before.* As he left work at 5:40, he had noticed a man standing near the bank doors, jotting notes in a personal planner. When he saw the witness watching him, he had quickly gotten into a blue, American-made van with tinted windows.

The teller described the man as being in his late thirties, white, around six feet tall, with brown receding hair combed straight back. He had a neatly trimmed reddish brown moustache. He wore a brown jacket and sunglasses.

Had he seen Scott? Quite possibly. Had he seen what Scott *really* looked like? No. He had only seen one of Hollywood's many disguises.

Although the investigators in Seattle didn't realize it, Hollywood had pulled *eleven* bank robberies—not ten. Just three weeks before—in June—he had failed miserably in Portland, Oregon, 165 miles south of Seattle. Initially, his plan seemed sound enough. He had arranged for someone—still unidentified, but not Steve Meyers—to buy two vehicles for him in the San Jose area. One was a Nissan station wagon and the other was the dark blue Ford Aerostar van.

Scott had Steve drive the van to Portland, while Scott drove the station wagon. They left the station wagon there. Although Scott wasn't very familiar with Portland, he had picked out a bank to rob, and he needed a drop car waiting in that city.

Maybe he was riding on a winning name, because he chose the *Hawthorne* branch of the First Interstate Bank. He and Steve Meyers drove down to Portland a couple of times to sit surveillance on the bank. Scott decreed that June 24 would be the day they expanded their operations into Portland.

It was a fiasco almost from the beginning. Scott picked up the station wagon and they drove separately to the bank. The weather was good—a bad sign according to the Scott Scurlock bank-robbing checklist. Steve drove around the bank with his scanner set to the Portland Police Bureau's frequency. He was too nervous to park; so many of the streets were one-way and he didn't want to risk getting caught too far away from Scott.

That was a good decision because Scott wasn't inside the bank very long before the robbery alarm was broadcast over the police frequency. Steve picked up the radio and called to Scott inside, "Get out!"

Someone had apparently seen Scott going in and called 911 on a cell phone. Scott got out, but without any money. The teller hadn't been able to open the vault, and Scott hadn't had time to get the other tellers to empty their cash drawers.

They abandoned the Nissan station wagon where Scott had parked it and headed for the bridge over the Columbia River and into Washington State. They barely spoke as they headed north on I-5 for Olympia.

So, in the summer of 1994, there *were* cracks in the

perfect facade of Hollywood. He'd failed in Portland, and he'd been seen with his blue Aerostar van *twice* at the Queen Anne First Interstate Bank.

Steve went back to San Francisco and his flight attendant girlfriend, Sari. In August, they moved to Sonoma. Scott flew down to help them move. This was something he had always done for his friends—Kevin, Steve, even Mark. Aside from their necessary close association when they carried out their carefully orchestrated bank robberies, Steve and Scott were still friends. Scott saw his friendship with Steve as comparable to the closeness he saw between movie bank robbers—a fantasy version of true male bonding. He and Steve climbed mountains together, fixed up houses together, drank together, helped each other move, and robbed banks together. Steve was now as close to being Scott's best friend as anyone could be; he had long since replaced his brother, Kevin.

It was two decades past The Shire days in Hawaii and the world had changed.

The lines on Scott's handsome face had deepened noticeably, but his thick hair had no gray strands, and he was in virtually the same physical condition he had been in in his twenties. He had done none of the things that make a man grow up: he was father to no one; husband to no one. He traveled when he liked and answered to no one. He was still in awe of his own father and was always anxious to please him.

The Swiss banker was as close to a steady girlfriend as any woman could be to Scott. She lived with him in Olympia for about a year during 1993 and 1994. She must have known that the large amounts of cash he gave her to launder in a Swiss bank account under *her* name had come from some murky source, but she didn't comment on it. A percentage of the money was hers to keep. Scott paid his mortgage and his credit card bills through her account.

Like many women before her, she loved Scott Scurlock. If being with him meant that she ignored parts of his life, she accepted that.

Kevin came back to Seattle, and he and Ellen and her girls still visited the treehouse occasionally. They sometimes came down when Scott was off on one of his journeys around the world. One time, the girls were exploring and found some of the white masks they had made with Scott years before. "They remembered how Scott had showed them how to make masks, and how much fun they all had. We used some kind of plaster of Paris stuff," Ellen remembered. "Now, they looked like death masks. One of my girls said, 'Look at this one. It looks like Scott.' And it did."

During the times when Scott was home, Ellen noticed an uncharacteristic anxious, strained quality about him. Nothing seemed to make him happy and he was often short-tempered. He confessed that he wasn't sleeping well, that he was haunted by nightmares. He felt as if something was following him—or *waiting* for him.

When she asked what, he couldn't or wouldn't say. Maybe he didn't know. He still looked like a movie star, despite the dark circles that purpled the skin beneath his eyes. It still seemed to cheer him up when Ellen brought flowers to the treehouse. He handed her a hundred dollars once, and told her to bring as many flowers as it would buy. She brought back armloads. He gave her more money and asked her to buy things for the treehouse kitchen. She bought dishes, pots and pans, and small appliances, and rearranged the kitchen shelves, hoping it would make Scott happy, as if flowers and neatness might erase the worried lines from his face.

Ellen's daughters didn't realize that Kevin and Scott weren't the buddies they had once been, although of course Ellen did. They went through the motions. The couple brought the girls down to clean up Seven Cedars. Afterward, they would still have bonfires. They made what they called "electric dogs"—hot dogs cooked with two nails and a piece of wood, hooked up to raw electric power with live wires. It was a little dangerous, but the adults didn't let the girls hold them. The wieners were cooked in seconds.

One night, Scott gobbled down four hot dogs, but he was still hungry. Ellen cooked another one for him, but it slipped off the nails and fell to the ground. Scott didn't notice. "I picked it up, wiped off the dirt, put catsup on it and popped it in a bun for Scott," she said. "He said, 'Man, what did you do to this one? This is better than the others.' We all laughed."

For a moment, everything was OK again. Ellen and Kevin packed up the sleepy kids and were walking toward the car when they looked back to where Scott had been piling debris on the campfire.

He had always had an obsession with fire, building

bonfires that were just at the edge of being dangerous. *This* one was beyond being on the edge. Now, Scott was urging Steve to throw on stacks of bone-dry boards, paper, and boughs higher and higher over the flames. With a *Whoosh,* the fire soared toward the lower limbs of trees.

"The whole place is going to go up," Kevin yelled. "Stop! STOP!"

Already, sheets of flame were heading for the barn. Kevin and Ellen headed back to help. Working with shovels, boards, and a single garden hose, it took them all night to get it under control. It almost seemed that Scott had meant for Seven Cedars to go up in flames.

And, in a sense, it may have been better if it had.

26

The officers, detectives, FBI agents, and private bank security companies that were searching for Hollywood were primed for him to hit again in the second half of 1994. But after the July 13 robbery at the Queen Anne Interstate, he seemed—once again—to have gone into hiding. They figured he might have been spooked because he'd been seen not once, but twice. The off-duty bank teller's hard look in the parking lot the night before the robbery could not have been lost on him. And he must have noticed the woman gardening in her front yard who stared at him as he ran from the bank with a laundry bag full of money in his hand. True, he was in disguise both times, but he was used to being completely invisible. Until Queen Anne, no one had spotted him before or after. Worse, perhaps, the witnesses both described a dark blue minivan—a Ford Aerostar.

Scott had no need to risk another bank robbery in the latter half of 1994. His three Seattle hits earlier in the year had netted him $240,000. He could afford to lay back in the weeds and wait.

Although Hollywood would soon become Mike Magan's obsession, he wasn't the criminal who initially prompted Mike Magan to search out bank robbers—it was another group of robbers who used disguises. In the late fall of 1994, Seattle detectives and FBI agents were still looking for the gang dubbed the Abe Lincoln Bank Robbers, six individuals, all of them dressed like Abraham Lincoln, who were hitting north end banks with annoying regularity. Some of them were clearly men; others might have been female, and there were probably accomplices working outside the banks.

The Abe Lincoln gang had obviously planned their robberies well, and they were successful in at least thirteen bank jobs. They had made some of their escapes in a green van.

"Their disguises were actually kind of comical," Magan recalled, "but what they were doing wasn't."

Since Mike and Chris Gough knew the north end so well, they began to work with the FBI on the "Abe" cases. "We developed an informant," Magan said, "and we brought her down to the FBI. She knew who one of the Abe Lincoln suspects was."

Their informant led them to others who knew who the "Abes" really were. Armed with the names that the two bike patrol officers had provided, the FBI and Seattle Police units carried out surveillance on another suspect vehicle. They arrested a man named David Fresonke, who ultimately pleaded guilty to five bank robberies.

Mike Magan and Chris Gough were also able to find the green van. They helped the FBI search the vehicle and found a fake beard and the latexlike material that had been used to make mock scars. They also found documents in the name of a female whose name had been mentioned by their informant. Later that day, they arrested the woman on two warrants. She matched the description of a bank robbery accomplice who had fled in the green van after a dye pack had exploded in it. Before midnight, they arrested still a third suspect.

Sergeant Monta commended his officers. ". . . The work of Magan and Gough in breaking this case for the FBI is far too extensive to adequately detail . . . the end result is that they are ultimately responsible for identifying six bank robbery suspects and several accomplices."

Mike Magan was in the FBI offices with one of his informants in December 1994, when the Supervisory Special Agent of their bank robbery squad, Mike Byrne, asked him, "Would you be willing to come help us on the Violent Crimes Task Force when it starts up?"

It was a question that almost any street cop would have shouted "YES!" to and Mike Magan felt a surge of optimism. He could not hope for anything more. "I thought that would be *great!*" he remembered. "And I said, 'Sure,' but I wondered how I was going to pull that off."

As much as he wanted it, Magan knew that this was an assignment that would surely go to a robbery detective. And it wasn't even up to him to accept the offer; if it should ever become an official offer, it would have to go through all the steps of departmental policy. So, at this point, it was really just an "Atta boy" that felt wonderful.

Mike went home and told Lisa, and they celebrated the vote of confidence. It wasn't Christmas yet, and the Violent Crimes Task Force wouldn't be operational until after the first of the year. Still, Mike made a few phone calls to see if officers higher up than he might call Seattle Police Chief Norm Stamper and put in a good word for him.

"Everybody I called said, 'No.' Actually, they said, '*Hell,* no!'" he joked. "I started to lose a little faith. And then I heard that the task force was definitely slated to start in March of 1995."

Initially, only one Seattle Police detective was selected to start on the Violent Crimes Task Force—that was Sergeant Ed Striedinger, who had been a detective in both homicide and robbery.

There would be other slots opening up, and Mike Magan hoped that Mike Byrne would send a letter of recommendation to Chief Stamper. Then he might at least be able to get a face-to-face interview with the Chief and *apply* for a spot on the task force.

Christmas passed, and it was 1995. By the end of March, new "pattern robberies" had begun to break. The Abe Lincoln bank robberies had stopped, but there were others to take their place. Mike Magan had long since learned—as all good investigators do— that hitting the bricks, or what cops call "heel and toeing it"—was often the best way to develop suspects. He had talked to business owners, motel and hotel managers, and street people constantly for years, handing out his cards. Sometimes they called in a week, or a month, or even a couple of years later. Sometimes they never called. But he had made scores of arrests because of a network of contacts he had built up over time.

Occasionally, the best tips came from former suspects who Mike had treated with respect—even as he was arresting them. He was like a fisherman who dropped hundreds of lines in the water and hoped for a few nibbles.

The Puget Sound Violent Crimes Task Force had started up in March 1995, and without Mike Magan. While he waited to find out if he had any chance at all to get on the task force, he kept busy. He was following up leads on bank robbers and just plain robbers who were striking in the north end of Seattle.

In April, a pattern robber was committing commercial robberies there. Armed with a vicious-looking, large folding knife, he specialized in robbing small businesses where women worked. He not only took the store's money, but he robbed the employees and customers, too.

He soon had a nickname: "The Buck Knife Robber." Women who had no choice but to go to work in convenience stores and other small operations were terrified. The Buck Knife Robber was suspected in at least forty robberies; it seemed only a matter of time until someone resisted or moved too quickly and he used his knife.

The Seattle Police Robbery Unit asked Mike and Chris for help in locating the suspect, who seemed to be under the influence of drugs during most of his robberies. They knew the neighborhoods he was hitting so well that they were able to set up stakeout sites. Mike sat on many of the stakeouts himself, watching and waiting. On May 18, he waited near a store that fit the profile of Buck Knife's prime targets. While he waited, he thought about the task-force job. Rumor had it that the next appointment would be announced on June 1. He still wanted it.

Mike looked up and spotted a car that looked like one they were looking for. He called for backup. The driver was a dead-ringer for Buck Knife. They moved in and arrested him, along with his girlfriend.

It was the Buck Knife Robber. When detectives, including Mike Magan, searched his apartment they found a large folding knife, along with other items of evidence that connected him absolutely to more than three dozen robberies.

It seemed that Mike was wearing a detective's hat as often now as he was a bike cop's uniform. He had slipped into it so easily, but he still felt as though he'd be spending his life waiting to become a detective. Detectives in the Robbery Unit invited him to their offices on the fifth floor of the Public Safety Building, showed him around, and wrote him still another commendation letter. All it did was whet his appetite more.

Mike Magan kept thinking *"June 1. June 1. June 1."*

Magan's Lieutenant, Linda Pierce, and his Captain, Dan Bryant, urged him to approach Chief Stamper. He was reluctant. Chances were that Stamper would look at him like he was a kid, untried—not ready. He went ahead anyway and made an appointment.

In truth, Norm Stamper is the most approachable of police chiefs, an amiable man who has none of the stiff-necked pride that old-time chiefs had, even though he sports a "cookie duster" moustache that gives him the look of a lawman from another era. Stamper is fiercely devoted to his officers. He tries to know all of them personally. He is so good at his job that most of them are in awe of him.

What Mike Magan didn't know was that his wife, Lisa, had already talked to Stamper when she sold the chief a bottle of perfume for his wife. Lisa hadn't been at all shy about praising her husband. Mike was embarrassed when she told him, but she reminded him that, at least, Stamper would know who he was now—and he wouldn't be just another faceless street cop.

Magan had other boosters too. Lt. Pierce totaled up his arrests and was amazed to find he and Chris had cleared *eighty robberies* in six months. "I don't think any deed should go unnoticed," she told Mike. "Captain Bryant and I think I should go with you when you meet the chief—and, by the way, I got you an earlier appointment."

The meeting with Norm Stamper was pleasant and friendly, but it ended without any promises. Stamper mentioned that he had had a nice talk with Lisa Magan, and said he would look into the situation with the task force. He didn't mention that he had already pored over Mike's personnel file and read his commendations and his entire history with the Seattle Police Department.

Wheels that Magan knew nothing about were already turning.

Mike was off duty on June 1, 1995, when his phone rang a little before eleven. It was Linda Pierce.

"See you later," she said cryptically.

"What do you mean?"

"I'm just calling to tell you that you got the spot."

"You're kidding me."

"No, it's yours."

Mike couldn't stay home. He called Lisa and told her that he had been assigned to the Puget Sound Violent Crimes Task Force. She suggested he might as well go to work in his new office. And so he did. For the first time, Mike Magan walked into the Violent Crimes Task Force offices. He picked out a desk and that made it seem real.

It was June 1, 1995. Sixty miles away, there was a man breaking the law and getting away with it. One day soon, he would find out who Mike Magan was. Catching the Hollywood Bank Robber wouldn't be just Magan's goal, of course. The elusive, masked man would become the number one quarry of every investigator on the new task force.

27

When the task force started up in the spring of 1995, they saw that Hollywood hadn't been seen in Seattle during the last half of 1994—not after the Queen Anne bank robbery in July. His pursuers wondered if he had retired. But they knew that was wishful thinking. He had gone underground before, and no one on the new Violent Crimes Task Force believed that he was gone for good.

And, of course, he was not. Scott Scurlock had spent the summer and most of the fall of 1994 traveling. His last two bank jobs had netted him well over a hundred thousand dollars apiece, and his expenses had been minimal—cash for two cars in California, a car rented for Steve Meyers for the Queen Anne bank robbery, some makeup, and the almost miserly $5,000 he had given Steve after each robbery. Whatever they then made gambling was just the frosting on the cake.

There were good reasons for Scott to lay low—beyond the fact that his yen to travel was calling to him. He was infamous now, and he'd seen his picture (in full makeup) in the newspapers several times. He acknowledged that he had lost the advantage he once had as a fledgling bank robber. He was *Hollywood* now. Part of him must have enjoyed his notoriety, even as he realized that he would have to plan even more carefully than he had before. But being anonymous wasn't nearly as important as being an expert was. And he *was* an expert now. Scott had continued to study banks and bank security, and there wasn't much he didn't know about where the big money—and the danger—were.

From the very beginning, he had been careful never to purchase the theatrical makeup himself. He had bought it through the mail, using the address of a friend in Olympia who knew nothing about the bank robberies. His friend wasn't sure what it was that Scott picked up at his house, and he asked no questions. He did tell Scott that he was never, ever, to have guns or ammunition sent to his house, and the packages from Los Angeles were too light to be guns.

Scott had even created a hidden makeup room in the big barn where he applied his disguises. Unless someone knew it was there, he was sure they would never find it.

So many of Scott Scurlock's friends suspected that he was up to no good, but few guessed what he was actually involved in. Probably no one—beyond Steve, Mark Biggins, Bobby Gray and Kevin—knew about the bank jobs. Unless you had been befriended and groomed by Scott, it was almost impossible to understand what loyalty he evoked. He made each person in his circle feel so special, as if he had never had a friend he admired more.

No one was caught up in Scott's friendly web more

than Steve Meyers. His life continued to be one of upheaval and change. His live-in girlfriend, Sari, was hired by United Airlines and that meant she had to go to Chicago for training only three months after she and Steve moved to Sonoma. Before she left, the couple drove a truck up to Scott's place and dropped off most of Steve's possessions. He was still living a peripatetic life where he *had* no real home, other than Scott's house and treehouse in Olympia. In truth, Steve had never had a permanent home—not even when he was a little boy back in Kansas and Texas.

There was little time now for him to sculpt or paint, since planning bank robberies and laundering money wasn't conducive to artistic excellence. Sometimes, Steve let himself think about the way things really were. All Scott had to do was crook his little finger and he expected Steve to come running. He no longer deluded himself into believing that Scott needed him as a friend. Scott didn't need him until he was out of money and it was time . . . again.

It still galled Scott to think of the fat zero they'd scored in the aborted bank robbery in Portland, Oregon, in June of 1994. They'd run home to Olympia with their tails between their legs, and he wanted badly to erase that humiliating memory. Five months later—shortly after Thanksgiving—Scott had told Steve that they were going to hit Portland again.

Scott figured the Ford Aerostar would be good for one more robbery—but not in Seattle. It was described on wanted bulletins there. Scott would drive it to Portland, and Steve would drive his car. Scott thought that the Ford minivan would probably have to be left behind; like an old horse, it had served its purpose.

They hit the U.S. Bank, the Woodstock branch, in Portland on December 20, 1994. Although this trip to Oregon was more successful than the one in June, it was not a complete triumph. They didn't get much money—not by Scott's standards. Scott didn't get into the vault, and when he left the bank, somebody followed him out and got the license plate number. It wasn't registered to Scott, but it would soon be broadcast over police channels. Scott had to jettison the Aerostar sooner than he'd planned, and he left it behind an apartment complex in Portland. They drove home in Steve's car.

Scott was in a lousy mood, frustrated and angry. A 200 mile round trip was a long way to go to get only $22,000, hardly enough for Christmas shopping—not to mention the stake he needed to carry him over the next six months or so. He gave Steve ten percent of the take.

Steve found himself trying to cheer Scott up and he stayed on with Scott in Olympia. On weekends, he flew to Reno to launder the Portland money. He spent New Year's Eve, 1994 at Scott's place.

With the New Year, they began planning the next bank robbery. Scott seemed to brighten up with the new challenge. He, of course, knew nothing about the impending mobilization of the Violent Crimes Task Force. He was confident that things could only get better in his career as a bank robber. If he'd been able to score big when he knew a lot less than he knew now, he should be able to steal a virtual fortune.

Pointing to a map of Seattle, he showed Steve his top pick for a January hit: the First Interstate Bank in Wallingford.

He liked the Wallingford District because he'd never robbed a bank in that area before. It was due west of the University of Washington. Although Wallingford had once been a fairly stodgy neighborhood, it had undergone a resurgence and had become fashionably funky in the nineties. Scott chose it because he liked the fact that it had a thriving commercial area with popular restaurants and shops as well as streets lined with old houses.

Scott took Steve out to eat at an Italian restaurant and, as they lingered over Chianti and biscotti, they watched the First Interstate Bank. There was something exhilarating about planning a new project, something not unlike the thrill they both felt when they walked into a Nevada casino. Like all gamblers, they didn't think of losing; they thought only of winning big.

They made two or three trips to Wallingford to check out their new robbing grounds. And it either didn't bother Scott, or he didn't know, that the north precinct of the Seattle Police Department was located in Wallingford.

If he succeeded in his next robbery, Hollywood would be stealing the cheese from directly beneath the rat's nose. Perhaps that made the game even more challenging.

Scott had two mechanics in Olympia—unknown even to Steve—buy the station wagon and Chevy Astrovan that they would use in Wallingford.

Everything was set. Scott was anxious to erase the

memory of the last trip to Portland and eager to get a new cache of money that would allow him to travel away from the Northwest during the rainy season. He appreciated the rain, however, on Wednesday morning, January 18, 1995; pelting rain, drenching rain— it was all perfect bank-robbing weather.

By this time, Scott Scurlock approached a bank robbery almost as an athlete would prepare for competition. He had to be *up,* in top form mentally and physically. He always popped a tape into the deck of his van, something that energized him as he headed north on I-5 in his now-familiar makeup. Not surprisingly, he preferred the soundtracks from action movies. Even someone who knew him well could never recognize him behind the translucent salmon mask, with the beaked nose and jutting chin. He had truly mastered the ritual of putting on his makeup, and enjoyed the long process of becoming Hollywood. A whole new persona emerged during the drive from the treehouse to whichever bank he had selected, an invincible man who could make crowds cower and do whatever he asked of them.

A little before 10:30 A.M. on this Wednesday morning, Scott parked the station wagon on Densmore, the street next to the west entrance of the Wallingford bank. Now that he had had time to think about it, he was no longer upset that he'd been seen near the Queen Anne Bank six months before; it was good, really, for witnesses to see the vehicle he drove up in since he would be switching cars later. Then the cops would be looking for the wrong vehicle.

It was 10:40 when the woman teller in the Wallingford bank looked up to see that a man waving a gun had taken over the bank. He pushed a customer toward others who had been herded into the center of the bank.

As she felt prickles of shock, he turned the gun on the teller, and she looked at him, this strange unhuman figure whose face was not really a face at all. He asked first for "hundreds and fifties."

Even in the midst of her fear, she thought what a wonderful, deep voice he had. Later, she would describe it "like a radio disc jockey's. A classic voice."

She took large bills out of the drawer and placed them carefully on the counter. "I want twenties, tens, and fives, too," he said, scooping them into a blue nylon bag. "I want all your money."

Now the robber saw that there was a dye pack in his bag, and for the first time he seemed nervous. "Will the dye pack set off an alarm?" he asked.

"No," she answered.

"Nobody pulls an alarm or I'll shoot," he said roughly, his voice even deeper. "Who's the vault teller?"

The other bank employees pointed to the teller he was already talking to, and she told him she had to get her key. He grabbed her arm and walked her toward the vault.

Earlier, he'd ordered another teller to get off the phone, and she had appeared to respond. But, instead, she only set the phone down on her desk. As soon as he turned his back, she picked the phone up and whispered, "We're being robbed. Call 911."

He didn't hear her.

He stood at the vault, ready to make a substantial withdrawal for the first time in many months. But he didn't get that far; the teller and a customer service rep heard a disembodied voice coming from his coat pocket, a voice shouting in panic, "You're out of there! You're out of there!"

It was, or course, Steve—who had just picked up the Seattle 911 operator dispatching police units to the bank.

The tellers realized now that the robber carried some kind of radio or walkie-talkie. In an instant, he was gone, carrying his blue bag with the dye pack *and,* unknown to him, a pack of bait bills.

A number of things had already gone wrong, although Scott Scurlock didn't know about all of them. He hadn't seen the teller on the phone, nor had he seen a customer who slipped out of the bank. That customer had warned another woman not to come in, and *she* had hurried to a clinic and called 911. She had also observed a man rush out the side door, turn left and jog south. She would describe him as: "a white male, wearing a tan coat and a brown hat."

The description wasn't much help—but it was a piece of a mosaic that would, hopefully, be filled in by more witness statements. The FBI team's procedure was always very thorough; soon, they would talk to *everyone* who had the slightest bit of information about this bank robbery.

The jogging man had disappeared down Densmore Street. There, a woman sat with her son in a parked car. She looked up and saw the running man and watched him for several seconds. She saw him head to an old, yellow station wagon. Just as he neared the driver's door, he swung his arm wide and flung a bag on the ground *away* from his vehicle. Almost instantly, a red cloud enveloped the bag—but not the man. He jumped behind the steering wheel and drove off.

All of the money Scott had just stolen—$11,924—was in the abandoned bag. It would have done him no good, anyway—it was stained with bright orange, indelible dye. His luck, such as it was, was still holding. If he had been holding the bag when it exploded, his skin, hair, clothing and car would be colored with the stuff that no amount of scrubbing would remove—not for days.

Steve Meyers had already headed south. His police scanner picked up a police dispatcher who was describing the station wagon Scott was driving. Things weren't going well at all; Steve wondered if he would ever see Scott again. This was the worst situation they had ever been in. He headed for their prearranged meeting place, south of Seattle, not really expecting Scott to be there. There was nothing else for Steve to do, and he tried not to panic.

A mile away, Scott was anxious to dump the yellow station wagon; he had never planned to drive it back to Olympia, anyway—and, now, he knew he had been seen. In one searing moment, his eyes had met the eyes of the woman waiting in the car. He had noted the recognition in those eyes—not of *him,* personally—but they must have known that he had just robbed a bank. As brief as the encounter was, it seemed to take hours, and she had had plenty of time to get his license number. As he headed south on Stoneway, he wondered if the yellow vehicle bore telltale streaks of orange. Why did it have to be *yellow?* The dye wouldn't have shown up so much on a dark car.

He still wore his makeup. He didn't dare risk stopping to wipe it off. He was grateful for the rain that rolled down his windshield and the driver's window.

Against all odds, Scott made it back to where he had parked his van. He leapt from the Chevy wagon and into the van. Once the exchange was made, he felt better, although his heartbeat sounded in his ears. He had the rag to wipe his makeup off—but he still didn't use it. If he *was* stopped, it would be all over. And that would be ironic—to be captured after a bank robbery where he got no money at all.

Nobody stopped him. Scott caught up with Steve Meyers on Highway 99 South, the road that paralleled the I-5 Freeway. There, finally, Scott took the time to peel off his chin, nose, the clear mask, the wig and moustache. With trembling hands, he wiped a rag over the spirit gum that still marked his face.

And then it was OK. He was Scott Scurlock again, driving a different car than the bank robber had, wearing his own face again. He was so confident that he wouldn't be recognized, in fact, that he and Steve Meyers stopped at a restaurant near the SeaTac International Airport. As they ate lunch, they talked in low voices. Scott told Steve about getting the dye pack. "This was the first time I *ever* grabbed a dye pack," he said incredulously.

They didn't know how much Scott had had in the blue bag. He knew he had never gotten near the vault money, but he was unaware that he'd risked so much for only $11,000. All he knew for sure was that, for the second time, they had nothing. And this wasn't Portland, Oregon; this was Seattle, where he knew the streets, the banks, the demographics. If anything, Scott had planned the Wallingford job more meticulously than any robbery yet.

His beginner's luck seemed to have worn off completely.

Scott had been clever to dump the wagon as soon as he could, even though he still had his mask and makeup on. Several witnesses *had* memorized the license plate number of the 1981 Chevy Malibu. FBI Special Agent Don Glasser ran the Washington plate through the Department of Motor Vehicles. Glasser and Special Agent Dawn Ringer visited the address in Tacoma that the department's computers had spit out.

The homeowner there nodded and said he had once owned a yellow Chevrolet wagon. However, he had sold it two months before by placing an ad in the free *Auto Trade* magazine. Anyone in western Washington could pick up a copy in stores and supermarkets.

Glasser asked who had bought the station wagon, not really hoping for much helpful information. Nor did he get it.

The seller shrugged. "A man phoned, and then he came to our house on foot—after dark. He was white, very polite, good grammar. He said he wanted a car to haul things in. He gave me $800 cash. He took the car and the title with him."

The seller couldn't describe the man any more than that. The car? Just a six-cylinder Chevy with automatic transmission, air conditioning, and a tape player. It had once been brown, but he'd painted it yellow.

Obviously, the new owner had not bothered to change the title. He had had good reason *not* to put his name and address in the state computer bank. Who he was or where he lived was anybody's guess.

Scott had never been worried that authorities would find any evidence inside the Chevy Malibu that would lead back to him. He and Steve had wiped it down with care, not once but several times. There was nothing there at all—he was confident about that. He was right. The FBI found it, processed it, and gleaned absolutely nothing of evidentiary value.

28

While Scott was evaluating the failed takeover of the Wallingford Bank, more than a thousand miles away in California, Mark Biggins and Traci Marsh were getting ready to move to a house in Oxnard. For Mark, it was almost as if the two bank robberies in Washington State in 1992 had never happened. Nearly three years had gone by and no one in their new world knew the truth. Traci and Mark hadn't seen Scott Scurlock at all during most of 1993 and not once in 1994.

Traci continued to care for disabled patients and Mark worked at various low-paying jobs. Sometimes he sold squid that would become calamari in upscale restaurants; sometimes he worked in a leather clothing factory. The money he'd buried after the Olympia robbery near Christmas of 1992 was gone, but his relationship with his daughter, Lori, was wonderful and that was all that was really important to him. He, Traci, and Annie continued to share parenting, although they lived in separate homes.

There was a downside to Mark's life, however. Mark and Traci had never broken the addiction to methamphetamines, an addiction begun during Scott's treehouse work parties. It was an expensive habit in two ways: it cost money they didn't have, and it gave them false energy and flawed their reasoning.

Mark still wrote poetry, and he still dreamed of better days. He wasn't using his college education. He seemed to have lost the drive that he had once had. He couldn't seem to find a job teaching. Maybe he didn't try.

On soft nights, he played his guitar, gazing out into the dark. It reminded him of his favorite painting: Vincent Van Gogh's "The Starry Night."

Mark Biggins was the most likable guy anyone could hope to meet; he still had his strong compassion for others, and he was the last person in the world that anyone might peg as a criminal, much less a bank robber. But he was a melancholy and indecisive man who abused substances that took the edge off the feelings of depression that threatened to destroy him.

Up in Seattle, at the end of January 1995, Scott Scurlock was worried. Once the buried money from his last big robberies was gone, he was edgy and anxious. His lifestyle depended on his being able to travel whenever he wanted. Now, he lived only for adventure, physical challenge, instant gratification, and—as strange as it may sound—his friends.

In his own mind, it is likely that Scott still viewed himself as the benevolent leader of his own particular pack, the man who was always there when his friends needed him. He apparently had no feelings of guilt about his secret life.

"No one ever robs a *bank*," he once said. "He only robs an *insurance company*." And Scott insisted that everyone knew insurance companies were fat cats, well able to lose a little of the cream off the top of their profits. He told Kevin that he didn't see anything morally wrong with robbing a bank.

"But you put yourself in a category by how you use your energy," Kevin had countered, wondering if Scott was going to come right out and admit the truth. "When someone pulls out a gun and shoves it in someone's face, he becomes a bully. I don't honor bullies. If I ever saw anyone robbing a bank, I would make a split decision. In fact, I've already made up my mind. I'd tackle the son of a bitch. If he kills me, I get killed. I don't go out for no reason—and I saved the day."

Scott was silent, his face unreadable. "Of course," Kevin laughed, trying to lighten the moment, "I suppose I could say, 'Pardon me sir, can I help you carry all that money to the car?'"

Scott forced a grin, and changed the subject.

The fact was Scott Scurlock was out of money. There were no more hidden stashes to dig up and send to Vegas with Steve. Only nine days after the debacle of the Wallingford First Interstate Bank, Scott was ready to move again. Not only was he stone cold broke, he could not stand the ignominy of losing his proceeds in a cloud of orange smoke. He had to hit again, and quickly.

All Scott needed was just one solid robbery and he could lay off for months—maybe even for a year. He knew now that many factors influenced the success of any one mission. He could not control people outside his line of sight. For every fifty people who were frightened into submission by the rattlesnake-scary sound when he chambered a round of ammunition, there might be one who would make a run for it—or for him. Somebody like Kevin who had to be a damn hero.

This time, Scott planned even more carefully. The makeup was fine; he was sure no one could identify him. The vehicle switching was working. They needed only, perhaps, to stakeout the target bank a little longer.

Scott had selected the Seafirst Bank in Madison Park. Again. Third time had been the charm for the Hawthorne Hills Bank, and, although he would never admit it, Scott was superstitious. The Madison Park area attracted Seattle's young movers and shakers. It had popular bars and restaurants, but more than that, it was close to one of the most upscale residential areas in Seattle. Some estates were gated, and there were dozens of magnificent homes fronting along quiet tree-lined streets with magnificent views of Lake Washington from back terraces and decks. There was money in Madison Park. You could almost smell it in the air.

He had been there twice before, and neither time

had ended in a memorable yield, but Scott had a feeling. The time he selected was his favorite—late in the day on a Friday: Friday, January 27, 1995.

Scott Scurlock and Steve Meyers had barely paused for breath after the abortive robbery on January 18. They watched the bank in Madison Park on several different days. They knew when the busy times were, who the tellers were, and, basically, who the customers were. Again, they had three vehicles. Steve never saw one of them—a small Japanese-made car—because Scott drove it up to Seattle and left it within a few blocks of the bank. He planned to park his Astrovan near it, and drive the little car to the bank just *before* the robbery.

On Friday, with everything ready, they retraced their route. This time, Scott was in his old-man makeup. Steve parked to the east of the bank near some tennis courts, empty now in the dark cold of January. Indeed, it had been dark for almost two hours when Scott parked the small car in an alley behind the bank.

Even though it had been two and a half years since Scott had first robbed this bank, the operations manager recognized him the minute he strode through the back door. It was Hollywood in full regalia, and he entered, shouting, "This is a robbery!" He pulled a handgun from his jacket and raised his arm in the air so that everyone could see it.

This bank had beefed up its security after the first two robberies; now the tellers were locked behind a bullet-proof enclosure. Hollywood demanded that they open the door, and one of them did.

Moving fluidly and efficiently, he scooped money from the tellers' drawers into the bag he carried.

"Where's the vault teller?"

The operations manager and the branch manager, both women, stepped forward. One had the key; the other the combination.

"You don't want me to hurt anyone in the bank," Scott said, "and I won't have to—as long as everyone cooperates with me."

The woman with the combination in her head fumbled slightly, and spun the lock around to begin again. He was impatient with her. "Get it open, and hurry," he said coldly. "I don't want to hurt either one of you. . . . If you're not able to get it open . . ."

The door to the vault finally swung wide, and Scott pushed both women into the vault in front of him. He was watching both of them closely while they led him to where the money was.

He took it all, so much cash that he had to stuff it forcibly into the bag he carried.

"Now," he said, "all of you! Wait twenty seconds before you activate the alarm. If you do it early, I'll know." He pointed to something clipped on his belt.

He was gone. Out the back door.

This time, Scott and Steve had decided *not* to race away from the bank. They would wait—as pedestrians—in the neighborhood. What better place to hide than close to the cops? It was a rainy Friday night, with all the rush-hour drivers heading home to the suburbs. Rather than risk being caught in the inevitable traffic jams, they would stay put.

Steve knew that Scott was safely out of the bank; he

had radioed him that everything was fine. Steve locked his car and walked down Madison to the restaurant where they planned to meet. Scott abandoned the little foreign car and switched to his Astrovan. He stashed the bag with the money, and deftly removed his mask and makeup.

It was Steve's idea that they wait in the area. For an hour and a half, while sirens screeched and wailed outside and police traffic filled the streets around them, they managed to appear to be only casual diners. Then they split up as they left the cafe—Steve walking across the street to buy a bottle of wine, and Scott heading up the hill on Madison. When Steve got back to his car, he radioed Scott—but he got no answer. He hoped that Scott had only turned his radio off.

Steve Meyers arrived back in Olympia an hour before Scott did. Experience had taught him not to panic, yet when Scott finally came driving up, he felt the tension go out of his body.

In the damp coolness of the cavernous barn, they began their tally of this latest bank robbery. They started to grin as they gazed at the stacks of bills. It sure looked as if their luck had finally changed.

It had, indeed. Scott Scurlock had carried $252,466 away from the Madison Park branch of the Seafirst Bank.

Steve had had more invested in this robbery than any before; the police bulletins now reported that there were *two* individuals involved in Hollywood's robberies. Steve had explained to Scott that, since he was in more jeopardy now, he needed to get at least ten percent of the take, not just $5,000.

FBI agents located the Japanese-made car that Scott had abandoned. Indeed, they had spotted it even while Scott and Steve ate a few blocks away. Shawn Johnson did not really expect to find much of evidentiary value and he was right. Every surface has been wiped clean of even a partial fingerprint. The car was pristine and it was as anonymous as a vehicle could be.

Still, Shawn felt the ghost—the *shade*—of the faceless man who had been in this car only ten minutes before. The odor of perspiration—faint, but detectable—was still there. For an instant, Johnson felt a presence and tried to lock onto it. But then it was gone—gone like Hollywood was gone. Who was he? Why was he doing what he was doing? Someday, somehow, Shawn Johnson hoped to ask him all those questions.

Within days of the January 27 robbery, Steve Meyers left for Reno with a large chunk of the bank loot. He stayed at the Hilton and watched the Super Bowl on a big screen TV. It was a great time to be gambling; everyone was betting on the game. He laundered money for Scott, and he put $10,000 of his own down and won $22,000 more. It was as if he couldn't lose. Scott and his Swiss banker showed up in Reno, too. Among them, they were able to move a good deal of the bank take through the casinos and pick it up clean.

Steve's girlfriend, Sari, finished her training in Chicago, and her request to be based out of San Francisco was granted. So Steve Meyers packed up his things and drove a rental truck down I-5 back to northern California. This time, he didn't stay; he only dropped off the furniture and appliances Sari needed. Scott had told Steve he wanted him to move to New Orleans.

While Steve would recall that Scott had become more and more dependent upon him, it was actually Scott who was making all the major decision in Steve's life. If Scott scheduled a bank robbery, Steve had to be there—no matter what other plans he might have had. All Scott had to do was pick up the phone. Steve had never planned to live in New Orleans; his girlfriend had finally returned to San Francisco, and that was where he *wanted* to be—but if Scott wanted him in New Orleans, that was where Steve would be.

Scott had been to New Orleans once for the Jazz Fest and had been intrigued by the city. *He* didn't want to move from his idyllic spot in Olympia—but he liked the idea of having a kind of outpost in New Orleans.

Steve drove his car to New Orleans and arrived just before Mardi Gras. He stayed at a bed and breakfast while he looked for an apartment. Despite the events of the last year in Seattle, he still thought of himself as a man whose life's work was that of an artist. New Orleans was humid, sultry, full of flash and dazzle, but saturated with history. The cemeteries were replete with statuary marking the above-ground graves of the city's dead, buried high to escape flood waters.

Steve Meyers thought New Orleans might be a place where a sculptor could thrive. And something in him must have ached for an end to his constant travels.

Steve found an apartment in the Lower Garden District. He paid $620 a month in rent and began to look for property where, once more, he could set up a studio. It took him three months to find what he wanted. Steve paid $95,000 cash for a home in late April 1995. He wouldn't lose this house the way he lost his Virginia rental or his Chicago studio. This house was his. The money came from Steve's personal bank account—not Scott's—every cent he had saved from his bank robbery proceeds, his gambling winnings, and the few thousand dollars he'd received for his artwork.

Back in Seattle, Mike Magan had come aboard the Violent Crimes Task Force. Shawn Johnson, the BRA (the Bank Robbery Agent) was the principal special agent working the Hollywood case. Everyone on the task force knew about Hollywood now. He had crept insidiously up the list of their most-wanted felons in Seattle. But he had disappeared once again. They assumed he didn't need money for a while since his last robbery had netted him a good quarter of a million dollars in cash.

None of the task force members were going to find much satisfaction in the spring of 1995. There were bank robberies all right, and all manner of other violent crimes, but the bank robberies were "ordinary," if such a thing could be. They were the kind where guys walked in and handed tellers a clumsy note. They were not take-over robberies like Hollywood's. The task force worked some difficult cases and some not so difficult, they caught the bad guys, closed the cases. And waited.

All during the summer of 1995, through the autumn, the Puget Sound Violent Crimes Task Force investigators waited to hear word of another Hollywood bank hit. But none came. They didn't allow themselves to be lulled into a false sense of security. Somewhere out there, circling, planning, there was a man who was picking his spots. Sometime, on some rainy evening at the end of a week, he was going to surface again. If they were very lucky, he might just hit at the bank where one of them was watching, slumped down in a car behind a tree or sitting on a bench reading a newspaper and "waiting" for a bus. With just the right synchronicity, they would have him.

Shawn Johnson read over all the reports, all the witness statements from each bank that Hollywood had hit. He saw that the slippery robber was smart—and inordinately lucky. There were times when he had come closer to being caught than even *he* realized. "On one occasion," Johnson said, "there was someone in the bank who had a loaded gun pointed at Hollywood—but the man decided not to use it for fear of endangering the other people there. And Hollywood never knew."

Judging from the amount of money taken in each robbery, it seemed to him that Hollywood's standard of living and/or his pattern of spending required approximately $20,000 a month. Johnson also felt that it had to be more than just the money that drove this particular bank robber. "I thought that, over time, he had become addicted to the adrenaline rush that came with the act of robbing," Johnson recalled. "He was learning a lot as he went along—starting from the first robbery where he and his accomplice actually depended on a stolen car for their getaway. That was what an amateur might do, but he wasn't an amateur any longer."

Shawn Johnson added up figures, trying to establish Hollywood's budget. "Going on the assumption that Hollywood was spending $20,000 a month, and deducting that sum for each of the months after his last robbery on January 24, 1995," he said, "I picked three dates when I believed he was going to hit again. One of them was January 25, 1996."

29

Throughout 1995, Scott Scurlock was traveling, and shedding parts of his life. The Swiss banker, who endured her nickname of Swiss Cheese, was really named Sandra. Scott's friends noticed that she was no longer in residence in Olympia, nor did she commute from Europe to see him. She had left her home, her family, and her country to be with Scott. But he had often disappeared for a day or two—or more— without even telling her where he was going. Without Scott there, the night shadows crept in on her. She was lonely and frightened, especially because she couldn't speak English well. She felt terribly isolated on the treehouse property and she was desperately homesick. Her relationship with Scott had finally come to a point where it either had to move forward or end, and it ended. Perhaps they had shared too much shady history for a lasting love to survive, but he grew tired of her. One day Sandra was there; the next, she was gone.

If Scott experienced pure friendship with any woman, it was with Ellen. Ellen was lovely to look at and innately good, and when Scott was frightened, he turned to her. She didn't know what it was that was haunting him, although she was smart enough to perceive that he had to be involved in something on the dark side of the law. He never seemed to work, and he always had enough money to do whatever he wanted. But, like Marge Violette before her, Ellen could not picture Scott doing anything beyond fraud or drugs. She knew from Kevin that Scott had occasional outbursts of anger. But violence? No. If Scott was involved in something violent, Ellen was sure she would know. When she asked Kevin what was going on, he always just changed the subject.

Ellen was a listener and not a judge. Despite her thick taffy-colored hair and large blue eyes, she seemed unaware of how attractive she was. She was not drawn to Scott in a sexual way; she saw, instead, a troubled soul. She would have liked to see him with a woman who loved him, but he had told her many times that he could never be with the kind of woman he most admired.

"It's one of the sadnesses of my life that I have to deny myself the company of women I *really* want. I have to have 'ditzy' girls," Scott told Ellen. "I can't be with a woman who is going to size things up and start asking me questions. I can't afford that luxury."

She looked at him without comprehension.

"Ellen, you *know* that I have to have dumb women," he said again, "—women who won't question me or want to be too involved."

"Why?" Ellen asked for the twentieth time. "What is it that you're hiding?"

"You don't want to know."

She didn't—not really. When she didn't know, it was easier to see him as just *Scott.*

By 1995, no one close to Scott wanted to come out and ask him a direct question. They all feared the truth. Again, Scott gave his parents a large gift of money. When his father asked where the money came from, he had responded, "You don't want to know."

Instead, Scott had muttered something about starting a Geoduck harvesting business in Washington, and investing in construction back east. Geoducks are immense clams that dot Northwest beaches. They can dig down faster than most humans can follow. They are much sought-after, and commercial ventures in the Olympia area use hydraulic suction pumps to pull them from the floor of the sea. Had Scott actually invested in Geoducks, he might eventually have made more than he had stolen.

Whatever Scott told the Reverend William Scurlock probably would not have mattered. His father seemed to look upon Scott as a golden child who was beyond reproach. His whole family had adored Scotty from the moment he was born and, in their eyes, he could do no wrong. They certainly would not pursue answers to questions that would mar the image they had of him.

In May 1995, Scott headed down to New Orleans again for the Jazz Fest. There he met friends who lived on the East Coast and they all stayed in the Lower Garden District for a week. Scott Scurlock had a wonderful time wherever he was. His whole life was a vacation; if he became satiated or bored, he simply moved on.

He traveled once more to New Orleans during the summer of 1995. There was a flood while Scott was there, and he sat in a bar one afternoon, lifting his eyebrow quizzically in an expression that was familiar to his friends, watching water roll through the door and rise to the first rung of his stool. He only grinned and took off his shoes and socks.

Everyone left the bar except the bartender and Scott, and a slender woman with flyaway blond hair. She was thin and delicate looking, an almost plain woman with glasses and a pageboy haircut that lay flat against her skull. Even without makeup, her features were quite perfect.

Outside the sky turned black and the water continued to rise. The woman was so attracted to Scott that she scarcely cared that the muddy water had risen up to their knees as they clung to bar stools. She laughed and took off her shoes too. She and Scott talked for hours as the water rose higher.

Her name was Sabrina, and she told him she was from Phoenix and that she worked in a jewelry store there. Sabrina Adams* must have felt as if she had stepped into the pages of a romance novel. Scott

Scurlock was incredibly handsome, and the only sounds she heard were the gentle slosh of floodwaters that rose around them, and his soft, deep voice. They talked and drank and Sabrina fell in love.

She wasn't a gorgeous woman; she had a certain rabbity quality that kept her from that—but she was appealing in a small-boned, dependent way. And she had enough guts to ride out the flood with a stranger. Scott was quite taken with her; he saw that she trusted him absolutely and that she also had a careless—almost hedonistic—air about her. She was enjoying this adventure as much as he was. He invited her to come to the Seychelles Islands with him, and she said yes without hesitating.

Afterwards, when Scott told his friends about meeting Sabrina, he sometimes described encountering her one way, and sometimes another. Once he went into great detail about how he had met her "in a jewelry store in Phoenix." He said he had gone in to case the store for a planned robbery, but, instead he had stayed to talk to Sabrina and become entranced with her. His friends could believe Scott as a jewel thief or cat burglar. He probably was imagining himself right into Cary Grant.

However it happened, meeting Scott was the most romantic thing that had ever happened to Sabrina. After their trip to the Seychelles, she became his new woman—not his new love—but his new woman. So many women had moved through Scott's life, and yet he hadn't been able to hold on to any of them. He might have said that was the way he wanted it; he let go deliberately before any of them could hurt him.

Sabrina had clearly fallen totally in love with Scott

the first night she met him. At first she and Scott enjoyed a temporary monogamy of sorts. They posed for pictures with their arms around one another, their bodies almost one. They cuddled together up in the treehouse, watching videos, listening to music, smoking pot. Sabrina kept the rooms there and in the gray house spotless, she cooked what Scott liked, and hung on his every word.

Probably because he was by this time constitutionally unable to be totally honest with any woman, Sabrina never really grasped what it was that Scott wanted. But she did her best to decipher his mixed signals and tried to interpret them. She believed he actually *liked* the Greeners, the hippies and the latter-day flower children, who had crept back onto Scott's land while he was away, because they appreciated nature and trees just like Scott did. She even tried to emulate the ragtag visitors. She let her hair grow long and never wore makeup. She even stopped shaving her body hair.

Kevin and Ellen visited in the summer of 1995 and felt a little sorry for Sabrina. She didn't know yet that Scott was certain to grow bored with her and send her away. Even though he didn't say it aloud, Sabrina obviously thought he was as much in love as she was.

"He liked having her there all right," Kevin recalled. "He told me that she was the best housekeeper he ever had—that's all. But then he said he wanted to get rid of her—but he'd miss having her clean."

Sabrina had no idea that Scott spoke that way about her. It was possible that he *did* love her, but that he had cultivated his cavalier attitude toward women for so long that he could never admit to tender feelings about Sabrina. How he *really* felt about Sabrina was anybody's guess.

Sometimes, Scott asked her how much she would give up for him. It was either a head game or a test of her love: *Would she give up everything? Her family? Her identity? Her life in America? Would she simply disappear with him—for years, if need be?*

For him? Of course, she would. *Anything.*

More often now, Scott spoke of leaving everything behind and disappearing. If he went away, Sabrina knew she would have to follow him. She could not bear the thought of being without him.

Was the bank robbing over? Had Scott Scurlock proved to his own satisfaction that he was the best?

Down in New Orleans, Steve Meyers was finally getting established in his own place, and he was beginning to focus again on his art. Kevin drew his first deep breath about his brother in a long time. Maybe it *was* over.

30

It was far from over.

Scott Scurlock did a lot of traveling in mid-1995, and he spent the rest of the time home in Olympia. But he knew that even the big haul he'd carried away from the Madison Park Seafirst Bank wouldn't last forever—not considering his lifestyle. It was only a matter of time until the white plastic pails he'd buried would be empty.

His friends had heard him muse about what the life of a cat burglar who stole jewelry might be like. Maybe he was thinking of changing specialties. Perhaps he was only teasing Sabrina. Any reasonable man who had survived fourteen bank robberies without being caught would have to wonder if he had pushed the law of averages too far. And Scott had had some close calls. It would have been tempting to look for the kind of robbery where he didn't have to confront dozens of people.

Was he tempted to give up stealing completely? Probably not. Weighing who Scott Scurlock was, how far he had come along the path to amoral behavior, it's unlikely that he could have gone back. And back to *what?* The only real jobs he'd ever had in his life were the landscaping work in Hawaii and his short stint as a building inspector in Reston. He had never gotten his college degree. He was forty years old. How was he going to explain all those years of no visible employment to a future employer?

Too late. His tastes were much too opulent for him to accept the kind of job he was qualified for—barring a career as an actor. He had the looks, the charisma, the voice, and how he would have loved it. But he had never tried; he was another kind of Hollywood now.

Scott was having a strange summer. He was smoking too much marijuana and drinking too much. One moonless night as he walked along the path to the treehouse, he saw something just ahead of him. It wasn't human; it wasn't anything he could explain. The thing had red, glowing eyes that stared at him.

He was utterly terrified. He blinked once, twice, three times—and finally the thing on the path disappeared. It had either run away or vaporized. He ran to the treehouse and clambered frantically upward. He called Ellen and babbled to her that he was frightened. Would she come down?

Kevin was away, painting—and Sabrina was in Arizona. Scott, who had never been a solitary man, needed company now more than ever. Ellen drove to Olympia and listened as Scott talked all night. He didn't sleep until the first pale strands of dawn pierced the black lace of the cedar trees.

Scott was fine when he woke up. He didn't want to talk about the red-eyed creature any longer. He thanked Ellen for being his "friend, therapist, listener, advisor," and she smiled faintly. Yes, she listened and she gave him advice, but she knew that, in the end, he always did exactly what he wanted to do.

When Ellen mentioned Scott's strange encounter to Kevin, he nodded as if he was not surprised. Twenty years earlier, in another lifetime for all of them, Scott had been frightened by something similar. Kevin had always believed that Scott's luck would carry him through *anything,* and yet he had watched him move along "a dark path." Now, Scott had quite literally walked along a night-shrouded path and encountered something that sounded demonical.

Scott had always been superstitious and afraid of unseen or unexplainable things. As much as he loved movies, there were a few extremely popular films that he avoided. One was *Ghost,* starring the same actor who had played Bodie in *Point Break:* Patrick Swayze. However, in *Ghost,* Swayze played a murder victim who came back to help his fiancée escape the man who had killed him. One scene in *Ghost* involves the villain's death and his screams as black, amorphous, creatures carry him to hell. When that scene came on, Scott turned pale and left the room. He refused to watch the movie ever again.

Kevin was almost relieved that Scott was finally frightened. Now, maybe he was scared enough that he would walk away from what could only end in disaster for everyone.

One night, when Scott was so intoxicated that he could barely walk, he and Kevin went for a run. Scott had always been able to keep going—out of sheer will, if need be. Kevin understood that. He was the same way himself. Now, Scott fell again and again, and Kevin urged him to stop and just sleep it off. He was horrified when he looked at Scott's knuckles and saw that, when he'd fallen, the gravel and sharp stones had cut them so deeply that the bone beneath was visible. Whatever Scott was running from, it had to be more than the alcohol that clouded his thinking, and worse than the pain in his hands.

As they jogged together through the starry night, they talked—their voices bursting forth in panting sentences—but Scott still didn't tell Kevin exactly what he was involved in. He did say something that chilled Kevin's blood. Scott boasted that he had donated $50,000 to Amnesty International.

Amnesty International? Why not, "Save the Trees," or "Save the Whales"—all those causes to protect the environment that Scott had always been so passionate about? Kevin wondered if Scott was even telling him the truth. If he had, indeed, given that much money to amnesty, Kevin couldn't help wondering if it was insurance against his own future.

As they ran, Scott confided less to Kevin. He never mentioned seeing the creature with red eyes. Maybe that was why he wouldn't allow himself to go to sleep drunk. Was he afraid that the thing he had come to fear most would creep into his dreams? The pain in his bleeding hands had to be excruciating, but Scott kept running. They ran for seventeen miles; it took that long for Scott's head to clear. It was daylight when they came back to the treehouse. There was nothing there to be afraid of. It still looked like every boy's dream fort in the woods.

Kevin knew that Steve was having nightmares too, although he wouldn't elaborate about the images that came to him. But Steve always slept with his late sister Dana's blanket as a talisman against danger.

Finally, Steve admitted to Kevin that he had a recurring dream where his legs were cut off. He would look down to see that he couldn't walk and would awake in a cold sweat. Odd. Steve needed his *arms* to create his art, his hands to shape marble and wood into the images in his head, but in his dreams it was his legs that were severed. Maybe he wanted to run away from what his life had become—but he couldn't.

Despite the terrifying creature that stalked him after the sun had set, Scott went ahead with his next project. He planned to be flawless at his craft, at his *crimes.* He watched every movie he could find that involved robbing banks. He watched the daily television news and he scoured the papers. When he pinpointed some mistake that ended in a bank robber's arrest—or death—he committed it to memory. He believed that he had been blessed with uncommon good luck, but he continued to refine his game plan. He renewed his focus on bank security. He had decided one thing; he didn't want to go into the banks by himself anymore. There was just too much going on for one man to handle, even with Steve on the outside. Scott had also decided to move into larger banks; that would make a partner essential.

Scott had struck out with Bobby Gray and Kevin Meyers; neither one of them wanted anything to do with his latest "projects." And he was already using Steve as the outside man.

Now, Scott knew who he needed. *Mark.* Mark had been with him on his first bank robbery, and he was trainable. He hadn't seen Mark Biggins for two years, but he knew just where to find him; he would be close to his daughter Lori.

Mark hadn't heard from anyone in Washington for a long time. Part of him hoped that it would stay that way; another part strained against the poverty that had dogged him since he'd come to California. It was November 1995, when Scott showed up unexpectedly at Mark and Traci's house in Oxnard. He said he'd been traveling, and had even stopped in to see his ex-wife. He was the same old Scott, and Mark couldn't help being glad to see him. Scott brought energy and laughter and the possibility that life could only get better. He stayed a few days and they caught up on what was going on in each other's lives. Almost casually, Scott said, "I'm *working* again."

"Oh?"

"Yeah, with Steve."

Scott told Mark that he and Steve had planned to rob a bank in Chicago. They'd even gone back there to chose which one. But then some husband and wife bank robbers started making headlines all over the place and the heat was on in Chicago. Steve and Scott had dropped their plan for the windy city.

Scott said he wanted to give Mark a plane ticket to come up to Washington. Mark tensed. He knew what Scott was building up to. He had almost been home free; he had another life now. But he had no money, and he could barely meet his bills. He wondered if Scott could read it in his face.

Mark Biggins flew to Seattle in late November or early December of 1995, and something crucial died in Mark on that trip. There was no bank robbery at that time, but he and Scott did a lot of talking, and Mark obliged Scott by buying an older model station wagon that had been advertised in *The Seattle Times*.

Although he was home for Christmas, he knew he would go back. In January, Mark caught another plane to Washington. This time, Steve Meyers was there, too. Steve wasn't anxious to continue robbing banks; he told Mark he had a feeling that they were close to being caught. There had been some dicey situations already. Nevertheless, Steve said he was in on the next job.

Scott had decided to rob either the Seafirst Bank in the Wedgwood area on Thirty-fifth NE or the First

Interstate Bank, which was close by. He had never robbed either bank before, but he'd robbed a bank two blocks away in January—two years earlier. He had robbed a First Interstate before and gotten almost $112,000, and he had hit *six* Seafirst banks. One of the target banks in the Wedgwood neighborhood was good-sized—the Seafirst Bank—but Scott didn't want to attempt it unless he had someone who would go inside with him.

That someone would be Mark Biggins. Scott, Mark, and Steve made several trips to Thirty-fifth NE to observe the two banks. They not only watched from the outside, they mingled with the customers inside. After they had done their surveillance, they would retire to a pool hall or a restaurant in Seattle to discuss their strategy. They agreed that Mark would be crowd control, and Steve would continue to be electronics, on the outside.

Scott said that the robbery would come down on Thursday, January 25—almost exactly a year after his last job on January 27, 1995. But he explained to his accomplices that he wouldn't decide *which* of the banks he would hit until they got there. This made Mark and Steve more nervous than ever.

Nevertheless, with Mark and Scott in full makeup, they headed for Seattle on that Thursday morning, arriving around eleven. Scott and Mark were in Scott's white van and Steve drove a blue Mazda that he had rented in Portland. They had parked an unobtrusive beige 1984 Chevrolet station wagon near the bank the day before.

They had agreed beforehand that if anyone saw an armored car near either bank, the code word would be

"Stagecoach." "The Seafirst Bank would be "Number 1" and the Interstate was dubbed "Number 2."

Steve dropped Mark and Scott off at the old Chevy wagon and they cruised the area, observing both banks. They spotted the armored car at the Seafirst bank; it was leaving—which meant that the big money was going with it. Scott picked up his Motorola and said, "The stagecoach is pulling out. We're going for Number Two."

They had picked one of Shawn Johnson's three unlucky days, the dates he had checked on his calendar, based on how fast Hollywood spent money. But Johnson was sitting on a stakeout at a bank two miles away from the First Interstate branch, a lone FBI agent with a hunch.

Mark Biggins carried a Smith and Wesson and a pistol with a fifteen-round magazine, Scott had his Glock, and they had also brought a rifle in a guitar case. That, Scott told them, was to shoot out the engine of any police car that might try to stop them. Although they had always carried weapons, no one had ever talked aloud about actually *firing* them at anyone. Mark, who had been away from this world for so long—felt sick to his stomach.

And, then, it began again. Inside the Interstate Bank, the head teller was assisting a customer when she caught a glimpse of a man in a theatrical mask out of the corner of her eye. She heard his voice; she would describe it later as an "an actor's voice." He held a black handgun and she saw that his finger was not on the trigger, but held straight above the trigger guard. That was only small comfort.

"Ma'am," he said, politely, as he pushed a male

customer out of his way, "this is a robbery. I want your fifties and hundreds."

He looked familiar—if a man in makeup and a mask *could* look familiar; she had seen the flyers describing Hollywood and she knew who this man was. He seemed to know exactly what he was doing as he moved to another teller.

She saw now that there was another man in disguise, a taller, bigger man, who was herding customers toward the center of the bank.

The first robber leapt effortlessly over the gate and into the tellers' area. He asked the first woman and the other tellers about specific security devices; he appeared to know so much about the inner workings of banks. He scooped money out of a teller's drawer, leaving the dye pack behind. He studied a wall of alarms that was usually hidden from customers' view, as if he knew what to look for. A phone shrilled. The bank was so quiet that it sounded like a siren.

"If that's the alarm company," he ordered, "tell them that there is nothing wrong."

"I'm sure it's just a customer," a teller answered. "Why don't we just let it ring?"

He seemed to consider that for a moment, and then he nodded. "Let it ring."

All during this time, customers were entering the bank unaware of the robbery—and the second masked man was directing them toward the center lounge area. Now, the first man—the smaller, slimmer man, asked for the vault teller.

A woman stepped forward and identified herself as the vault teller. He nodded. "OK, come with me and bring your keys."

In the vault, she bent over the lock, fumbling a little as so many women had before her when they were next to the man in the mask, her fingers leaden with fear.

"Don't fuck with me, lady," the robber hissed.

To her immense relief, the vault door finally swung open.

"Turn around and face the wall."

She complied, but she could see that he was taking stacks of money out and slipping them into a dark canvas bag. She could hear him muttering, half to himself, half to her, "Oh. Dye pack," he said softly. "I've had enough of *those* in my lifetime."

Did he *want* her to know how savvy he was about bank robbing? He seemed to. She recognized the sound when he opened a cardboard box that was in the vault. She knew there were dye packs inside. And so did the robber. He sounded annoyed as he said, "Oh, *more.* . . ."

She heard him place them on top of the vault.

Was he through? No, he turned to her once more, and said, "OK. Now open the ATM."

She lied to him, explaining that it was a very complicated procedure that involved several bank employees. She hoped that he didn't know as much about the ATM's workings as he obviously did about the bank itself.

They walked toward the ATM, and she felt her heart pounding. Suddenly, there was a squawking sound that sounded like the squelch button on a scanner. A strange, almost robotlike, sing-songy male voice said, "Five, four, three, two, one. End—you're out of there."

Both of the masked robbers instantly moved toward the west exit doors, but the man with the bag of money turned briefly and said, "Thank you, ladies! See you later!"

The moment they were out, she locked the doors behind them. She watched them cross the street and get in a small Chevrolet station wagon with a silver luggage rack.

One of the other tellers took down the license number: 645BPM. It had Washington plates.

So they had a beat-up old tan station wagon. Now, they also had $141,405.

A few miles away, as Shawn Johnson watched and waited, his radio crackled with the report that police units were responding to a bank robbery. *Damn!* He had almost tossed a coin between the First Interstate and the bank he'd picked, and he was frustrated that he had guessed wrong.

It wasn't only the bank robbers who felt the adrenaline rush. Shawn Johnson turned his car around and headed for the crime scene, but he was too late.

Mike Magan was already there. A retired naval officer was telling him about the masked man who had pushed him aside as he waited in a teller's line, and of how easily he had leapt over the gate to get to where the money was. "He was like a gazelle," the man marveled. "He went over that gate with no effort at all."

And the bank robbers had escaped clean. If there was one word that would sum up the task force's feeling about Hollywood, it was *frustration*. "I was so far behind this guy," Magan said. "And then I remembered my days as a defensive lineman. When a runner got too far ahead of you, you had to cut him off at an angle. That's what I had to do with Hollywood. I just wasn't sure how."

The license number wouldn't do the task force much good; Shawn Johnson traced the number to a Tacoma, Washington, address. The owner told the FBI agent that he had once owned the station wagon, but he had advertised it in *The Seattle Times* in November. A man named "Tim" had called him from a car phone. Two hours later, he showed up with another man in a gray Chevy Blazer. The driver had let "Tim" off and driven away. Tim had asked only to drive the station wagon around the block. Satisfied, he said he wanted it.

"He paid the $1,200 in cash," the former owner said. "All $100 bills. I wanted to go to the license office to change the title right away, but he said he could do it without me. Then I asked if we could do it the next day, and he said that was OK. But he didn't come back the next day."

"What did he look like?" Johnson asked.

The man shrugged. "White, maybe thirty to forty, six feet, 200 pounds, short hair—and a stubbly beard."

"What was he wearing?"

"Sports coat—gray, maybe. Button down shirt. Gloves—dirty yellow gloves."

"Can you remember anything else about him?"

"No, he was just a guy—an ordinary-looking guy."

Ordinary or not, Shawn Johnson had an FBI artist sketch the man as the car owner described it. He believed that the man might very well be one of Hollywood's accomplices.

Next, Johnson had the seller look at the recovered station wagon. "Is there anything different about it— since you sold it in November?" he asked.

The man walked around it, looked under the hood, and then he nodded. "Yep," he said. "It has four brand new tires. And the battery's new too."

Johnson traced the tires to a Les Schwab dealer in Tacoma. But no one remembered who had bought them. Nevertheless, it established another transaction involving Hollywood that was south of Seattle.

There was a silent war going on, a war between combatants who didn't even know each other. The Puget Sound Violent Crimes Task Force knew in their bones that Hollywood was planning his next bank job. Although $141,000 was a big bundle of cash, it was not nearly as much as Hollywood had gotten in January a year earlier. They doubted that he would wait a whole year before he hit again.

The investigators tabulated every bank robbery that they had attributed to Hollywood. They noted the date, time, day of the week, bank location, amount stolen, and whether he had brought an accomplice into the bank. They added notations on whether a vehicle was recovered, whether a dye pack or marked bills were taken, and counted how many days passed between robberies. They knew every disguise he'd ever worn down to his shoes: they had dozens of surveillance photographs.

Every human being on earth has certain behavioral patterns, most unconscious. Hollywood was no differ-

ent. If something worked, he repeated it. If it didn't,
he dropped it. And, all the while, he was creating a
profile that allowed his trackers to get a narrower fix
on him.

This they had come to know about the man known
as Hollywood:

- He was white, five feet ten inches to six feet
  tall, of medium to slender build.
- He spoke as an educated man would, and he
  had a deep voice.
- He had thick dark hair, covered always by a
  reddish blond wig that was streaked with
  gray.
- He was probably between thirty-five and forty-
  five years old, although he moved like a much
  younger man.
- He worked with at least one "outside" accomplice. Twice, he had used an "inside" accomplice.
- He probably had several vehicles available to
  him, all of them prosaic, common makes that
  would not draw attention.
- He probably lived south of Seattle.
- He preferred to hit banks at the end of the
  week during the late morning, noon, or late
  afternoon hours.
- He had never robbed a bank during March,
  April, or May. He had hit the most in January—four times.
- The shortest time between robberies was eight
  days; the longest 370 days.
- He "cased" the banks he was going to hit
  beforehand.

They might have added that Hollywood was smart
as hell, as cunning as a fox, and slippery as an eel. He

seemed to rob banks not only when he needed money, but when he needed an adrenaline rush. He also appeared to know what *might* happen before it actually did and prepared himself for any eventuality.

Shawn Johnson thought of a father-son team who had run rampant through banks back in Wisconsin. They had been the same way; there wasn't a trick in the book of bank security that they hadn't anticipated, and they'd been almost impossible to catch. Hollywood was another take-over robber made of the same cloth. He wasn't going to be easy; he clearly enjoyed the game too much.

Shawn had sat behind the wheel of the cars they had recovered and tried to *think* like the man who had sat there before him. Surely, someone who had been revved up by the excitement and fear that had to come with the act of robbing a bank at gunpoint must have left some essence of himself behind. But he came up with nothing beyond his own sense of frustration.

The task force members took a map of Seattle and put flags in the spots where the target banks were. The flags clustered in the northeast sector, but then there were a few scattered miles away. However, there were none at all in the south end of Seattle. Did he hit the north end because his friends, business connections, and home base were all south?

Mike Magan wanted to *catch* Hollywood so much he found himself thinking about him day and night. He wanted the satisfaction of putting handcuffs on him and leading him out of a bank—some bank, *somewhere*.

Mike's concern was that Hollywood would escalate

the violence that had to be just beneath the surface of his take-charge attitude. He had always shown a powerful handgun to his victims, and now he'd added a Taser. Witnesses of the later robberies had described Hollywood as impatient and easily annoyed. Worse, he had actually racked the cartridge into firing position. All it would take was a change of position of his trigger finger and someone could die.

"What he was capable of doing," Magan said, "was far more important to me than who he was. I didn't want to see anyone die."

Shawn Johnson certainly wanted to catch Hollywood too—but his obsession was on finding out *why* Hollywood robbed banks. From what Shawn could tell, he didn't fit the profile of most bank robbers who robbed to get money to buy heroin or cocaine. From experience, Shawn knew that most bank robbers spent only about thirty seconds to a minute inside the bank—but Hollywood was almost leisurely in comparison; he was usually inside for three, four—even five minutes. He had to have somebody outside who could alert him when a silent alarm went off.

Shawn wanted to know what drove the man, what Hollywood's learning curve had been. He was no garden variety bank robber. Shawn longed for the day he could sit across an interview table from Hollywood, unmasked, and ask the questions that burned in his mind.

When he was assigned to the task force, Shawn Johnson had posted a print that symbolized a Kwakiutl Indian legend over his desk. It was called "The Owl and the Wolf":

The two most revered hunting creatures among Northwest Coast Native Americans are the Wolf and the Killer Whale, neither of which were hunted for food. A person who acquired Spirit Power from the Wolf would become a very adept hunter. Native Americans tell of several incidents where wolves were seen herding game towards a hunter with exceptionally strong spirit alliance to Wolf. Owl is a supernatural being of the forest able to sense the proximity of game and watch over a hunt to insure its success.

Shawn knew intuitively that it was going to take almost "a spirit alliance to Wolf" to beat Hollywood at his own game.

31

On the evening of January 25, 1996, Mark Biggins, using an alias to buy his ticket, boarded a Greyhound bus headed for Eugene, Oregon. He would stay there overnight and catch a train for California the next day. Although he didn't know it, he was a patsy; he'd believed Scott when he said the take from the Wedgwood Interstate Bank was around $68,000. Mark had no idea it was more than twice that much. Scott gave him some of "his share," and promised him more after the money was laundered in Las Vegas.

Once again, Mark had proved to be a less than adept accomplice. During the robbery on January 25, Scott had yelled at him because he wasn't standing near the doors as instructed. Of them all, Scott was the only one who seemed to come alive during the actual bank invasions; Steve had a modicum of safety because his only connection to what was going on inside was the radio, but Mark had been immobilized with fear—just as he had been the first time.

Steve didn't know the true amount of the take either. He thought it was about $120,000. Scott gave him his "ten percent"—$12,000. Although Steve still trusted Scott, he was annoyed that he had brought Mark Biggins back into the picture. Steve liked Mark well enough—but he didn't trust Traci Marsh. He knew Mark would tell Traci everything about what had happened in Seattle, and that could be dangerous to them. The fewer people who knew, the better. And Steve feared that telling Traci was akin to telling a dozen people.

After the First Interstate robbery, Steve drove to Portland, returned the rental Mazda van, and caught a plane for Las Vegas. Scott and Sabrina had already flown out of SeaTac International Airport. By nightfall, Scott and his two accomplices had all left the state of Washington. Steve met up with Scott and Sabrina at the Sands Hotel.

Steve and Scott talked about when they should schedule the next bank robbery. Scott wanted to do it in May, and he wanted to hit another First Interstate. There seemed to be no breathing space. With one down, another popped up. Now, all three of their lives—Scott's, Mark's, Steve's—revolved around the next project, the next bank robbery. In between, they had enough money to live exactly as they liked—but none of them had any real freedom any longer.

For the moment, though, the three partners scattered. Steve went back to his house in New Orleans, and his mother came to spend Mardi Gras with him in February. Mark went back to Oxnard, Traci, and Lori. And Scott and Sabrina went again to the Seychelles Islands.

The Puget Sound Violent Crimes Task Force took no vacations. Whether looking for a bank robber or a serial killer, there are basically only two approaches for detectives to take: reactive and proactive. So far, the task force had *reacted,* responding to the Hollywood bank robberies and gathering every morsel of information they could. But after fifteen robberies, evidence and information gathering techniques had produced so little. They had the bank cameras' pictures of Hollywood—but even his own mother wouldn't have recognized him from those. They had no fingerprints; he always wore gloves. They had no car identifications since he clearly used drop cars.

Mike Magan was a *proactive* detective. His natural energy didn't allow him to sit and wait for the next time Hollywood hit. The January 1996 robbery had shown him that Hollywood's aggressiveness had been upped several notches; there were two men now and two more guns. His hunger for cash was becoming insatiable, too.

One of the other special agents on the task force,

Don Glasser, a onetime standout football player from Utah and an ex–Navy Seal, had watched the escalation of Hollywood's activities carefully, and he too was worried. Glasser had served on the FBI's Hostage Rescue Team and on the security staff for the FBI's Director, and he sensed an impending disaster. Glasser told Mike Magan, "This could be a Miami in the making," referring to a deadly shoot-out on April 11, 1986, in Florida where two FBI agents—Ben Grogan and Jerry Dove—had been killed, and five others badly injured because they had underestimated the dangerousness of two particularly brutal bank robbers: Michael Platt and William Matix. The four-minute encounter has been called "the deadliest firefight in the history of the FBI." Platt and Matix would no longer rob banks; they died in the gun battle too. Don Glasser warned Mike, "You need to be careful. This guy is deadly."

Even though he had never actually fired the Glock handgun he used to threaten bank personnel, no member of the task force discounted Hollywood's potential for opening fire on anyone who came after him. Nor did Seattle Police Chief Norm Stamper, who told reporters, "God help anyone who points at one of my officers."

Magan went to Bob Gebo, a longtime Seattle homicide detective who is particularly skilled in profiling unknown felons. Magan grinned, "All it cost me was a cup of coffee—and I got some of the best advice I could hope for."

Magan pored over every report and follow-up that he could find about Hollywood, and he asked Gebo what it all meant. As he listened, he nodded his head.

Gebo was verifying everything that Mike believed to be true about the elusive bank robber, "He's white," Bob Gebo theorized. "He's about forty. He's well disciplined—he's a man who invests in himself—his physical condition, how his actions will affect him. His cars are so clean that they've probably been through the car wash thirty times, and he's willing to abandon them if he has to. You say he's left a couple of them behind, already?"

Magan nodded, and the Seattle Police profiling expert continued.

"He's been doing surveillance on the banks; he knows where the vaults are, he knows employees' names, the key personnel, and about the alarms."

Bob Gebo continued. "He takes complete command. He starts out with a firm voice, but he escalates his demands if anyone balks or delays—and then he intimidates them."

"Bob," Magan said, with some hesitation. "I think he may be a cop."

Gebo didn't blink. "What makes you think so?"

"The way he positions his trigger finger—he indexes it on the barrel the way we're trained. He knows when the shifts change, and he hits around then when cops are at Roll Call. He knows that Union and Charlie sectors are the busiest we have, and he hits there. He knows how to set his lookout's scanners to police frequency." Magan paused. "He's a cop or a true professional."

"So what you're saying is that, if you corner this guy, he just puts on a cop coat and blends in?"

"He could," Mike nodded. "I think he has a van stashed someplace. I showed the bank pictures to my mother—she teaches drama—and she says he'd need time to put on that carefully sculpted makeup that he uses—probably forty-five minutes to an hour at least. Some of the tellers said it looked real enough to be a bad plastic surgeon's job. But my mom said that he could remove it all quickly with the right solvent. He could do that in a van."

Picturing Hollywood as a cop was an awful supposition. If Hollywood was one of them, then they were going to have to keep their strategy within a relatively small group so that they wouldn't alert him to their plans.

"You're not just looking for one guy," Gebo said. "You have to realize that you're looking for at least three—maybe four. And they're going to be armed with heavy artillery. They're going to have an advantage over you. What are you prepared to do?"

"I guess I need to have the SWAT team," Magan said.

"I'd bring them on board immediately."

When Scott returned to Washington State, he was gearing up to strike again. Steve had been summoned from New Orleans and Mark was on his way up from Oxnard, California. Although Mark spent a few days in Olympia, Scott sent him home; he and Steve had decided on a bank that didn't need crowd control: the First Interstate on East Madison.

Scott and Steve used the same fool-proof MO they had successfully employed so many times before. The decoy station wagon was in place, and Steve circled the bank with his scanner on while Scott went in. As he watched and waited, his radio crackled with the news of a major fire with dozens of police units responding. How fortunate for Scott. He couldn't have known about the fire that would draw police patrols away from the bank just as he robbed it. It was almost as if some arcane force was giving him a hand.

Hollywood waltzed out of the bank with his duffel bag full of $114,978. He had been pleasant enough as he said to people who stood anxiously in the center of the bank, "Stay there in the middle. Don't push any alarms. Don't watch me leave, and I won't be back to bother you. If you do, I will have to come back and hurt you."

Bother was an ambiguous word, that usually sounded fairly innocuous—but coming from a bank robber with a gun in his hand, it was enough to keep everyone rooted to the spot.

Steve and Scott were on the freeway headed south within fifteen minutes. What Steve didn't know was that Scott had actually driven back through the area of the bank he'd just robbed. He was in a different vehicle, of course, his own Astrovan, and he had his makeup off. But something in him craved that danger-ous gesture of defiance. It had been such a rush to drive by police cars and think, *Watch me, you dumb cops. I'm right here and you don't even recognize me.*

Trained detectives would have recognized Holly-wood's need to raise the stakes in the game; they had seen serial killers take similar chances. Ted Bundy had taken *two* victims on one July day at a park where the Seattle police were having their annual picnic. When the excitement factor dipped, criminals addicted to a certain high deliberately dared police to catch them. And, if they got away with it, it was only a matter of time before they upped the ante again.

On May 23, Shawn Johnson distributed a press release that might have pleased Scott Scurlock. It read:

> This robber has been nicknamed "Hollywood" because of the heavy costume makeup he wears to disguise his face. "Hollywood" has become the Seattle area's most sought-after bank robber, having now robbed 14 banks in the last four years. A $50,000 reward is being offered for information leading to the arrest and conviction of the robber. . . .

Mike Magan was successfully clearing more than eighty percent of the three dozen cases that had been assigned to him since he'd joined the task force, but it was Hollywood he was fixated on. Mike wasn't even officially assigned to Hollywood's case, but he didn't care; he had made up his mind to catch him.

In February 1996, FBI Supervisory Special Agent Ellen Glasser had replaced Mike Byrne as the head of the Puget Sound Violent Crimes Task Force. Ellen was Don Glasser's wife and half of an FBI special agent couple. Ellen Glasser was a petite woman and a mother of four—the very antithesis of the image most laymen have of an FBI agent. She was exceptionally good at her job, and had a great deal of field experience and a perceptive eye. Her forte was in administration and in placing the right people in the right assignments. She saw that Mike Magan was champing at the bit, so she turned him loose on the Hollywood case.

Magan wasn't alone. Everyone on the Puget Sound Violent Crimes Task Force had a personal theory on the best way to catch the elusive bank robber. By returning again and again to the same banks and/or the same neighborhoods, he was almost asking to be caught. Or he was thumbing his nose at them.

From the time they were in junior high school, when Mike Magan and his brother Jake had been faced with seemingly insoluble problems, they always told each other, "Don't think horizontally—think *vertically.*" It didn't make much sense—to anybody but the Magan brothers, but it meant they had to step back and look at a puzzle from a different angle. Sometimes, that worked. Often the solution was right there, but they had to look at it in a different way to see it.

Now, Mike stared at the photographs taken by all the bank cameras over the prior four years. He had them blown up and enhanced and looked again. The clothing Hollywood wore varied slightly, but the face was almost always the same.

"It was as though he was inside a glass ball," Magan recalled, "and I couldn't get in. There was something there that nobody had seen yet—and I was trying to find it."

Concentrating on the enhanced photographs, he could see that Hollywood carried a number of tools: a knife, a radio clipped to his belt (the way a lot of cops did), an ankle holster with what looked like a .22

caliber gun in it, the 9-mm Glock in his hand. Mike noted the somehow bowlegged stance of the man he sought. The gloves. Some of the witness statements suggested that the real color of his hair was black or dark brown. He looked like a caricature of a person, but that caricature had become a personality itself. Mike Magan began to see the man in the Converse All-Stars in his sleep. It was almost as if, if he could just concentrate hard enough, he could see it all.

He saw everything . . . but the face.

On May 23—a day after the last bank robbery— Magan returned to Madison Park. With the help of the Seattle Police Department's Community Police teams, he figuratively put a net over the area of the First Interstate Bank in Madison Park. It wasn't that he expected Hollywood and his accomplices to still be there; instead he hoped to find the people who were routinely in the area around noon on a weekday. People tend to forget those they see every day; they become the background in the painting of their worlds, becoming almost invisible.

"I was a delivery man myself in college," Mike recalled. "I drove the beer truck and people saw me and my truck without *really* seeing me. But throw a net over a section of blocks at 11 A.M. on a weekday morning, and you'll see who's trying to get in or out. Then you may find a witness who's seen someone suspicious."

The officers who fanned out over the Madison Park neighborhood talked to scores of people. "Were you here this time yesterday?" "Did you see anyone who looked peculiar to you?" "Did you see a man running?" "Did you see a man carrying a blue duffel bag?" "Did you know the bank across the street was robbed?"

Painstakingly, the officers jotted down bits and pieces of memories and observations. They handed out 800 flyers with Hollywood's picture and with a composite sketch and a description of a second man—the bigger man who had been seen twice. The flyers mentioned that, at one bank robbery, Hollywood had yelled at his accomplice to watch the doors—and he had called the second man "Mark."

One of Mike Magan's goals was to keep Hollywood away from Madison Park. He asked the media to cover Hollywood intensely. Between the nightly television news and the flyers, he doubted that Hollywood would have the guts to come back to the Madison area. But Magan did not delude himself into believing Hollywood would just go away. He would be back, and Mike guessed that he would probably surface again somewhere in the north end.

32

Steve Meyers saw one of the flyers about the Hollywood bank robbery. When he read about the $50,000 in reward money, his heartbeat faltered. He didn't know how many people—beyond Mark and Traci, Bobby Gray, and possibly his own brother,

Kevin—knew that Scott Scurlock was Hollywood. There were the guys Scott had paid to buy the expendable station wagons, but Steve had no idea who they were, or if they knew what Scott wanted with the wagons. There was the guy in Olympia who let Scott use his mailing address, and he didn't know much about him either. But $50,000 was a lot of money. All it would take would be one anonymous phone call.

Steve confronted Scott, and held out the flyer. "You never told me about this."

Scott shrugged, and lifted his hands, palms up. He didn't seem worried.

"You goofed. Somebody heard you call Mark by name."

"There are a lot of Marks in this world."

Steve wanted to walk away, but he felt "hooked." He was caught in the robberies too tightly to extricate himself now. If he couldn't get Scott to stop, sooner or later it was all going to come crashing down on them. Steve begged Scott to end it while they were still free and in one piece. Even so, Steve took the packets of money Scott gave him and flew home via Reno, where he exchanged the bank cash for casino money. He felt a little better when he was finally back in New Orleans.

Kevin Meyers *did* know about Scott and his brother. Most of the time, he tried not to think about it. But, in the summer of 1996, he became aware of the $50,000 reward money, and he even thought it might be a way for him to end the nightmare. If Scott and Steve went to jail, they wouldn't get hurt or killed, and, better, they wouldn't be able to hurt anyone else.

"But I couldn't do it," he remembered. "I couldn't turn in my friend, and I sure couldn't turn my brother in. I didn't want the money. That would be blood money. All I could do was try to convince them that what they were doing was wrong—that it was going to end with somebody dying."

Kevin's pleadings didn't make much of an impression on Scott. Like so many other things in his world, he had always pictured dying as it happened in the movies. Kevin remembered how Scott had watched *First Blood* over and over, fascinated with the way Sylvester Stallone's character was depicted. In the film, Stallone spoke graphically about how parts of his friend's body literally exploded in battle and how he had tried to put him together again. Of course, Stallone washed the blood off when the director yelled "Cut" and lived to be shot at again in movie after movie. Kevin wondered why Scott didn't realize that dying in movies wasn't like *real* dying.

But then, Scott didn't expect to be caught, or shot. He was beefing up his own arsenal to include powerful, metal-piercing automatic weapons. He was also studying up on new anti–bank robbery devices. He had heard that there were things beyond dye packs that could be hidden in stacks of money—various devices that could tie robbers to their crimes. He didn't know if such high-tech equipment really existed or if it was only something on the "X-Files" or in spy novels. It didn't worry him that much; it was only another challenge, part of the very sophisticated "chess game" that his entire life had become.

Now that he was *the* most sought after bank robber in Seattle, Scott assumed that the cops would bring out everything they had to stop him. It didn't matter; he wasn't about to quit, not until he carried out such a memorable bank robbery that nobody would ever forget it.

Sabrina still lived with Scott in the treehouse, although she made frequent trips to Arizona. She had learned never to ask questions about his activities, but she knew he was in danger. He had told her that someone might come after him, and that they would have to be ready. She didn't know that Scott had been talking about being ready for years—all she knew was that Scott was involved in a massive "experiment" and that it required a big cash investment. In the long edgy summer of 1996, Scott told her he was running a little low on money and asked her if she would get a cash advance on her credit cards for him.

She had good credit, and she had loaned Scott money before. He *always* paid her back twice what she had loaned him. This time, Sabrina was able to get over $30,000 for Scott. Borrowing that much was a little scary—she had never been in so much debt before—but it didn't matter; she loved Scott, and they had been together for more than a year now. She thought they would probably be together for as long as they lived. Her money was his money, and, anyway, she had every reason to trust that he would pay her back when his latest project came through for him.

Sometime in high summer, Scott traveled to see Steve Meyers in New Orleans. During the week that Scott stayed in Steve's home they discussed their future plans. Scott seemed to consider Steve's worry that they were running out of luck. Both of them had always played long odds and won—but they also knew that no one won forever.

Scott told Steve that there would be only one more bank robbery. Steve felt a tremendous sense of relief. But Scott held up his hand, "I meant, we're going to do one last *day* of bank robbing."

His plan was to hit three banks in one day. Bing. Bang. Boom. The cops would never expect that. While police cars were clustered around the first bank, Scott, Steve, and Mark would already be in the second. That would leave the police and the FBI reeling—and then they would be in and out of the third before the men and women on the task force ever put it all together.

Steve Meyers stared at Scott, wondering if he had lost his mind. *Three banks in one day?*

"It will be a big job," Scott continued smoothly. "We'll get at least a million—maybe two."

"I'd need twenty percent," Steve said, "for something that risky."

"No problem."

Scott explained that he was approaching this job with more preparation and study than ever before. It would be a three-man job. He had already consulted with technicians who might be able to help them circumvent any new security the banks might try to throw at them, and he had even figured out a way to lose police helicopters.

Steve asked about Mark. Mark had made mistakes in each of the bank jobs he had participated in so far. How did they know he wouldn't get nervous and mess up again? What if he got caught?

"If he's wounded—I wouldn't leave him behind," Scott said flatly. "I'd kill him, because he would talk."

"What about me?" Steve asked in a hushed voice.

"You wouldn't get caught. Nobody ever sees you."

"But what if I *did* get caught?"

Scott said nothing.

For all his calm exterior, Scott seemed to sense that everything was spinning out of control. Did they need two million dollars? Was it worth the risk? Was *anything* worth the kind of risk that Scott was suggesting?

Scott went ahead with his plans, brushing away any questions or objections. He called for a summit meeting in Olympia. Steve was there and so was Mark Biggins. Scott outlined the possible targets: the Seafirst Bank in the Roosevelt district; the Seafirst Bank in the Green Lake district; and the Seafirst Bank in Lake City.

They were all in the north end of Seattle—the first two in the *near* north end, and the latter near the city's northern border. They were all neighborhood banks.

Bing. Bang. Boom.

While Scott Scurlock was holding *his* summit meeting with his accomplices, there was a similar summit going on among the detectives who stalked him. Not only was he the main focus of the PSVCTF, he was also a special target all by himself for the Seattle Police Department. He had finally attained a kind of infamy not unlike the movie rogues he so admired.

Whether Scott saw the irony in the fact that he, who was obsessed with movies, was now dubbed Hollywood by lawmen is an interesting question. Most likely he himself didn't realize how skewed his thinking had become. Film and reality had merged in his thought processes, and he could no longer differentiate between what was real and what was fantasy.

On August 30, 1996, with the help of Sergeant Paul McDonagh of the Seattle Police Emergency Response Team (the SWAT team) Mike Magan prepared an official memorandum for the Seattle Police Department. It did not go out to the entire department; there was enough support among the brass for Mike Magan's theory that Hollywood might actually be a working cop that the information was disseminated in as confidential a way as possible. Not even the patrol units would know the extent of the proposed operation.

Those organizing the joint all-out effort were: Supervisory Special Agent Ellen Glasser, Special Agent Shawn Johnson, Sergeant Kevin Aratani, Detective Mike Magan (all from the task force); Lieutenant James Pryor, SPD Robbery Unit Commander, Sergeant T. C. Miller, SPD Robbery Supervisor; Lieutenant William Moffatt, SPD Special Patrol Unit Commander; Sergeant Tim Moellendorf and Sergeant Paul McDonagh, SPD SWAT Supervisors (all from the Seattle Police Department).

Because he had been so prolific and had already stolen $1,500,000, because he was thought to be a profound threat to both the public and to police officers, and because the "level of sophistication" he had attained was so impressive, everyone agreed that it was vital that Hollywood be taken off the streets and, especially, out of the banks.

The memorandum read (in part):

During the past four years, sixteen banks, 14 in Seattle, two in Portland, have been robbed by an individual or group of individuals. . . . Officers should be aware that "Hollywood" may wear any number of different disguises. . . . In the past, he has worn loose fitting clothing, which usually includes a brimmed hat, sunglasses, a sport or Gortex coat, dress pants and gloves. He is armed with a semi-automatic handgun which he displays early into the robbery. This weapon is carried in a shoulder holster. "Hollywood" also has an ear piece in his ear which is believed to be connected to a two-way radio. He—or his accomplice—may have access to a police scanner. The mask the robber uses appears to be made of plastic or a putty. The makeup is designed to create an extended chin and nose. The mask has a mustache. . . . the suspect is a W/M, 35–40, 5'10", 160–179 lbs. He appears to have some knowledge of bank security procedures such as alarms and dye packs . . . once inside a bank, he commands all occupants into an area where he can control them. He removes money from the teller drawers and the vault, spending considerable time inside the bank. "Hollywood" appears very athletic in his movements and has vaulted counters. Upon leaving the bank, it appears he may walk a block or more before entering his getaway vehicle. Officers should use caution as "Hollywood" may have one or more accomplices acting as lookouts. There is little information as to what kind of threat they may pose. . . . "Hollywood" is believed to use older model station wagons in the commission of the robberies and switch to vehicles with possible tinted windows. Two non-recovered vehicles of interest are: 1) 1980's Blue

Ford Aerostar, and 2) 1980's Gray Chevrolet Blazer.

Concept of Operation: The Seattle Police Department will assign members of the Special Patrol Unit, and when available, members of the FBI and SPD Robbery Unit to monitor area banks. These members will work within the city limits of Seattle in two to four unit teams. Upon notification of any bank robbery or robbery in progress, these units will respond and work with marked patrol units to increase the probability of suspect apprehension. All members of the Hollywood Detail will have police identification with them which will be visible during a response.

The last directive was desperately important. There would be so many lawmen responding to the next robbery that one of them could be mistaken for one of the bank robbers—unless they all wore blue "Police" raid jackets. If plainclothes officers raced to a suspected Hollywood robbery, they were instructed to have blue bubble lights, to put on raid jackets and plainly display their badges. Everyone expected there would be gunfire—and they sure didn't want any of the "good guys" shooting each other.

Suspects may possess large caliber weapons—including shotguns, hunting rifles, and military style rifles. These afford the suspect greater fields of fire, and superior penetration to a handgun. A rifle round will easily penetrate a patrol car door. Remember to stay behind cover whenever possible when confronting a possible suspect. . . .

Beginning in August 1996, task force members began staking out banks in the Madison Park and Northeast Seattle neighborhoods on the last three workdays of the week: Zone 1 (considered most likely) was the Wedgwood/Roosevelt area, Zone 2 (considered less likely) was Madison Park, and Zone 3 (considered least likely) was West Seattle.

On Wednesday, the stakeouts would be manned by the Puget Sound Violent Crimes Task Force members and Seattle Robbery Unit detectives. On Thursday, the Special Seattle Police Patrol (Tact Squad) would sit on the banks, and on Friday, it would be the FBI's Special Operations Group (SOG). *Someone* would be watching likely target banks between 9:30 in the morning and 1:00 P.M.

The memorandum warned that the men and women who were about to begin a six-month all-out campaign to trap Hollywood must *never* attempt an arrest without backup.

They would be out there rain or shine until February 1997—or until they caught Hollywood.

For hours, officers sat in their cars observing customers go in and out of a long list of neighborhood banks. Any cop who has ever participated in a stakeout will verify that they are not pleasant. In the winter, it's cold; in the summer, suffocatingly hot. Joints and muscles ache, and eyes blur from looking for something and seeing nothing. Cops get thirsty and hungry and their bladders come close to bursting.

Despite the best efforts of dozens of law-enforcement personnel throughout August and September 1996, the long stakeouts ended in disappointment. Nothing happened.

School started, maples and alders turned from green to gold, and stores put out their Halloween merchandise. As far as those on stakeouts could tell, the Hollywood gang wasn't even casing banks. They didn't see the vans they'd been told to watch for. That didn't mean much, however. Nobody could be sure what he was driving now.

Mike Magan's dad, Frank, was worried. He was an old cop himself and he understood how consumed Mike was with catching this bank robber. But he looked at his younger son and warned, "There'll be shots fired when you find him, Mike."

Magan tried to reassure his father; he had no intention of going after the guy by himself; the way they had it figured, there would be cops all over the place when they finally caught up with him.

"They're the best in the West, Dad," Mike said. "We've got the most highly trained SWAT team. They're highly motivated and they're always there for us."

Without telling his parents, Mike Magan began to train for a confrontation he believed was inevitable. Some day—or some night—he knew in his bones that he was going to face Hollywood eyeball to eyeball, and he planned to be ready. He spent more time at the firing range, focusing on MP5 submachine guns and AR15 rifles. He spent hours practicing pursuit driving and felony take-downs. He ran three nights a week; if he ever found himself in a chase with Hollywood—who was obviously a trained athlete— Mike didn't want to lose him because he was out of shape. He kept telling himself, *If Hollywood's as disciplined as Gebo says, then I'll have to be twice as disciplined.*

He went over possible situations and what his reaction should be so many times that his response would be automatic. "Every step Hollywood took," Mike recalled, "I would take two. If he went straight, I'd go diagonal. In a car chase, I'd find a way to cut him off. I knew that, one day, I was going to catch up with him."

Still a good Catholic boy, Mike prayed every day that he would catch Hollywood. He also prayed that no one would get hurt while he accomplished that.

Mike Magan's thirty-fourth birthday was on September 21, 1996—the first day of fall. He blew out all the candles on his cake and made a silent wish. On the way home, his wife Lisa looked at him and said, *"I know what you wished for."*

"What?"

"To catch Hollywood."

"How did you know?" he asked, surprised.

"I know *you.*"

She was a little frightened for him, although she never said so out loud. He had assured her dozens of times that, whatever happened, he would have plenty of backup.

The Puget Sound Violent Crimes Task Force was getting more help than they ever imagined. The men and women sitting on bank stakeouts began to recognize faces—those that belonged there, those that seemed strange or different—even if no one had yet spotted Hollywood.

The King County Police's air support unit, Guardian One, with Steve Kometz and Randy Shoutk aboard, worked with Mike Magan to improve communication among and between the units who would most likely respond to the scene of the next bank robbery. They would work off the Tact Squad's channels and a few others—and try to keep police communication scrambled before it reached Hollywood's scanner.

Mike contacted a ham radio genius known as "Rich the Glitch" and showed him a photo of Hollywood, pointing to the radio clipped to his belt. "You recognize that?" he asked. "How do I intercept the communication between Hollywood and the guy he's talking to on the outside?" he asked.

"They're probably on a UHF Itinerant Frequency," the Glitch said. "I'll hook up an antenna and a scanner in your car—you'll be able to hear them if you're in the area, too."

That, of course, would have been a dream come true. But, in reality, what Mike heard on the frequency was small talk; people on cordless phones discussing their ailments and symptoms, their boyfriends, their pets, their in-laws and recipes. Before long, he wished he'd never heard of that frequency.

The Wedgwood area was totally familiar to Magan; he'd grown up there and he'd worked there. Now, he made it a high priority to get to know the bank employees in the area. Some of them had already met Hollywood, and he was afraid that more of them would meet him in the future. He told them that he was always available if they had thoughts about who the elusive robber might be, or if they saw something that didn't seem quite right.

Something didn't seem quite right one day in one of the Wedgwood banks on NE Eighty-fifth and Thirty-fifth NE when Magan stopped in to talk to the employees. A candidate for All-Time Loser of the Year: (bank robbery category) came in. A woman robbed the bank while Mike was standing there, and as he chased her down the street, a dye pack exploded. He got a good look at her, and even though he lost her in some thick shrubbery and a cloud of dye, she was stained bright red. She was arrested soon afterward and charged with two bank robberies.

It wouldn't be long before the autumn rains started—Hollywood's favorite weather for bank robberies—and everyone on the task force began to brace for the next robbery. Things had been too quiet for too long, and it made them all hinky.

Whenever Mike Magan ran out of ideas, he went to more experienced lawmen for advice. His boss, a former task force supervisor, Ed Striedinger, was a great source of knowledge, as was Agent Don Glasser. Mike asked Glasser about his experience with other serial bank robbers, and he recalled a man the FBI had dubbed "The Shootist." His MO was to enter a bank and fire a round into the ceiling—which not only got everybody's attention but scared them all witless. The Shootist was colorful, but he made mistakes. He always drove an easily recognizable perfectly restored vintage red Alfa Romeo. At some point, he realized that he and his Alfa Romeo weren't suited for surveillance, but he apparently couldn't bring himself to give the car up—so, Glasser recalled, he switched to observing banks at night. Still, he never came close to stealing as much money as Hollywood had. The Shootist was not a detail man, and that made him a third-rate bank robber.

Glasser's comments about The Shootist's nighttime robberies gave Mike Magan an idea. Maybe Hollywood wasn't doing daytime surveillance at all; maybe he prowled after dark.

"Every Friday night," Mike remembered, "my partner, Sheila Bond, and I checked out the banks on the list. We looked in the windows after they were closed to see what someone could find out from *outside*. We discovered that often *we* could see the camera locations, the alarms, where people sat, and where they went in and out. If we could see it—so could Hollywood. That meant he didn't have to risk being seen during the day."

Mike went several steps further; he climbed up on bank roofs in the wee hours of the morning to see what he could tell from up there, fully expecting he might set off a bank alarm. He was always careful to wear his jacket with "POLICE" on the back.

"I made noise—no response. I shouted—no response. When I got back to my car, I revved the engine—no response," he said. "That told me that anyone wanting to hang around a bank at night would have free rein. Nobody in the neighborhoods called 911 or came out to see what was happening.

"One night at 2 A.M., I dragged a couple of guys with me—and probably annoyed the neighbors," Mike recalled. "We aimed our headlights in different directions, looking at the reflections of lights in the bank windows. Looking for angles, clear shots of what you could see behind the teller counters, the alarm positions. *What* was *he* seeing? Maybe I even had a glimmer of hope that we'd see a suspicious car—*his* car—parked close." They never did. One night, Mike drove to all the banks that had been robbed—all fourteen. "Why was he hitting them? I began to look at manpower allocation, possible escape routes. And, again and again, I kept asking myself: *What are we missing?*"

Sheila Bond was a former New York Police Department officer—but she had switched to the DEA, and she represented that agency when she joined the violent crimes task force in the spring of 1996. She came on initially as a tough-talking, no-nonsense officer with an East Coast accent. She was all of those things, but she was also one of the best partners Mike Magan would ever have. Like everyone else on the task force, she had an opinion of who Hollywood was. Mike thought he was a cop; Sheila thought he was probably ex-military.

"No, Sheila," Mike argued with her. "If he was ex-military, he'd have a 9-mm Beretta. And you can see in the bank photos that he's carrying a Glock. *We* all carry Glocks."

Like Shawn Johnson and the rest of the task force, Mike and Sheila were well aware that they were looking for a very special criminal. "Ninety-five percent of the people we arrest are dopers," Magan said. "The other five percent are thrill seekers, gamblers, professionals, or people who act out of sheer desperation. Hollywood was in that minute one percent of professionals. He kept reinvesting in *himself,* buying cars, making sure those cars were up to snuff with new tires and batteries, full gas tanks, oil changes. They were clean as a hound's tooth when we found them. He bought the clothing he liked—those trademark Converse shoes. He had good weaponry and expensive Motorola radios."

Sheila Bond and Mike Magan were only required to work stakeouts one day a week, but they decided that they would sit on all the banks they could, whether they were scheduled to or not. They even discovered a few banks hidden away in quiet spots that weren't *on* the lists of "most likely to appeal to Hollywood and Company."

Mike noticed that certain banks tended to close their blinds during the day when the sun hit the windows. That would effectively render whatever might be happening inside invisible from the street; a bank robber could be confident that he wouldn't be observed. Magan had established such a close liaison with *his* banks that all he had to do was call them and say, *"Open your blinds!"*

Eventually, the bank employees in his stakeout sector were so convinced of the importance of open blinds that Mike told detectives to call him if they *ever* saw a bank with its blinds closed. That would mean trouble inside.

Although no one had so much as glimpsed Hollywood since May, there were other criminals out there, plenty of them. And they got caught, too. The surveillance teams caught a number of bank robbers, including two men who had accosted a bank manager at home and forced him to drive to his bank. Kevin Aratani and Mike Magan tracked them down and arrested them in Bellevue, a suburb on the other side of Seattle's floating bridges.

But these bank robbers had nothing whatsoever to do with Hollywood.

Just in case Hollywood *was* a rogue cop, the specifics of the massive dragnet and surveillance schedule were still a secret to most Seattle police officers. Magan didn't even tell his longtime bike patrol partner, Chris Gough, what was going on. Chris called him one day and said, "There's an FBI stakeout in the neighborhood. You guys are just coming out of the woodwork everywhere!"

Indeed, they were—at least in North Seattle, West Seattle, and in Madison Park. Feeling somewhat disloyal to his old partner, Mike told Chris that the FBI was there because some neighborhood kids had been robbed.

Kids were one of the things that worried the task force the most. Many of the banks in the target area were located near schools, and they dreaded the thought of a gun battle near one, particularly since Hollywood had often favored the noon hour, a time when a lot of children would be walking home for lunch.

On Friday, November 22, there was a robbery at the Wells Fargo Bank's Laurelhurst branch. A lone robber had come in wearing a ski mask and a fake beard. He'd robbed both the tellers and the vault. He had gotten away with $40,000. It didn't sound like Hollywood's disguise, and $40,000 was small potatoes for him. Detectives had followed the Wells Fargo robber—and lost him as he turned corner after corner and then disappeared.

Still, Mike Magan wondered. Could the Wells Fargo bank robber have been Hollywood—but a Hollywood—who, for his own reasons, was varying his pattern? The bank was definitely in the northeast section of Seattle where Hollywood had struck so many times before. On a hunch, Magan drove the route that the robber had taken from the bank. If the guy was heading for the freeways, he took such a circuitous route to get there that Mike figured he had to be from out of town.

If the man in the ski mask had been Hollywood, Magan's retracing of his getaway route validated something he felt instinctually; he had never believed that Hollywood lived in the north end of Seattle. For that matter, he suspected he didn't even live in Seattle at all. Mike and Shawn Johnson both felt that he lived south, or that he had connections there. He had bought his throwaway cars in Kent, Tacoma, Auburn—all south of Seattle.

Both of them realized that they were only guessing. And it was more difficult than counting the number of pennies in a gallon jar.

The "Hollywood Detail" was in its fourth month of surveillance in November without one sighting of the man they wanted. If interest flagged, nobody would blame them. Mike Magan was afraid that enthusiasm to catch Hollywood was going to dissipate as the fall wore on. Maybe *he* knew they were waiting for him and he was getting the last laugh, again. "Even the merchants recognized us," Mike laughed. "And we recognized them. That wasn't all bad. That meant that we were sure going to spot any strangers who showed up."

But nobody lost interest. Besides Shawn Johnson and Mike Magan—the two task force members who probably wanted Hollywood the most—everyone involved was in it for the long haul. But they all knew it couldn't run at this pitch forever. The law of diminishing returns was bound to factor in. It had happened with the Green River Killer Task Force; when they failed to find the serial killer in two years, taxpayers grumbled and financial support collapsed, leaving the probe terribly understaffed.

Ellen Glasser talked to Magan in late November. "We may have to taper down . . . or go to the media again, Mike."

He begged her for more time at full throttle. "Just a few more weeks," Magan asked. "Hollywood loves it when it rains. And it's raining."

He pointed out that they'd had lots of luck with other cases because of the surveillance teams. He reminded her about the Wells Fargo bank robbery in Laurelhurst—right in Hollywood territory on November 22. Even though the MO and the description didn't fit, that surely made it a good argument to keep the teams active.

"Hollywood could be gone, Mike," Ellen Glasser pointed out. "He could be on the other side of the country. He could even be dead."

Magan knew that. But he argued that Hollywood had laid low for more than a year before. And he had always popped up again. He had hit *twice* before in November.

Finally, Ellen agreed to give the detail some more time at full strength.

Two days later, all hell broke loose.

33

In 1996, Thanksgiving Day fell on November 28. By the twenty-seventh, people all over Seattle were in a holiday mood, getting ready for a feast and a four-day weekend. Ellen Glasser called off the usual Wednesday-Thursday-Friday surveillance. It had been raining so hard and so steadily that even someone directly across the street from a bank wouldn't be able to see what was going on. After four solid months of stakeouts, everyone craved—and deserved—a couple of days off.

Kevin Meyers was in Virginia spending the Thanksgiving holidays with his mother while Ellen was near Seattle with her daughters, getting ready to cook the holiday meal. Marge Violette Mullins was in Missouri, trying to keep her three sons out of *her* way while she made pies for the next day. Sabrina Adams was in Arizona, but she planned to catch a flight to SeaTac International Airport on Thanksgiving Eve so she could be with Scott for the holiday. He had promised he would pick her up on Wednesday evening, the twenty-seventh. Steve Meyers was in Washington State, and Mark Biggins had made a quick trip up—although he planned to be home in plenty of time to have Thanksgiving dinner with Traci and Lori.

Both Steve and Mark were relieved that Scott had dropped the plans to do a three robberies in one day. Something had changed his mind.

Everyone seemed to be taking time off—cops and robbers alike. Except for homicide detectives, who know all too well that a certain percentage of families cannot deal with much holiday togetherness without violence, and state patrolmen who have to cope with the fatal highway accidents that proliferate after holiday parties, most law-enforcement officers can expect a spate of calm over Thanksgiving and Christmas. Shawn Johnson left the Puget Sound Violent Crimes Task Force offices a little before 5:30 on that Wednesday afternoon, and headed toward his West Seattle home, looking forward to family time with his wife and two small children. Mike Magan's partner, Sheila, left the task force office early that afternoon to go home and stuff her family's turkey. Mike planned to play basketball with a bunch of the guys from SEAFAT (the FBI's Seattle Fugitive Apprehension Team), but he had forgotten his gym bag, so Lisa brought it down to him. After the game, the players were going to meet at the Metropolitan Grill in Seattle's Pioneer Square neighborhood to have a couple of beers.

"I played lousy that afternoon," Mike recalled, "and I stopped at the office before I went to the Met. The only members of the task force still there were Ellen Glasser, Kevin Aratani—and Pete Erickson, a Mercer Island detective assigned to the task force."

Far below their twenty-eighth floor offices, on the streets and freeways of Seattle, traffic was backed up—because of the rain and the fact that it was the beginning of a long holiday weekend. The wind-driven storm was so full of water that it seemed that half of Eliott Bay on the west of Seattle and Lake Washington on the east were caught up in it as it drenched hapless pedestrians and impatient commuters alike.

At 5:40 P.M., Kevin Aratani wished Ellen, Pete, and Mike a happy Thanksgiving and left the office.

At 5:41 P.M., the tones of a silent alarm sounded. The Seafirst Bank in Lake City was being robbed.

"Fuck!" Magan shouted. "It's *Hollywood!*"

What had begun as one of the most meticulously planned bank robberies in the annals of crime in America had already started to disintegrate. Before Hollywood was even inside the bank—and before Steve Meyers had switched on the police radio frequency—one of the tellers had spotted him and pushed a silent alarm button—not once, but twice. The bank's cameras were set a minute fast, but they began efficiently and mechanically taking pictures of everything that was happening in the hushed bank.

The two robbers, one lithe and athletic with a weird

masklike face and a hooded jacket, and the other taller and bulkier, his face, too, disguised, knew about the cameras and were unconcerned. With their make-up, their hoods, and their dark amber aviator-style sunglasses, they were confident that they were fully disguised.

The one in command, the smaller man, walked up to a teller—whose first name was Scott—and said calmly, "Don't touch any buttons. Don't set off any alarms—or I'll take a hostage."

It was, of course, already too late—but Steve had not picked up the "Bank robbery in progress" call on his scanner.

Now, the robber shouted for the vault teller, and the teller, Scott, said that he could assist in opening the vault.

"OK then, let's go."

The customer service representative and Scott, the teller, waited at the entrance to the vault as the robber hopped over a partition and a gate. He seemed infinitely familiar with their bank, and calm. He walked through the safe deposit room to the vault entrance.

The robber apparently knew that there was more than one section to the vault itself, and he demanded that they all be opened. He readied his navy blue duffel bag.

"This cash is new," he said, his voice disappointed.

Did he expect them to apologize for having crisp new bills? Nevertheless, he began grabbing bricks of bills and shoving them in the bag.

"Don't let me take any dye packs," he cautioned. Odd. It was as if somehow he believed that they were all working together in his assault on the bank. The teller and service rep said nothing.

There was a cardboard box in the top vault, and the robber looked at it, and then dumped its contents into his bag, along with another brick of $20 bills.

He had seemingly lucked out once more. He hadn't picked up any dye packs, though he did have a stack of bait bills.

He had been in the vault only a very few minutes. As he came out, he called to his accomplice, asking what sounded like, "Is she here? Did you hear the call? Any alarms been set off?"

"No alarms."

"We're out of here."

The two men left through the door on the south side of the bank building. They had not seen Steve Woods, who had been standing in line, as he'd moved to the window where he could watch their escape. He stared after them as they walked west on NE 125th Street and then turned north around the bank. He himself exited through the north side of the building and followed them. They weren't running. He watched, marveling at their self-control, as they walked rapidly through a library parking lot and then past a park up a hill. He wasn't far behind but he was hidden from them by the darkening sky.

After Woods had crossed through the park himself, he noticed a blue station wagon with Washington, or maybe Idaho, plates—it looked as though it might have been a Subaru—speed out of the church parking lot next to the park. The driver was reckless and took an abrupt left turn onto NE 125th Street—a busy thoroughfare—and disappeared. Woods, on foot, lost sight of them. He could not swear that the bank robbers were in the station wagon, but he somehow knew that they were.

The moment that the alarm tones had sounded in the task force office, Mike Magan was halfway out of the office. Pete Erickson was right behind him, and Mike turned back to ask Ellen Glasser if she wanted to come.

"I said 'yes,'" Ellen Glasser recalled. "I grabbed my fanny pack (which held her gun) and together we all ran out of the office immediately, and got into Magan's car on Second Avenue."

Ellen got in the rear seat right behind Mike Magan, and Pete Erickson rode shotgun. They were in downtown Seattle and they had to drive ten miles to get to the Lake City Bank. In the middle of the afternoon on a sunny weekday, it would have been a piece of cake. But this was the night before Thanksgiving, there was a virtual monsoon out there, and the entrances to the I-5 freeway were like parking lots.

Mike Magan slapped a bubble light on the roof of his unmarked car, hit the siren, and called the FBI radio center on his portable radio. "Call 505 at home!" he shouted. "Tell him that Hollywood has hit!" Shawn Johnson was 505.

Magan asked SPD radio to notify the Special Patrol Unit. Sergeants McDonagh and Rolf Towne, monitoring the call on Tac 1, reported that they were on their way to the scene.

If they could just get through the massive traffic jam, the FBI, the Seattle Police Department, the rest of the task force, and Hollywood and Friends just might meet up in Lake City. A patrol officer was at the scene and he was reporting by radio that the robber inside the bank had worn heavy makeup and carried a Glock. When word of this came over the air, there was little doubt that Hollywood had, indeed, hit again.

Mike could see that he wasn't going to get on the freeway going north; all the lanes were full and, even if drivers tried to move over, they had no place to go. "I took the shoulder the whole way—at sixty-five miles per hour," he remembered. "I looked in the rearview mirror and Kevin Aratani was right behind me—he'd picked the calls up on the radio, too."

The SWAT team had been training at the old Sand Point Naval Air Station all day, and that put them closer to Lake City than Mike, Ellen, and Pete, though they were closing in. Mike was glad now that he had practiced pursuit driving, but he realized his bullet-proof vest was in the trunk of his car.

He doubted he would have time to put it on when he reached the crime scene. And, at the same time, he realized that he probably had never needed it more in all his years on the Seattle Police Department.

As they raced north, the police radio spat out bits and pieces of information. There was a possibility that the bank robbers had driven off in a blue Subaru station wagon—possibly with Idaho plates.

Unfortunately, there had never been a direct linkage between the Seattle radio channels and the FBI's, so there was no way—beyond a walkie-talkie radio and a cell phone—for SSA Ellen Glasser to notify the FBI office that she was with Mike Magan and Pete Erickson. Most of the information on the bank robbery was coming from Seattle Police dispatchers.

When they arrived at the Lake City Seafirst Bank location, they found organized chaos. Seattle Police patrol cars blocked escape routes now, but no one really thought that Hollywood was still in the area, although Mike Magan would not have been surprised if he had taken one triumphant sweep down the street before he headed for wherever his sanctuary was.

No, he would be gone by now. One tip was that a citizen had seen two men run into a pizza restaurant, but Seattle police had already checked them out. Neither of them was Hollywood.

Mike Magan was full of both adrenaline and despair; they could not have gone through all the organizing, planning, training, daily briefings, endless stakeouts, only to lose their quarry now. Hollywood couldn't have had *that* much of a headstart. The silent alarms had gone out before he was even in the bank, and the customer who had followed the two robbers had seen them on foot less than ten minutes before Magan arrived on the scene.

Mike knew they would have to get their makeup off; they couldn't risk being stopped in their full bank robbery regalia. And Hollywood and his crew would have to find their way to the freeway in a blinding downpour. Mike figured Hollywood wasn't going to have any better luck in the traffic jams than he himself had had, but if *he* tried to drive on the shoulders, some Seattle cop would pull him over. That thought gave Magan a chill. He didn't want any state trooper or local cop encountering Hollywood unaware. That had always been his fear, but now he stood by his decision to keep full disclosure from the whole police department. He still suspected that the most prolific bank robber in decades might be a cop himself.

Mike knew he had to find Hollywood before any uniformed officer stopped the getaway vehicle. Convinced as he was that Hollywood had come from outside Seattle, Mike figured he couldn't begin to know all the shortcuts and circuitous streets in the northeast section of Seattle the way he himself did. Mike had *grown up* here, dated a girl here, and been on patrol here. All these streets were his backyard.

With the radio chattering in their ears, Mike headed south on Thirty-fifth Avenue NE. They had just about reached NE Seventy-fifth when, up ahead, they spotted a white Astrovan. That was near enough to one of the vehicles that Hollywood was believed to drive to warrant a closer look. The van turned west, then south, and then west again. Magan didn't know if the driver knew he was being tailed.

He was just behind it when the van stopped at a four-way intersection at NE Seventy-fifth and Twenty-fifth Avenue NE. The van appeared to be in the process of turning left once more when Mike pulled up behind. He moved in so close that no one inside could open the rear doors of the van. Another inch and their bumpers would have locked. If this white van was Hollywood's getaway vehicle, he didn't want anyone bursting out of the back.

He could see the license number—a Washington plate, LT-1198, and he asked the dispatcher to check it through WASIC computers. Mike, Ellen Glasser, and Pete Erickson could see the heavy condensation on the van's rear windows as if someone inside was breathing heavily and sweating. The dome light was turned on in the back part of the van, and it looked as if someone was moving a flashlight back and forth. They could see something flickering and glowing.

Mike Magan had always believed that Hollywood used a van for his "second" getaway vehicle, but since it was the "first" getaway car that was left behind, he could not be sure that this supposition was correct. He radioed that he was about to make a "felony stop."

And then the red light changed to green and the white van turned left, with the trio of task force members right behind, and now eight Seattle marked patrol cars joined the grim parade. Mike clocked the van at fifteen to eighteen miles an hour. It turned right onto Twenty-fourth Avenue NE, a residential street that was narrower than NE Seventy-fifth, with cars parked along both curbs.

It was not the kind of neighborhood where people expect a police chase. Hillary Lenox* stepped out of her house at Seventy-fifth and Twenty-fourth at 6:23 P.M. She had to walk her dogs, even though the wind was blowing so violently that garbage cans were bouncing and rolling across the sidewalks and into the street. She had barely started down the walk when she heard sirens and the sound of cars racing.

"I heard the tires squeak on the pavement," she said, and described looking up to see a white late-model van stop sideways against the curb. She was only thirty feet from the driver of the van who got out and stood by his door.

Mike Magan had seen that the van had moved more and more slowly. He wondered if he had guessed wrong, especially when it stopped suddenly. He saw no brake lights; it looked as though the driver had let the car coast to its spot against the curb.

He slammed on his brakes. His car was fifty to sixty-five feet behind the white van, and a little to the left. He glanced in his rearview mirror and saw that his backup was there. All those marked patrol cars behind him. *The Best in the West.* He had always known he could count on them.

If somebody hopped out of the white van carrying a turkey and a bag of groceries, Mike Magan was going to feel pretty foolish. But he *knew* with the instinct that lives in every superior cop's guts that if anybody got out of the van, it wouldn't be a turkey they were carrying.

There was no turkey. Hillary Lenox half-crouched, frozen in place as she saw the police cars, knowing instinctively that she was in the wrong place at the wrong time.

Mike squinted through his rain-streaked windshield. He couldn't see the driver's door of the van. He slid out from behind his steering wheel, drawing his Glock 40 caliber pistol from its holster, and taking cover behind his car door. He could see a man standing outside the van now at the driver's door. He was white, slight in build, and had a moustache. He was also holding a semiautomatic rifle at port arms. It seemed to Magan that the man was waiting for him to get out of his car. The man took aim at him, placing the rifle on his right shoulder. He seemed to be pulling the trigger, but there was no accompanying boom, even though the man's body jerked forward as if he was anticipating fire.

Mike ran toward the rear of his vehicle, shouting to

the officers in the patrol car behind him, "*Automatic weapon! Automatic weapon! Get down! GET DOWN!*"

Hillary Lenox heard him yell, and she saw one officer move forward and crouch behind his car. She started running when she heard gunshots.

From his position behind the right door of Magan's car, Pete Erickson had seen the sliding door on the right side of the van open; he couldn't see the man outside the van with the semiautomatic rifle, but he heard Mike scream at the patrolmen to get down. Ellen Glasser had pulled her weapon and was behind the back door on the left side of their car. She heard Mike's warning, dove across the back seat and heard the first booms of powerful rounds. She notified FBI radio that they were "taking fire."

In actuality, they weren't. The bullets came from Mike Magan's gun. He had seen the man next to the white van getting ready to fire again as he held the assault rifle's barrel up toward his right shoulder with his left hand, with the stock placed against his upper right thigh. He was racking the slide back and forth, getting ready to fire. And then he had disappeared from Mike's view. Mike was afraid that the man, and whoever was in the van with him, were about to pull "the old bear trick" and come around behind them and wipe them all out. Mike's intent was to eliminate the driver from the equation. He wanted him disabled so that he couldn't shoot or drive away.

Mike Magan lifted his Glock and fired straight into the left rear door of the white van. Six times, maybe seven. Then the van doors closed and it started up again, slowly, heading north along the quiet residential street. Mike had no idea if his bullets had struck anyone, but he leapt behind the steering wheel and told Ellen and Pete to hold on as he kept pace with the van.

It turned west on NE Seventy-seventh. He tried to find his radio to call "Help the officer," but in the chaos of gunfire, it was out of reach somewhere on the floor. "But we don't quit," Magan explained, remembering the terror of a firefight. "It was 'Go! Go! Go!' Your training just kicks in. I knew I had to pop the guy hard the first time—and I'd popped him. I had the uniformed guys with me; I was in Union 2, my old district."

Magan's car followed the white van as it moved slowly around a traffic circle—a little island of trees planted to slow down drivers on Ravenna Avenue NE—and stopped diagonally in the intersection, but he had shut off his lights.

Mike stopped a hundred feet behind, jumped out of the car and took cover behind it. Now, he heard four to six rounds of semiautomatic rifle fire coming at them from the van. He could hear 9-mm rounds buzzing by his head. He returned fire. And so did the officers in the first patrol car behind him. Seattle Police Officer George Basley and K-9 Officer Ed Casey and his Police Dog, Beethoven, were inside.

The windshield of Basley's patrol car exploded in a shower of glass as it took fire from the van. But neither Basley nor Casey—nor Beethoven—were injured.

The van took off again, moving as ponderously as a wounded turtle along Seventy-seventh NE and headed north on Twenty-first Street. There, Mike hoped to cut it off. Driving past rolling garbage cans, he stopped just below the crest of the hill, and ran back to Basley and Casey. "Shut off your headlights and your emergency lights!" he shouted. He didn't want them to be easy targets, and he didn't want to be backlit himself.

Mike opened his trunk, grabbed his shotgun, and ran back to a position at the front of his vehicle. He heard bullets whizzing past his ears. He flashed on the firefight in Miami—he'd read the Forensic Analysis of that encounter Don Glasser had given him. Don must know by now that his wife was in the middle of another firefight. Mike knew that Ellen was, at least for the moment, safe in the back seat of his car. But he didn't know what was coming next.

And then he heard voices up ahead, beyond the crest of the hill and out of his line of sight, shouting, "Get on the ground! Get down on the ground!"

Mike raced up the hill and saw that the white van had struck a house. It appeared to have coasted to a stop against a brick chimney and a giant rhododendron bush. He racked a round into the chamber of his shotgun as he drew near. He wasn't sure how many rounds he had fired from his handgun, so he removed the magazine from his Glock and saw it only had two rounds. He reloaded with a new magazine and put the used clip in his pocket.

Mike Magan reached the driveway of the house where the van was, not trusting that any of them were safe yet. He took the safety off his shotgun and aimed at the driver's side door. He could see that several officers were moving in on the passenger side.

"The van's clear," someone called.

Mike ran around the van and saw two white males,

handcuffed and lying facedown on the sidewalk. Now, he recognized Officers Tom Mahaffey and Curt Gerry from the East Precinct Anti-Crime Team, and Officer Michael Thomas from the North Precinct.

Along with the entire Puget Sound Violent Crimes Task Force and what seemed like most of the cops in Seattle, Mahaffey and Gerry had responded to the bank robbery and were well aware of the chase that was going on. Mahaffey knew that officers were being fired on with an automatic weapon. He had turned right onto NE Seventy-seventh, and seen the Astrovan headed straight for the unmarked car he was driving. The van had veered to the left to avoid a head-on collision, and he and Gerry had watched the driver bail out while the van was still moving. He had run off in an easterly direction. Even before the van hit the house, the sliding door on the passenger side opened.

"As it hit the house," Mahaffey said, "I could see a guy inside with his hands at his waist in a crouched position. He looked like he was looking at something in his hands."

Mahaffey knew that whoever was in the white van had just shot to kill other cops. "I exited my car and yelled to the suspect that I was the police and to come out of the van with his hands visible—Gerry was yelling too."

At that point the suspect moved farther back into the van, almost as if he intended to jump out the rear doors. They could barely see him as he turned away and then whirled, his hands still in the position of someone about to fire a handgun. He wasn't responding to their commands.

Mahaffey said he fired two rounds. Still, the man in

the van wouldn't come out. Mahaffey yelled again, and finally the man came out, clutching his hands at his waist. He lay on his back and side, rolling around in pain.

Another white male had come from the van then. He fell to the ground on his face and barely moved. Gerry and Mahaffey had approached them both, and, with Thomas, had handcuffed them. Thomas had advised both of their rights under Miranda. The first man acknowledged that he understood, the second seemed to be past understanding.

Mike Magan approached the two men on the ground, halfway expecting that he might recognize them—he had been one step behind them for so long. "It appeared to me that both had been shot," Magan recalled. "I saw blood coming from one—right shoulder and arm. The second white male was bleeding from the right side of his stomach, and it looked to me that he was not conscious—and maybe dead. Then I realized that the third suspect, the driver, had jumped from the van while it was still moving and had run southbound down an alley."

Mike rolled one of the wounded men onto his back so he could see his face. When he did, he had an instant stab of recognition. "It was the man who was standing on the driver's side with the automatic weapon—the man who had fired at me. He was pleading, 'Please shoot me. *Shoot* me in the head. This hurts. Put me out of my misery.'"

Mike leaned down and asked him what his name was. "Are you Hollywood?" He wondered if, at last, he was looking at the man he had hunted so long.

"I'm not Hollywood. I'm Steve," the man moaned.

"Steve *what?*"

"Steve Meyers."

Mike looked again at the unconscious man. He was a big man, husky, with very curly light brown hair. He was far too big to be Hollywood.

Mike went to an unmarked police vehicle, picked up the radio and asked that Medic One Units be dispatched immediately. He advised the paramedics that there were shooting victims, and he gave them directions to the scene.

Then he called his Captain, Dan Bryant, and his Lieutenant, Linda Pierce. Both responded that they were enroute to the scene, too.

Mike Magan knew that he had had backup when he needed it, but he wouldn't find out until later just how many units had responded, and were still responding. The man who was the chief dispatcher for 911 had been in his job for twenty-five years. For the first time in his career, he had broadcast an "all city–all precinct 'Help the Officer!' call." And help had come pouring in from all over Seattle. The SWAT team, on duty or off—in uniform or not, had raced to the scene. There were 165 law enforcement units in the area or on their way.

The firefight was over—at least for the moment. Two of the suspects were down, and one had escaped. No one had any assurance that the third man wasn't out there with a semiautomatic weapon. They didn't even know yet *who* the third man was.

Mike knew he needed to set up containment of the area. They would place patrol cars and K-9 officers and their dog-partners around the perimeter of a ten-block area. Magan asked for Guardian One to bring the King County Police helicopter into the area of NE Seventy-seventh and Twentieth Avenue NE so that they could search for the third suspect from the air.

It was perhaps most important to keep the van itself inviolate. The key was still in the ignition and the headlights were on. And there it was: a blue nylon duffel bag stuffed with money. There were scattered bills and the torn paper bindings that had held them on the carpet of the van, most of them stained now with blood.

"I don't know why," Magan recalled, "but I thought there was only a couple of thousand dollars there. However much it was, I knew that there would be people crawling all over the place in a minute, and that it had to be guarded so that nothing inside was touched." He strung yellow crime scene tape around the van.

There was a plastic bag with two bottles of mineral spirits inside, another with a damp washcloth, and grotesque-looking pieces of what looked like real flesh, but, on closer inspection, were only a fake nose with a moustache attached and a false chin.

After so long, and so many disappointments and frustrations, it was all there in front of Mike Magan. This had to be Hollywood's van.

He looked at the back of the van and saw eight bullet holes in the left door.

His shots.

The van's right rear window was shattered, but the force appeared to have come from the *inside.*

Magan was hyperalert now. He peered again into the back of the white van. He saw the .308 caliber assault rifle that had been aimed at him only minutes before. It was on the front passenger seat; a semiautomatic shotgun was near an open guitar case on the floor behind the driver's seat; a 9-mm semiautomatic pistol was on the floor near the back doors, its slide locked open; a clear plastic bag with a number of 9-mm rounds inside. Three portable Motorola radios and a police scanner were also on the floor. Any one of them—Ellen, Pete, Basley, Casey, Mike himself, or Mahaffey and Gerry—could have been killed. Easily.

One of the paramedics looked closely at Mike, evaluating his state of mind. "Do you want to talk about it?" she asked.

He didn't. "I snuck away for a couple of minutes," he said. "I checked my clothes for bullet holes, and I didn't find any—but then I started feeling my arms and legs to see if I'd been shot. It just seemed to me that some of those bullets had to have hit me."

Miraculously, he had no wounds. But he knew he was going to lose his job. He turned to Ellen Glasser and Don Glasser—who had shown up at the scene— and said, "Well, that's it. I'm fired on Monday."

They looked at him stunned. "You're not going to be fired," Ellen said. "You did a good job. You did exactly what you were supposed to do."

Mike shook his head. "I killed one guy. The other one wants *me* to kill *him*. Another guy's loose out there someplace. No, I'll be fired on Monday, all right."

He meant it. He knew he would be accountable for every round he had fired. And it had all happened so fast.

People kept asking him what he was feeling, and he recalled later that, "I was feeling pissed that *I* had caused all this mess."

Mike watched the paramedics working over the two wounded men, and hoped that they weren't dead or dying. Ellen Glasser was beside him now, and so was Shawn Johnson. Shawn had materialized from somewhere on the other side of the blue van. They watched the comatose man silently; his stomach was swollen, a sign that the blood in his body was pooling there. Mike realized that he was trembling, and he looked at Shawn and saw that he, too, seemed to be vibrating.

Although it wouldn't truly hit any of them until later, it is a well-respected axiom that the cop who has to shoot someone is wounded just as badly as those who take the bullets. It doesn't matter that he may have had to shoot because his life and other lives were in danger, and it doesn't matter that the wounded or dead are in the act of committing a felony, the aftermath of a shooting is emotionally shattering. At this point, no one could be sure *whose* bullets had struck the two suspects. Officers behind the van and in front of it had all fired. And all of them turned over their service weapons—40 caliber Glocks—to ballistics experts.

Each officer on the scene had done everything right; they had two suspects in custody, and more than enough evidence to tie them to the Lake City robbery. Still, Mike Magan knew that Hollywood himself was out there and still dangerous.

Mike suddenly needed to talk to his wife, so he called Lisa at work on his cell phone. She wasn't available, and he left a message for her that it was an emergency and she should page him. His phone rang almost immediately. This was 1990s technology; it would be hard to imagine an old-time gunfighter or even Elliot Ness calling home from a shootout. Lisa Magan is an incredible wife for a cop, level-headed and not given to excess emotion. But she had heard reports that something big was going down in the Northeast sector of Seattle. She was scared. Now she heard Mike's voice, and she knew he was alive.

"What's going on?" she asked Mike.

"I've been in a shooting."

"Hollywood?"

Mike can't remember if he nodded or said yes. "I'm watching a man die right in front of me," he said, his eyes steady on the paramedics and the unconscious man on the ground.

"How do you feel?"

"Lisa, I did what I had to."

Lisa told Mike that she would call his parents, and they hung up.

Seattle Homicide Sergeant Dave Ritter arrived, and gave Mike one of the sharp looks he was becoming accustomed to.

"You OK?" Ritter asked.

"I'm fine, but I don't know about those guys," Mike said, pointing to the wounded suspects.

Dave Ritter reached out and tapped Mike on the chest. "Where's your vest?"

"In the trunk of my car."

Ritter looked at the unmarked car near the van. "This your car?"

"Yeah."

"I don't see any bullet holes," Ritter said, grinning. "You are one lucky SOB!"

Mike led Ritter over to the van and showed him the weaponry inside, explaining which had fired and which had jammed. The homicide sergeant's grin faded. It seemed a miracle that none of the police officers had been killed—that they hadn't even been wounded.

Chief Norm Stamper and Assistant Chief Harvey Ferguson arrived. For a very brief period, ten of the brass of the Seattle Police Department stood at the scene. Everyone seemed to be asking, "You OK? You OK?" and the officers involved in the shooting kept nodding and saying they were.

"Then we'll leave you to do your job," Stamper said. "So far, you're doing just fine."

Mike Magan felt better, but he still needed to be reassured that he had done the right thing. It was lucky that there was a lot to be done, and he felt better when he was moving. The rain beat down now like a tropical monsoon—only colder—and the SWAT team needed someplace to change into their uniforms. Mike found a homeowner nearby who offered his garage as a dressing room.

Seattle Homicide detectives scoured the spots where gunfire had taken place, picking up casings and taking photographs. They checked out the bloody van and saw the virtual arsenal in the back: a Beretta shotgun (loaded with two rounds in the tube and one in the chamber), a military 308 assault rifle with its serial numbers ground off (loaded with one round in the chamber, but with the bolt open and jammed), a

Ruger P89 9-mm pistol (its action locked back and an empty magazine still inserted), a Smith & Wesson 9-mm pistol (loaded with one round in the chamber and a loaded magazine inserted). There were almost sixty rounds of live ammunition for the automatic assault rifle in the back of the van. That kind of fire power could blow up a squad car's engine, or blow a cop right out of his seat.

But one gun was missing: the Glock that Hollywood always carried wasn't there. He was still out there and probably armed. He was on foot, and he had to be desperate to escape; there was liable to be another shootout.

He had told both Steve and Mark that this would be his last bank robbery.

Had he meant it?

34

Shawn Johnson had barely arrived home that Thanksgiving Eve when he got the call that Hollywood had hit the Lake City Seafirst branch. He, too, had raced to the north end of Seattle through the pouring rain and throngs of preholiday traffic. On the way, he, too, had wondered if this was the night when he would be able to put a face to a name. Was he finally going to meet Hollywood?

While Mike Magan, Pete Erickson, and Shawn's supervisor, Ellen Glasser, were pursuing the white Astrovan along NE Seventy-fifth, Shawn was north of them, heading toward the area where patrol cars were swarming. He had arrived to find the van nosed into the rhododendron bush. Seattle cops had two men on the ground, and Mike Magan was running up the hill with his shotgun at the ready. It would take a while to sort out who was who.

Don Glasser, Ellen's husband, had been buying pizza for their four children when he heard over the FBI radio that she was involved in a pursuit. Luckily, Ellen, crouched on the floor of the back seat, had been able to keep the FBI operator apprised of what was happening. Don knew as soon as possible that she was OK.

When Mike Magan disappeared beyond the crest of the hill, Ellen had jumped in the front seat to move his car closer to give him cover. But the keys were gone. Then she had heard the radio report that two suspects were in custody and one had fled on foot.

It was 6:28 P.M. It seemed impossible that so much had happened in only forty-seven minutes. Only forty-seven minutes since the tones had sounded in the task force offices, tones alerting them to a bank robbery ten miles away.

No one knew, really, how many bank robbers there were. Shawn Johnson and Mike Magan had discussed the possibility that someone might even try to waylay the caravan of aid cars on the way to the hospital. With lights flashing and siren wide open, Shawn followed the aid cars to Harborview Medical Center.

He had a Seattle Police squad car right behind him, and uniformed officers rode *inside* the aid cars beside the patients/prisoners.

The medics shook their heads as they worked feverishly over the taller man; it was questionable that he would even survive the transport to the hospital. Johnson hoped that he might be able to talk with the other man.

Although the FBI and the Seattle Police had not verified it yet, one of the men who was being treated in the ER Triage Unit of Harborview Medical Center *was* Steve Meyers. Though he had suffered extremely painful and disfiguring wounds to his right arm and left front shoulder, they were not fatal. The doctors told Shawn Johnson that he could talk to Meyers as soon as he received emergency treatment. Steve Meyers wore a black T-shirt, black sweater, and blue jeans—all sodden with his blood now. He had a black shoulder holster, $545.81 in bills and coins, two Ford keys and an automobile light bulb in the pocket of his jeans.

The other man? He was in extremely critical condition. His wounds were all on his right side; he had been shot in the right thigh, right arm, and through the back into the stomach. They were trying to get him stable enough to undergo surgery to stop the hemorrhaging in his gut.

Medical personnel cut away the unconscious man's clothing—a green jacket with a hood, green corduroy pants, a green shirt, all heavily stained with blood. He had worn two pairs of brown leather gloves, beige boat shoes, and a belt with a black nylon holster, which held a Taser stun gun, and three semiautomatic magazines with 9-mm ammunition. In one of his pockets, they found his false nose, chin, cheeks, and his false moustache. He hadn't had time to get all the makeup off, though, and he still had strips of latex on his forehead, down the sides of his face and on his chin.

Still unidentified, the big man was wheeled on a gurney to the basement for surgery. And, at last, Shawn Johnson was told that he could talk to the man named "Steve."

South of Seattle, after a bumpy, crowded flight from Arizona, Sabrina Adams was looking forward to her holiday reunion with Scott. She could hardly wait to deplane and she hurried to the luggage carousels on the bottom level of SeaTac airport. She stood outside the doors, watching for Scott's white van as all manner of vehicles moved through the passenger pickup zone's four lanes. Often, she saw a white van—and sometimes even an Astrovan—but it was never Scott's. Despite the rain, she stood out near the curb so that she could see him the moment he drove up off the ramp.

Minutes and then hours passed. But Scott Scurlock never came.

Sabrina waited for a very long time, going through feelings of disappointment, annoyance, anger, and, inevitably, anxiety. *Where was he?* Finally, she realized that something must have kept him from picking her up and that he hadn't been able to get a message to her. She took a cab to Olympia, fifty miles south of the airport, half-expecting to find him waiting there.

But no one was home—not in the treehouse and not in the gray house. Exhausted and worried, Sabrina climbed the steps and ladders to the treehouse and fell asleep in the bed she usually shared with Scott. He would probably wake her when he got home with one of his perfectly logical explanations, and they would spend Thanksgiving together.

More than sixty miles away, Seattle detectives and patrolman were going door to door, talking to residents to determine if they had seen anyone running in their yards, or even if someone might be inside, holding the homeowners hostage. They worked their way up and down the street where the van had crashed, and found nothing unusual, even though they were careful to evaluate possible witnesses carefully. Did they seem nervous? Were they trying to signal that someone was behind them, holding a gun? Everyone seemed calm enough, wanting to be cooperative—but with nothing solid to contribute. It was an odd dichotomy; they were walking down stormy streets where a desperate fugitive was probably hiding and yet, when the doors opened, smells of pumpkin and mince pies drifted out.

The driver who had bailed out on his two wounded partners had been swallowed up in the night. The rain continued to fall and high winds were gusting. In dark clothing, he would be almost invisible. There were a thousand places to hide; the streets in the containment area had only pale overhead lights. No one searching for him had the slightest idea where he was, or, for that matter, *who* he really was.

* * *

Scott had always warned his accomplices that helicopters would be major impediments to their escape from bank robberies. They had heard one overhead as they drove away from Lake City, but it wasn't Guardian One from the King County Sheriff's Office or any official law-enforcement agency; the whirlybird was from a local television station. The police helicopter hadn't been able to get airborne in time. But "The Hollywood Bank Robber" was headline stuff, and a television crew was circling above the action.

Two of the bank robbers were shot up, and the entire plan had turned sour. No one will ever know what the third man was thinking on that Thanksgiving Eve, 1996. But he must have been shocked that something planned out with such meticulous care could have gone so badly. When he leapt from the van, had he believed that his friends were dying—or already dead? Or was he running away to fight another day?

Scott had once told a confidante that he would come back to kill Mark if he was ever wounded—so he wouldn't talk. Mark was the weak link, Scott believed, who would spill his guts if he was captured. Although the investigators didn't know about that statement, they had already placed several armed guards next to both prisoners as they were being treated at Harborview Medical Center.

Mike Magan stayed behind to wait with the homicide detectives, and to help set up further containment of the area. For all he knew, the third man might be wounded too. If he was, they would probably find him soon. But it was a scary situation; there were thousands of families in the area, many of them with company arriving for the Thanksgiving holiday. Hopefully, the police sirens and lights, and the steady *thrub-thrub-thrub* of helicopters overhead had warned them that something was going on. And if they turned to the news channels, they would be alerted not to open their doors to strangers.

Four or five blocks from the crash site, a resident who kept an art studio in a small cottage on the back of her lot was startled to see a man run through her property. He was white, dark-haired, and of average build. Their eyes met for an instant—and then he was gone. She had been so busy painting that she hadn't been listening to the radio or television, and she didn't know about the huge police dragnet that had dropped over the streets around her home. Only later did she suspect who it was that she had encountered.

Hillary Lenox saw no reason to call the police about what she had seen. There were so many police cars around when the bullets started sailing by that she figured there couldn't be anything she could add to what they had seen with their own eyes.

K-9 dogs located a green, hooded jacket in the alley where the third man had disappeared. They also found a white shirt that might or might not be connected with the fugitive.

Where could anyone hide within such a heavily manned containment area? In the past, Hollywood and his friends had either raced away from the area where they had just robbed a bank, *or,* as they had done in more recent robberies, they had stayed close by, playing pool or eating dinner, expecting that police would check out any cars that tried to leave. Scott had even enjoyed the sensation of driving past the clusters of squad cars, knowing that they had no idea who he was. But *then,* he had been in his car and had the capability of easing onto a freeway.

Scott was in magnificent physical shape and he could jog twenty miles without collapsing. Still, a running man in a crime-besieged neighborhood would stand out as if he were lit by neon. However, he *could* make his way through the heavily treed back-yards to the edge of the containment area, and with some of his clothing jettisoned, walk south, toward home. He could call friends, perhaps, to come and pick him up. The police were sure the "third man" probably had a gun with which to commandeer a driver.

In the end, cops figured that the most prudent thing for him to do was to go to ground and hide until they dispersed. An open cellar door or a garage, or even a parked car that wasn't locked might hide him from the officers and the dogs who trailed him. He had only to risk the telltale rattle of a door knob or an unsuspected car alarm.

The fact was, that, as the hours passed, there was no sign of the man who had bailed out of the white van. Wherever he had chosen to hide, it had worked.

Because Mike Magan had been able to get word to Lisa that he was all right, he was comfortable staying at the command post where he walked Seattle homicide detective Kevin O'Keefe through the intersections and streets where the shootouts had occurred. "There wasn't an inch of ground that we didn't cover," he remembered. And he *was* able to account for all of his rounds. The casings were exactly where they should have been.

Mike pointed out where Basley and Casey—and Beethoven—had been, and where he had been. It was late and stormy, he hadn't eaten since lunch, but he barely noticed; he was running on nervous energy and the shock that follows a close encounter with death. Later, he said, "If that automatic weapon hadn't jammed, there would have been several officers' funerals."

He did not say that, in all likelihood, his own would have been one of them.

On First Hill, above downtown Seattle, Shawn Johnson sat next to Steve Meyers' bed, trying to get a fix on him. Although Steve had given his real name, he was very reluctant to say who his partners were. He explained that he was a sculptor whose pieces sold for anywhere from $500 to $15,000, and that he had never before been involved in a bank robbery. He seemed inordinately loyal to the men who had been with him a few hours earlier. Gradually, Shawn got Steve to see that, whoever had leapt from the van, he was no friend. He had left Steve and the other man to die, either in a shootout or when the van crashed.

At length, Steve admitted that the man who had run from the scene was named Scott Scurlock.

"Where does he live?" Shawn asked.

"He lives in the biggest treehouse in the world."

Shawn stared at Steve, wondering if he was disoriented by painkillers. But Steve insisted he was telling the truth. He said the treehouse was in Olympia. "You'll see. It's the biggest treehouse in the world."

The FBI agent left the room to have someone check the name Scott Scurlock through the Department of Licensing, and an address came back for a *William* Scott Scurlock on Overhulse Road in Olympia. He asked Steve Meyers if that was the correct address.

"That's it," he said. "He has twenty-some acres down there. I helped him remodel his house."

Steve said that he himself had been in the Northwest for only a few weeks, and that he had tried to talk Scott out of the Lake City robbery, but that Scott was "getting greedy."

"He told us that if there was a shootout and anything happened," Steve said, illustrating how persuasive Scott had been, "he would come to the hospital and break us out. Or if we ended up in custody, he'd get us out of jail."

"Who was driving the van?" Shawn asked.

"I was. Mark was in the right front seat. Scott was in the back looking through the money for dye packs or something—just before the shooting started."

Once Steve began to talk, he was voluble. In the end, he would talk to Shawn Johnson for dozens of hours, detailing all of the bank robberies, the preparations, the escapes. But not on this first night; he was doing his best to portray himself as a neophyte bank robber, recruited only to drive.

Shortly before midnight, Seattle Police homicide detectives Greg Mixsell and Walt Maning joined

Shawn Johnson in Steve Meyers' hospital room. Once more, he listened as his rights were read, but he said, "I don't have a problem answering questions. The chess game is over."

At least it was half over. Steve recalled the way he had met Scott through his younger brother, and that he had come to Washington to help remodel Scott's house. But he said he had no idea what Scott's "business" was until six months earlier. Even then, Steve said, he knew no details. Scott had always told him it was better if he didn't know too much.

"Where have you been living before you came here a few weeks ago?" Mixsell asked.

"In New Orleans, on Constance Street. I had a girlfriend living with me there at one time, but she's gone. I live there alone."

"What was your involvement in tonight's bank robbery?"

"I was to be the driver of one of the vehicles—I was offered twenty percent of the take for that and to scan police frequencies. I was supposed to say, 'You're out' if I heard police dispatched to the bank."

He told the three investigators that he was to pick Scott and Mark up after the robbery. He said Scott bought all the cars they used, and all the guns. He stressed again that this was the very first bank robbery he had ever participated in. Scott had chosen it because he wanted a large bank, and because he knew that banks loaded up on money before a long holiday weekend.

"What does this Scott do with his money?"

"He gives a lot of it away—to environmental

causes. And some of the money he gambles with in Reno and Las Vegas. I think he belongs to Green Peace."

Shawn Johnson, Greg Mixsell, and Walt Maning would have no idea at this point that Steve Meyers was giving them only about forty percent of the truth. This had not been his first bank robbery; it was closer to his tenth. As it was, they were puzzled; he was making this Scurlock guy sound like a combination of Robin Hood and Mother Teresa.

They pressed him, asking him to explain again how the vehicles had been obtained. Shawn had sat in two or three of the cars and he wanted to hear more about them.

Meyers sighed. Yes, he admitted, he *had* purchased cars and vans for Scott to use in bank robberies in the past. He remembered a little yellow Renault.

So did Shawn Johnson. "When was that?"

"Several years ago," Meyers said. "He gave me a thousand dollars to buy it and we never changed the registration."

"And you never participated in any prior robberies?"

"This was the first."

Of course, it wasn't, nor did the three men studying him believe him. They changed their line of questioning to his personal life. He said he had been married once, and had a daughter, fifteen, from that marriage. Sadness washed over his features when he mentioned his daughter, but he didn't go into detail about her.

"Any other cars down on that Olympia property?" Walt Maning asked.

"There's an old red Ford pickup and a blue Dodge van."

They asked him to tell them about the hours leading up to the bank robbery in Lake City. For Shawn Johnson, particularly, this was like opening a box full of treasures—it was, finally, a chance to learn how the bank robbers thought. Mike Magan would always be frustrated that he was not been in the room, listening, but he was needed more out where they were searching for the third man.

Steve Meyers said that Scott, Mark Biggins, and he had left Olympia midafternoon. "Scott and Mark were in the Chrysler, and I was following them in the white van—"

He stopped for a moment, and said nothing. Finally, he admitted, "You'll find out soon enough what the other vehicle was. There wasn't any Chrysler—Scott and Mark were driving the blue Dodge Caravan. It has California plates. It's not down in Olympia."

"Why would you lie to us about that?" Shawn asked.

"I was the one who bought it—about six months ago in California. I didn't want to say I'd bought one of the rigs we used in the robbery."

"Where is it now?"

"It's about three or four blocks north of the bank—by a big lot full of school buses."

(Shawn Johnson left the room and relayed the information about the Dodge Caravan to FBI agents and officers at the scene. It had already been located, reported to 911 by a citizen. Officer T. J. Havenar found the blue van parked on the east shoulder of

135th and 32nd NE. Its sliding door was wide open. The key was still in the ignition. He reached in the window and turned it and the engine purred. He called for a tow and it was taken to the police garage to be processed later.)

The three investigators urged Steve Meyers to continue his narrative. He said that, because of the heavy traffic on the freeway, they hadn't arrived at the Lake City bank until about 5:30. By the time they got there, Scott and Mark already had their makeup on. "Scott put his own face on, and I'd helped Mark with his. We all wore gloves whenever we were in the vehicles, and we always wiped the cars down three times afterward, anyway."

Steve said that he'd known Mark for about a year and a half, and that he thought he had been brought in because they were hitting a large bank with a lot of customers inside.

"How much did Scott think he'd get from that branch?" Shawn Johnson asked.

"He told me to expect three, four—maybe five—hundred thousand dollars," Steve recalled. "But once we saw the money when we were looking through it, we thought it could be seven or eight hundred thousand."

Steve Meyers stressed that he had never been in real trouble with the law, nothing more than kid stuff where the police gave him a ride home.

"What do you have down at the Olympia place?"

"I have a bag there with some cash in it."

"Any firearms there?" Shawn asked.

"An old shotgun. Maybe some small arms."

"Tell us a little more about Scott," Shawn asked.

"He's a scientist," Steve said. "He's always reading scientific journals."

Mixsell, Maning, and Johnson exchanged a look. What was a scientist doing robbing banks? For that matter, what was a nature lover doing robbing banks?

"What did you plan to do, Steve," Greg Mixsell asked, "after this robbery—if things hadn't ended this way?"

"I was going to drive to Portland, take a plane to Reno, and then get a rental car to drive to Louisiana."

That was the end of their interview with Steve Meyers; a nurse came in and said he had to be transported to surgery. They went up to the seventh floor and found the man that they now knew was named Mark Biggins in a single room there, guarded by uniformed Seattle patrol officers. They attempted to talk to him, but he was still too sedated after surgery to respond.

If Mark Biggins and Steve Meyers were in Harborview Medical Center, that validated the investigators' belief that the man who had escaped was William Scott Scurlock, forty-two, allegedly a scientist, a conservationist, a philanthropist, and perhaps one of the most cunning bank robbers they had ever encountered.

It was midnight. Greg Mixsell and Walt Manning went back to the Homicide Unit on the third floor of the Public Safety Building to start their paperwork. Shawn Johnson went to the PSVCTF office on the twenty-eighth Floor of the FBI Annex. He hadn't eaten, and he would not sleep this night. He had to prepare arrest warrants and a search warrant for the property on Overhulse Road in Olympia, Washington, where—according to Steve Meyers—FBI agents would be searching "the biggest treehouse in the world."

Lieutenant Linda Pierce, who had lobbied to help Mike Magan get a spot on the task force, was Scene Commander out where the van had crashed, and she was busy coordinating scores of officers who still combed the area. Just before midnight, Sergeant Ron Smith came and took Mike Magan away from the scene to get a hamburger.

It was only then that Mike realized he had not called his partner. Sheila had been as anxious as he to catch Hollywood, and hours had gone by where he was too occupied to think about calling her.

"Sheila?" Mike was tentative; Sheila Bond could be one tough partner.

"What's up, baby?" she asked.

"It happened, Sheila," he said, "and it's over."

"What happened?"

"Hollywood. . . ." Mike went through the evening once more for Sheila. She wasn't mad—she was disappointed that she hadn't been there, but she told him she had spent the whole evening in the kitchen, and that she hadn't even turned the radio on.

At Seattle Police Homicide offices, Mike attended a debriefing. There were more than fifty people there, and for the first time, everyone learned what everyone else had been doing.

Also for the first time, they learned just how much money the Hollywood gang had stolen: *$1,080,000!*

Somebody asked, "How much does a million and eighty thousand dollars weigh?"

"Fifty-six pounds."

Mike Magan finally headed for home at 3:00 A.M. on Thanksgiving morning. He stopped off at the North precinct to see how things were going. Then he drove past Lake Washington toward the house where Lisa and his two cats were sound asleep.

"The storm had knocked the power out," he remembered. "The wind was still blowing across the lake, raising whitecaps, and I could see those, but the streetlights were out and there were signs that had been knocked down rattling in the street. It was eerie, like a ghost town. When I got home, there were no lights and I could hear our smoke alarm chirping. I checked on Lisa, and then I came downstairs. I was too tired to sleep. I still needed to talk to somebody so I called the FBI radio room at the Federal Building.

"They said it was quiet. They were getting ready for a search warrant in the morning. I asked them if Hollywood would make their Top Ten, and they said if we didn't catch him tomorrow—today really—he probably would."

Finally, with the smoke alarm still chirping, Mike went to bed. He lay there, staring into the dark until morning. He didn't sleep, nor did he try to.

At 7:30, the phone started to ring: officers, old partners, friends, and then Shawn Johnson, updating Mike on the interrogation of Steve Meyers.

Hollywood was still free.

35

Quietly, throughout the night of November 27–28, FBI SWAT team members and other agents staked out the address on Overhulse Road in Olympia, Washington. They saw no one arrive and no one leave the property. Sabrina Adams was sleeping high up in the treehouse deep in the woods. She had arrived before the FBI team got there. They didn't know she was back there, and they were far too quiet for her to hear, even though she awoke often to listen for the sound of Scott's van approaching.

By Thanksgiving morning, Shawn Johnson had obtained a search warrant from U.S. Magistrate Judge Philip K. Sweigert of the United States District Court, Western District. Two FBI Evidence Response Teams were assigned to sweep the property at Overhulse Road, to look for evidence that would further connect Scurlock and his wounded accomplices to the crime. Don Glasser headed for Olympia at 8:00 A.M. to join them. Every item of interest they uncovered would be photographed, marked, and meticulously logged so that the chain of evidence would remain unbroken. They would also take photos of this remarkable compound.

Despite the fact that he had had no sleep since

Tuesday night, Shawn Johnson joined the search. The teams who had guarded the property all night were still there. They had seen no one approach during the night, though, but it was possible that Scott Scurlock had made his way home under cover of dark. There had to be other ways to get in, especially for someone who had reportedly lived here for a dozen years or more. And none of them knew about Sabrina Adams. Since she had arrived at the treehouse property by taxi, there was no vehicle indicating she was there; there was only the old red pickup Steve Meyers had mentioned and a nondescript sedan with California plates.

The FBI agents approached the gray house first. It looked like a pleasant farmhouse from the exterior. When no one responded to their knocks of shouts of "FBI!" they kicked in the glass-paneled door and it shattered, its shiny wooden frame breaking into pieces.

Sometime during the night, Shawn Johnson realized that he had come to think of the man still missing as two people; one was Hollywood, the bank robber— and the other was a man he hoped to meet: Scott Scurlock. *Both* of them had lived in this house.

It was a perfect Thanksgiving day; the winds of the night before had blown the rain clouds away, and the sky was blue. Everywhere he looked, Shawn saw hundred-foot cedar trees reaching upward.

This was where Hollywood reportedly had lived, planned, and plotted. This was where he took refuge after each bank robbery. (Or, if Meyers hadn't been lying about the biggest treehouse in the world, this was where Scott had created it.)

This house, Steve had told Shawn, was the guest house where Scott welcomed family and friends. The farmhouse had obviously been remodeled; the kitchen and bathroom, particularly, were works of art with tile work that Steve had described. Some of Steve's marble sculptures were in the yard among the sword ferns and fallow vegetation.

The FBI searchers found a dozen pairs of Converse All-Stars—black, blue, red, wine, even pink—the canvas shoes that Hollywood had worn into banks so many times, and tan boat shoes—*exactly* like those in a number of surveillance photos. There were extra portable radios, a number of books, magazines, and technical articles about shortwave radios and a frequency directory that included police channels.

Steve's bag was there, as he had said—stuffed with stacks of crisp $20 bills. Many, many stacks of $20 bills. They found a passport in the inside pocket of a Versace sports jacket, more passports, baseball caps, maps of far-off places, mineral spirits, a catalogue for knives and optics, aviator sunglasses, rubber gloves, duct tape. There was a rifle in a pink Velcro case, and packets of ammunition.

The house looked for all the world as if the occupants had only stepped away for a few minutes. The bed covers were thrown back and dirty clothes were piled on the floor just like in any bachelor's pad. There was a bottle of wine on the kitchen counter, a tea kettle full of water on the stove, and a bouquet of fresh flowers.

There were any number of banking records for William Scott Scurlock, 1506 Overhulse Road. He banked, ironically enough, at a Seafirst branch. His credit cards were there, and, in a desk in the dining-room, they found a vial with a white powdery substance that they field-tested and found to be codeine. Nothing sensational; it could have been prescribed for a toothache. While they searched, the phone rang and they listened while a man named Doug* asked the answering machine, "Where is everybody?" and then left his phone number. They jotted down the number.

Was Scott on his way home? It was hard for them not to jump when cars approached. A search warrant is an intensely personal invasion, granted only when there is probable cause to believe that evidence connected to a crime will be found. Such a search plunges law-enforcement officers into the middle of someone else's daily life; the sounds, smells, tastes, and habits of a stranger are there to be touched and experienced.

Something that they didn't find that Shawn expected were newspaper clippings about the bank robberies. Since Hollywood was such a showman, it seemed a given that he would have saved the headline accounts of his handiwork. "There was no scrapbook of his 'achievements' at all," Shawn said.

Of course, they had only searched the gray house; there was still the treehouse, the barn, and all of the outbuildings.

They found books on a number of unusual subjects. One was called *How to Bury Your Goods*. Riffling through the pages, they could see demonstrations of how to establish landmarks and triangulate measurements so that someone could go back and pinpoint where he had hidden valuables in the ground. Another, along the same lines, was *U.S. Army Special Forces Caching Techniques*. Other titles included *New I.D. in*

America, Credit Secrets, Serious Surveillance, and *The Heavy Duty New Identity Book.* Far more troubling was a book titled, *Kill Without Joy!: The Complete How to Kill Book.*

Clearly the games that Scott Scurlock was playing were becoming more and more intricate. After the gray house, the FBI search team swept the barn. The entry room was a jumble of equipment, tools, building materials—the kind of storage that any builder or handyman might have.

The room beyond the first room had a massive safe and more storage-type items. But, here, the team saw what looked like a plywood trap door in the floor. They pried it up, wondering nervously if the man they sought was down there with a gun aimed at them.

But there was no one there, only a huge underground room beneath the barn. It was a concrete, bunkerlike space, with plenty of room for several men well over six feet to stand without bending.

There was no cash in the safe, but there were weapons. Indeed, every place they searched on this sylvan property was rife with guns. They moved around a corner, and past a curtain made of two army blankets. Now they seemed to have found Scott Scurlock's makeup studio. It was fully equipped with both makeup and ammunition. There was bright track lighting over a counter that held mirrors, several shades of theatrical makeup, fake hair, powder brushes, adhesive, gloves, knives, guns, and bags and boxes of rounds of high-powered ammunition. Kleenex apparently used to apply makeup the day before was still wadded up in a cardboard box beneath the counter.

(Later, during the many long conversations he would have with Steve Meyers, Shawn would realize that this barn room must have been where he and Scott had come to count their money after a bank job.)

If there was a "war room" in Scott Scurlock's compound, this had to be it. There was even a huge stereo system in the barn, perhaps used to blast out the music that would get their juices going for what lay ahead. Curious, Shawn reached over and turned on the system. A CD was in place, and the room was instantly filled with the sound track from the movie, *Top Gun;* the song "Danger Zone" that played whenever Tom Cruise and Anthony Edwards soared in their jet fighters. The music boomed for a few moments, and then he switched it off. It was very quiet again as they searched the barn, finding more ammo, and more evidence that chilled them as much as the November cold in the unheated barn.

Shawn Johnson kept thinking that whoever had set up this room had been totally committed to what he was doing. It was a completely professional operation. All of it. Perfect makeup. Careful planning. Untraceable cars, according to Steve at least, wiped clean three times.

"We finished with the house," Shawn said. "We finished with the barn. The treehouse was way, way back in the woods. You had to walk a long way down this wooded path. I remember walking back there. I was trying to find this thing—expecting a small treehouse. All of sudden, I looked up—and there it was."

It rose up out of the mossy forest floor as though it

had burst from the earth. It might not have been the biggest treehouse in the world but it was *big*, three stories built *above* its tall "legs" of living cedar trees. He saw that it might have known better days. The exterior looked weathered and somewhat jerry-built, as if one of its decks or ramps could drop off at any minute. There were walkways extending hundreds of feet into the trees; Shawn was amazed that anyone had managed to build them way up there.

Some of the other FBI searchers had found the treehouse before Shawn got there. They had shouted up to what appeared to be the living quarters, not really expecting an answer, but far above, a slender blond woman had peered down at them, disappeared for a moment, and then come back wearing glasses. Her face was a study of shock, panic, and sadness as she followed their commands to come down.

"I saw all these FBI guys," Sabrina remembered sometime later, tears filling her eyes and her voice choking. "I thought that everything Scott had ever warned me might happen *was* happening." She didn't say if he had told her *why* someone might invade their perfect world, but it was obvious he had made some attempt to prepare her for disaster.

After she clambered down the steps, the team waiting for her shouted up for Scott to come down, too.

"He's not here," she said softly. "I don't know where he is. Do *you?*"

And, of course, no one did.

They began the search of the treehouse next, and were greeted by a smiling Buddha statue at the bottom of what seemed to be endless series of stairs and ladders. It was a little hairy climbing up, since most of the stairs had no railings, and some of them appeared to be flimsy. It could even have been booby-trapped, with the ladders designed to collapse under a man's weight. Once inside, the FBI agents found the first two floors "very well done." The living area had a new couch covered with a fleecy Alpaca throw, a rattan trunk, lamps, and floors covered by colorful Southwestern rugs.

The interior walls were expensive cedar, carefully dove-tailed. As in the gray house, there were book-shelves everywhere: novels—from Tom Clancy to Louis L'Amour—numerous books on nutrition and biology, the Bible, *Liar's Poker, Sahara, Of Wolves and Man, Warrior, Stress and Tension, Circle of Fear.* There was a Whitley Streiber book about alien beings. Scott Scurlock was obviously an eclectic reader and something of a scholar.

Shawn saw that he *had* saved one newspaper clipping; it was the 1986 *Seattle Times* article that featured his treehouse, entitled, "A Treehouse with a Guest Bedroom." The man in the photograph was clearly the same person whose image was tacked on the wall or in picture frames around the treehouse—but much younger. In 1986, he had looked like a very handsome kid. Later pictures showed a still-handsome, masculine man who might have been a model or movie star.

The FBI team soon discovered a cache of private photographs. Scott had saved dozens of photographs of naked girls, most taken with the treehouse as a backdrop. Some might have been taken surreptitiously, some were posed, and some were of Scott and several different woman engaged in sexual acts.

There were Tiffany lamps, huge expanses of window, sculptures, and paintings. Scott's oak desk was in the corner next to a Chinese hooked rug, and nearby a dolphin statue rested on a slab of wood suspended from the ceiling by four ropes.

The kitchen was as nice as the one in the gray house, with high-end Calphalon pots and pans hung from a beam over the stove. Spoons and cooking utensils were stuck in white pitchers with cobalt blue trim, and the canister set was cobalt blue. There was a small refrigerator, a microwave oven, a sink. But the stove was cold; there were no preparations for Thanksgiving dinner. Most of the FBI agents searching had forgotten it was a holiday, themselves. Few of them had eaten, nor did they even think about eating.

The treehouse had every eventuality covered; there was even a bathroom up there, albeit an open air bathroom out on one of the decks. It had a toilet, sink, and shower (a garden hose snaked up one of the cedars). A toothbrush rested next to the sink.

Up a ladder, they found the bedroom where Sabrina had slept, waiting for her lover to come home. It was a small room, and the bed took up most of the floor space. A telephone sat on the bed itself. She probably had kept it close so she could grab it when Scott called. There were books there too; someone had recently been reading *The Call of the Wild* by Jack London. Above the bed, a poster of N. C. Wyeth's classic illustration of *Robin Hood and his Merry Band* was tacked to the cedar wall.

There was a third floor, although it was still in the

construction stage. When the wind blew, the searchers could feel the whole "house" move. It was almost like an eagle's nest built at the top of an evergreen. Maybe Scott Scurlock had felt that too; there were a number of photographs of eagles in flight on the cedar walls.

The treehouse was heated, in a somewhat cannibalistic manner, by a wood stove.

This treehouse reflected the soul of a romantic, someone who craved adventure. It could have been the realization of a lot of dreams, but now it seemed to be only part of a nightmare for the young woman who waited below, huddled in despair.

What had Shawn Johnson expected to find? He wasn't sure—but not this, certainly. He had long since learned that bank robbers were usually hooked on drugs and lived in low-rent apartments or cheap motels. This place and the gray house showed taste and planning. It was an odd sensation to be walking through the rooms where the man the task force had sought for so long had moved and breathed less than twenty-four hours before.

The treehouse was not all whimsy and good taste; they found more guns—a handgun and a rifle—and ammunition. Had Scott Scurlock been waiting for lawmen to come after him here, he would have had a perfect eagle's eye view from the treehouse, sighting down the path as someone approached. The agents recovered a 30/30 caliber lever action carbine rifle, loaded with silver tipped bullets, with boxes of dozens of rounds of extra ammunition, and, in the sleeping area in the second-story loft level of the treehouse, a .38 Special Colt Cobra six-shot revolver.

Shawn walked out on one of the long ramps that led out into the woods, ending in space. "I wondered how far he intended to go with them," he said. "They swayed in the wind and creaked."

But in spite of the almost palpable sense of him they got in the treehouse, Scott Scurlock was not there. The FBI teams had searched all the nooks and crannies—and there were dozens of them. They had explored high above the ground in the treehouse and deep under the floors in the hidden room beneath the barn.

Wherever Scott was, they were convinced he was nowhere on the twenty acres he owned in Olympia.

Shawn interviewed Sabrina Adams. She bit her lips to keep them from trembling as she denied any knowledge of Scott's connection to bank robberies. She seemed to be in shock. If she wasn't, she was an excellent actress, but Shawn Johnson felt that she really had not known what Scott was doing.

She did not tell him that she had recently loaned Scott more than $30,000 with advances from her credit cards. Her mind must have been racing. Would she not have wondered why Scott needed *her* money if what the FBI agents were telling her was true?

Shawn wondered if the guns had been out in the open when Sabrina was around. Hadn't she ever noticed them? She seemed pole-axed by the events he laid out for her. Maybe she really was in the dark about all of this; maybe she had simply trusted her lover too much to ask questions.

* * *

The search was over shortly after 1:00 P.M. Thanksgiving afternoon. Since Shawn Johnson was the case agent assigned to the Hollywood bank robberies, they loaded everything of evidentiary value into the trunk of his car and he headed for FBI headquarters in Seattle. He called Greg Mixsell in the Seattle Police homicide offices and told him that he was on his way back from the treehouse.

He told Mixsell that they had found a number of weapons, a room devoted to makeup and disguise, *and* $30,000 in cash. There was little question in either of their minds that they had found, at last, Hollywood's lair. Mixsell said that Walt Maning and Sergeant Cynthia Tallman had gone back to the scene of last night's shooting to look for more evidence in the daylight.

As Shawn Johnson drove north, he realized he was hungry. He thought he might get to stop at home after he delivered the evidence and get something to eat—not a whole turkey dinner—but maybe a turkey sandwich. He might even get to take a nap.

He pulled into the basement of the FBI building around 3:00 P.M. and was just about to call for a cart to get the stacks of evidence upstairs when his radio crackled. He heard a Seattle Police dispatcher say, "Shots fired. . . . Unidentified subject in camper at Seventy-fifth and Twentieth NE . . ."

He never even turned the engine off, and instead wheeled his car around and headed to the north end of Seattle for the second day in a row. The address given on the radio was only five blocks from where Hollywood had vanished twenty hours earlier.

36

Thanksgiving Day, 1996, was no holiday for the Seattle FBI office and the Seattle Police Homicide Unit. Steve Meyers had admitted that the other wounded suspect in Harborview Hospital was named Mark Biggins and that he was from California. The FBI wondered if there might have been a fourth man—the man who left the message on Scott's answering machine during their search of Seven Cedars. He had left a San Jose phone number, and they asked a special agent in California to check that number. It turned out to belong to a latter-day Monterrey hippie commune where no one in residence admitted to knowing anyone named Doug. It was a lead that went nowhere.

Trent Bergman, a Seattle police patrolman, was assigned to guard Steve Meyers in the hospital. He sat outside his door, but walked into the room to see what the football score was.

"Seven to seven," the prisoner said, and winced in pain.

"Where did you get shot?"

"In the arms."

"You're lucky to be alive."

Steve Meyers shook his head. "No, I'm ready to die, ready to pass on to the next life. I've been there already on several occasions and I'm looking forward to it."

Bergman stared at him, wondering if he was under heavy medication. "What do you do for a living?"

"I'm a sculptor," Meyers said bitterly. "What did you do before you became a cop?"

"I studied to be a pastor."

"Scott's dad is a Baptist minister."

"I don't know who Scott is," Bergman said truthfully.

"Scott is *Hollywood,*" his prisoner explained, stretching out the infamous name. "He hired me to work at his house and be a sculptor—I met him through my brother. He had me buy cars for him, and I found out he used them in bank robberies. This time—my first time—he asked me to be his driver. I was going to get twenty percent—somewhere around a hundred thousand dollars."

"What would you have done with the money?" Bergman asked, wondering how anyone could risk his entire future for money.

"I would have built a studio, and I would have given the rest to my daughter."

Earnestly, Steve explained that he hadn't even been in it for the money. He and Hollywood had robbed banks, he said, to get back at the political leaders who were dragging America into chaos. His hatred for the government seemed intense, and he said Scott shared his feelings, that Scott had actually given most of the money *he* stole to environmental causes.

"How'd you get caught?" the young cop asked, more interested in the football game, really, than in the prisoner's life story.

"I should have been the one to get away," Steve said. "Scott took over the driving after the robbery—when *I* should have been driving."

Bergman didn't see how it would have mattered who was driving, and he didn't comment. The man in the bed was obviously bitter that he was the one who had been captured, and that this Hollywood/Scott was still free.

Scott *had* bailed out on his friends, and now Steve, a brilliantly talented sculptor, had two mutilated arms. In the repetitive dreams he had told his brother Kevin about, it was his *legs* that were lost. He wondered now if he could ever again use his arms to create anything beautiful.

Mark Biggins miraculously survived surgery, and near midnight on Thanksgiving Eve, he had spoken to the officers guarding him—Chris Gray and Shane St. John. He admitted to them that his name was not Patrick John O'Malley—which he had given earlier—and said that he'd given the wrong birthdate, too.

"My name's really Mark Biggins."

"Where do you live?" Chris Gray asked.

"I won't tell you that."

"What's your phone number?"

"I can't tell you that either."

"Are you married?"

"Yes."

"What's your wife's name?"

Mark shook his head weakly. It wasn't Annie or

Traci or himself he was trying to protect. It was Lori, his daughter. But he would not say her name or give any information that might lead them back to her. He was deluding himself, of course. There was no way now for him to protect Lori.

Now, it seemed very unlikely that either Mark Biggins or Steve Meyers would ever go home to their daughters—at least not until their girls were middle-aged women. No one has ever doubted that each of them loved their daughters more than anything in their lives, and yet they had allowed their weaknesses, their bitterness, their excesses, their debts of honor to make them vulnerable to the ultimate manipulator.

Scotty Scurlock was yet to be found. He could be in Canada, or east of the Cascade Mountains and headed for Montana. It was easy enough to cross the border into British Columbia without a passport; Washington's relationship with that province was so friendly and relaxed that it was almost like crossing a state border. Scott didn't have his passport. That had been labeled and bagged as evidence down in Olympia and was now in the trunk of Shawn Johnson's car.

Still, by early afternoon on Thanksgiving Day, it appeared that Scott Scurlock might have made it out of the dragnet untouched. There had been remarkably few reports of suspicious characters from the neighborhood around NE Seventy-fifth. Shawn Johnson had been heading to Seattle from Olympia, of course. Mike Magan was getting ready to go to his parents' home for Thanksgiving dinner. He still had the strange eerie feeling, leftover emotion, maybe, from the power outage that had made his own neighborhood seem like a ghost town. Maybe it was just because he hadn't had any sleep.

FBI agents were attempting to locate Bill and Mary Jane Scurlock in Sedona, Arizona. They phoned Special Agent "Mac" McIlwaine in Arizona and asked him to check the elder Scurlock's home on Eagle Lane. He reported back that he and Sedona police officers had been to their home and found no one there. "The neighbors told us they were out of town for Thanksgiving."

There were a few Scurlocks living in the Seattle area. Sergeant Kevin Aratani, who had been right behind Mike Magan's car as they raced up the shoulder of I-5 the night before, checked out a Scurlock family who lived in the same general neighborhood of the gun battle. But they had never heard of a Scott Scurlock. A former Bellevue, Washington, police department employee was named Scurlock, but she knew no Scott.

Even now that they knew his name, Scott remained a phantom.

Seattle detectives Walt Maning and Cynthia Tallman were in the 2200 block of NE Seventy-seventh, looking for the casings ejected by Officers Basley's and Casey's weapons as they fired at the fleeing van. As they worked, a woman who had witnessed the shootout approached them. She made arrangements to give a formal statement. Then they walked to Seventy-fifth and Twentieth NE to take a statement from another female witness who had been taking out her garbage the night before when she heard a short siren blast, followed by shots.

It was now ten minutes to three on Thanksgiving Day.

A passerby stopped the two detectives as they moved along the sidewalk, still searching for casings or other evidence. "My son found a twenty-dollar bill and a casing last night," a resident told them. "But one of your patrolmen has already picked them up."

Cynthia Tallman and Walt Maning were standing in the 7700 block of Twentieth NE. They had seen two patrol cars with sirens screaming earlier, but thought nothing of it; the neighborhood had been riddled with Seattle police cars since the evening before. Suddenly, they heard several volleys of shots south of them. As they stood, listening, they heard more shots.

It was starting all over again.

The two homicide detectives moved into the street to stop all civilian traffic going southbound on Twentieth NE, and advised radio that they were in the area in plainclothes. Maning and Tallman waited until enough patrol units arrived to surround the area and then they moved down the street toward the sound of the shots.

By this Thanksgiving Day, everyone in the neighborhood was aware that one of the bank robbers was still loose, and they worried that he might be someplace close by. An elderly woman living on Twentieth NE watched the news and read the morning paper. She lived alone, although her grown sons visited her frequently. She'd lived in her own home for decades, and she didn't want to move. She had her garden and her friends there.

Her "boys" were due for Thanksgiving dinner, but she felt too nervous to start cooking, not knowing who might be down in the basement or hiding out in her yard. She surely wasn't going down the basement to get any of the jars of canned goods she stored down there. After worrying about it for a while, she called her fifty-three-year-old son, Robert Walker. "If you boys want Thanksgiving dinner," she said, "you'd better come over here and check things out for me. I'm not going downstairs until you check it out and make sure everything's safe. That bank robber could be right here in the house with me, for all I know."

"I'll be over early, Mom," Walker said. And, true to his word, he showed up a little before ten. He and his girlfriend and another friend checked his mother's basement, garage, and the large backyard. They looked under the deck and even walked around a camper belonging to Robert's brother, Ron. It hadn't been used for a while, and it was sitting up on saw horses in the back corner of the yard. Everything looked fine.

"We even looked at the camper door and it still had the cables locked over the door," Walker said. Reassured, Mrs. Walker went about cooking a turkey and making pies. The basement didn't look nearly so menacing once her company was there. At 2:00 P.M., Ron Walker showed up for dinner. He and Bob talked about the slight possibility that anyone might be hiding in his camper.

"Did you actually look *in* the camper?" Ron asked his brother.

"No, the door was locked."

They discussed it a little more, and Ron pointed out that there were other ways to get into the camper than through the main door. There were small access doors

low on the sides that were never locked. He didn't
bother locking them because no one could see them
when the camper was loaded on a pickup truck and in
his mother's backyard the camper was pretty much
hidden by trees.

As Bob Walker told Detective Walt Maning later,
"We went back out there and double-checked the door
again. And I walked around to the back side of the
camper—or the furthest away from the house—and
took a look at the door there, and there was a little
spring clip holding it closed. . . . So I used the palm of
my hand and hit the top apart right where the spring
clip is (supposed) to spring the door open—so I could
stick my head in there and look around. I hit it two or
three times hard with the palm of my hand, and it
didn't budge at all."

Bob Walker said he'd picked up a two-by-four and
hit the access door several times at the clasp area, but
it still wouldn't move. "I was just getting into position
to hit it where the whole latch would come all the way
off. Just about that time, my brother whispered down
to me, 'Bob, *Bob!* He's in there.'"

Bob Walker set down the two-by-four very carefully.

Ron Walker had taken a ladder over to the other
side of the camper where one window's drapes were
open. It was over the bed. He had climbed up two or
three steps and looked in. He was shocked to see that
there *was* someone inside. He had not been able to see
the man's face, but he saw the back of his head, the
curly dark hair, and a portion of his shoulders. While
he watched, he could see the man's shoulders tense.

With exquisite delicacy, the two brothers moved

away from the camper, speaking to each other only in
sign language.

In their mother's house, Ron called 911, while Bob
kept an eye on the camper. Nothing changed. No
doors opened. If there hadn't been two of them, it
might have been easy to think Ron had only imagined
someone huddled inside.

In less than five minutes, the first patrol cars
arrived. Some came up the alley near the trailer, some
stopped in front. And soon, there were Seattle police
officers everywhere.

Mike and Lisa hadn't left for Susan and Frank
Magan's house yet. They were just beginning to gather
up things when the phone rang. It was Chris Gough,
Mike's old partner from his bike patrol days.

"Mike," Chris said, "I think they got your guy. Get
on the radio."

Mike left the house with lights whirling and siren
shrilling. "I wanted to see how it would end," he said.
"I couldn't stay away."

He was carrying a gun; before he had left Homicide
the night before, one of the sergeants had given him
one. It was a vote of confidence, a sign that they knew
he had fired his own Glock only because he had no
other choice. There would, of course, be a shooting
review board—as there always is when a Seattle
Police officer fires his gun at someone. Mike hoped to
God he would not have to shoot on this day.

When Shawn Johnson arrived at Mrs. Walker's
house, he saw a seemingly endless stream of blue
whirling lights. "I don't think I've ever seen so many

police in one spot in my life," he remembered. He parked on the south side of the surrounded property. "I'm thinking I've got to get my MP5 (a shoulder weapon) out of my trunk—but I opened the trunk and it was still so stuffed with the evidence from the treehouse property that I couldn't get to my gun."

He looked again at the waves of squad cars and the personnel standing by and realized they probably didn't need an FBI agent who had been on duty and hadn't eaten or slept for thirty-six hours. He also realized it would be a long time before he got home. Of course, he would not have gone home if someone had ordered him to. He had to be where he was just as much as Mike Magan did.

They were finally coming to the end of something that had consumed them for a very long time.

37

Sergeant Howard Monta had been off duty the evening of the bank robbery. He heard about the shootout and knew that his men who were under fire. He had offered to come in and help, but Radio Dispatch had told him they already had enough commanders on the scene.

Monta *was* scheduled to work second watch on Thanksgiving Day. At his squad's roll call at 11:30

A.M., the main topic of discussion was, of course, the bank robbery and shootout of the night before. Since he was a sergeant in the neighborhood where it had all happened, Monta expected that he and his officers might have a pretty busy day answering calls from nervous residents. It looked, however, as though the fugitive bank robber had managed to get away under cover of darkness.

Monta's wife and son promised him that they would wait to have Thanksgiving dinner with him after his shift ended just before 8:00 P.M.

At 2:36 P.M., Monta heard two units on his squad receive a call to check out a possible prowler in a backyard on Twentieth NE near Seventy-fifth. "I decided to respond," Monta said. "Even though I believed that Hollywood was long gone. The intense search that had been conducted made it highly unlikely that he would still be in the area."

Monta was the first to arrive at the address given. Ron Walker came out to meet him and explained what he had seen. Monta asked Walker what the best approach to the camper would be—just in case someone was inside.

"Are you *positive* you saw someone in there?"

"I can't be absolutely positive," Walker said, wondering now if he had only imagined a man inside. "But I thought I saw a curtain move—and now the curtains seem to be in a little different position. But then we've had trouble with kids getting in there in the past."

Monta suspected Ron Walker was reacting to the general panic in the neighborhood. He had been a cop for a very long time, was just about to retire, in fact.

Howard Monta knew that the power of suggestion made people see things.

The patrol units in his squad arrived, and Monta directed them to the backyard of the Walker home. While his officers moved to surround the camper—just in case—Ron Walker led Monta, Officers Jon Dittoe and Mike Cruzan, J. Johnson, and Student Officer Sjon Stevens to the camper.

Monta and Walker went to the camper door while the patrol officers took up positions near the huge fir trees at the back of the yard. Monta could see that the cable lock on the camper door was securely fastened and the curtains along the side windows were drawn tightly shut. The window at the north end of the camper was covered by either a couch or a chair cushion.

"I knocked on the east window and the door of the camper," Monta recalled, "and said 'Seattle Police.' Even though I thought there was no one inside, I was still careful in positioning myself to the side of the door and window—just in case."

One of the patrol officers yelled toward the camper, saying that the police were outside.

There was no response at all. They hadn't really expected one.

"You think Scurlock's in there, Mike?" Monta asked, half joking.

"Hey, Scurlock," Cruzan called from behind the tree where he aimed his weapon for cover fire, "if you're in there, you'd better come out!"

Nothing.

Ron Walker showed Sergeant Monta the storage hatch on the right side of the ten-foot camper. "Some-

399

body could have crawled through there," he said. "It's blocked from the inside, and it shouldn't be."

Thinking that "somebody" would have to be pretty slim and agile to get in that way, Monta asked Ron Walker to remove the lock from the door, but Walker said it was also locked from inside. "And I've lost the door key."

Cruzan stretched up to a small window on the north side, opposite the door, and shined his flashlight in. He could see no person or movement inside. Just a cold camper with built-in upholstered benches, a stationary table, an over-cab bed.

Monta cracked open one of the louvered windows and called, "Come out—or it's going to get uncomfortable."

Nothing.

Almost positive that the camper was empty, but loath to leave without being sure, Monta pulled two canisters of Oleoresin Capsicum Spray (pepper spray) from his jacket. As it happened, he was the pepper spray instructor for the Seattle Police Department, and he knew its effects all too well. If anyone was inside, they could not possibly remain in such a confined space without crying out or coughing when the spray came in.

He emptied a canister of pepper spray into the louvered window.

There was no response at all.

Just to be absolutely sure that the camper was empty, Howard Monta emptied the second canister.

Nothing. There wasn't a cough, a shout, even a sigh, from inside.

"With no sound at all from the camper," Monta

said, "that convinced me that no one was in the camper—that it was safe enough to break in."

Howard Monta almost decided not to check out the camper. But as long as they were there, he reached through the window to open the door, knocking aside the cushion. He lifted his flashlight, prepared to shine it into the corners of the shadowy camper, and heard—incredibly—the boom of a gunshot.

"I thought I was dead," he remembered. He ran for cover, hearing multiple gunshots behind him. He dove toward a large fir tree about ten feet west of the camper, but the student officer was already there. "I didn't think it would be quite fair to pull rank on the kid and kick him out of there, so I broke and ran for the next tree. I had only taken a few steps when rapid semiautomatic gunfire rang out again."

Monta hit the ground and crawled. He looked back and saw the curtains moving in the camper's windows. He radioed that shots had been fired and asked for backup.

When he reached another large tree, Jon Dittoe, who had been covering Monta, yelled to ask for cover fire so that *he* could move farther away from the camper.

Monta fired several rounds from his 357 Magnum revolver, and another officer fired his 9-mm semiautomatic. Mike Cruzan and J. Johnson also fired to cover Dittoe.

The backyard where Mrs. Walker had taken such pride in her flowers and bushes rang out with the sound of gunfire. Monta and his men were using cover fire to allow all of them to get as far away from the camper as possible. "My biggest worry," Monta recalled, "was that Hollywood was going to get desperate and charge out with automatic weapon fire. We had used a lot of our ammunition; one officer had used both of his clips. I called for more ammunition on the radio. I also called for assistance from a television news helicopter that was overhead, (asking them) to watch for an attempted escape into the yard east of us."

It didn't seem possible that anyone could get out of that east window—but then it hadn't seemed possible that someone had been inside, waiting with a gun drawn, someone who had the self-control to breathe in two canisters of pepper spray without making a sound.

Sjon Stevens, the student officer, was able to scramble out of the backyard and return with a shotgun. Monta had him train it on the door of the camper, with orders to shoot immediately if Hollywood—or anyone else—came out that way with a weapon in his hand.

Ron Walker had gone back into the house to get a screwdriver to open the door or a window when he heard gunfire. He went into the bedroom where he could observe the backyard. He saw three officers with their guns drawn as they tried to keep the trees between themselves and the camper. He watched one officer fire into the camper and thought he saw return fire.

Walker stood, frozen, by the window for about fifteen minutes. There was one more spate of gunfire during that time, but he could not tell who had fired.

The Seattle Police Emergency Response Team arrived. Mike Magan directed newly arrived patrol units, suggesting several ways to surround the backyard where the camper sat. Most of the units responding had been his backup the night before.

Officer Jennifer McLean, who had found the discarded jacket at the shootout scene the night before, reached the Walker house at seven minutes to three on that Thanksgiving afternoon. She was a trained negotiator.

The camper was contained; the man inside could not possibly get past the dozens of law-enforcement officers who took up positions around the Walker property. To help the Emergency Response Team, Jennifer McLean had Ron Walker draw a detailed sketch of the exterior of the house, the backyard, and the camper itself.

How long could Scott Scurlock—if it was, indeed, Scurlock in the camper—survive in the camper? She asked Walker what was inside the camper that might be useful to him.

There was virtually nothing. No electricity, no food, no television, no radio, no phone, no heat, no batteries, no cooking utensils or knives. No blankets, no first aid supplies. There was some water in a twenty-gallon tank.

If Scott Scurlock was trapped in there, how ironic that the man who liked to go first class all the way, who drank Dom Perignon and ate at the best restaurants, was holed up on the traditional day of feasting in a beat-up little camper. He was surely cold, hungry, and desperate. He might even believe that both his friends were dead, and feel remorse. And it had all been for nothing: $1,080,000 had slipped from his grasp.

But the Scott Scurlock who could hike the Grand Canyon and climb Mount Rainier in tennis shoes and shorts, without food or water, might be capable of waiting out the police. If and when he surrendered, it would be on his own terms. He had trained his body to be his most important weapon, and he had survived before on far less than most men could.

Shawn Johnson got a cup of hot chocolate from the mobile food station the fire department had set up for the officers. He tried to drink it, but his hands shook so much it kept spilling. He stayed at the command post with his supervisor and with Burdena Pasenelli, the Special Agent in Charge of the Seattle FBI Office. People kept telling Johnson, "Go home—go home," but he shook his head.

Mike Magan wondered what was happening at his folks' house. Were they having dinner? Every officer there had someplace to go, and somebody missing them on this day. But nobody moved.

At the downtown FBI offices, Special Agent Faye Greenlee received a phone call from Reverend William Scurlock. He said that he and his wife, Mary Jane, had learned from someone in Seattle—probably Sabrina Adams—that his son was being sought by the FBI.

Bill Scurlock was calling from Denver, from the home of one of his daughters. He seemed concerned, of course, but sounded genuinely amazed that it might be *his* son the FBI wanted. Greenlee told Scurlock that she wanted him to hang up—that Bill Waltz, one of the Seattle Police Department's hostage negotiators, would be calling him immediately. It was essential that Waltz talk to him.

After the hostage negotiators had learned whatever they could from Scott's father that might help them bring him out of the camper without anyone being injured further, Faye Greenlee talked again to Reverend Scurlock. He said that he knew now that police had surrounded an area where his son was believed to be hiding. They also believed, apparently, that Scott was a bank robber who had shot at police. He said it was "unthinkable" that Scott would ever try to kill anyone. He didn't think Scott would shoot at anyone—unless, perhaps, he was faced with prison.

Scurlock described his son as a gentle, caring, charismatic, and personable man. He told Faye Greenlee that Scott had many friends of both sexes—but that he was also a loner who sometimes enjoyed being by himself. He hurried to point out, however, that Scott was certainly not an isolationist.

As far as any experience Scott might have had with guns, all his father could think of was a time, when Scott was given a round-trip ticket to London for a high school graduation present. On the trip, he had spent time on an Israeli kibbutz near the Golan Heights. When he came home, he told his father that he had received training from the military there, including weaponry and self-protection, and the protection of others in the kibbutz.

His father said that Scott hadn't visited their Sedona home since June, but that they were expecting him in December. He had never talked about financial difficulties. His parents thought he earned his living as an "entrepreneur" and in carpentry and logging.

A bank robber? *Never!*

From the way his father described him to the FBI, Scott Scurlock sounded like the all-American son. As far as Bill Scurlock knew, Scott never drank hard liquor. He had stopped smoking marijuana years ago. No, he would not do something like this for publicity or as a way to get attention.

If he had not deliberately set out to get attention, Scott Scurlock was certainly getting a great deal of it. Now, for the second day in a row, a peaceful family neighborhood in the northeast part of Seattle was a war zone. A few stray bullets had zinged through a dining room wall where turkey was being served. Most of the block's residents had either evacuated by choice or at the Police Department's request.

A huge armored vehicle lumbered into the backyard where the camper sat with its shattered windows and bullet-pierced shell. The mammoth thing looked like an armadillo crouched over some of Mrs. Walker's prize rosebushes.

The afternoon wore on, and everyone watched the red and white camper. There had been no movement at all from inside, no response to the negotiators. It would be dark soon; Seattle was only three weeks away from the shortest day of the year. It would be full dark by five.

Mike Magan's attention was drawn to some FBI

agents who were escorting a woman toward the edge of the yard. He wondered who she was. She was blond and slender, slightly tan—something that stood out in Seattle in late November. And she seemed terribly upset. He watched her, curious to see what part she might play in this endless drama.

"I glanced at her shoes for some reason," Mike recalled. "And she was wearing high-top Converses. And then I knew who she was—who she *had* to be. *That's his girlfriend!* I thought."

She was. FBI agents had brought Sabrina Adams to the scene in the hope that she might be able to convince Scott to surrender and come out of the camper without any more shooting. His parents couldn't fly from Denver in time to help, so Sabrina was it.

"She was sobbing," Mike said. "And biting her nails, pleading with Scott to give up."

It had been such a long day. Mike looked at Jon Dittoe and Mike Cruzan. They had been part of his backup last night, and now they'd been involved in the gunfire on Thanksgiving Day. He saw that their faces were chalky with fatigue and emotion. They had all gone without sleep for too long now.

Mike watched the girlfriend, and, as hysterical as she was, as fervent as her shouted pleas were, she didn't seem to be getting through to Scott. There was no response from the camper at all.

It was finally completely dark, and still nothing had happened. They could not risk spending a long night out here with no action. They had decided to force the barricaded fugitive out of the camper. At 6:00 P.M. on Thanksgiving Day, the crowd hushed as Phil Hay from the SWAT team fired a tear gas canister toward the camper. It pierced the metallic skin on one side, went straight through and came out the other side.

Some people can survive pepper spray, but no one can breathe with tear gas choking them. And Scott Scurlock was hiding in a tiny camper. The sound of the shot faded and then everyone watched to see the door burst open and a choking man tumble out.

But nothing happened.

Sabrina Adams stood at the edge of the crowd, silent. And then she turned and moved to an area where she could use a phone. She called Bill and Mary Jane Scurlock and told them what had just happened. Bill put another call in to the FBI, and wanted to know if it was true that the police had fired tear gas into the camper where his son was supposed to be—and that Scott had not come out. He needed to know what that meant.

Faye Greenlee could not tell him because she didn't know. She was not on the scene. Even if she had been, she wouldn't have been able to tell him. No one could be sure.

At 6:20, Phil Hay fired another tear gas canister into the camper. And, again, there was no response. Now, there was no question in anyone's mind that, if there was a man inside, he was dead.

Sergeant Paul McDonagh, head of the Emergency Response Team, walked slowly toward the bullet-riddled camper. It was brightly lit by auxiliary lights. He moved past the tall fir trees, across wet grass strewn with autumn leaves, and then past the still-lit flashlight that Howard Monta had dropped just after the first shot was fired hours before.

With his team covering him, McDonagh opened the camper door. No one breathed. His voice came over the radio, "We don't see anything . . ."

That could not be. There was no way that Scott Scurlock could have gotten out of that camper. Not if he had been in there when Howard Monta pushed aside the cushion and looked in shortly before three.

A deeper silence gripped the crowd now as McDonagh moved around inside the camper. Out of all of those hundreds listening for some word from the SWAT commander, no one held their breaths more than Mike Magan and Shawn Johnson.

And then McDonagh's voice said, "There's a lot of blood . . . a lot of blood. But we can't find a body."

Shawn actually thought, *What is this guy—a ghost? There's got to be a body in there. What do they mean there's no body?*

They could see the flicker of floodlights and shadows inside the camper, and then, finally, McDonagh said, "We have a body." After a long pause, he said, "It appears to be that of a white male in his late thirties."

Paul McDonagh had not been able to see the man at first because he was almost hidden *beneath* a tiny dinette table that sat on a stainless steel pedestal. The dead man had wrapped himself in blue and red gingham print plastic table cloths, a bedspread, and upholstered cushions, effectively disappearing in the protective coloration of the camper decor.

He was positioned on his right side, the right side of

his face lying on the built-in seat beside the table, and his legs tucked below. Only his left hand rested on the table top.

The body in the trailer wore a dark green shirt, gray pants, and beige boat shoes, and the deceased had a profusion of curly dark hair. His face was not disfigured.

McDonagh called for someone to bring a picture of Scott Scurlock down to the camper so that they might make positive identification.

Mike Magan realized he didn't want to go. It was over at last. "I figured he was dead," Mike said. "It had been so long, and there were so many bullets. And, now, with the tear gas, when there was no response—he had to be dead. I didn't particularly want to see his body."

Shawn Johnson could hear other officers saying, "We got him. It's wrapped up. It's over."

"Not in my mind, it wasn't," Shawn said. "I had some pictures of Scott that I'd taken from the search that morning. One was in my pocket and I'd given one to the Seattle Police Department to put up on the bulletin board at the command post. Until that day, nobody *really* knew what Hollywood looked like. I realized that I needed to go down to the camper to see who this was."

On strangely wooden legs, Johnson made his way down through the fir trees. He had seen only one other body in his career, and that had been another bank robber who had been fatally shot after robbing a Wedgwood area bank.

Homicide Detectives Greg Mixsell, Walt Maning, and Cynthia Tallman had been at the command post all afternoon, and they had been joined by Sergeant Don Cameron, and detectives Sonny Davis, Al Gerdes, and Cloyd Steiger. The task of determining the sequence of events was now up to the Seattle Police Homicide Unit. There was no more danger from the man who half lay/half sat behind and beneath the camper's table. There was no possibility any longer that he would escape.

Don Cameron, something of a legend in the Seattle Police Homicide Unit, had been there longer than anyone assigned to homicide. Big enough to dwarf most patrol officers, Cameron had forgotten more about unveiling the mysteries of violent deaths than most of his detectives knew. He was a familiar—and reassuring—sight in his tan raincoat. The crime scene was in his experienced hands now.

Cameron glanced at the photograph Shawn Johnson held out and nodded. The dead man was undoubtedly William Scott Scurlock. How and when he had died would take a little while longer to determine. No one could stay inside the camper for more than a few seconds because it was permeated with tear gas fumes. It would be at least an hour before they could start processing the death scene. Even then, the homicide detectives would have to wear gas masks.

Johnson glanced at the body of the man who had been Hollywood. He wanted to say, "Wake up, and talk to me!" but he knew he would never get to ask the questions he had been saving up. The lights, the blood, the acrid, choking smell of tear gas, and so many hours without food or sleep made it all seem surreal.

Shawn Johnson turned and walked away. He still

had evidence to deliver to the FBI downtown, and then he could go home.

As he drove, he remembered how he had talked to his wife about celebrating when they finally caught Hollywood and his accomplices, how they would have a big party at their house and invite everyone who had worked on the twenty bank robberies.

"I didn't feel like celebrating," he remembered. "There was nothing to celebrate."

Mike Magan watched Paul McDonagh walk up from the camper area, after he'd turned it over to Don Cameron. McDonagh came over to Mike, and said, "It's all over, Mike. I appreciate your help. And I'm glad you're alive."

"It's your training that kept me alive," Mike said. And it was. McDonagh had drilled his men and the task force to be ready for anything. And when "anything" happened, Mike had been ready.

It was close to eight. Mike headed, finally, over to his parents' house. His dad "debriefed" him, listening to every detail of the past twenty-seven hours. His mother cried, and filled a plate for him.

Finally, on Thanksgiving Night, Mike slept.

Bill Scurlock had waited all afternoon for word from the FBI in Seattle. Faye Greenlee had called and told him that it was true that tear gas had been fired into the camper where his son had barricaded himself.

"Then he must be dead, or he would have come out," Scurlock said, with no hope in his voice.

"I don't know," Greenlee said. "But I promise you I will call you as soon as I do have any definite word."

At 8:00 P.M., Faye Greenlee called the Scurlocks in Denver and told them that a body *had* been found in the camper. A positive identification could not be made until the King County Medical Examiner arrived.

Scott's father said he would be flying to Seattle the next morning. Greenlee suggested he contact the Seattle Police Department Chaplain for assistance in dealing with the tragedy that had stunned his family. But Bill Scurlock wanted no contact whatsoever with the Seattle Police Department.

38

It was 7:40 P.M. on November 28, 1996, when Sergeant Don Cameron escorted a senior Seattle Fire Department Paramedic into the red-and-white camper. At that moment, William Scott Scurlock was officially pronounced dead. He had been dead for hours, although it would take a postmortem examination by the Medical Examiner to say how many hours.

Wearing gas masks, the homicide detectives began to process the camper and the area around it. They would be there until midnight; any homicide crime scene requires many hours of investigation, tedious collection of the most minute evidence, and photographs of *everything*. Although some of their reconstruction of the shooting could be done with computer software later, they had to gather the information while the scene was cordoned off and untouched.

They began with the outside of the red-and-white camper, noting that the east side almost abutted the fence. The front of the camper was about about seven feet from the alley. The homicide detectives could see now that copious amounts of blood had dripped through the floor onto the grass beneath.

All the windows on the west side of the camper were shattered, as were the front windows in the cabover sleeping section. There were sixteen bullet "defects" in that portion, all within an eighteen-inch diameter.

"That would account for Jon Dittoe's return of fire—to cover Monta," one detective commented.

The west side of the camper—which had faced the first officers at the scene—had twenty-six bullet holes on that side. These were consistent with the covering fire that Cruzan, Monta, and Johnson had provided to allow Jon Dittoe to get out of the line of fire that might come from the camper.

There were twelve exit defects on the other side of the camper, and two at the rear.

The homicide detectives went inside and jotted down their description of the little camper that had become an abattoir: "With the entrance door open, there is a small dinette/eating area, with a small table and cushioned bench seats to the left . . . to the right of the door is storage. Forward on the right are cabinets and a sink, and to the left a small 'reefer' (refrigerator) and cabinets. . . ."

The interior of the camper looked as though some giant had picked it up and shaken it vigorously. Drawers had been pulled out and were lying on the floor. The cupboard doors were open and their contents strewn all over. "There is broken glass, blood, and powdered CS chemical agent (from the tear gas) covering almost every horizontal surface," Sonny Davis noted.

Scott Scurlock's body remained where he had died. The most severe visible wound was just beneath his chin. Except for the blood, he looked as if he had fallen asleep at the table and slid sideways on the bench. He looked much younger than the age given for him—forty-two—and there was no gray at all in his curly dark hair.

An examination of his body revealed a black nylon shoulder holster attached to his belt. There was a magazine pouch with two loaded clips, and a hunting knife in a scabbard. On his right ankle, he had a black nylon ankle holster that contained a Beretta .22 pistol.

Scott's body rested in the trajectory of many of the bullets that had penetrated the camper shell. Only an autopsy would reveal how many wounds he had sustained, and whether they had occurred before or after death.

At 10:30, Dr. Norman Thiersch and Investigator Don Marvin from the King County Medical Examiner's Office arrived to begin their examination of the body. The hands were bagged with plastic baggies before the body was moved. As the ME's men lifted it, a spent 9-mm casing and three projectiles fell to the floor, along with two keys and a banded packet of cash.

Scott had been dead for hours, and his body was in full rigor mortis. The core temperature of his body had dropped to 95.93 degrees.

There were obvious postmortem wounds, but Dr. Thiersch found what appeared to be a contact wound beneath the chin and a corresponding exit wound just in the hair line at the top front of the forehead.

The body was removed at 11:30 P.M. The camper was impounded and taken to a long-term storage facility, and the Seattle Fire Department came to wash the scene clean of any sign that a man had died violently in this quiet corner of a gentle lady's backyard.

When Cameron and his crew drove off, the streets were dark and quiet. The police, the FBI, the onlookers, the reporters, the helicopters, all gone now.

Thanksgiving Day, 1996, was over.

Down in Virginia, Kevin Meyers had had a good holiday with his mother. When the phone rang that Thursday evening, he had expected it to be Ellen—calling to share a little bit of the day with him. He had not expected to hear her sobbing so violently that she could barely speak. He begged her to calm down, and finally she was able to blurt out the words that Kevin had been dreading.

"Scott's dead," she said, softly, "and Steve's been shot. He's in the hospital, and he's under arrest. They robbed a bank."

Kevin glanced at his mother. She had been through so much that he couldn't bear the thought of what he had to tell her. Dana was dead, his stepfather was dead, Randy was in Europe. At least Steve was still alive.

That was small comfort, but it was some.

Ellen was the kind of woman who cried if her cat killed a mouse; she bled for the whole world. Whatever Scott had been, Ellen had hoped that he would change, that he would tap some well of goodness inside himself. She had tried to talk him through his night terrors, but now she remembered how frightened he was of the dark, red-eyed, creatures who lay in wait for him, and she began to sob harder, gasping for air.

Kevin asked her to put her daughters on the line. He told them that they must help their mom—that she was very, very sad because of Scott—and because of Steve. They weren't little kids; they would be able to help her until he got home.

And then he turned to his mother, took a deep breath, and told her the news that no mother should ever have to hear. Ellen said that Steve had been shot in his arms and his shoulders. Kevin looked at the pieces of his brother's sculpture in his mother's house, and he asked himself: *How could he have sacrificed the wonderful talent that God gave him in a search for gold? And now God had taken away his arms.*

Marge Violette Mullins was startled to hear her phone ring late on Thanksgiving night. And more surprised to hear Kevin's voice on the line. "Scott's dead, Marge," he said. "And Steve's all shot up. They got caught robbing a bank."

After a moment of shocked silence, Marge remembered Scott telling her about his being involved in something about banking. She had never imagined *this*.

"Where are your boys?" Kevin asked.

"They're asleep."

"Wake them up, Marge. Wake them up and tell them."

"Why, tonight?"

"I want to be sure that they know that crime doesn't pay. Somebody told us that once, but I guess Steve didn't believe it."

"OK, I'll wake them up."

And she did. When she had finished explaining what had happened to the man who had been so good to them, the man who lived in the treehouse, her oldest son looked at her with a dawning expression of understanding.

"Mom," he said, "that's where he got so much money, isn't it? That's why he could give us twenty-dollar bills and not even care. Because it wasn't his money at all, was it?"

"No, it wasn't."

Marge sat 2,000 miles away from Seattle, and remembered a night in Hawaii from two decades past. Try as she might, she could not understand how the sensitive young man she knew then—the man whose biggest ambition was to save someone's life—had ended up dead in a gunfight with the police.

Ren Talbot was returning from Thanksgiving dinner at her parents' home in Olympia with a friend when the news came on. She was surprised—but not shocked—when she heard that Scott Scurlock was dead and how his life had ended. But then, the report continued, and she heard Mark Biggins' name. She was more than shocked, more than stunned. She hadn't seen or heard from Mark in many years, but the man she remembered could not have changed enough that he would become a bank robber. The Mark she remembered was the gentlest man she had ever known.

Friday, November 29, was still a holiday for most people, but the Seattle Homicide Offices were open for business at 7:45 A.M. Mike Magan had spoken with Traci Marsh, who said that she was Mark Biggins' common-law wife. He told Greg Mixsell that apparently Mark and Scott had been friends at Evergreen College and that Mark had gone to Olympia to work in Scott's "construction business."

At Harborview Hospital, Mark was ready to tell all of the truth. With tears in his eyes, he admitted to Cynthia Tallman, Greg Mixsell, and Walt Maning that he lived in Oxnard, California, with Traci and his teenage daughter. He had tried so hard not to involve Traci and Lori, but the worlds that he thought he could keep separate had collided. How had he thought that they would not?

Scott Scurlock's autopsy took place at noon on Friday, with the trio of homicide detectives observing. Dr. Thiersch pointed out the chin wound, and the distinctive contact impression of the muzzle of a Glock pistol. It was clearly a self-inflicted wound, one that would have been instantly fatal as the .40 caliber slug tore through the frontal lobe of the brain, causing multiple fractures of the skull as it exited.

There were six other wounds, all of them attributable to bullets fired by someone else, and almost surely, they were postmortem. One bullet had entered the back of Scott's neck, fracturing the cervical spine at C3. Had he lived, he would probably have been a quadriplegic. The third bullet entered the back and caused hemorrhaging into his left lung. Another had pierced the back and fractured his spine at the L5 level, and the last three sliced through the soft tissues of his arms and legs.

It would be of some comfort to the many people who loved Scott Scurlock to know that he never felt anything after he placed the muzzle of his Glock beneath his chin and fired.

The legend of Hollywood was over, although people in the Northwest would talk about his exploits and his motivations for years to come. His crimes and his death made headlines in Reston, Virginia, and in cities all over Washington State. Ironically, one *Seattle Times* headline read, "Scurlock: Known for his Looks, Charm, and His Big Tips."

A photograph accompanying the article showed a handsome, bare-chested Scott. It was a shallow memorial to a man whose whole life was modeled on the movies.

His memorial service was in Olympia, on the twenty acres where he had built himself a perfect world. Mourners built a huge bonfire in his honor. There were many, many people who had loved Scott

Scurlock and most of them were there. They spoke of how he was now free.

And, in a sense, he was. But the two friends who bought into his dream were not. For Mark Biggins and Steve Meyers and for all the people who loved them, the years ahead loomed ominously.

Epilogue

By the time Steve Meyers and Mark Biggins had recovered enough to be transferred from Harborview Hospital to the King County Jail, the Christmas season was well under way. But not for them. They saw the world now through the slit-like windows in the jail that sits high on a hill above Elliot Bay. What had seemed unbelievable was all too real.

Ren Talbot hadn't seen Mark for years, but she remembered the sweet guy she had known in Olympia. She was working as an investigator for Seattle criminal defense attorney, Fred Leatherman, and she hoped that she could help Mark. "I went up to the jail to see him," she recalled. "At first, I barely recognized him, but then he saw me and he just hung his head. He was so ashamed."

Fred Leatherman agreed to defend Mark, and Steve retained defense attorney JoAnn Oliver. The prisoners faced serious federal charges. Katrina C. Pflaumer, United States Attorney for the Western District of Washington and William H. Redkey, Jr., Assistant United States Attorney, filed the charges: One count of Conspiracy to commit armed bank robbery; one count of Armed Bank Robbery; two counts of Assault on a Federal officer; and one count of Use of a Firearm (a semiautomatic assault weapon-shotgun).

The maximum combined prison time for the five charges was fifty years for the first four, and an additional ten years on the firearm charge—a mandatory term and which, by law, had to run *consecutively* to the other sentences. In addition, there could be fines totaling a million dollars. Somewhat ironically, the smallest monetary penalty called for one hundred dollars (on each count) to be paid to the Crime Victims Fund.

If Mark and Steve went to trial, they each faced the possibility of spending sixty years in prison, and they could be fined almost as much as they had stolen. They had no money, so that was moot—but they were over forty, and, if they should receive the maximum penalty for their offenses, they would have to serve virtually a life sentence.

Usually mitigation packages are used only in cases where convicted killers face the death penalty. Now, Ren Talbot and Kevin Meyers set out to show the federal prosecutors and Judge William Dwyer the kind of men Mark Biggins and Steve Meyers had been before they became involved in Scott Scurlock's plans. They encouraged family and friends to write letters, they gathered photographs and remembrances, incorporating them in two albums. They were albums that reflected the most positive aspects of two lives, lives that anyone could be proud of.

Would it be enough to spare Mark and Steve from life in prison? No one knew. Both men had admitted their complicity in the Lake City bank robbery.

Despite her better judgment, Ren Talbot found herself drawn to Mark Biggins. She had always liked him, and now she tried very hard not to love him. She watched as his daughter Lori came to visit for Christmas. His agony as he realized that he wouldn't be there for Lori any longer was painful to see. When Traci Marsh abandoned Mark—and Lori—Ren did what she could to convince him not to give up.

The intertwining of lives continued, only at a muted pace. Scott Scurlock, who may have believed that he would live forever, died without a will. His parents hired an attorney to oversee the assets that were now theirs. Bill Scurlock was anxious to look through the property that the FBI was holding from their searches and impounds of Scott's homes and vehicles. He contacted Shawn Johnson, who told him he was quite welcome to do that. Scott's father and one of his sisters appeared a few days later to catalogue what now belonged to them.

With the FBI agents, the elder Scurlock was cordial. He still refused to talk at all with the Seattle Police Department, apparently blaming *them* for Scott's death.

The Scurlocks allowed Sabrina Adams to stay on in the treehouse and she became a sad and lonely caretaker. Her hope was to buy the property. However, the asking price was reported to be over $300,000, far beyond her assets. She still owed $30,000 on the credit card loan she had taken out to give Scott.

At night, intruders with shovels and flashlights prowled Seven Cedars, enticed by rumors that Scott had buried thousands of dollars around his land. And, indeed, he had. The question was, was there any left?

The $114,000 taken in the May 1996 robbery was probably gone by November. And the $40,000 from the Wells Fargo robbery only five days before the failed Lake City robbery was pretty well accounted for after the FBI search. If there *was* any buried treasure out among the cedar trees, no one has ever admitted finding it.

Sabrina stayed on in the treehouse until the spring of 1998, even as it deteriorated around her. There were no more work parties to repair it and, finally, it became too dangerous to live in. Now, only the squirrels and the birds perch on its decks. Renters live in the gray house.

Seven Cedars is still for sale.

In February 1997, Steve Meyers and Mark Biggins entered into a plea bargain agreement with federal prosecutors. In return for the U.S. Attorney's promise not to file any additional charges on other assaults or robberies, they agreed to plead guilty to one count of Armed Bank Robbery, two counts of Assault on a Federal Officer, and one count of Firearms Violation. (King County, Washington, prosecutors would not file charges on the assaults on the Seattle police officers.) In doing this, Mark and Steve gave up their rights to a trial. They were sentenced to twenty-one years in a federal prison. Steve Meyers is serving his sentence at the federal penitentiary in Sheridan, Oregon, and Mark Biggins is incarcerated at a federal prison in Terminal Island, California.

With good behavior, they could be out in another seventeen years, although they are currently seeking a reduction in their sentences to a point where they would have only twelve years to serve.

Lori Biggins visits her father whenever she can. He helps her with her homework still, but over the phone, now. Traci Marsh lives somewhere on the East Coast, and Lori lives with one of Mark's brother's family.

Kevin Meyers did his best to help *his* brother avoid a long prison sentence, to no avail. It was Kevin who went to New Orleans and packed up Steve's belongings and sculptures. Then, on Steve's instructions, he sold the New Orleans house and studio, and banked the money—for Steve. But even after all of Kevin's efforts, Steve was angry with him. They no longer speak or write. The fall of 1996 continued to be a season of loss for Kevin Meyers. Two weeks after Scott committed suicide, Bobby Gray was burning some trash outside his Florida home when a spark ignited the gas can in his hand. The ensuing explosion knocked him unconscious, and when he came to he was on fire. He rolled down a rock-strewn driveway into a palmetto grove, trying desperately to smother the flames. It was too late; he was terribly burned over most of his body.

Bobby Gray lived only eighteen hours, and for the second time in as many weeks, Kevin lost a friend he'd known for more than thirty years. He flew back to Florida to give the eulogy at Bobby's funeral. It seemed to Kevin that death was everywhere he looked.

Kevin and Ellen have stayed together, both of them shell-shocked and grieving at first, although they have come to a quiet acceptance of what they cannot change. After a while, Kevin started painting again. His later work is more spectacular than anything he has ever done. His dearest wish remains, as always, to have a studio that belongs to him, a wish that eludes him, still.

Mike Magan went back to duty on December 5. That was the day that Seafirst Bank gave a luncheon to honor the officers who caught Hollywood, and his accomplices. Mike had permission to pick up Lisa in a squad car that day. They were headed for the Four Seasons Olympic Hotel to join 150 other Seattle Police officers and FBI agents for a belated Thanksgiving feast when Mike's radio sounded bank robbery tones. The Wells Fargo bank at 1620 Fourth Avenue had just been robbed.

"I kept waiting for someone else to respond," Mike said, laughing, "but they were all at the luncheon. Finally, I turned off the freeway at Roanoke to go after the robber."

The radio dispatcher reported that the robber had hopped on a bus headed north, and gave a precise description. At that moment, Lisa Magan looked in the window of a bus just passing them and said, "Mike, there he is!"

The robber gazed back at them from the bus window. There didn't seem to be any other patrol units around, although Mike could hear the rotors of Guardian One overhead.

Over her protestations, Mike stopped and left his wife on the parking strip and then peeled out with siren wide open after the bus. He caught it just as Lt. Linda Pierce and Captain Dan Bryant—also on their way to the Seafirst luncheon—pulled up. The three of them split up and entered the bus front, middle, and back. They arrested still another bank robber.

In the meantime, a patrol car had picked up Lisa

Magan and driven her to headquarters to wait for Mike. But when they brought her in, everyone thought *she* was the suspect. She and Mike finally got to the luncheon, but they were late.

Mike Magan served three years on the Puget Sounds Violent Crimes Task Force, and he is currently a detective assigned to the Domestic Violence Unit. He still reacts to the "tones" that signal a bank robbery until he remembers that he is in another phase of his police career.

Shawn Johnson finished up his eleven years in the Seattle FBI office in September. His next station will be in Wisconsin. Although he and his wife are happy to be going "home," they will miss Seattle. Shawn still regrets that he never got to talk to Scott Scurlock, the man he sought so long who died before he could explain *why*.

No one will ever really know what made Scott Scurlock run. Scores of people *thought* they knew him well and they were shocked to find that they did not. In death as in life, he remains an enigma. Seemingly, he had every quality it takes to become a success, to be happy, to make the world a better place. He should not have died only halfway through his life. People who loved him *still* love him, even though they know now his hidden side.

As an author who never knew him, I found myself delaying the time when I had to write the end of Scott Scurlock's story—as if, somehow, it might change before I came to the night of November 28, 1996. I didn't want him to die. All of us want to like someone who is physically beautiful, charming, and fun to be with. Perhaps we all secretly admire the rascal adventurer. Certainly, we want to believe that, underneath, they really do care about other people.

But some of them really don't.

Was Scott Scurlock a man without conscience and a complete hedonist? Probably. He left behind a trail of broken hearts, broken friendships, and damaged lives. He always knew the probable consequences of what he was doing, but he didn't stop. Quite likely, he was more afraid for himself when Captain Pat was murdered than he was remorseful. But Scott only changed gears, dropping the manufacture of crystal meth and beginning another illegal activity.

Although he was generous to his friends, he had no compunction about robbing them of the things that meant the most to them. In the end, like all sociopaths, Scott seemed unable to feel anyone else's pain. If he had had the empathy that others possess, he would not have coaxed Steve away from his art. He would not have taken Mark away from his daughter. And he would not have abandoned his friends as they lay bleeding.

But there are degrees of sociopathy, and I think Scott Scurlock was only moderately afflicted, and not a killer. Ironically, it is Sergeant Howard Monta, the Seattle police officer who was the last person in the world to speak to Scott (although he didn't answer) who denies that Scott was completely without conscience or regret. "I always wanted to write to his parents," Monta says. "He wasn't all bad. I wanted to tell them that their son had every opportunity to kill me, and he didn't shoot. I was as good as dead when I went up to that camper door, but he didn't kill me; he killed himself instead."

Kevin Meyers still misses the best friend of his life. He looks away as he tells of talking with one of the women who used to visit Seven Cedars.

"She said to me, 'You know, Kevin—we'll never hear the crow calls down there anymore.' And she's right," Kevin says quietly. "We never will. Nothing will ever be that safe or happy again."

The
Peeping Tom

The victim in this case was happier than she had ever been in her life. All of her dreams were about to come true; she was planning her wedding to the man she loved. Why then did she feel that she was in danger? There was nothing to substantiate her uneasiness and she knew that it was an irrational fear, but it seemed to her that someone was watching her.

Tragically, someone was.

Even though I have written about more than a thousand homicide cases over the last thirty years, I remember every one. Some of them are more unsettling than others, and they come back to haunt me at odd moments. They will probably trouble me until the end of my life. This case is one of the saddest of all, and certainly one of the most baffling to solve.

When Salem, Oregon, detectives found the key to a seven-year puzzle, they realized that a young woman's wonderful dream was sacrificed to fulfill the basest of human desires. The identity of the man they finally arrested was a complete surprise to everyone involved.

Kay Owens was so happy in July of 1971. She was twenty-six years old, and she had the world by the tail. She was in love and about to be married, she liked her job, and she had just been admitted to the law school at the University of Oregon in Eugene. Kay was a classically attractive brunette, tall with a willowy figure. She was also very intelligent; her brilliance and her skill had won her the position as the only female employment analyst in the Oregon State Welfare Department. Kay enjoyed her job so much that she almost hated to leave to go to law school, but she had wanted to be an attorney for a long time.

The Oregon State Welfare Department—like all state facilities in Oregon—was headquartered in Salem, its capital city. Situated in the fertile Willamette Valley, Salem is one of the loveliest cities in the west, and Kay loved living there. Her wedding was scheduled for August, and she was busy making the arrangements, getting ready to move to Eugene with her bridegroom, and working full time. Yet she was haunted by a fear of something unnamed and unknown, something that moved just beneath her conscious awareness. Perhaps it was because she felt her life was too good to be true. Many people are superstitious when their lives get so close to perfect and fear that such bliss can't last.

Kay had lived in the rear unit of a duplex at 1830 Court Street NE in Salem for two years. It was located in a neighborhood mostly comprised of rental property, probably because it was so close to the state office buildings. She shared her meticulously clean duplex with her two cats. She had an understanding landlord, she could walk to work, and her living quarters were so close to other units that she knew if she ever needed help, her neighbors were only a few steps away.

Kay's fiancé, Dan Stone,* was an attorney who lived in Eugene, sixty miles south of Salem, but he spent as much time with her as he could. He stayed over with her Wednesday nights and every weekend. Before long, they would be together all the time.

But, for the moment, Kay was all alone with her cats four nights a week. She had never been ill at ease before, but as spring passed into summer, Kay Owens' niggling fear became more specific. She was disturbed by her sense that someone was watching her when she was alone at night. If she had tried to verbalize her premonition, it would have sounded too bizarre to be believed. How could she convince anyone that she was being watched when she'd never seen anyone, never heard a quiet footfall in the cedar chips outside her bedroom window? She only sensed that someone was there.

Kay was a most rational woman who hated to admit that she was frightened by shadows in the night, but she finally told her fiancé about her fears.

He tried to comfort her, assuring her that she wouldn't be living in her apartment very long.

Oddly, it was only when Kay was in her apartment that she was frightened. She often had to work late but she was never scared there. Nor was she uneasy about walking home alone even if she left her office after 11:00 P.M. The well-lit streets of Salem didn't scare her at all. It was almost as if she knew that the thing she feared waited for her at home.

Kay took precautions; she locked her doors tightly at night and placed dowels in her windows so that they couldn't be opened more than a few inches. She kept her blinds closed as tightly as she could.

On Thursday, July 29, 1971, Kay Owens left her office shortly after five. Dressed in a navy blue jumper and a white, long-sleeved blouse, her long, dark hair caught up in a bun, Kay strode home along streets whose parking strips were ablaze with roses. It would be daylight until 9:00 P.M., and Dan would be coming up the next night. Her fears faded on this sunny afternoon.

Kay stopped to talk to the elderly woman who lived in the other half of her duplex. She said she was going to drive to the store to buy cat food and asked if she could pick up any groceries for her neighbor. Other neighbors recalled hearing her laugh. "You couldn't mistake Kay's laugh," one of them remembered later. "It was such a musical laugh."

It was a quiet Thursday night. Kay must have come home and put away her groceries, but no one saw her.

On Friday morning, Kay Owens didn't show up for work, nor did she answer her phone when her supervisor and one of her fellow workers called to see if she was ill. They watched the clock anxiously. Maybe somebody else might decide to take a day off without reporting in, but not Kay. She was as dependable as the seasons.

Kay's friend Cindy Clark* waited an hour before she left work and walked the short distance to Kay's apartment. She knocked gently and then pounded on the door. There was no answer. Cindy went to a neighbor who had a spare key to Kay's front door. The key slid in, the tumblers meshed smoothly, and the door opened.

It was very quiet. Feeling like an intruder, Cindy stepped inside. She would be really embarrassed if she found Kay and Dan asleep in the bedroom. She almost backed out, but then she turned resolutely and walked through the living room, calling softly to Kay.

Kay had recently installed bifold doors so that she could close off the bedroom from the living area, but now Cindy saw that they were open. And then she saw two long, slender legs on Kay's bed. She forced herself to walk toward the bedroom.

Kay Owens was there. She was naked, sprawled on the bed with a pillow over her face. Cindy rushed to pull the pillow off, but Kay didn't move. Her face was swollen and suffused with a bluish-purple tinge. Almost unconsciously, Cindy placed the pillow over Kay's pubic area to protect her friend from strangers' eyes. And then she stumbled back to the elderly neighbor's duplex, crying, "We need an ambulance! We have to call an ambulance!"

The two women were so distraught that they couldn't find the number of an ambulance and called the Salem Police Department instead. But Cindy had yet to accept a terrible truth; she told the police dispatcher that there was an "ill woman" at 1830 Court.

It was 9:44 A.M., and Patrolman R. D. Marsh was dispatched to the scene. "Is she ill—or dead?" Marsh asked Cindy Clark.

"I don't know . . . I'm afraid to look," the tearful woman answered.

Marsh entered Kay's apartment through the screen door that led into the living room. He saw the woman lying very still on her bed in the room just beyond. She was on her back, with her left arm resting on her breasts and her right arm thrown up next to her head. As he came closer, Marsh saw that something made of a yellow or beige silk had been knotted tightly around her neck.

Fearing that it was far too late for medical help, Marsh nevertheless checked for a pulse in the woman's left wrist. There was none and her body was already locked in full rigor; the slender woman on the bed had been dead for many hours.

Marsh asked Cindy Clark to stand by outside the front door while he called for detectives. At 9:53 A.M., more patrolmen arrived to help cordon off the death apartment and the surrounding area. By 10:00, the homicide detectives on duty, Sergeant Delmar Johnson and E. Hoadley, began the crime-scene investigation.

There was absolutely no sign of a struggle in Kay Owens' bedroom. The only odd elements were a makeup mirror on the bed, and a candleholder tipped over on the nightstand. The cloth that had cut into the flesh of the victim's neck appeared to be a shortie nightgown or a half-slip.

It was impossible to tell without an autopsy, but Kay Owens had probably been strangled by ligature. There was no blood visible either on the body or on the bedding beneath it.

"It's possible that she was asleep," Johnson surmised. "She's a good-sized woman, and she would have put up quite a struggle if she'd had any warning."

Cindy Clark told them that Kay's two cats had been sound asleep and curled up next to their mistress's body when she arrived.

It was eerie; everything in the place was normal—furniture in place, doors locked. Whatever had happened to Kay Owens had happened very quickly and probably very quietly.

Ten minutes later, a Salem Police detective, Lieutenant James Stovall, who was assigned as Liaison Officer to the Marion County District Attorney's Office, arrived with Assistant DA Jim Hearn to join the investigation. Standing in the quiet duplex, they, too, wondered how a woman could have died silently and apparently without a struggle so close to help.

Kay Owens' little duplex was sandwiched between a large apartment building and a private residence. Her bedroom window faced the private residence. A narrow strip of ground with evergreen bushes and shredded bark was all that separated the two buildings.

Detectives noted scuff marks in the bark as if someone had stood outside the victim's window peering in. They found a bright orange scarf, which later proved to be Kay Owens', caught in the branches of a bush.

The Salem investigators divided up; some worked at the crime scene and others began a canvass of the neighbors. Many of the residents in the adjoining apartment house knew Kay Owens by sight and had often exchanged casual greetings with her. She was described as a good neighbor; she'd never had a noisy party, and no one could remember any of her visitors. She had been friendly—but quiet—and hadn't mixed too much. "She came out every night at ten, though," one woman remembered, "To call her cats in."

A man named Burt Cowan* recalled that he'd seen Kay Owens the night before between 8:30 and 9:00. "I was carrying some shrub trimmings out to the back of our apartment building to dump them," he said, "and I saw her sitting at a table by the window. She was writing letters, and she had on a long-sleeved white blouse. Her hair was in a bun."

"You say anything to her?" a cop asked.

"Nope—just went on by."

Burt Cowan was a husky blond man about thirty. He said he'd finished the yard work and then gone down to the first floor of his building and visited with a girlfriend. "We talked and sang songs until about ten-thirty or eleven when I went back to my apartment and went to bed."

"You hear anything unusual last night?" a detective asked.

Cowan shook his head. "Not a thing. Nothing suspicious all night."

The elderly woman who lived in the other side of Kay's duplex told the detectives that she had awakened about 2:30 A.M. and had seen a figure darting across her front yard. She couldn't tell, however, if the person had been male or female. She couldn't describe the person in any detail.

Burt Cowan interested the investigators. He apparently kept an eye on everything around the apartment complexes, and he loved to talk. He told them he'd lived in the apartment house next to Kay Owens' duplex for only a week; he was unemployed and depended on odd jobs from the apartment house owner.

Cowan told detectives that he'd seen Kay Owens talking to two men in a blue pickup with a bubble top on Wednesday night. It seemed to the detectives that he had spent a lot of his time watching her.

When the Salem Police investigators talked to the apartment owner, he said he'd come over to do some maintenance work at about 8:00 P.M. the night before. "Kay's car—it's that VW wagon—was parked outside her place. But I didn't think anything of it because she usually walks or rides her bike."

"Kay's lived here for two years—ever since we built the duplexes," he said. "I've never had one complaint about her, or *from* her for that matter. She was just a really nice lady, minded her own business, paid her rent, you know."

"How about other tenants?" Johnson asked. "Have you ever noticed anything peculiar?"

The man thought a moment. "One thing. About three yesterday afternoon, I was talking to one of the young women in the big apartment house. This guy Cowan that just moved in came out and offered us both a beer. So this young gal says she's going swimming and Cowan says great—he'll go with her. She told him 'no,' but he wouldn't take 'no' for an answer, and he went back to his place and came back wearing his swimsuit.

"He's really pushy, you know. I could see she was trying to get away from him without being rude. She went into her apartment and then she told him that she'd just had a phone call and she had to go to work. I figured she was making an excuse to get out of going swimming with him."

Burt Cowan was the only person who'd seen Kay Owens late on the evening of the twenty-ninth, and he seemed to have quickly earned himself a reputation as a would-be Romeo. He had clearly been fascinated with Kay Owens. A young woman tenant told the Salem Police that she had been sitting outside a few nights earlier with Cowan and some other tenants listening to his portable stereo, which he'd turned up loud.

"Kay Owens came out about ten and asked us to turn it down. She wasn't mad or anything," the girl recalled. "She was real polite. When she walked away, Burt made a comment about what beautiful long legs she had, and he was asking if she was married and things like that. He was calling her 'Legs' when he talked about her."

Detectives talked to Lily Peele,* the woman Cowan had visited the night before Kay Owens was found. Lily said she had lived in the apartments for almost a year. "I knew Kay as a neighbor," she said. "We talked in the yard, but we've never been to each other's apartments. I heard her come home between five-thirty and six last night. I didn't see her, but I heard her laugh in the parking lot. She had a great laugh. The last time I really talked to her was on Wednesday, and she was telling me about her wedding next month."

Lily Peele said that Kay's boyfriend had been with her on Wednesday night. She had noticed that his pickup was parked outside Kay's duplex the next morning. "He was just leaving about seven."

"Was Burt Cowan at your place on Thursday night?" a detective asked.

She nodded. "He came over and ate dinner and then he got his guitar and came back and we sang Beatles songs. When he left about a quarter to midnight, I saw that Kay's porch light was still on."

"Wasn't it always?"

"No, that was unusual—but that was all that was different."

"Hear anything during the night? Anything at all?"

"No. Everything was normal, and quiet."

One of the Salem detectives talked to two young male roommates in the apartment building. The men, both lawyers from Indiana, said they'd each been out very late the night before. The last to arrive said he'd come in at 3:30 A.M., and he admitted that he had been somewhat intoxicated. He'd found his roommate asleep. "I went right to bed myself," he added.

Neither had heard anything out of the ordinary

during the night. Both of them knew who Kay Owens was. "There isn't a male in the entire complex who hasn't noticed her," one said. "She's gorgeous and she's very nice."

The retired couple who lived in the house facing Kay's bedroom window said they'd been up reading until 2:30 A.M., but they hadn't heard or seen anyone around Kay's duplex.

It seemed impossible that of all the people living close to Kay no one had heard a disturbance during the night or a cry for help. The closest thing to a witness was the old woman on the other side of the wall they shared, but she had only seen a wraithlike figure.

Now, the investigators' best hope lay in the findings of criminalists from the Oregon State Police Crime Lab. Lieutenant Manuel Boyes, Corporal William Zeller, and Corporal Chuck Vaughn processed Kay Owens' apartment while Salem detectives photographed the victim and the premises. Kay's body could not be moved until all of that was accomplished.

It looked as if Kay Owens had gone to bed before her killer entered her room; her contact lenses were in their container in her bathroom. There were frustratingly few pieces of evidence: the makeup mirror found on the bed that might have good fingerprints on it, the orange scarf caught in the bushes, samples of the bark outside Kay's bedroom window, and the candleholder.

On closer examination, the detectives found a long slit in the window screen just above a table in the dinette area. Someone could have reached through it and removed the dowel that Kay Owens had put there and then opened the window wide.

The State Police criminalists found very few prints in the bedroom and bathroom. It looked as if someone had made an effort to wipe off telltale marks. They *did* find the imprint of a bare foot on the top of the toilet seat, not a usual spot for such a print.

After photographs of the original scene were taken, the victim's body was rolled over. The distinctive purple-red striations of postmortem lividity (or livor mortis) were all along her back. When the heart stops pumping, blood sinks to the lowest level of the human body. If the body is not moved, the striped pattern becomes fixed after several hours; if a body *is* moved before this happens, a secondary pinkish striation will appear. But this lividity pattern showed that Kay Owens had lain in the same position until she was discovered.

When Kay Owens' body had been removed to the morgue, a detective there examined the garment that had been around her neck. Someone had cut her shortie nightgown up one side to make a square and then tied the opposite corners tightly around Kay's neck. A purple bruise was evident on the left side of her throat where the delicate fabric had cut into her neck. The nightgown garrote had been tightened so cruelly that it had left deep grooves in her flesh.

Dr. Larry Lewman of the Oregon State Medical Examiner's Office began the autopsy on Kay Owens at 2:00 P.M. on Friday, July 30. He found very little bruising on the body beyond the contusions around the neck. However, he did find three small bruises on the victim's right hip and some blood in the vaginal vault. Microscopic examination of fluid found in the vagina indicated the presence of dead sperm cells and seminal fluid. (In 1971, there was no such thing as DNA matching, although blood types could be determined from body fluids.)

Kay Owens had either been unconscious or dead when the sexual assault took place; she did not have the expected bruising to the inner thighs usually found in rape victims. There were no defense wounds, which would be expected if she had fought her attacker. Her hands weren't scratched and her fingernails were unbroken.

Kay Owens had apparently died of strangulation by ligature. The characteristic petechiae (small hemorrhages in the eyes, heart, larynx) were present, although the hyoid bone at the back of her throat was intact. Her killer had probably not been very strong; strangulation often crushes the hyoid bone and causes deep bleeding into the strap muscles of the neck. The minimal damage to Kay Owens' throat also indicated that she had been either asleep or unconscious when the killer choked her. Had she fought, much more pressure would have been necessary.

At postmortem exam, Kay Owens measured five feet, nine and a half inches tall, and weighed 137 pounds. She could have been a formidable adversary for any man had she been able to fight back.

Samples of her head hair, pubic hair, and blood were preserved, along with scrapings from under her fingernails, her fingerprints and her footprints. Someday, they might be connected to the man who had killed her.

There was another horrific assault to Kay Owens. As her body was being prepared by mortuary attendants, they were shocked to discover that her killer had gagged her with tissue paper. Facial tissue had been jammed deep down in her throat so forcibly and deeply that it hadn't been found at autopsy. It, too, was retained for evidence.

Now Salem detectives tried to learn as much about Kay Owens as they could. Was there someone in her life she feared? Had she been involved in relationships that troubled her? Had she, perhaps, been bothered by unwanted attention, obscene phone calls? Was there *anything* that might have provided a motive for her violent death?

They learned that Kay Owens had been married once before. Apparently, the divorce had been amicable. Coworkers recalled that her ex-husband had phoned her at the office just to talk a half-dozen times in the year before her murder.

Nevertheless, the investigators located the ex-husband and checked out his whereabouts on the night Kay was murdered. He had a firm alibi for the entire night of July 29–30.

Kay's fiancé, Dan Stone, told detectives that she had planned to quit her job in August and move in with him in Eugene after their marriage. The distraught man said that he had called Kay around 10:00 P.M. on Thursday night. At that time, she hadn't sounded in the least upset or worried.

"We made plans to look for a house in Eugene over the weekend," Stone said sadly.

Dan Stone had last seen Kay on Thursday morning. "We always spent Wednesday night together," he explained. "This Wednesday night, my brother and I—he's with the Oregon State Police—had dinner in her apartment. My brother left after dinner and I stayed the night and got up at five, because I had to be at work in Eugene by eight."

Asked if Kay was afraid of anyone, Stone said Kay had suspected that she had a window peeper, and she had insisted that the bamboo blinds in her bedroom be pulled down securely. "But it was hard to get that shade all the way down. You could sort of see in through the side, I guess, because it didn't hang quite straight."

Detectives Hoadley and Johnson checked the blinds and saw that they would not go all the way to the window's edge. A man of average height would have been able to peer in.

The motive behind Kay Owens' murder had apparently been simple lust. Everything else had been eliminated. It wasn't robbery; Kay's expensive watch, her red wallet with money inside, her TV, stereo, and jewelry had all been found in her apartment. She didn't have an enemy in the world, and she never argued with her neighbors or coworkers.

Kay Owens had been very beautiful, with a lovely figure. She could have been a woman that a man with a sexual quirk desired beyond all reason.

The name that kept coming up was Burt Cowan's. He had been fascinated with Kay's long legs and he'd pestered other people in the apartment complex with questions about her. He was definitely a flirt, a man who came on to women around the apartments, and he was apparently the last person to see Kay alive on the night she died.

A check into his background unearthed information that he was sexually kinky. His first wife had divorced him because of what she termed his perverted sexual practices; she had caught him molesting his own children. According to both his first and second wife (who was currently estranged from him) he was a man with an extremely small penis—a condition they blamed for his sexual attraction to young girls—and boys. Burt Cowan's exes listed sexual aberrations that included such bizarre practices that they might have come right out of Krafft-Ebing's study on aberrant sex.

Burt Cowan emerged as the prime suspect in Kay Owens' murder. Although Cowan had left his new girlfriend before midnight on July 29 and apparently gone directly to his apartment and turned on his stereo, there was no reason to assume that he could not have slipped out to peer into Kay Owens' bedroom window. And then, inflamed at the sight of her, he might have cut the screen over her dinette table and gone in.

One question niggled, though. If Cowan really had an abnormally small sex organ, would he have been capable of raping a woman so violently that he made her bleed?

As it turned out, Burt Cowan was arrested on August 5—but not for the murder of Kay Owens; he was charged with the sexual assault of his own three-year-old son. While he was incarcerated, Cowan was given a polygraph examination concerning the death of Kay Owens—and, in police jargon, he blew ink all over the walls. To the layman, he flunked the lie-detector test.

On August 6, Lt. James Stovall interviewed Burt Cowan. Stovall was a skilled interrogator, and he not only listened to what a subject had to say, he observed physiological signs as the subject responded.

"I watch for their rate of breathing, for an increased pulse beat in the throat or wrist, for perspiration," he explained. "It often tells me as much—or more—as what the subject is saying."

Stovall's interview with Burt Cowan was extremely interesting; he soon saw that what Cowan said aloud and his body language didn't mesh. As expected, Cowan denied that he had killed Kay Owens.

Jim Stovall used a time-honored technique to get a suspect to talk; he allowed him to become an "expert" giving advice to a puzzled detective. He asked Cowan his theories on how Kay Owens might have been killed and how someone could have silenced her so that no one had heard her cry out.

Cowan said, "Well, she could have been gagged with something."

"Like what?" Stovall probed.

"Oh, something like . . . paper, maybe."

It was an electrifying statement. Nobody outside the investigation knew that tissue paper had been forced down Kay Owens' throat.

Still, something about Burt Cowan didn't fit. Stovall studied him and saw that he was absolutely calm. He wasn't sweating; the pulse in his throat beat at a slow, steady pitch; and he wasn't even breathing heavily. In short, Burt Cowan was reacting like a completely innocent man who was merely surmising what had happened to his pretty neighbor.

Despite the lie-detector results, and Cowan's mention of paper used as a gag, Stovall wondered if he was looking at a man who, although culpable in other sex crimes, might very well be innocent of this one. If not that, Cowan's emotions were so flat that he hardly felt them at all.

Any good detective has had a few cases where he was convinced that he had found a killer, where everything fit but one small piece. And any layman would have sworn that Cowan was the killer of Kay Owens.

Stovall wasn't so sure.

Criminalists tested some hairs found in the orange scarf in the bushes outside Kay's duplex against hairs that had been found on her body. They matched, but neither sample matched Burt Cowan's hair in class and characteristics when they were placed under a scanning electron microscope. This mismatch well-nigh eliminated Cowan from consideration.

The footprint lifted from Kay Owens' bathroom didn't match Burt Cowan's feet. Kay herself had left it there. And there wasn't a single fingerprint in the apartment that couldn't be traced to either Kay or her fiancé.

There was absolutely no physical evidence that linked Burt Cowan to Kay Owens. Although Burt Cowan's past perversions made him a good suspect, nothing but circumstantial evidence connected him to her murder. Yes, he had certainly had the opportunity to spy on her through her bedroom window. He could have let himself into her duplex, and he had the physical strength needed to strangle her; he weighed over two hundred pounds. But there wasn't enough to go into court with murder charges against Cowan.

The Marion County District Attorney and the Salem Police had only Cowan's "guesses" about how Kay died and a "guilty" polygraph reading. But lie-detector results are not admissible in court unless the defendant agrees to let them in. Why would Burt Cowan agree?

The State declined to file murder charges against Cowan. He was put on probation on the sexual molestation charge involving his son and released from jail.

Still, Salem Police detectives kept track of Cowan. They learned he had gone from jail to the waiting arms of Lily Peele, the woman he'd spent the evening with the night Kay Owens died. The two lived together for a few months and then moved to another Oregon city where Cowan took classes at a community college using his air force benefits. He studied practical nursing and got a job in a nursing home.

When Salem detectives visited him, Burt Cowan told them that he had "gotten religion" and he wished them well in their continuing probe of the Owens case. They accepted his good wishes bleakly; if ever a man looked good for a homicide, it was Burt Cowan. Only Jim Stovall felt that Cowan was probably not Kay Owens' killer. A sexual weirdo, yes—but his demeanor during Stovall's interview with him had not been that of a man guilty of the crime he was being questioned about.

Homicide investigations are rife with unexpected twists and turns. A detective with tunnel vision who focuses on only one suspect is liable to miss seeing the forest for the trees.

But they were back to square one. If Burt Cowan

hadn't killed Kay Owens, who then? A lot of men had wanted her. Her first husband was in the clear. Her fiancé had never been a suspect; he was miles away on the night she was killed, and besides, it was obvious how much he had loved her. Everything the investigators had turned up indicated that she had been absolutely faithful to Dan Stone. He was the last man in the world who might have wanted to harm her.

However, as they dug deeper into Kay's past and talked to her friends, detectives learned of a very prominent—and married—professional man. He had reportedly been obsessed with Kay Owens. He'd courted her assiduously before her engagement to Dan Stone, and he'd had the means to do it. He had showered her with unwelcome gifts and flowers—to no avail. Kay Owens had had no interest in being the secret love of a married man. She didn't need a backstreet romance. With her beauty, brains, and personality, she could have any man she chose. She had told the married man "no" and "no" again.

Discreetly, detectives checked the man out. They found he *had* been entranced with the tall brunette and might even have been angry at being rejected. But they also were able to account for his time on the night of July 29–30. The married suitor was so relieved to be cleared that the Salem investigators doubted that he would ever wander far from home in the future.

The detectives continued to track Burt Cowan. When they looked for him in January, 1972, they found him in a Portland hospital—not as a nurse, but as a patient. He had undergone a complete colostomy after being diagnosed with colon cancer. Physicians at the veterans' hospital said he would recover.

The Salem investigators had worked every lead on the Owens killing that came up. In truth, homicide detectives work ten times as hard on a case they wryly term "a loser," as they do on the cases where a successful arrest and prosecution ensue. It seemed as if they had been so close to Kay Owens' killer, and it galled them that he still walked free.

But there were no more cases in the Salem area where the MO matched that used in Kay's murder; there were no helpful witnesses or informants. They'd been over every aspect of the investigation not once but a half-dozen times, and they'd come up with nothing. Although the Owens case was no longer mentioned in Salem papers, it was far from forgotten by the Salem detectives. Jim Stovall pulled the thick case file out every six months to see if he had missed something that might show up on rereading.

Some Salem detectives still felt that Burt Cowan was the guilty man; others were not so sure.

But, by 1978, any hope of a definitive solution to the Owens case was pretty dim. Seven years had gone by. Kay Owens would have been thirty-three years old, probably an attorney and a happily married woman if tragedy had not intervened.

None of the detectives or patrolmen who had gone to 1830 Court on that misty morning in July of 1971 had forgotten Kay. But they knew that if a case isn't solved soon after a murder, the chances that it ever will be diminish proportionately as time passes. And a lot of time had passed.

By 1978, Jim Stovall was the commander of the Salem Police Department's Criminal Investigation Unit, and two former patrolmen—Vern Meighen and Tom Mason—had become detectives. Stovall asked the new detectives to read the Owens case.

Meighen and Mason learned that Kay Owens had been alive at 10:00 P.M. on July 29, 1971, and dead some four to six hours later. She had been raped and strangled with her own nightgown. And she'd been dead for almost seven years. The trail left by her killer was ice cold.

However, Jim Stovall wasn't the only one who thought often about Kay Owens. It was Friday, May 12, 1978, when an inmate in the Marion County Jail approached jailer Walter Tappy. "Hey," the prisoner said, "one of the guys in my cell is talking about some rape-murder he did about seven years ago. He's talking about a lot of other sex crimes too."

"Which man is it?" Tappy asked.

"I don't want to be a snitch," the informant hesitated.

Tappy convinced the inmate that if the other con was telling the truth, it wasn't something that could simply be forgotten. "OK," the man sighed. "The guy's Ivan Miller*. He's been getting weirder and weirder ever since that guy in the next cell hung himself two weeks ago. It freaked us all out because he did it so quick we couldn't stop him, and we all saw him strangle. But Miller, it hit him harder, and he really flipped out. Something's eating at him. His conscience is bothering him bad."

The prisoner said that Ivan Miller had told him he was in jail for molesting a little girl. "And I says to him, 'Hey, it's not like you killed somebody or something,' and then he says he *did* kill some chick and raped her and all."

Tappy got as much information as he could and then he called Detective Jan Cummings of the Marion County Sheriff's Office. Cummings checked the county's list of unsolved homicides and found nothing that sounded like a match. She suggested that Miller might be confessing to a City of Salem case.

Walt Tappy went to the cell that Ivan Miller shared with the informant, hoping to get a more precise fix on his alleged confession.

"Tell Tappy what you told me over the weekend," the informant urged. Suddenly Ivan Miller erupted with words, "I did it," he said. "I killed a girl when I was about seventeen years old, and I've done a lot of other sex things. I have to tell somebody about it."

This torrent of words was more than Walt Tappy had expected. He told Miller to write down as much as he could remember about the killing, but to say no more. Then he hurried to call the Salem Police Criminal Investigation Unit.

"This guy said he killed a girl in Salem when he was seventeen—and he's twenty-four now," Tappy said. "Do you have an unsolved murder from about seven years ago?"

Vern Meighen had no trouble pinpointing the murder Miller was confessing to. The only rape-murder in Salem seven years before was Kay Owens'. Meighen and Tom Mason drove the few blocks to the Marion County Jail in minutes. The young prisoner who wanted to confess to a murder was brought out to an interview room. They saw that Miller was an unprepossessing figure, a very short skinny man who hardly looked capable of a brutal murder.

Since there was virtually no physical evidence gleaned from the Owens crime scene, Vern Meighen and Tom Mason had a delicate interrogation ahead of them. Ivan Miller would have to tell them details about the victim and the inside of her apartment that no one but the killer could know. Otherwise, they would have to write him off as just another chronic confessor.

It was 5:00 P.M. on May 15, 1978, when the answers to the mystery of Kay Owens' murder finally came. Vern Meighen, Tom Mason, and Walter Tappy listened to one of the most incredible confessions any of them would ever hear.

After the two Salem detectives advised him of his rights, Ivan Miller began to talk into a tape recorder. He evinced relief that he was finally able to get the murder off his conscience. And then he appeared to be in a trance as he recalled in chilling detail the night Kay died. It was not just a confession; the investigators were watching a man whose mind was back in Kay Owens's bedroom, a man who was reliving an ugly crime.

"OK, Ivan," Meighen said. "We want to talk to you specifically about a girl who was killed at 1830 Court Street. Do you know her name?"

"Yeah. I read it in the papers. It was a real pretty name: Kathryn Owens. I'm not sure of the address, but I can show you where it is. It's close to the Deluxe Ice Cream on State Street."

It was indeed.

Miller said he'd been living with his parents and

sister during the summer of 1971. He gave an address less than a mile from Kay Owens' apartment.

"Have you talked to anyone about this crime until the last few days?" Meighen asked.

"No. *Yes*—but only once in Arizona. I confessed it to a priest. He didn't know my name, and he didn't even see my face. I must have been about nineteen or twenty then."

Miller said he had dropped out of school when he was fifteen and had stayed home, not working, from then on. He thought he'd been about seventeen when Kay Owens died.

"What caused you to go to that particular house?" Meighen asked.

"Well, I'd been looking in windows since I was about thirteen or so. I came to her house, and a couple of others nearby. I saw her in there and I went back two or three times. One night, I saw her in the bedroom with a man. They were making love, and I watched. It wasn't too long after that I went inside myself. Maybe a few days later. See, I never saw her undressed and I wanted to, so I kept coming back to look in her window. That night that it happened I did see her undressed."

"How could you see into the room?"

"The curtain—it was kind of bamboo and you could see in if the lights were on—and it didn't come quite down to the bottom."

Miller said that Kay's apartment had become a regular stop on his nocturnal rounds of window peeping. He correctly described her car as a dark blue Volkswagen station wagon with a square back and recalled where she had parked it.

"Her apartment was just off the alley to the west," Ivan Miller said. "She lived in the back half of a duplex; the front door was on the east and there's a window on the south that goes into the dinette, and then you go into the front room and the bedroom's on the left."

He was absolutely right.

Miller said that on the night of July 29 he'd arrived at Kay Owens' bedroom window later than he usually did; until this night, he'd never been there to see her prepare for bed. By the time he got there on the weekend before the murder, the man had been there, and he'd gotten up and pulled the curtains tight and Ivan Miller couldn't see in the room anymore. But, now, he was determined to see Kay Owens nude.

"I got there just after sunset. You could still see light on the horizon but the sun was down, and it was pretty dark. I was at her place from then until two in the morning. It was clear, and it was real quiet and the stars were out. I looked through her bedroom window on the west side of the house. She took off all her clothes after awhile and went and took a shower. She walked around for a while naked and I was masturbating."

Miller's eyes took on a faraway, glazed look as he finally told in detail the story he'd carried in his head for seven years. He told of waiting "a real long time" until Kay Owens turned out the light and got into bed.

"When she went to bed, I waited. I wanted to go home, but I wanted to go in too. I tried to make up my mind. I stood there smoking a cigarette and finally I decided to go in. I had a pocketknife and I cut the screen on the window. She'd left it open a little bit.

She'd had it shut and then she opened it just before she went to bed."

Even though what had happened could not be prevented all these years later, the men listening tensed. It was terrible to think of the woman in danger, oblivious to the man watching her.

"There were plants just outside the window," Miller said. "I stepped on them and they were squishy. When I got in, there was a table underneath the window."

Miller recalled how he'd sat down in a chair near the folding door that separated Kay's bedroom from the living room. He was able to describe that bifold door perfectly. He told of sitting quietly outside the bedroom as Kay Owens slept, unaware of his presence.

"It seemed like I sat in that chair for a pretty long time. The door was hooked on the inside—the bedroom side. The chair was nice. It felt nice to sit in. I couldn't see anything because it was dark.

"I couldn't open the door [the bifold doors] right away. I had the fishing knife, and I found I could open up the hook on the door. I pushed it aside, and I went in the bedroom. I couldn't see anything but I knew about where the bed was and I went up to it and just stood there, real nervous. It was so dim that I couldn't see her. She was sound asleep and snoring.

"I was trying to find her. I reached out with my left hand and reached down and felt around. I found her that way. I stood up again and waited. I didn't want to wake her up. I'm not sure if she jumped or not when I felt her—I'm trying to remember. She wasn't covered up. She was on top of the covers."

The jail interview room smelled of sweat and cigarette smoke. The detectives waited for Ivan Miller to continue his terrible story.

"I turned on the light—and then I jumped on top of her," he said. "I put my hands around her throat and I wanted her not to wake up. I wanted her to be unconscious. While that was going on, she was fighting me and then she went unconscious—or pretty close. I remember putting some paper down her throat."

Burt Cowan had guessed this detail, but it was clear that Ivan Miller knew what had happened.

"She was fighting and awake and I remember opening her mouth and putting the paper in," Miller continued, his voice tight.

"What kind of paper was it?" Meighen asked quietly.

"It felt soft, pretty soft, like tissue paper. It was right by the bed on the bedstand. I think maybe I must have put the paper down her throat before I turned the lights on. Then, after she was unconscious, I turned the light on—it was a chain light that hung from the ceiling."

So Kay Owens had never seen her killer. She must have been unconscious by the time the light was turned on, choked with Miller's hands and the Kleenex that blocked her throat.

"I started to do things to her," Miller continued, his words bubbling up under pressure. "I moved her around on the bed and touched her, and things like that, maybe making love to her."

Miller said his victim had still worn her nightgown,

and he described it as a peach or yellow shortie gown with white lace at the top.

That was right too. How many times had he gone over this ugly crime in his mind over the years? He knew every detail precisely.

The two Salem detectives hoped that Kay Owens was already dead at this point. At the very least she was mercifully unaware of the actions of the teenager who had crept into her apartment.

As the graphic confession continued, there were more particulars that tied this suspect tightly to the murder. He said he had inserted a candle into the victim's vagina. He had taken her makeup mirror from the bathroom and held it at an angle so that he could watch himself as he raped her. "I got this mirror and was making love to her, and I was holding it so I could watch myself."

Ivan Miller said he thought the victim had been breathing while he was raping her. "I remember when I was through with the mirror, I was just kind of pretending that maybe she was alive. I couldn't have an orgasm at first—so I was pretending that she was alive."

He said he had tried to remove the Kleenex gag from her throat but that she'd swallowed it and he'd been unable to get it out.

"What did you do with her nightgown?" Tom Mason asked.

Miller said he'd choked her with it, but he didn't know why he'd done that.

"Do you remember how you did it?"

"I put it around her neck, and I was like mad or

something, and I felt like doing that. It was kind of knotted. It was only one time, but I pulled real hard. I don't know why, because she was unconscious, but I did that and then I made love to her."

The detectives winced as Miller referred to rape as "making love," but they fought down their revulsion and continued to question him on specifics. Thus far, he had demonstrated that he knew everything that had gone on in Kay Owens' apartment so many years before.

After he'd achieved orgasm, Miller said he'd tried to loosen the garotte from around Ms. Owens' neck, but that it had been too tight. "She didn't have to have it on anymore, but I couldn't get it off.

"I looked inside her purse—it was like a straw fishing creel—and I took out her red wallet. I took a little bit of money out of it and put it in my pocket."

Miller said that then he had started "feeling different" and that he'd found an orange cloth (Kay Owens' scarf) and wiped off everything he had touched. The mirror, the phone, the window. He erased every trace of himself with his victim's scarf.

He said he'd thrown the scarf onto a bush between the duplex and the house next door. It had undoubtedly been Ivan Miller that Kay Owens' elderly neighbor had seen at 2:30 A.M.

"Where did you go then?" Vern Meighen asked.

"Home." Ivan Miller explained that he always crawled out of his bedroom window and returned the same way, so that his family wouldn't know he was out. On the night of the murder, though, his father had replaced the screen. "I had to go in through the front door. My family was up and I made up a story about going to some coffeehouse I'd heard about."

He said he had told no one about what he'd done. Shortly after Kay Owens' murder, he left Salem to drive to Minnesota with relatives.

It all fit. Ivan Miller knew the complete layout of Kay Owens' apartment, and he knew about the Kleenex, the mirror on the bed, the orange scarf, the color of her nightgown, the plastic bifold door, the cut in the window screen, her purse and wallet, the hanging lamp over her bed. None of this had ever been released to the media.

Meighen and Mason stared at Miller. He couldn't weigh over one hundred fifty pounds or stand more than five foot seven. Had Kay Owens had any warning, she probably could have handled him. She had been taller than he and almost as heavy. If she had screamed, a dozen people would have come running. But she never had a chance. One moment she'd been sound asleep, the next she'd been gagged and strangled.

Ivan Miller had planned his attack on Kay Owens carefully; he was intrigued by fetishes. He told them that he had worn a shirt he'd deliberately dyed black. "When I went out looking in windows, I figured I wouldn't be seen if I wore black."

"Have you ever killed anyone else?" Meighen asked suddenly.

"No."

Miller did admit to several other sexual offenses, however. He recalled entering one house and hiding under a bed because he planned to attack the two sleeping occupants of the home one at a time. While he waited, he'd felt the urge to urinate and he had done so—into the mattress, awakening his planned victims. They had discovered him and chased him from the house.

He confessed that he'd been fishing on the north fork of the Santiam River once when he saw a little girl riding a bicycle. He had enticed her down onto the riverbank and into his car, where he disrobed her and fondled and kissed her. "But I didn't rape her," he said.

He had never been apprehended in either case.

In another incident, in downtown Salem, Miller said he had parked his car and debated taking his knife with him when he went in search of a female. He had decided not to take the knife, but he'd approached a woman telling her he had a knife. He ordered her to come with him to "have intercourse." She'd screamed, and he'd been frightened off.

Ivan Miller had watched a woman through her window as she took a shower. Like a scene from *Psycho,* he'd opened her door with a knife and surprised her in the shower. He forced her to perform oral sex. "But I didn't rape her because she told me her boyfriend would be there any minute."

After he had signed his confession, Ivan Miller led the two Salem detectives on a grim tour around Salem. He pointed out Kay Owens' duplex and the sites of his other attacks.

Vern Meighen and Tom Mason did a psychological background check on the confessed killer. They learned that Ivan Miller had been a loner most of his life, deeply involved in drugs and pornography. As a teenager, he had been sullen and untalkative and he'd refused to go out during the daytime hours. His family knew he sneaked out at night, but they had had no idea of the awful scope of his wanderings. They told the detectives that they had never connected him to the headlines about Kay Owens' murder.

Miller had never had a girlfriend until he'd moved to Arizona when he was about nineteen. There, he became obsessed with a go-go dancer who had just broken up with her husband. Their affair lasted only a few weeks before the dancer reconciled with her husband, leaving Miller distraught. "One night," a relative recalled, "He was drinking and he got quite unmanageable at our house and started throwing things. He went into the back bedroom and we heard a gunshot. I ran back and found he'd tried to fake a suicide attempt."

Tom Mason learned that Miller had eventually married a woman who was also named Kay, either by coincidence or by design. She had children from an earlier marriage, and her relationship with Ivan Miller soon foundered, principally because she would not allow him to discipline the children. And, like the first suspect in Kay Owens' murder, Miller had been arrested for sexually molesting his stepchildren. It was *that* charge that had placed him in the Marion County Jail.

When the two Salem detectives talked with the inmate to whom Miller had originally confessed, they got a broader picture of the intricacy of his fantasies. Ivan Miller had bragged that after Kay Owens' murder he had been consumed with the idea of having sex with another woman who was unconscious. "He said he never wanted to kill anyone again," the informant said, "but that he wanted to find some way to drug a woman instead of having her awake when he had sex with her."

The physical evidence in the Owens case—as meager as it was—had been held for seven years in a secure locker in the Salem Police Department. Now, Oregon State Police criminalists found matches with the hair samples and isolated Ivan Miller's blood type in the semen he left behind.

Kay Owens' death had been explained, solved. Had it not been for Ivan Miller's conscience, it might have remained a tragic mystery forever. The killer didn't know his victim, he left no evidence that could be traced to him. There was no way that a connection could have been made between a beautiful, vibrant woman and the disturbed teenager whose chief preoccupation was voyeurism. It was the kind of case that every homicide detective dreads.

Miller told his cellmates that Kay Owens was the kind of woman he'd always dreamed of having, and the only way he could possess her was to kill her. Sadly, her seemingly irrational fear that someone was watching her and waiting for her had been all too accurate. Ivan Miller had been a voyeur for half his life—since he was twelve. It is a common misconception that window peepers and exposers are not dangerous. In truth, many murderers begin with just that kind of aberrant behavior and escalate to far more dangerous assaults. Ivan Miller is a prime example of the dread progression of violent sexual behavior.

During the summer of 1978, Ivan Miller pleaded guilty to second-degree murder and was sentenced to twenty-five years in the Oregon State Penitentiary. But prison sentences are rarely finite numbers and even life sentences seldom mean *life*. Ivan Miller was released from prison in 1990 at the age of thirty-six and remains free at this writing.

The Girl Who
Fell in Love with
Her Killer

Almost everyone has someone who cares about
them, looks after them, and even loves them. So it
may be almost impossible to comprehend the overwhelming need of the victim in this case simply to
have someone notice her. She was so needy that she
was willing to forego love and concern. She had
taken care of herself since she was a child, and she
thought she knew how to survive. But she ached for
someone who would pay attention to her and reassure her that she wasn't invisible. Attention, however, can be both positive and negative, and
psychological studies show that human beings do
better with even negative attention than they do
living in a vacuum.

The teenager in this case had set off on a desperate journey to find the man whom she believed to be
her father. Her mother didn't want her; she barely
knew the man who had long since deserted his
family. She was young, and she had led a sad life

thus far. But she had a dream and she was willing to risk being cold and hungry and lost to make it come true: she was going to find her father.

Unfortunately, when she met someone who noticed her during her fruitless search, he gave her the worst kind of attention. She was so hungry for any crumb of notice that she was perhaps the most psychologically vulnerable victim that I have ever written about.

It was bitterly cold in Granite Falls, Washington, on Wednesday evening, November 7, 1973. Snow had already begun to fall in the mountain foothills, and soon sleet would whip the barren stretches of frozen farmland of Snohomish County. The frail girl seemed unaware of the cold as she clambered up from the ditch where she had regained consciousness. Her head hurt and she felt dizzy, but she remembered now what had happened to her, and she knew she dare not give in to her impulse to huddle on the ground until she felt better. *He might be coming back for her.* She felt the blood—strangely warm and metallic tasting—as it coursed down her face.

She didn't know where she was, but she knew she had to get help. She forced herself to crawl up the muddy embankment, losing one shoe in the process. There was nothing up above but thick brush and blackberry vines, and she ran in circles trying to find a way out. Thorns snagged her clothes and scratched her arms and face. Every so often, she stopped and listened for a sound that might rise above the steady wind. His hopped-up car had a loud muffler, and she thought she would be able to hear it if he came back to see if she was really dead.

Finally, she found a dirt road. Far off in the distance, she could see the lights of a farmhouse. Sobbing, she headed in that direction. Her head felt as if it wasn't even part of her body anymore but a balloon full of air, and she wondered if she would make it.

She couldn't stop to rest. He had wanted to kill her. She remembered his eyes looking at her over the gun as if she was a rabbit in a trap. All of her begging and pleading had fallen on deaf ears. The last thing she remembered was a loud boom. She tried to focus on the lights ahead, but they blended into a blur of red as blood continued to pour from her head.

It was a minute after 9:00 P.M. on that Wednesday night when Snohomish County Deputy Jim Eiden and Detective Roger Johnson responded to a call from the Cascade Valley Hospital in Monroe, Washington. The sheriff's dispatcher had radioed that a young girl suffering from several bullet wounds had been brought into the hospital a few minutes before. She was in the emergency room, and it was questionable that she would live.

The officers looked suspiciously at the nervous man who had driven her to the hospital. He identified himself as Alf Johansson* and said he was a farmer who lived by himself out near the Jordan River Trail Estates between Arlington and Granite Falls. He said that he'd heard a faint pounding on his door, thought it was his imagination, and then heard it again.

"I'm so far out in the country that it startled me,

you know? I just don't get that many people knocking on my door after dark, and I hadn't heard a car engine or footsteps or anything. Then I heard this little voice crying, 'I've been shot—and raped.' I looked out and here's this girl—real young girl—and she's got blood all over her."

"You ever see her before?" Eiden asked, sensing truth in the man's voice.

"No, sir. Never have," Johansson said. "But if I had, I wouldn't have recognized her the way she was. I guess I should have run out and picked her up—but I was so shocked myself to see her that way. I grabbed my keys and a blanket and told her to get in the truck. I feel bad about that now, but she was sitting up in the cab of the truck when I came running out. I'll tell you I just got her in here as quick as I could."

The ER physicians told the sheriff's men that the victim appeared to have two bullet wounds—one in the scalp and one in the right cheek. Amazingly, she was still conscious. "You can talk to her, if you keep it brief."

Johnson and Eiden looked at the trembling young victim. She had suffered a bullet wound in her right cheekbone and there were black powder burns around the wound. This gun barrel debris indicated that someone had held the weapon virtually against her cheek and fired.

She told the investigators that her name was Barbie Linley* and she was fifteen years old, "—but put down *sixteen* because it's almost my birthday. This guy picked me up while I was hitchhiking. And then he raped me," she said tearfully. "After that, he shot me."

It seemed impossible that she was still alive, and the Snohomish County investigators were careful to keep their own horror at what had happened to her out of their voices. She could go into shock at any moment.

"You didn't know this man?" Johnson asked. "You're sure it wasn't the man who brought you into the hospital? You're safe here, Barbie. You can tell us the truth. You're sure you've never seen him before?"

"No," she shook her head faintly. "That man was helping me. The other guy stopped when I was just hitching a ride up to look for my dad in Marysville. And he picked me up."

It was a familiar story to the Snohomish County officers, as it was to almost every lawman in the country. The first thing most parents teach their youngsters is, "Never get in a car with a stranger." Yet, in the seventies, America's teenagers had embraced hitchhiking wholeheartedly. In most states, hitching was legal, and the kids translated that to mean *safe*. In many cases, they got into cars with exactly the kind of people their parents had warned them about.

One detective sighed in frustration. "We're working on the murder of a teenager who was last seen hitchhiking. We put out a teletype asking for information on cases with similar MOs. We got back a dozen answers—just from the Northwest. It's an epidemic. But the kids keep right on hitchhiking. They don't think it's going to happen to *them*. There are guys out there just cruising around looking for a girl hitching."

* * *

The Girl Who Fell in Love with Her Killer

Barbie Linley was lying on her stomach in the emergency room as the deputies talked to her. The doctor treating her pointed to her wounds and said that, despite the copious blood, there were only three. They all looked as if they had entered from the front. "One bullet's still lodged in her cheek and the others exited out the back of her head."

He showed them the X-ray film, and they could see the large bullet—probably a .45 caliber slug—clearly. Barbie's right cheekbone was shattered.

Detective Jerry Cook arrived at the hospital and joined the investigators talking with the critically injured girl.

"Do you know who shot you—I mean, do you know anything at all about him?" Cook asked.

"Yes," was the amazing reply. "He told me his name was 'Easy.' I laughed, and he said people called him that, and then he said his regular name was Brandon Oakley.* He picked me up in Everett, but then he drove me down a dirt road out in the country."

Barbie turned her face away and took a deep breath. "Then he—he raped me, and he shot me. I remember I felt three bullets." Barbie Linley was very brave and very observant. By all rights, she should have been dead, but almost miraculously none of the .45 slugs had struck her in a vital spot.

She said that the man called "Easy" drove a fairly new Camaro and that it was either green or blue. "I think he's about eighteen years old, probably about six feet one inch tall, and he has a big nose."

The doctors ended the interview then. Barbie had

to be transferred to Providence Hospital in Everett for surgery.

The sheriff's men had heard the name Brandon Oakley before—although he usually used his nickname: "Easy." Brandon Oakley had been arrested only a week before on a burglary charge and promptly bailed out of jail. Why would he have told Barbie Linley his real name? The only answer was a terrible one: he had never expected her to live to report him to anyone.

Eiden and Johnson headed to Granite Falls to see if they could locate Oakley. Granite Falls' population was only twelve hundred, and they figured Police Chief Charles Curtis probably knew everyone in town. If Brandon Oakley lived there, Curtis probably knew his life story all the way back to kindergarten. They asked radio to locate Chief Curtis.

While Barbie Linley was en route to Providence Hospital, Snohomish County Chief Criminal Deputy Glen Mann and Detective Doug Engelbretson were notified at home. The message was cryptic: "A girl's been shot and raped—she may not live."

Engelbretson and Mann rushed to the hospital. Reserve Deputy Leslie Miller, who worked full time as a laboratory technician at the hospital, assisted the detectives as they recorded a statement from the injured girl. Barbie told the same story that she'd whispered to deputies earlier.

A nurse gave the detectives the clothing that Barbie Linley had worn to the hospital. They bagged the blood-soaked items into evidence: dark blue velvet jeans; a T-shirt imprinted, somewhat ironically, with

"Try it; you'll like it"; a zodiac pendant; a bra; panties; and a one-dollar bill.

Although she was in amazingly good condition for someone shot three times in the head, surgeons said they couldn't operate on her without endangering her life. The bullet which had shattered her cheek had lodged in the hinge of her right jaw, making it impossible for her to open or close her mouth completely. She would have to be treated vigorously with antibiotics to prevent infection before surgery began.

One wound in the back of her head had not penetrated her skull, and the other proved to have come from a ricocheting bullet, and it was neither an entry nor exit wound. However, both had caused severe bleeding. Barbie was fortunate that she had an unusually thick layer of bone in the back of her skull.

She had, indeed, been raped. Detectives wondered how anyone could have treated such a skinny little kid so brutally. There was no logical reason that she should be alive. Now, physicians worked to prevent an infection that might well be fatal if it reached the brain itself, which was only inches from the bullet in her cheek.

After talking with Barbie Linley, Mann and Engelbretson were satisfied that there was probable cause to arrest Brandon "Easy" Oakley on charges of first-degree assault with attempt to commit murder and for armed forcible rape. They radioed detectives who waited in the Granite Falls vicinity.

In the meantime, Deputy Ron Cooper and Detective Dick Taylor tried to find where the attack itself had taken place. It was full dark and finding physical evidence would be a challenge in the black and frigid November night. They found a spot that matched Barbie Linley and Alf Johansson's directions. It was off the Jordan Way Road and along an old logging road. With flashlights, they found recent tire tracks about five hundred feet up the road. The tracks were extremely wide and were from snow tires.

Next, the investigators located a purple-and-white knitted stocking cap and four hundred feet farther a small shoe imprint. There were two cigarette butts on the ground, along with a gum wrapper. All of these items were dry, although the road was wet and muddy.

The bank that Barbie had crawled up had seemed steep to her, but the ditch was really quite shallow. Now Cooper and Taylor found her purse at the bottom. It had fringe and two shades of brown suede squares sewed together. They figured the victim had lain in the ditch some time because there was a pool of blood next to the purse. They could also see where Barbie's hands had dug into the mud of the bank as she crawled out.

Carefully, they retrieved the items in the ditch, slipped them into bags, and labeled them.

Nearly three miles away from the bloody ditch, Snohomish County detectives approached a farmhouse on a twelve-acre farm near Granite Falls. They noted the customized metallic-green 1969 Camaro in the driveway. It had orange and black "Happy Faces" glued to the back windows.

It was five minutes to ten that night when they

knocked on the door and a woman answered. She looked distressed when they asked to talk to Brandon Oakley.

"He's home," she said. "But he's in bed asleep. He just went back to duty at Fort Lewis today, and he was tired when he came home."

Chief Curtis and the Snohomish County deputies followed the nervous woman to Oakley's room. When she switched the light on, a lanky young man sat up in bed; his eyes were bleary as if he'd been asleep for hours, and he appeared confused.

The officers advised Oakley of his rights under Miranda and informed him that he was under arrest. He stared straight ahead at the wall, refusing to acknowledge the rights' warning until Eiden asked him several times if he understood. Finally he nodded his head scornfully.

Asked if the clothes hanging over a chair in his room were the same ones he'd worn during the evening, Brandon Oakley nodded. The detectives took the clothes for evidence, and told him to put something else on. Oakley gave verbal permission for a search of his car. The woman homeowner said that they could search his room. This initial search turned up nothing that could be linked to the attack on Barbie Linley but Brandon "Easy" Oakley was transported to jail. His flashy Camaro was impounded and hauled to a local towing company, where it would undergo a thorough processing later.

Before they handcuffed him, the arresting officers cracked open a GSR (Gun Shot Residue) test kit and swabbed Oakley's hands to see if he had fired a gun recently. The tests were positive.

The "Easy" Oakley that Barbie Linley had described was, indeed, the same Brandon Oakley who had been arrested on the Halloween just past for second-degree burglary, and then released on his own personal recognition. Although just past his eighteenth birthday, Oakley already had had more bizarre run-ins with society than many men three times his age.

Chief Chuck Curtis knew "Easy" far too well. A Granite Falls citizen had once muttered to the chief, "He's going to kill someone if you cops don't do something." Around town, Oakley's classmates had described him as "immature," a "show-off," and "a creep." He had always been fascinated with fast, eye-catching cars and he bragged that he'd driven 130 miles an hour on the freeway and gotten away with it. There had been an incident where he'd deliberately swerved his car at a pedestrian. Luckily, the target had leapt out of the way in time. Teenagers in town had told Chief Curtis that Brandon went out of his way to run over animals.

Brandon Oakley had five older brothers, the oldest a dozen years older than he was. Since his father had left the home some months before his birth, his brothers had tried to fill in as surrogate fathers. But he had resented their telling him what to do, and he'd been something of a behavior problem since he was ten.

Despite his sadistic antics, "Easy" Oakley had friends, most of them a few grades behind him, kids who were impressed with his rebellion against authority. When he wanted to be charming, "Easy" had one of the most winning smiles in Granite Falls, but when he was feeling hostile, he had thought up some fairly rotten tricks to pull. On one occasion in high school, he had deliberately run a board full of nails through a planer in Shop, ruining the planer blade.

While Brandon Oakley waited in jail for his arraignment, Doug Engelbretson questioned more of his friends. They had heard "Easy" was carrying a .45 in a shoulder holster when he returned to Granite Falls from serving overseas in the army. They recalled that he had always carried a gun—even in high school. He liked to pull his car parallel with another vehicle on the road and fire at the occupants with his gun, only he had it loaded with blanks.

"Easy" Oakley hadn't graduated from high school. He had joined the army at the age of seventeen. After basic training he had been sent to Germany, where he was a truckdriver. He reportedly enjoyed this duty, but something happened during his second month in Europe that landed him in jail. Oakley's barracks mate, a soldier named Curran, was found strangled. "Easy" claimed he knew nothing about how Curran had come to be choked to death in their barracks room, but army authorities held him for court-martial proceedings.

Six months later, Brandon Oakley was acquitted of the murder charges. Through the efforts of his family and the intervention of Washington Senator Henry "Scoop" Jackson, he was ordered back to the States and reassigned to Fort Lewis sometime in October of 1973. He had also been granted a thirty-day leave that was scheduled to end on November 6, one day before Barbie Linley was attacked. According to his family—and Fort Lewis authorities—he had reported for duty but had been driving home in his new Camaro each night.

Now, only two-and-a-half months after his acquittal on murder charges in Germany, "Easy" Oakley was facing serious charges once again.

On the early morning of November 8, while Barbie Linley fought for her life in Everett's Providence Hospital, Snohomish County investigators returned to the lonely logging road where the she had been attacked.

They approached the shooting site on the logging road just as Barbie and her attacker would have the night before. As their vehicles moved slowly along the road, they videotaped the scene. When the road narrowed, they parked their cars and walked up the logging road. It was an area which had been clear-cut and reseeded with small firs, and much of it was still piled with slash. At the end of the logging road, it split into a *Y*. It was here that the assault appeared to have taken place.

In the daylight, they could see a set of small footprints that led from the bloody ditch up the bank through mud and heavy brush. For 120 feet, the tracks went in a circle and then went back to the road, and finally to the blacktop. These had to be prints Barbie had made as she struggled to find a way out.

There were the tire tracks too, extremely wide tire tracks measuring almost seven and a half inches wide. And they were distinctive. The outer rim of the tread had been worn down almost flat while the inner rim still had thick tread.

The air was so frigid that the detectives had to build a fire before the plaster moulages they made of the footprints and tire tracks would set up. As they worked, sleet drove needles of ice beneath their collars and cut into their faces. It seemed even more impossible now that a terribly wounded girl could ever have made her way out of this deserted area.

Two days after she was shot, Barbie Linley's doctors finally said she was strong enough to withstand a longer interview. Doug Engelbretson and Detective Vivian Griffiths went to Room 425 in Providence Hospital to talk with the 110-pound girl. Because she could not yet open her mouth with the slug caught in her jaw, it was painful for her to talk. But Barbie was able to tell them that she had already completed her high-school requirements and was attending an Everett secretarial school. At six o'clock on the evening of November 7, she had been hitchhiking on the corner of Hewitt and Broadway in Everett.

"I was standing there about five minutes and a blue and green Camaro stopped to pick me up."

"Can you describe anything else about the car?" Engelbretson asked.

Barbie gave the two detectives an amazingly detailed description of the vehicle. "The inside of the car was black," she said. "And a strap used to pull the driver's door closed was broken. There was a white scarf hanging from the rearview mirror, and a little stuffed dog. It had bucket seats with a console between them. He had marijuana in there."

Barbie enlarged upon her first description of her

assailant. "He was tall and thin, and his hair was pretty short. The only part that was long was in the front, and that hung down over his eyes."

"What was he wearing?" Vivian Griffiths asked.

"Faded Levis."

Barbie said she had told the man that she was on her way to Marysville, about seven miles north. That was OK with him, but, as soon as they left Everett, he had turned in another direction. "I know it was dumb," Barbie said, "But I liked his car and I didn't say anything. We talked, and he told me his name was 'Easy,' and then that it was Brandon Oakley. He told me he'd only lived around here for six weeks."

"Easy" had offered Barbie marijuana and she'd accepted. "But then he kept telling me to roll more joints, and I didn't want to. I wasn't holding the smoke in my lungs—I blew it out quickly so it wouldn't affect me."

While he drove, "Easy" Oakley had smoked several joints.

Barbie realized then that she was way over her head, and getting in deeper. As the Camaro hurtled toward Lake Stevens, Oakley asked her if she wanted some cocaine. She had never had cocaine, but she wanted to appear worldly, so she said, "OK, sure."

"OK. We'll go to my house and get some," "Easy" had answered.

But the drive to his house had ended up on a lonely country road instead. Explaining again that he hadn't lived in the area long, "Easy" Oakley backed the Camaro out and turned into an even narrower dirt road.

"He said, 'Oh, heck, I've got the wrong road again,'

when he came to a *Y* in the road," Barbie remembered.

But now "Easy" made no pretense of backing out. He turned off the engine and the radio and remarked, "Doesn't the quiet sound good?"

The quiet sounded frightening to Barbie Linley, and she asked him to turn the radio back on. He did, but then he grabbed her and started to kiss her. She tried to push him away.

"I begged him not to," Barbie said, thinking back to the moment she realized she had gotten herself into a scary situation.

She said that "Easy" had leaned back and she thought that he was just going to sit there for a few minutes. But then he said a strange thing, "Do you like your head?"

She thought he was kidding her in some odd way and mumbled, "Sure."

Then he was kissing her again, and she felt something moving down the front of her T-shirt. She thought it was his hand and she reached to move it away.

It was a gun.

Holding the gun against her, he said, "Do you want to lose your head? No? Well, just be cool."

He had asked her for oral sex and she said, "No. *Please,* no!" But he was forcing her down, his hand on the back of her neck. She asked if he was going to choke her, and he said he knew a better way to die and touched her again with the gun. Sickened, she complied with his request.

And then he had peeled off her clothes and pushed her between the seats, where he raped her. It seemed to last for an hour as the icy rain drummed on the top of his car.

When he was finally finished, Barbie had asked, "Can you take me home now? I won't tell anybody."

He seemed to agree and he even offered to let her drive. She got out and started to walk around to the driver's side. But he met her outside the car, removed her blouse, and forced her back into the car where he raped her for the fourth time. Still he was not satiated. Barbie got out and tried to put her clothes on as she edged toward the passenger seat. Suddenly, "Easy" had snaked out his arm, grabbed her and pulled her shirt over her head.

It was then that she felt a blow on the back of her head. The force knocked her off balance. She realized he was hitting her with the gun. Desperate, she pretended to collapse on the ground, hoping he would think he'd hit her hard enough to knock her unconscious and would just would go away.

Barbie said she'd lain there on her stomach for a long time, with her legs drawn up under her. "It got really quiet," she told Griffiths and Engelbretson. "I couldn't hear him, so I risked a quick look over my shoulder."

"Easy" Oakley was standing above her, smiling, his legs spread wide apart, holding a large handgun in both hands. It was pointed straight at her head.

She said she'd cried out, "No! Please! No!"

But "Easy" only squeezed the trigger. "I felt such a tremendous force hit the back of my head," Barbie remembered. "It lifted me up off the ground and flipped me over onto my back. I felt like I was flying."

Her ordeal was far from over. She had been

knocked into some kind of ditch or depression, but she could see "Easy" looming over her. He was still aiming the big gun at her. She thought she was going to die. Too scared to speak, she watched him slowly squeeze the trigger. A bullet slammed into her face, and a geyser of blood spurted from her cheek.

"It felt as though someone hit me in the face with a hammer, and the pain was so bad I didn't think I could stand it."

Barbie Linley was sure that "Easy" was going to shoot her again. Maybe she was already dead. It was hard to tell; there was so much blood, and so much pain. "But he walked away from me. He opened the car door and took out my purse and my coat, and he threw them on top of me. I lay there so still. I wanted him to think that I was dead, and he didn't need to worry that I could tell anybody what he'd done to me."

She said she had waited until she could no longer hear the sound of his car's motor. Then she had struggled to her feet and crawled out of the ditch. "First, I put my coat on," Barbie said, her eyes mirroring remembered fear. "I pulled my shirt down and I started toward a light. I saw the light and I sort of walked toward it, but there were all kinds of tree stumps and everything, little sticks and water and stuff, and I was stumbling over them as I started to walk back to the road."

"Do you know how far you went out in the brush?"

"Oh, I didn't walk very far. Maybe seventy-five or a hundred feet. I turned around and started walking back, because it was too hard. I kept falling and hitting my head. I was scared that guy, Brandon, would come back. So, when I made the road, I was sort of sticking along the side of the road so he wouldn't see me if he did."

Somehow, Barbie had made it to the farmhouse in the distance and to safety. She had stumbled more than six hundred yards.

Brandon "Easy" Oakley's car was thoroughly processed in the impound garage where it was being held. Just as Barbie Linley had described, a white knit scarf and a yellow-and-black stuffed dog hung from the rearview mirror. Detectives found a bag of marijuana, cigarette papers, and matches in the console between the bucket seats. A "roach" was still in the ashtray.

In the trunk of the Camaro, they found a somewhat odd item; it was the complete transcript of Oakley's murder trial in Germany.

They did not find the .45 handgun that had fired the bullet into Barbie's head. However, on that day, they were about to get some help in that area. A psychology class in one of the local high schools was discussing the vicious assault when one of the students said, "Yeah, and they've arrested Brandon Oakley, too."

This was electrifying news to another boy. He hurried home after school and grabbed the evening paper that headlined Oakley's arrest. He said nothing to his family; he didn't want to worry them—but he had something in his possession that he thought the sheriff's office should know about. At a quarter to six that evening, he walked up to the front desk in the Snohomish County Sheriff's Office and asked to talk to a detective.

"It's about 'Easy' Oakley," the nervous teenager said.

Doug Engelbretson hurried into the office from his home. He could see the kid was scared.

"I've got a gun in my car, sir" the boy said. "Brandon Oakley gave it to me last Wednesday night. He handed me the gun and a shoulder holster and said, 'Can my heater!'"

"Did you get rid of that gun?" Engelbretson asked.

"No sir. I still have it. Would you like to see it?"

Engelbretson most assuredly would. The boy handed over a bag. Inside, there was a .455 six-shot Webley revolver-Mark VI. Ballistics tests would prove that this was the gun used to shoot Barbie Linley.

The cooperative teenager who brought the gun in assured Doug Engelbretson that he'd had no idea that a girl had been shot when "Easy" gave him the weapon to dispose of. But he admitted that Oakley had attempted to involve him in burglaries. "He said all I had to do was be a lookout, but I told him, 'No way!'"

Doctors at Providence Hospital were cautiously optimistic about Barbie Linley's recovery. They had managed to forestall any infection, and they were considering leaving the bullet in her head because surgery to remove it would be so dangerous. In the end, they had no choice. Unless they got the .45 slug out, she would never have normal mobility of her jaw. She couldn't go through life with her mouth locked half open. They operated and gave her massive doses of antibiotics and gradually she began to recover.

At first it had seemed that her cheekbone had

shattered irreparably, but she had been lucky. Although she would always have a scar to remind her of the awful night on the logging road, her face healed.

The detectives who had found her assailant were unaware that Barbie had an overwhelming need to find out why "Easy" Oakley had wanted to hurt her. Secretly, she wrote him a letter in jail. And he wrote back.

Oakley was a challenge for jailers in the Snohomish County Jail. Soon after he went in, he met another prisoner who had once been committed to Western Washington State Hospital for a mental evaluation. Oakley set out to learn how to appear insane. He told his cellmates he planned to go "the crazy route." He spent one whole day staring at the ceiling of his cell, then remarked to another inmate, "Do you have any idea how difficult it is to just sit and stare at the ceiling all day and not talk to anyone?"

Evidently the catatonic imitation was too much of a bore, so he tried active disruptions. He set fire to his mattress and started fights with other prisoners. At various times he announced that he was James Bond, a Communist agent, and, later, an American spy who had gone undercover to fight foreign powers. He insisted to his fellow prisoners that he could not remember what had happened with Barbie Linley because he'd been "out on window-pane" (LSD).

Oakley decorated the back of another prisoners' jail coveralls with a grotesque ink sketch of a skull with a bullet hole cracking the bony structure. Underneath, he signed his handiwork: "Easy."

"Easy" Oakley was not popular with his peers. He was derisive and ridiculing. But little Barbie Linley, who had no one in her life who had acknowledged her existence in any real way, had had "Easy's" full attention for hours on the night he raped and shot her.

When she contacted him in jail, he had been pleasant to her. He, of course, had every reason to be; she was the prime witness against him. It was easy for him to convince her that he hadn't meant to hurt her—that he had been so attracted to her that he lost control of himself. She, on the other hand, blocked out the memory of the gun in his hands. In order to even begin to understand her self-delusion, it is necessary to remember that Brandon Oakley came upon Barbie when she had left a home where she wasn't wanted in a pitiful attempt to find a father who had never wanted her. She was cold, broke, lost, and miserable. And "Easy" had talked to her and given her a ride. She remembered the good part about that evening in November and pushed the awful part away.

Barbie continued to write to him.

Why "Easy" Oakley raped and shot the slender fifteen-year-old is a mystery. He already had a girlfriend who told deputies that they had traveled all over the state and spent nights in motels together. And he had never touched her sexually. It may have been that his sexual desire was aroused only when a female was terrified. Barbie Linley had certainly been afraid of him. When he was satiated, shooting Barbie may have been no more upsetting to him than swerving off the road to run over an animal.

A forensic psychologist diagnosed Oakley as a classic antisocial personality. After spending hours talking with the prisoner, he wrote:

He unknowingly depicted a callous, hedonistic relationship with his peers. He was totally unappreciative of what his mother and brothers did for his well-being when he was confined in Germany and unappreciative of efforts to get him reassigned, as if this was all his obvious due. He felt himself innately lucky and deserving of continued good luck. He was blind to what he did not wish to see and flared to aggressive anger to terminate attempts to point out issues he did not want assessed. He was smoothly able to rationalize all of his behavior so that it appeared to him warranted, reasonable, and justified. He felt laws did not apply to him. He was incapable of guilt and felt himself a uniquely special individual.

In other words, "Easy" did what he wanted when he wanted and felt completely within his rights in doing so. He not only fit within the parameters that define an antisocial personality, he also had facets of the narcissistic personality disorder *and* the histrionic personality disorder. He wasn't crazy; he simply thought he was special and he loved attention, and it didn't matter who got hurt for him to have his own way—always.

While awaiting his trial for rape, sodomy, first-degree assault with intent to commit murder, and commission of a felony while armed with a deadly weapon, "Easy" Oakley continued his insanity charade. He cut a gash in his forearm; it bled profusely but it wasn't deep enough to do him much damage. He tied his neck to the bars with a towel and pretended to be hanging, but jailers could see that the terry cloth noose was not cinched tightly and that he was breathing quite comfortably.

"Easy" was often angry with his jailers. Once, he screamed at a guard, "I'm going to get even with you just like I did Curran [the victim in the strangulation killing in Germany]!"

"Easy" Oakley went on trial during the third week of January 1974. He continued his temper tantrums in the courtroom. During jury selection, it was necessary to handcuff him to his chair. When this didn't work, the judge warned that if he didn't stop misbehaving, he would be barred from his own trial. Three days later, "Easy" promised to behave himself and the cuffs were taken off.

During his trial, court watchers also saw flashes of Oakley's charming smile, which he could turn on at will. "Easy" had reason to smile; he had stolen the State's chief witness against him. Incredible as it might seem, Barbie Linley had *married* him. As his wife, she could not be forced to testify against him. The sixteen-year-old without a home had grasped at the only chance she had ever been offered to become part of someone else's life. The investigators shuddered at the thought of what her life would be like if her bridegroom should be acquitted.

But that didn't happen. Brandon Oakley was found guilty on all charges. His face turned scarlet with fury and he looked as if he were about to explode. Court deputies quickly slipped handcuffs on him for the long walk back to jail.

He faced two life sentences to run concurrently

(which meant a minimum of thirteen years and four months), a ten-year sentence on the sodomy charge and a mandatory five-year sentence on the deadly weapon charge.

Brandon "Easy" Oakley was released from prison after seventeen years. He is now in his early forties. No one was surprised when his marriage did not last.

An Unlikely
Suspect

Although this case happened more than two
decades ago, it might well have come out of the
headlines of today's newspapers. The suspect was
the last person the victim's family and the police
suspected. He was someone who seemed totally
incapable of violent murder.

He was to have been part of the dream of a
reunited family. In truth, he turned out to be the
destroyer of that dream.

It was shortly after midnight on Wednesday, October 2, when Deputy Mike Butschli was dispatched to a residential subdivision in the southeast part of King County, Washington. The only information he had was that there was a "possible dead body." He wasn't overly concerned as he headed through the night to the address given. Such a report can turn out to be anything: a pile of leaves or rags; a drunk sleeping it off who *looks* as if he's dead; a "natural" death, suicide, or, only rarely, a homicide. The neighborhood where the call had originated certainly didn't look ominous, and the neat, two-story white house with gray trim appeared peaceful enough from the outside.

Inside, it was another story entirely. A distraught middle-aged man met Butschli at the front door and apologized for his delay in answering. He said his dog was going nuts, and he'd had to put it in the garage first. He identified himself as Milton English,* the owner of the home, and he beckoned to the officer to follow him as he started upstairs.

Now expecting to find a dog-bite victim or even a

dead animal, Butschli followed English to a bedroom on the west side of the upper story. English said it was his son's room.

The door to the room was open and the deputy could see a partially clad woman lying face up on the floor. He hurried over to her, and knelt beside her to feel for a pulse in the carotid artery in her neck. There was none. And hers appeared not to be a natural death. There was an ugly cluster of wounds on the top of her head and blood had soaked her hair and the blanket beneath her.

Deputy Butschli backed carefully out of the room. He asked the ashen-faced man to take a seat in the living room and to refrain from touching anything until homicide detectives arrived. Sergeants Sam Hicks and Jerry Van Horne were already en route to help secure the scene.

In a broken voice, Milt English told Butschli that the dead woman upstairs was his twenty-nine-year-old wife, Vera. He said he'd found her on the floor when he returned from work at midnight. He worked the swing shift, and he had left for work as usual about three-forty that afternoon. Everything at home had been completely normal. His wife's two little girls by a previous marriage were playing outside and his son by a former marriage, John English, fourteen, was off somewhere on his bike.

"I kissed my wife, picked up my lunchbox, put on my jacket, and left," English said. "Like I always do."

He had called his wife's name when he came home and received no answer. He said she worked two nights a week in a gift shop at a nearby shopping mall, but the store closed at 9:00 P.M. Worried because she should have been home by then, he'd started to look for her. Then he'd noticed that her car was missing from the garage and assumed she'd been held up at work.

"Where are the children?" Butschli asked.

"The girls are here." English said that he'd checked on the little girls when his wife hadn't answered him. They were sleeping soundly in their room. "Since my son would have been baby-sitting if she was at work, I went to his bedroom to ask him where she was. But on the way, I saw my wife on the floor."

His teenage son was not in the house, and English was afraid that something had happened to him, too. The boy was always very conscientious about caring for his seven- and eight-year-old stepsisters. It just wasn't like him to leave the little girls alone in the house.

Within minutes, the gray and white house in the quiet neighborhood was alive with King County police cars. A deputy was posted at the door of the bedroom where Vera English lay; they didn't want her small daughters to see her body as detectives carried them to a neighbor's house.

The county homicide detectives surveyed the body of Vera English. Even in death, it was apparent that the slender woman had been extremely attractive. It looked as if she had been the victim of a violent sexual attack; her bloodied yellow sweater had been yanked above her full breasts, her bra had been ripped open, and her legs were splayed in the classic rape position. The lower half of her body was naked except for knee-length nylons. The dead woman's panties lay near her body—tied in knots. There was a belt and a multicolored garment of some sort tied tightly around her neck. A blue claw hammer just to the right of her shoulder was covered with congealing blood. Undoubtedly it had caused the terrible wounds to her head. Her purse's contents were dumped all over the floor.

Despite the fact that the thermostat in the house read seventy-four degrees, Vera English's body was cool. She had probably been dead for several hours.

While the patrol officers searched the exterior of the home and yard, Detectives Ted Forrester and Rolf Grunden photographed, measured, and processed the home's interior. They noted that someone had piled pillows taken from the master bedroom beside Vera English's body. This kind of attempt to make the body "comfortable" usually indicated that the killer had been someone close to the victim.

It was a puzzling case. Had a burglar known that Milt English worked late and that this was Vera's night to work? He might have come in to rob the home and been surprised by Vera English and attacked her with the hammer in a panic. It was possible that the boy hadn't even been home; he could very well turn up at a friend's house—but that possibility seemed less probable as it got later and he neither came home nor called.

Concern grew for fourteen-year-old John English. The little girls would have been no particular threat to a killer. They had probably slept through the whole attack, and he might not even have known they were in the house. But a teenaged boy would have tried to defend his stepmother when she ran to his bedroom for help. *He* would have been able to identify the killer, and the chances were good that he had been abducted by the murderer when he made his escape in the dead woman's car.

The King County detectives tried to calm Milt English, but they all knew there was a good possibility that his son had been killed too. He wasn't anywhere in the house or the rain-soaked yard.

Police radio broadcast a bulletin at once asking for reports on any sightings of the missing 1974 bronze Chevy Nova with Washington plates: IEG–508. Soon every lawman in the seven western states was watching for it, but the car didn't turn up. There were so many places in the Northwest where a car with a dead boy in the trunk could be hidden: bottomless bodies of water, old mines, almost impenetrable forests. Milt English had already lost his wife, and now he was frantic with worry about his only son.

He was not, however, out of the woods as a suspect himself. The first rule of thumb in a homicide investigation is always, "Look at the people closest to the victim." Only after detectives clear family, lovers, friends, and work associates do they look for stranger-killers. And they usually don't have to go that far down the list.

As Ted Forrester and Rolf Grunden processed the crime scene in the English home far into the wee hours of October 2, they discovered some bizarre items that seemed out of place in a nice suburban neighborhood. John English's bedroom was not the usual boy's room with sports posters and equipment.

There was a mobile hanging over his bed, but it wasn't made of colored disks or birds or butterflies; this one had anatomically correct naked dolls hanging from nooses around their necks.

The two detectives lifted the boy's mattress and found a profusion of pictures of nude women in various provocative poses, pictures obviously cut out of girlie and sex magazines. And they weren't *Playboy* centerfolds; they were hard-core pornographic photographs that included bondage and discipline.

As Grunden and Forrester proceeded through the home, they figured they had found the source of the kid's photo collection. There were a plethora of sexually oriented magazines in several rooms. The parents had obviously made no effort to hide them from the children. It wasn't surprising that John had collected dozens of pictures that depicted women as the objects of what could only be called kinky sex. It appeared that fourteen-year-old John English had been bombarded with sexual stimuli pretty heavy for an adolescent male.

Grunden and Forrester had seen some unexpected twists in homicide cases over the years and nothing surprised them much anymore. They continued to peek into closets and behind furniture, hoping to find some clue to what had happened in this house. When they pulled out a drawer in the bedside table in the master bedroom, they found all manner of ropes, handcuffs, and leather thongs fashioned into loops. Although they exchanged glances at the bizarre collection, they weren't there to pass judgment on the Englishs' sex life.

There were empty hangers in John English's closet, and it looked as though half the stuff was missing from his chest of drawers. No kidnapper was going to give his victim time to pack a bag.

A terrible suspicion had begun to insinuate itself into the investigators' minds. Was it remotely possible that there hadn't been an intruder at all? Could John English have killed his own stepmother? Most boys tend to view their stepmothers as nonsexually as they do their natural mothers, but Milt English told them that John had only been living with him and Vera for the last year. And Vera English was—or had been—an incredible looking woman. Maybe the kid had seen the pretty woman as a desirable female instead of as a mother figure.

Judging from what they had found in John's bedroom, it was clear that his interest in sex and the female body were more than a little precocious. The detectives hoped that their suspicions were wrong, but, either way, it didn't look as if there would be a good ending to the puzzle; if John English wasn't the killer, he himself was probably dead.

John English moved up as a probable murder suspect when the investigators found a number of people who could swear to the fact that Milt English had been at his job all evening. He would have had no time to drive to his home and kill his wife. Furthermore, John had seemed to be madly in love with Vera.

An update was added to the "want" on the Chevy Nova. Northwest lawmen were now told to approach fourteen-year-old John English with caution. According to his father, there was a .22 rifle missing from the family home, and all the money from the family's piggy banks. "And some handcuffs," he added. "At least one pair of my handcuffs are missing."

Again, Forrester and Grunden didn't ask why a man who worked at an airplane plant owned handcuffs. But they knew now that the Englishs' marriage seemed to have leaned heavily toward sexual bondage.

If fourteen-year-old John English was the killer, he could be suicidal once the enormity of the crime hit him. The King County police didn't expect him to get very far, however. He was two years below the legal driving age in Washington, and he should be easy to spot. He would probably run off the road ten miles from home, if he hadn't already.

When neither John English nor the missing bronze Nova had been spotted by dawn the next morning, the dragnet for the missing car was expanded. Information on the murder was released to all news media. It seemed impossible that the car could still be in Washington as the day passed. If it were, someone would have seen it. Rolf Grunden notified the border patrol at Blaine, Washington, and asked that the Royal Canadian Mounted Police be given the description of the bronze Nova in case the driver tried to cross over into British Columbia.

Either an unknown killer or John English probably had enough credit cards to pay his way to Europe, if necessary. None of Vera's cards had been in the jumble of items dumped from her purse. Grunden contacted the security units of Seafirst Bank's Master-Card, Texaco, Arco, and Shell and asked to be notified immediately if there were any "hits" on credit charges to the English accounts.

Although they had had no sleep at all, Ted Forrester and Rolf Grunden attended the postmortem examination of Vera English's body at 11:30 on that interminable Wednesday morning of October 2. Dr. Donald Reay, now Medical Examiner of King County, would perform the autopsy.

The five-foot-four-inch woman weighed only 107 pounds, and she had a perfect figure. Vera English had been a gorgeous, if somewhat flamboyant-looking woman. She had flaming red hair, and it looked as though she had just finished putting on makeup when she was attacked. Skillfully applied green eye shadow colored her eyelids and her orange lipstick was still fresh. She wore her wedding band and a ring in the shape of a flower on her silver-tipped fingers. She was very tan, with the only pale skin visible in areas that had been covered by a very small bikini bathing suit.

From her clothing, it looked as if Vera English had just come home from work when she was attacked; the flowered smock she wore to the gift shop still bore her name tag. Beneath her twisted yellow sweater, her bra, which fastened in the front, was torn apart at the plastic fasteners. Dr. Reay pointed out that the victim's extremely large breasts were the result of silicone implants.

Someone had done terrible damage to Vera English. There were twenty-three separate wounds on her head; many of the blows had caused depressed fractures and exposed brain tissue. In addition, she had been strangled by ligature, crushing her hyoid bone and causing extensive hemorrhaging into the throat muscles and soft tissue.

Vera English had obviously seen her killer, and she had fought for her life. She had sustained multiple defense wounds, fractures and cuts on her fingers as if she had tried to protect her head from the hammer blows raining down on it.

Surprisingly, she had not been raped, but there were some abrasions of the labia minora of the vulva that indicated rape had been attempted. The autopsy results suggested that the killer had been very strong and very, very angry.

Rolf Grunden searched out John English's friends and acquaintances. He quickly heard rumors that John had carried a gun to school, but he was unable to substantiate them. Both Grunden and Ted Forrester were determined to keep open minds. They still didn't know what John English's part—if any—had been in his stepmother's murder. The possibility remained that he, too, was a victim.

However, John's complicity in his stepmother's death became more suspect when Rolf Grunden talked to Vera English's employer. He learned that Vera had never arrived at the gift shop on the night of October 1. "Her stepson, John, called," the woman said. "He told me that Vera had the flu and that she couldn't come to work."

"Vera didn't have the flu," Milt English said. "She felt fine when I left for work."

Detective Judy Watson talked to Vera English's two small daughters and took statements from them about the evening before. The little girls remembered that everything had been normal the night before. Their mother had eaten with their stepfather and then served an early dinner to them and their stepbrother. "Then we went downstairs with John," the older girl said, "and we watched television in the rec room."

The girls remembered that their mother and stepbrother had gotten into a "little fight" over who was going to do the dishes. "They didn't yell, though, and my mom did them." After the dishes were done, their mom had gotten dressed for work. "She came downstairs to watch TV with us before she went to work, though."

The time line was essential in this case, and the detectives wondered if two small girls would be able to pinpoint certain events. They were very smart children, and they knew exactly when their favorite shows were on.

They said that they thought their mother had gone to work while they were watching *That Girl,* which was on from 6:30 to 7:00 P.M. At least, they didn't see her at all during that time. Right after that, John had gone upstairs, telling his stepsisters that he was going to do his homework.

"While *The FBI* was on, John came down and told us it was time for bed," the older girl recalled.

"What time was that on?"

"Right after the one about Ann Marie—from 7:00 to 8:00."

It was John who put the girls to bed, and they knew he was close by because they could hear him down in the living room. He was listening to the radio.

Sometime later, one of the girls said she'd woken up

because their pet poodle was barking. "And I heard the car leaving the garage. I went out in the hall and I looked for John, but I couldn't find him."

She said she didn't look in his room because she was not allowed to go in there. Sleepy, she had gone back to bed. Neither of the girls had awakened until the police woke them to move them to a neighbor's home.

Both of the girls said they liked John, and that he was good to them. "He yells at us sometimes," one said, "but he would never hit us."

"Did you hear anything at all during the night that scared you? Detective Watson asked. "Any sound you never heard before?"

"No."

"Did you hear anybody yelling or screaming?"

"No. We were just sleeping."

King County patrol cars began to check Texaco, Shell, and Arco service stations in a five-mile radius of the English home. Milt English was sure that the Nova's gas gauge had been on empty. Whoever had stolen the car—whether it was John or a stranger—would have had to get gas almost immediately. None of the regular employees contacted recalled having sold gas to someone in a bronze Nova.

With any homicide case that gets as much media publicity as the English case did, detectives expect scores of tips, sightings, and offers of help from those involved in the occult "sciences." This case was no different. One astrologer contacted the King County homicide detectives and told them that the configuration of the planets on October 2 indicated to her that John English was dead.

It began to look as if her prediction was right. He was either dead or he had managed to slip through an extremely tight blue line of cops watching for him.

And then Rolf Grunden received a call from Detective Don Dashnea of the Renton, Washington, police. Dashnea had received a phone call from the parents of a schoolmate of John English. The boy, Ben Brown,* had information on the English case. Grunden left at once to talk with him.

He met a very chastened and shocked teenager. Ben Brown knew exactly what had happened after Vera English was killed. He said that he had met John English during the first week of school in September. On about September 30, they had decided to run away to Oregon together. The plan was for John to get some food together, steal one of his parents' cars, and meet Ben in the parking lot of a hospital south of Seattle.

"I met John about 9:30 P.M. on Tuesday, October 1," Ben said. "He had a brown Nova. He was just sitting there relaxing in the car with his hands behind his head. I told him, 'Hey, man, let's go.'"

The two boys had driven south until about 2:00 A.M., reaching a little town along the Pacific ocean in Oregon. They got out and strolled along the dark beach for a while and then decided to drive farther. "John probably used his gas credit cards about five times," Ben said.

The whole trip seemed like a lark to Ben—until they got to Gold Beach, Oregon. And then John English had turned to him with a smile, and said casually, "Don't you wonder how I got the car so early?"

"And so I said, 'Well, how did you get the car so early?'" Ben told Rolf Grunden.

But John's reply had been a question so shocking that Ben could scarcely believe it. "Do you think if you hit somebody hard enough in the back of the head with a claw hammer you could kill them?"

"I don't know," Ben answered slowly. "What's that got to do with anything?"

"And then John told me, 'I got my mom in my room and then I hit her in the back of the head with a hammer once or twice.'"

"Do you think you killed her?" Ben said he'd asked.

"Yeah," he quoted John's reply.

Ben Brown had been sick to his stomach with horror as they drove on south toward the California border. He'd barely spoken for about fifty miles, and with each passing mile he was more convinced that he didn't want to stay with John any longer.

Ben said that when they reached Orick in northern California, he got out of the car and said he was going back. He'd called his parents in Washington and told them he was on his way home. As soon as his bus arrived, he told his parents what John had said, and they called the police.

Ben seemed bewildered by the turn of events. Under Detective Grunden's questioning, he said he'd never thought that John had any problems at home or any tendencies toward violence. He wasn't into drugs or alcohol, as far as Ben knew. They had just planned that John would wait until his stepmother got home from work Wednesday evening, and then he would load the car very quietly and drive it away. They were going to see California, Reno, and Las Vegas. But John English had changed their exciting trip into horror.

It appeared now that John English was not only alive, he was headed into Nevada with a .22 rifle in the trunk of his car. He had told Ben Brown that the gun "might come in handy."

It was 1974, and homicidal violence by minors was virtually unheard of. Although a "want" for fourteen-year-old John English went out over the western half of America, it still seemed impossible that a boy of his age could have committed murder. But investigators now had a witness who had seen John within minutes of Vera English's brutal murder. Everything pointed to him and they had to stop him before he hurt anyone else.

On October 7, Grunden sent an updated teletype throughout Washington, Oregon, and Nevada. He also alerted Arco, Shell, and Texaco to the fact that the fugitive teenager would probably be using their cards in the Nevada area. But it would be more than a week before the first information from the stolen credit cards paid off. Texaco's computer system registered a "hit" on Milt English's credit card in Benson, Arizona.

Rolf Grunden immediately called the Benson Police Department, the Benson County Sheriff's Office, the Arizona Highway Patrol, and the U.S. Customs Office on the Mexican border.

If John English was still in the state of Arizona, there was virtually no chance that he could escape the notice of authorities. Further, it seemed impossible that a boy so young and so inexperienced as a driver hadn't been involved in a traffic violation or an accident. But days passed with no word of him.

Somehow, he had gotten out of Arizona. There was no telling where he could be.

Grunden kept in daily contact with the oil companies and MasterCard security, but there were no more "hits." Texaco voluntarily prepared a special bulletin to all its dealers asking them to watch for a boy in a bronze Nova, but nobody spotted him. If John English had somehow managed to slip across the Mexican border, it was quite possible that he might never be apprehended.

And then, on October 17, Milt English received a curious call from his insurance company. The Chevrolet Nova had been recovered, but the company had no information about *where* it was. Thinking that English must have misunderstood, Rolf Grunden called the insurance company's headquarters. He got no further than Milt English had. *Someone* had the missing car, but there was nothing in their records beyond that tantalizing and frustrating information.

The use of computers in law enforcement was in its infancy in the midseventies. Glitches were more the rule than the exception. The failure of the insurance company's computers would considerably delay the capture of fourteen-year-old John English. Eventually, King County authorities would find out what had happened.

At 9:30 P.M. on October 16, Louisiana State Patrol Sergeant Maurice Roy was on routine patrol in unit I–76 on Louisiana State Road 93 near an exit of the I–10 freeway. Roy noticed a bronze Nova that was about to enter the freeway on an exit ramp. The driver appeared to be totally confused, and perhaps intoxicated. Sergeant Roy signalled to the car to pull over.

The driver complied, narrowly averting a head-on collision. When Roy walked over to the car, he saw that the person behind the wheel was only a kid who looked far too young to be driving. The Louisiana trooper asked for a driver's license, but the boy was unable to produce one.

"I guess I put it in my other shirt," the driver stuttered. "I can't find it."

Roy walked around the dusty car and saw that it had Washington State plates. The kid was a long, long way from home. He seemed very calm, and he was polite and cooperative, and there was no odor of alcohol about him.

"Whose car is this?"

"It belongs to my father, sir. He loaned it to me so I could take a trip to Florida."

"Do you have any identification?" Roy asked.

The boy dug in his wallet and produced a student-body card for a high school in Washington State and several credit cards in the name of Milton English.

While the driver waited with apparent nonchalance, Roy walked back to his patrol car and asked radio to check the Nova's license plates, and the boy's name through the NCIC (National Crime Information Center) computers.

Again, computer malfunction played into John English's hands. The NCIC computers at the FBI headquarters in Quantico were temporarily down and the Louisiana State Patrol radio dispatcher was unable to get a response.

"I'm afraid you'll have to follow me into headquarters until we get this straightened out," Sergeant Roy told the boy who said his name was John English. The kid nodded agreeably

Sergeant Roy headed east on I–10 and the Nova followed but another vehicle pulled between his patrol car and the Washington car just as Roy eased off the freeway at an exit. The Nova did not follow. Rather, it accelerated and raced on down the freeway. Roy wrenched his steering wheel and hurtled across a berm planted with bushes to get back on the highway.

The Louisiana trooper was in hot pursuit as the taillights of the Nova grew smaller ahead of him. He hit his siren and called for backup. His speedometer climbed above ninety miles per hour as he closed the gap between his patrol unit and the Washington car. And then, suddenly, the Nova spun out of control and crashed into trees in a roadside rest area. Roy leapt from his cruiser expecting to find the driver injured, but he wasn't even in the wrecked Nova; he had disappeared into the thickly wooded area.

By this time, several other Louisiana troopers had arrived at the scene and they fanned out through the brush. All to no avail; the youthful suspect had vanished.

The troopers surveyed the wrecked Nova and noticed that its trunk was tied down with cotton rope. Inside, they found two sets of handcuffs, a man's clothing, and a knife.

Sergeant Roy still held John English's student-body card, and he fed the name and the car's description into the computer at NCIC again as soon as he got back to his station. Only then did he learn that he had stopped a fugitive wanted all across the country. Roy contacted Rolf Grunden at once and told him that a widespread search for John English was currently going on all across Louisiana.

But once again, fourteen-year-old John English had managed to escape. However, now he was on foot. It didn't seem possible that a ninth grader could still be leading police on such a chase.

While the car was being processed by the Louisiana State Crime Lab, Grunden received a communication from the Barton, Alabama Police Department. They were investigating a homicide in which the victim had been shot several times with a .22 while handcuffed, and requested information on the handcuffs missing from the English residence. Grunden checked with Milton English and found that the stolen cuffs were a Japanese make. That eliminated young John English as a suspect in the Alabama case.

But where was John English? He had told Sergeant Roy that he was headed for Florida, and lab men in Louisiana had found an address in the wrecked car which listed a street in Tallahassee, Florida. Rolf Grunden requested a stakeout by Tallahassee police. This was set up, but English did not appear.

The days passed with no more word on the fugitive teenager. Grunden knew where he had been; he had, in fact, a complete chart of the route John had taken from the credit card hits that were now pouring in: Manzanita, Oregon; Eureka and Wasco, California; Las Vegas, Nevada; Tucson, Kingman, and Peoria, Arizona; and then three purchases in Benson. Almost miraculously, the kid hadn't been stopped as he moved through Deming, New Mexico; and San Antonio, Schulenburg, and Van Horn, Texas. All of the purchases had been for gasoline and oil. That was probably why he hadn't drawn attention to himself. If he'd tried to buy high-ticket items like tires or other auto accessories so that he could resell them to make money, John English might have raised suspicions among the station attendants, but he'd played it very carefully.

On October 27, John had been missing almost four weeks when Grunden received a phone call from the Miami Beach Police Department. They had John English in custody. Ironically, after being wanted for suspicion of murder, car theft, reckless driving, and evading arrest, it was a simple littering violation that tripped him up. Two Miami patrolmen had observed a man who appeared in his early twenties and a teenager tossing litter into the street. They walked over to talk to the litterers and asked them for identification. The older man said he was Bo Dennis* and that he lived nearby and worked at a local establishment. He had ID that verified this. The younger man had no ID at all. He said he was seventeen, but he looked to be much younger. He also looked like an unmade bed and appeared to have been on the streets for some time.

When the officers started to put the boy into their squad car, he broke and ran. After a foot and vehicle chase through nearby buildings and streets, the runner was apprehended.

At the station house, the youthful captive admitted that he was John English, fourteen—a runaway from Washington State.

"My mother's dead," he said. "And I live with my father." The arresting officers in Miami had no idea that, while his words were true, they told a far more grim story. English was transferred to a detention home pending correspondence with Washington authorities.

Bo Dennis said that he'd only been in Miami for three days when he met John English, who had told him he was seventeen. The teenager had been sitting on a park bench on the night of October 19, holding a blanket and looking forlorn. He told Dennis that someone had robbed him of his backpack, clothes, and fifty dollars in Mississippi. "He told me he had to jump out of a speeding car and that's what caused all those scratches on his arms," Dennis said. "I was down to my last ten bucks myself, so I offered to join up with him. We got a cheap hotel room and started looking for jobs the next day."

John English had given Bo Dennis a story of his life that sounded like something out of Dickens. "He's had a rough time," Dennis told the Miami cops. "His parents were both killed in a car crash and then he lived with stepparents who hated him and told him he had to leave."

Bo had felt sorry for the kid and taken him under his wing. They had spent the next few days at a friend of Dennis's. "But we were watching this prison movie on TV one night," he said, "and I noticed John was crushing beer cans with his bare hands. I kidded him about acting so violent, and he said, 'Yeah, I have a violent temper.' But I didn't think too much of it. I thought he was just trying to be tough."

The new buddies had gone to the Florida State Employment Agency looking for jobs and then to Traveler's Aid, where they were given five dollars apiece. A woman there asked John English if he was a runaway and offered to provide transportation home. She assured him that he wouldn't get in any trouble, but he told her that he was a high-school graduate and had his family's permission to be in Miami.

Bo and John had subsisted by selling their blood until John found a job as a stockboy at a dress shop. He had only worked one day when he and Bo went out "cruising around looking for girls." They found the police instead.

Bo Dennis told the Miami detectives that John had never mentioned any criminal activity in his past. "He told me he stayed overnight with a gay guy one night in Louisiana, but he said nothing happened."

Fourteen-year-old John English was nothing if not a survivor. Despite widespread BOLOs (Be On the Lookout For) from law-enforcement agencies, he had managed to drive the same stolen car thirty-four hundred miles from home. Now, the King County Prosecutor's Office began extradition proceedings to bring him back to face murder charges.

Two days before Halloween, Rolf Grunden flew out of the Sea-Tac Airport to bring John English back home. It was agreed between the prosecutors office and the sheriff's detectives that the boy was not to be interrogated, but if he chose, he could give a voluntary statement about the events of the evening of October 1 and his adventures since.

As it turned out, John English did want to talk. He had held terrible secrets inside for long, solitary weeks on the road. He agreed to a tape-recorded interview on the flight to Seattle from Miami. Rolf Grunden was careful to explain John's Miranda rights to him, and the teenager repeated them back, paraphrasing them to indicate he fully understood them.

As Ben Brown had said after he returned from California, the runaway plans had been a spur of the moment thing. On the morning of October 1, John said he had gone to school and heard that Ben wanted to run away. John said he'd offered to go with him and provide a car. After school that night, he had tried to figure out how he could get the car. Finally, he'd concluded that if he knocked out his stepmother and tied her up, he could take the car without interference. He had hidden the hammer in his room.

Just as Vera English was leaving for work, he had called her into his room and told her to look out the window. He recalled hitting her only a "few" times when she started to turn back toward him. He told Grunden he remembered that she tried to protect her head by putting her hands up.

He had been surprised when she had gone into convulsions instead of just passing out. That had apparently bothered him. "I used her belt to strangle her "because I didn't want her to suffer."

John English vehemently denied that sex had anything to do with his attack on his stepmother, but he admitted that he had taken her clothes off after she was dead because he was curious. The thought of rape had flashed through his mind then, he said, but he insisted he had decided against it.

While his stepmother was either dead or dying, he said he had left the room and began to pack his clothes. During this time, the little girls were downstairs in the rec room watching television and apparently thought their mother had left for work. John said he'd stopped to call the gift shop where Vera worked and told them she was ill with the flu and would not be in that night.

The boy steadfastly denied he had thought of his stepmother in a sexual manner. This question seemed to upset him far more than those about her murder. He said that there had been nude pictures of her in the house, but that she had never gone around nude.

"She did wear those see-through blouses a lot, though."

"One of your friends told us that you were always talking about what a great figure your stepmother had," Grunden said.

The teenager reddened, but shook his head. He said he hadn't really noticed. He described the atmosphere in his family as "very open," and said that his parents had never hidden anything from him.

Grunden asked him about the mobile in his room with the garroted nudes.

"That was just part of one that they had hanging someplace in the house," he said. "They said I could have it."

"How about all those pictures under your mattress?"

"Well, we had this family project to make a collage of different stuff. But nobody ever finished it, and I found them in a garbage can."

Grunden had no comment to that. Either the Englishes had an offbeat approach to family projects or the kid was making it all up.

John filled in the details of the one part of his flight that had not already been traced. He said that after he escaped from Sergeant Roy in Louisiana, he had jumped over a couple of fences and run into a field.

He took what money he had left out of his wallet and then threw away all of his ID and the wallet. "I just kept walking until I came to a road. Then I hitchhiked all the way to Miami. I met up with Bo there. I only ran away from the cops because they said Bo would go to jail if it turned out I was under seventeen."

After that, he figured he'd run about as far as he could and he just decided to give up.

John English wasn't very big—only five foot seven and 135 pounds. If he had not taken his stepmother completely by surprise, she might well have survived the attack.

He was booked into the juvenile detention facility in Seattle on charges of first-degree murder. Had he been two years older, the Juvenile Court system would probably have declined to try his case and he would have been tried as an adult. On November 15, 1974, however, John English appeared before Juvenile Court Commissioner Norman Quinn and pleaded guilty to second-degree murder. He was bound over to the Department of Institutions, Juvenile Division, until he reached the age of twenty-one. In 1981, he went free.

John English was far from the first "child" murderer in history, and, tragically, he was far from the last. He was simply a dread pioneer in a new category of killer. By the early nineties, of course, the phenomenon of murders committed by the very young was growing in America. Whether the open and permissive attitude about sex in the English home contributed somehow to the tragedy that occurred there is something that only forensic psychiatrists may be able to answer.

THE #1
NEW YORK TIMES
BESTSELLING
TRUE-CRIME AUTHOR
ANN RULE

All available in paperback from
Pocket Books

961-02